RAJ PATEL is an award-winning author, film-maker and academic. He is a Research Professor in the Lyndon B. Johnson School of Public Affairs at the University of Texas, Austin, and a Senior Research Associate at the Unit for the Humanities at Rhodes University (UHURU), South Africa. He has degrees from the University of Oxford, the London School of Economics and Cornell University, has worked for the World Bank and WTO, and protested against them around the world. In addition to his scholarly publications in economics, philosophy, politics and public health journals, he regularly writes for the *Guardian*, and has contributed to publications including the *Financial Times* and the *New York Times*. *Stuffed and Starved* is his first book and is published in eleven countries. He is also the author of *The Value of Nothing: How to Reshape Market Society and Redefine Democracy* and co-author, with Jason W. Moore, of *A History of the World in Seven Cheap Things*. www.rajpatel.org

From the reviews of *Stuffed and Starved*:

'Raj Patel's book confirms a widespread suspicion that the [global food] system is grotesquely out of balance – and not just because 800 million people in the world are undernourished. For the first time ever, there are actually more overweight than underfed people in the world. Patel argues that hunger and obesity are symptoms of the same global malaise. This exhaustively researched book demonstrates how the "choice" we get in supermarkets is an illusion: what we are offered is dictated by the reality of a market controlled by a few key players, and comes at an undisclosed cost to others. It also deconstructs the long accepted folk wisdom that "the poor are hungry because they are lazy", or, conversely, that the wealthy are fat because they eat too richly. Patel writes with a precision and clarity that make his unavoidably bulky suitcase of statistics accessible.' *New Statesman*

'This is one book above all I'd love to see at the top of the bestseller lists. A clear, hard-headed analysis of why and how half the world is stuffed and the other half starved. An important subject and brilliantly handled by Patel. I hope this book will be remembered as long as *Small is Beautiful* has been and gains as much influence.' *Publishing News*

'This critique of the world food system could not be better timed... Patel writes with passion and commitment.' *Scotland on Sunday*

'If you want to know the real cost of the food on your plate, read this book.' *Tribune*

'An important and radical contribution to the literature on the food we eat and the world in which we live.' *Socialist Review*

'Patel writes with an easy flowing eloquence as well as an urgency and commitment. He argues convincingly, that to change ourselves we need to change the world and to change the world we need to change ourselves; both are necessary; both are difficult... A must read.' *Morning Star*

'A captivating historical analysis of how corporate control of government food policy has generated the diet-related disease that plagues rich countries while also being the primary cause of the poverty and starvation that kill millions elsewhere every year... Essential reading.' *Management Today*

'Vital reading.' Craig Sams, Chair of the Soil Association and president of Green & Black's Ltd

Stuffed and Starved

FROM FARM TO FORK
THE HIDDEN BATTLE FOR THE WORLD FOOD SYSTEM

RAJ PATEL

GRANTA

First edition published in Great Britain by Portobello Books, an imprint of
Granta Publications, in 2007
This revised second edition published in the United States by Melville House,
Brooklyn, NY, in 2012 and published in Great Britain by Portobello Books, an
imprint of Granta Publications, in 2013
This paperback edition published by Granta Books in 2021

Granta Publications
12 Addison Avenue
London
W11 4QR

A CIP catalogue record is available from the British Library

9 8 7 6 5 4 3 2

ISBN 978 1 84627 479 4

Offset by Avon DataSet Ltd, Alcester, Warwickshire B49 6HN
Printed and bound by CPI Group (UK) Ltd, Croydon, CR0 4YY
www.granta.com

For the everyday heroines and heroes.

Contents

Preface to the Second Edition

When revising the first edition of this book in 2006, it was possible to be appalled that 800 million people were undernourished and a billion were overweight. International civil servants argued that if by 2015 we were unable to get the number of hungry down to 412 million, we'd have failed a generation.[1] Five years later, a billion are undernourished[2] and 1.5 billion overweight. Few people now see any drastic improvement on the horizon.

The global food system I describe in this book was engineered to create a world of increasing hunger and obesity. The Great Recession in 2008 kicked this system into overdrive, but there are other reasons why the recent past is prologue to future trouble. First, the weather. A series of unusual, and unusually strong storms, floods and droughts meant that about 1% less food was produced per person in 2008 than in 2007.[3] Although no single weather event can be attributed to global warming, a pattern of more, and more extreme, weather events is certainly consistent with everything we know about climate change. Climate change has already reduced global wheat harvests by 5% over the past 30 years, and no serious scholar of climate change expects this trend to do anything but deteriorate.[4]

The price of oil had obvious consequences for hunger in 2008, too. When the price of oil goes up, the economy slows down, and when the economy slows down, those just above the poverty line are pushed beneath it. Hunger increases during recessions, and since the current recession is likely to persist, so will its attendant undernourishment and food insecurity.

The price of oil also matters directly for farmers. When oil becomes more expensive, so does diesel – so transport, farm machinery and infrastructure cost more. The price of natural gas also goes up, and since fertilizer is primarily made with natural gas, the price of fertilizer goes up too. In the Great 2008 Price Spike, one of the agricultural commodities with the highest price rise was fertilizer, which more than doubled in price from August 2007 to 2008.[5]

There are subtler ways that the high price of oil has come to matter for the food system. Among the last laws signed by U.S. President Bill Clinton was the Commodity Futures Modernization Act of 2000, which unleashed 'over the counter' derivatives traders from government regulation.[6] The U.S. agency responsible for regulating this sort of exchange – the Commodity Futures Trading Commission – was now no longer responsible for monitoring the exchanges on which futures contracts were traded. This opened up a wild west of financial enterprise, in which billions were staked on anything that could be turned into a commodity. And that included bets on the price of food.

Food future contracts weren't just vigorously traded – they were brought into portfolios of commodity futures, such as the Goldman Sachs Commodity Index. Through financial engineering that has nothing to do with food itself, these indexes hitched the price of food to the price of oil.[7] In 2008, traders drove up the price of food independently of commodity indexes funds. When the oil price bubble burst in the middle of the year, 'hot money' ditched oil and moved into the one thing that people would need even in the middle of a recession – something to eat.

There is considerable debate among economists about whether speculators drive up prices. Economic models insist that there ought not to be any abnormal profit in speculation but rather that every winning trade has its losing counterpart. For every trader driving a Bugatti, another has lost his shirt, at least in theory. Reality is a little different. For their part, traders admit that they're gaming the system.[8] A major study by the United Nations Conference on Trade and Development suggests that commodities markets aren't working as they ought.[9] And this wouldn't be the first time in the past two years that reality has failed to live up to economists' expectations.

Another force behind the food price spike was a policy that was sold to the public as being something that could wean us off oil: biofuels. More properly termed 'agrofuels' – ('bio' meaning 'life giving' is argued to be an inappropriate name for an industry that causes such misery) this is an industry in which crops are grown not in order to eat, but in order to set on fire. Corn, sugar cane, jatropha and a few other crops are grown in order to be processed into ethanol. To stimulate the market, the EU and US governments legislated and subsidised purchasing targets for agrofuels. This encouraged farmers around the world to plant crops – particularly corn – that might be turned into ethanol, destined for the gasoline tanks of the world's richest consumers.

In a tight market, the land diverted to fuel drove up the price of other kinds of corn and cereals. There were few good environmental reasons to encourage the corn-to-ethanol industry. Although corn is renewable, it isn't sustainable. It takes more energy to produce than might be saved by simply burning diesel. But in a mid-term election year in the US in 2008, it was deemed better to burn American corn than Saudi oil. So prices went up. US President George Bush suggested that the contribution of agrofuels to food price inflation was 15%.[10] The World Bank said it could be 75%.[11] Most reasonable estimates are somewhere in between.

As I write, the planet's seventh billion person has been born, likely somewhere in a city in South Asia. Population growth has been fingered as a reason behind the food price rise.[12] George Bush himself, in perhaps one of the most controversial explanations of the food price crisis, offered this:

> ... the more prosperous the world is, the more opportunity there is. It also, however, increases demand. So, for example, just as an interesting thought for you, there are 350 million people in India who are classified as middle class. That's bigger than America. Their middle class is larger than our entire population. And when you start getting wealth, you start demanding better nutrition and

better food. And so demand is high, and that causes the
price to go up.[13]

The president overestimated the ranks of the Indian middle class
somewhat – a McKinsey Global Institute puts the figure at nearer
50 million.[14] And it isn't as if a large chunk of the Indian population decided to cast their Hinduism to the winds and chow down
on burgers. Per capita meat consumption in India is still twenty
times less than in the US, and growing relatively slowly.[15] India
was also a relatively small importer of food, causing far fewer rip-
ples in the international economy than the President assumed. If
there's a reasonable point buried in here, it's this: the western diet
is causing a 'nutrition transition', and with it a higher demand for
meat.[16] This is certainly one of the long term drivers of inequity
in the food system and therefore a chronic, rather than an acute,
cause for worry. It's not the people that are the problem. It is the
way we consume through this food system, which allows a few to
eat healthily, many to eat unhealthily, and many more not to eat
at all.

In an effort to stave off the worst effects of the crisis, some
governments reacted quickly to protect their citizens. Trouble is
that in a global economy, one government's actions on the international market have consequences for everyone else everywhere
else. India and Thailand, two of the world's largest rice exporters,
announced that they'd trim their contributions to the global market in October 2007. In response to rising rice prices the world's
largest rice importer, the Philippines, tried to buy 500,000 tons of
rice on the open market in mid-April. No supplier responded. So
the government tried to buy 650,000 in May,[17] sending prices to
over \$900 a ton (from a January price of less than \$400/ton).[18]
Similarly, in response to record fires in their grain belt, the Russian government announced a wheat export moratorium – a policy that served Russian producers and consumers well[19] – there
were food riots in Mozambique as a result.[20]

Every agricultural crisis is an opportunity, though, and many solutions have been suggested. The first is a renewed push for genetically modified crops. In a November 2009 declaration at the World Summit on Food Security in which world leaders declared themselves 'alarmed' by increasing hunger, the United States government did exactly what Monsanto asked, inserting language into the declaration that insists that it "will seek to mobilize the resources needed to increase productivity, including the review, approval and adoption of biotechnology."[21] Even if a growing number of studies show little to no improvement of GM over conventional crops,[22] the corporations behind the technology have friends in high places in government and in civil society. Philanthropic foundations, including the world's largest – the Gates Foundation, that sits on a $36.3 billion endowment – are staffed with acolytes of GM crops, and indeed, some invest in Monsanto.[23]

Countries and governments have also realized that they'll need land on which to plant crops for their customers and populations. With that realization has come a boom in the price of agricultural land worldwide. The cheapest land with access to water is to be found in Africa, and once again, there's a scramble for the continent. The United States has set up a military command unit – AFRICOM – to protect its resource interests on the continent. Private corporations from Asia have tried to make their mark, too. The South Korean firm Daewoo was in an agreement with Madagascar to obtain 1.3 million hectares of land to grow food for the South Korean market. The land would be given to the corporation for free, and the corporation's gift to Madagascar would have been to employ locals as farm hands. It was in part because of the inequities of this deal that the Madagascan government was overthrown soon after it was announced. But it's not just South Korean capitalists involved in land grabbing. Companies and governments from India, China, Saudi Arabia and the United States have all thrown their money at poorer parts of the world, where an acre of land and, most important, the groundwater beneath it can be had for a few dollars. Most of the 56 million hectares, an area the size of France, grabbed by foreigners in 2009 was to be found in Africa.[24] And this doesn't even count the far greater amount of land transferred away from the poor by local elites. This new scramble not only for African land, but for the resources of the poor, sets us up for a century of resource conflicts the likes of which we have never before seen.

The tragedy, of course, is that sustainable solutions to hunger are right beneath our noses. If we're concerned with fighting climate change, for instance, then we ought to heed the US-based Rodale Institute announcement that 40% of the world's carbon emissions could be sequestered if only we paid attention to improving our soil's health, and farmed organically.[25] Food policy councils are sprouting up in cities and towns across North America. Ecuador, Mali and Nepal have all adopted food sovereignty as national policy goals.[26]

People are also organizing to confront rising levels of overweight and obesity. The World Health Organization predicts that by 2015, 2.3 billion adults will be overweight.[27] Yet, around the world, consumers are developing a taste for local and seasonal food, pushing back against the food industry, and most importantly, realizing that they are more than consumers. Here in San Francisco, the local government has agreed to ban the inclusion of toys in Happy Meals, to help parents sway their children away from the fast food industry's marketing complex. It's a small act, but one that has the fast food industry scrambling to prevent similar legislation in other states because they can see in this token of citizen action the thin end of a very long wedge.

At a national level, our leaders are unlikely to provide the change in the food system that so many of us demand, but the current economic crisis provides an opportunity to organize for change. While industrial agriculture relies on things that will be in short supply in the twenty-first century – reliable water, cheap fossil fuel, predictable weather – we know that agroecological techniques are more robust in the face of climate change,[28] and higher yielding.[29] Farmers movements like La Via Campesina are in the forefront of these innovations, pointing out that 'small farmers cool the planet'. Indeed, these conclusions have been endorsed by an international high-level study funded in part by the World Bank – the International Assessment of Agricultural Knowledge, Science and Technology for Development. The peer reviewed analysis in the report was, however, subsequently repudiated by the United States, Australia and Canada for not being sufficiently enthusiastic about genetically modified crops and industrial agriculture.

There have been widespread protests against the high price of food. The Arab Spring followed protests beginning in 2008 against agricultural price inflation. In some cases, protests succeeded in amending government policy. In Mozambique in 2010, for example, the government backed down from a 30% increase in the price of bread. It is proof that the days of 'IMF riots' are far from over, but also that organized rebellion can work.[30]

I hope that a future edition of *Stuffed and Starved* will be able to look back on the first decade of the twenty-first century as the end of the neoliberal era, and the beginning of a more just global economy. The good news, writing amid an outbreak of #Occupy protests and the further building of a decade long food sovereignty movement, is that many of people are starting to see themselves not as witnesses to history, but as its authors.

San Francisco, October 2011

Introduction

Our Big Fat Contradiction

Today, when we produce more food than ever before, more than one in seven people on Earth are hungry. The hunger of around one billion[1] happens at the same time as another historical first: that they are outnumbered by the one and a half billion[2] people on this planet who are overweight.

Global hunger and obesity are symptoms of the same problem. What's more, the route to eradicating world hunger is also the way to prevent global epidemics of diabetes and heart disease, and to address a host of environmental and social ills. Increasingly, obesity and hunger are two points on a continuum of poverty. But the stuffed and the starved are also linked through the chains of production that bring food from fields to our plate. Guided by the profit motive, food corporations shape and constrain how we eat, and how we think about food. The limitations are clearest at the fast food outlet, where the spectrum of choice runs from McMuffin to McNugget. But there are hidden and systemic constraints even when we feel we're beyond Ronald McDonald's domain.

Even when we want to buy something healthy, something to keep the doctor away, we're trapped in the very same system that has created our 'Fast Food Nations'. Try, for example, shopping for apples. At supermarkets in North America and Europe, the choice is restricted to half a dozen varieties: Fuji, Braeburn, Granny Smith, Golden Delicious and perhaps a couple of others. Why these? Because they're pretty – we like the polished and unblemished skin. Because their taste is one that's largely

unobjectionable to the majority. But also because they can withstand transportation over long distances. Their skin won't tear
or blemish if they're knocked about in the miles from orchard to
aisle. They take well to the waxing technologies and compounds
that make this transportation possible and keep the apples pretty
on the shelves. They are easy to harvest. They respond well to
pesticides and industrial production. These are reasons why we
won't find Calville Blanc, Black Oxford, Zabergau Reinette, Kandil
Sinap or the ancient and venerable Rambo on the shelves. Our
choices are not entirely our own because, even in a supermarket,
the menu is crafted not by our choices, nor by the seasons, nor
where we find ourselves, nor by the full range of apples available,
nor by the full spectrum of available nutrition and tastes, but by
the power of food corporations.

The concerns of food production companies have ramifica-
tions far beyond what appears on supermarket shelves. Their
concerns are the rot at the core of the modern food system. To
show the systemic ability of a few to impact the health of the many
demands a global investigation, travelling from the 'green deserts' of Brazil to the architecture of the modern city, and moving
through history from the time of the first domesticated plants to
the Battle of Seattle. It's an enquiry that uncovers the real reasons for famine in Asia and Africa, why there is a worldwide epidemic of farmer suicides, why we don't know what's in our food
any more, why black people in the United States are more likely
to be overweight than white, why there were cowboys in South
Central Los Angeles, and how the world's largest social movement
is discovering ways, large and small, for us to think about, and live
differently with, food.

The alternative to eating the way we do today promises to
solve hunger and diet-related disease, by offering a way of eating
and growing food that is environmentally sustainable and socially
just. Understanding the ills of the way food is grown and eaten
also offers the key to greater freedom, and a way of reclaiming the
joy of eating. The task is as urgent as the prize is great.

In every country, the contradictions of obesity, hunger, poverty and wealth are becoming more acute. India has, for example, destroyed millions of tons of grains, permitting food to rot in silos, while the quality of food eaten by India's poorest is getting worse for the first time since Independence in 1947.[3] In 1992, in the same towns and villages where malnutrition had begun to grip the poorest families, the Indian government admitted foreign soft drinks manufacturers and food multinationals to its previously protected economy. Within a decade, India has become home to the world's largest number of diabetics.[4]

India isn't the only home to these contrasts. They're global, and they're present even in the world's richest country. In the United States in 2009, 50.2 million people didn't know where their next meal was coming from.[5] At the same time there is more diet-related disease like diabetes, and more food, in the US than ever before.

It's easy to become inured to this contradiction; its daily version causes only mild discomfort, walking past the 'homeless and hungry' signs on the way to supermarkets bursting with food. There are moral emollients to balm a troubled conscience: the poor are hungry because they're lazy, or perhaps the wealthy are fat because they eat too richly. This vein of folk wisdom has a long pedigree. Every culture has had, in some form or other, an understanding of our bodies as public ledgers on which is written the catalogue of our private vices. But the traditional language of condemnation doesn't help us understand why hunger, abundance and obesity are more compatible on our planet than they've ever been.

Moral condemnation only works if the condemned could have done things differently, if they had choices. Yet the prevalence of hunger and obesity affect populations with far too much regularity, in too many different places, for it to be the result of some personal failing. Part of the reason our judgement is so out of kilter is because the way we read bodies hasn't kept up with the times. Although it may once have been true, the assumption that to be overweight is to be rich no longer holds. Obesity can no longer be explained exclusively as a curse of individual affluence. There are systemic features that make a difference. Here's an example: many teenagers in Mexico, a developing country with an average income of US\$9,330[6], are bloated as never before, even as the ranks of the Mexican poor once again start to swell.[7] Individual wealth doesn't explain why the children of some families are more obese than others: the crucial factor turns out not to be income, but proximity to the US border. Omitting Mexico City, where obesity rates are the highest in the country, the closer a Mexican family lives to its northern neighbours and to their sugar- and fat-rich processed food habits, the more overweight the family's children are likely to be.[8] That geography matters so much rather overturns the idea that personal choice is the key to preventing obesity or, by the same token, preventing hunger. And it helps to renew the lament of Porfirio Diaz, one of Mexico's late-nineteenth-century presidents and autocrats: '¡Pobre Mexico! Tan lejos de Dios; y tan cerca de los Estados Unidos' (Poor Mexico: so far from God, so close to the United States).

A perversity of the way our food comes to us is that it's now possible for people who can't afford enough to eat to be obese. Children growing up malnourished in the favelas of São Paulo, for instance, are at greater risk from obesity when they become adults. Their bodies, broken by childhood poverty, metabolize and store food poorly. As a result, they're at greater risk of storing as fat the (poor-quality) food that they can access.[9] Across the planet, the poor can't afford to eat well. Again, this is true even in the world's richest country; and in the US, it's children who will pay the price. One research team recently suggested that if consumption patterns stay the way they are, today's US children will live five fewer years, because of the diet-related diseases to which they will be exposed in their lifetimes.[10] Another research team has indicated that at current trends, the number of overweight children in the US will double by 2030.[11] Some have suggested that half of all adults in the US may be obese by 2030 (with similar increases on the horizon for every other high and middle income country).[12]

As consumers, we're encouraged to think that an economic system based on individual choice will save us from the collective ills of hunger and obesity. Yet it is precisely 'freedom of choice' that has incubated these ills. Those of us able to head to the supermarket can boggle at the possibility of choosing from fifty brands of sugared cereals, from half a dozen kinds of milk that all taste like chalk, from shelves of bread so sopped in chemicals that they will never go bad, from aisles of products in which the principal ingredient is sugar. For instance, of the myriad branded breakfast cereals marketed directly to children in Britain, around 88% are high in sugar, 13% were high in salt, and 10% were high in saturated fat. Some cereals have the same amount of sugar as a candy bar, and others are over 50% sugar by weight.[13] What's more, this information is deliberately hidden from consumers and parents. There are 23 names for added sugar on ingredients labels that companies may use to avoid writing "sugar" as the first and most prevalent ingredient on the list.[14] It's hardly surprising, then, that one in three children between the ages of two and fifteen in the UK are obese or overweight.[15] The breakfast cereal story is a sign of a wider systemic feature: there's every incentive for food producing corporations to sell food that has undergone processing which renders it more profitable, if less nutritious. Incidentally, this also helps explain why there are so many more varieties of breakfast cereals on sale than varieties of apples.

There are natural limits to our choices. There are, for instance, only so many naturally occurring fruits, vegetables and animals that people are prepared to eat. But even here, a little advertising can persuade us to expand the ambit of our choices. Think of the kiwi fruit, once known as the Chinese gooseberry, but rebranded to accommodate Cold War prejudices by the New Zealand food company that sold it to the world at the end of the 1950s. It's a taste no-one had grown up with, but which now seems as if it has always been there. And while new natural foods are slowly added to our menus, the food industry adds tens of thousands of new products to the shelves every year, some of which become indispensable fixtures which, after a generation, make life unimaginable without them. It's a sign of how limited our gastronomic imaginations can be. And also a sign that we're not altogether sure how or where or why certain foods end up on our plate.

Arcadia Lost

> Old Macdonald had a farm, E-I-E-I-O,
> And on his farm he had a cow, E-I-E-I-O,
> With a 'moo-moo' here and a 'moo-moo' there,
> Here a 'moo', there a 'moo',
> Everywhere a 'moo-moo',
> Old Macdonald had a farm, E-I-E-I-O.
>
>   Traditional

The story of food production to which most of us can admit, almost as a reflex, owes more to fairy tales and children's television programming than anything else. Without a reason to revisit the creation myths of food we learned when young, we carry around unquestioned our received opinions of pastoral bliss, of farmers planting the seeds in the ground, watering them and hoping that the sun will come out so that the plants can grow big and strong. This is certainly one description of how food is grown. It's just one that glosses over the most important parts. The tales we tell about farming stuff a sock into the mouths of the world's rural poor. When food's provenance is reduced to a single line on a label, there's much we don't understand, nor even understand that we should ask.

Who, for example, is the central character in our story of food – the farmer? What is her life like? What can she afford to eat? If only we asked, we'd know: the majority of the world's farmers are suffering. Some are selling off their lands to become labourers on their family plots. Some migrate to the cities, or even overseas. A few, too many, resort to suicide.

The questions continue. What, for example, does a farmer plant? Most farmers' choice of crop is tightly circumscribed by the kinds of land they own, the climate, their access to markets, credit and a range of visible and invisible ingredients in the production of food. There is no moment of sucking a finger, holding it to the wind and deciding what it'd be nice to eat next year. If they're hoping to sell their crops for cash rather than eat them themselves, most farmers have few options, particularly those in the Global South (the term I use in this book to refer to the world's poorer countries).[16] They will have to grow the crops that the market demands.

The business of farming is, at the end of the day, constrained by the playing-field of the market. What this language hides, though, is that the terrain of the market isn't so much a playing-field as a razor's edge. If there's room to make planting choices at all, they are tough decisions based on optimizing multiple parameters, with little room for error. The market punishes poor choices with penury. For farmers who are already highly indebted, this means bankruptcy. Banks and grain distributors have developed novel ways for dealing with the subsequent insolvency. Contract farming or land rental arrangements, for example, reduce farmers to providing raw labour on what used to be their own land. Old MacDonald now rents his farm. Yet farmers are willing to subject themselves to these new farming arrangements because they have so little choice. With banks wielding the threat of foreclosure, any kind of farming, even the kind of farming that asset-strips the soil, is preferable to no farming at all.

As the farmer is forced into 'choosing' among these alternatives, other options are removed as possibilities. And at the same time as the set of choices for farmers is winnowed down, others – powerful groups, corporations, governments – expand the empire of their options. At every stage of the story of food, choices are made over a wide range of issues, from the obvious to the esoteric.

Who chooses the safe levels of pesticides, and how is 'safe' defined? Who chooses what should be sourced from where in making your meal? Who decides what to pay the farmers who grow the food, or the farm workers who work for farmers? Who decides that the processing techniques used in bringing the meal together are safe? Who makes money from the additives in food and decides they do more good than harm? Who makes sure there is plenty of cheap energy to transport and assemble the ingredients from all around the world?

These choices may seem impossibly distant, so removed from our experience as food shoppers that they might as well happen on Mars. Yet the very same forces that shape farmers' choices also reach to the stacked aisles of the supermarket. Who, after all, fixes the range of items that fill the aisles in the supermarket? Who chooses how much it costs? Who spends millions of dollars to find out that the smell of baking bread and the wail of Annie Lennox in the aisles might make people buy more? Who decides that the prices in the market are higher than the poorest can afford?

Here lies the crux. The narrow abundance of the aisles, the apparently low prices at the checkout and the almost constant availability of foods, these things are our sop. 'Convenience' anaesthetizes us as consumers. We are dissuaded from asking hard questions, not only about how our individual tastes and preferences are manipulated, but about how our choices at the checkout take away the choices of those who grow our food.

About Joe

A recent report from Oxfam provides fodder for thinking about where the power lies along the chain of food production. Consider the case of Lawrence Seguya, a coffee-grower in Uganda. He puts it like this: 'I'd like you to tell people in your place that the drink they are now drinking is the cause of all our problems.'[17] His assessment is widely shared. Salome Kafuluzi lives on a coffee-farm with her thirteen children, and she has this to say: 'We're broke. We're not happy. We're failing in everything. We can't buy essentials. We can't have meat, fish, rice, just sweet potatoes, beans and *matoke* [a kind of green banana mash] ... We can't send the children to school.' Salome's husband, Peter, links their situation quite directly to the price of coffee: 'I remember when *kiboko* [the local term for sun-dried coffee cherry] sold for 69 cents/kg. We slept without worries. We could support our families. For me, I'd need to see a price of at least 34 cents/kg. Even at 29 cents/kg we can't look after the land.'[18] The price at the moment is around 14 cents per kilo.

The laws of supply and demand would suggest that coffee-growers would move out of the market and do something else. This would presuppose that there *is* something else they can do. Too often, there isn't. The immediate result of low farm income – and this is a law to which anyone living on the breadline can attest – is a panicked self-exploitation. Rather than throwing in the towel and moving to the cities, or trying to grow something else, farmers grow *more* coffee, working themselves to exhaustion and scraping together whatever they can to be able to maintain some sort of standard of living, and sometimes, reluctantly, hurting the natural environment in a desperate bid to survive. This has resulted in a global coffee surplus of 900 million kilos. You'd think that with all that coffee floating around, we'd see the end-price of coffee go down. But there are a good few steps along the way from the fields to the bottom of the cup.

Lawrence and his family live in an area well suited to coffee – it's high-altitude, hilly terrain. This means that their land is unsuited to anything else. The choice that faces them is this: grow coffee or leave. With little else to go to, they grow coffee.

They sell to a local middleman at around 14 cents per kilo, who then takes the bag to the mill and sells it for 19 cents. The mill will process it for an additional 5 cents per kilo – which is barely enough to keep the mill going. Mary Goreti runs the mill in Kituntu to which the coffee is brought. 'The profit margins are so small right now,' she says, 'and the electricity is so high ... We have so few people bringing *kiboko*. Some farmers are just keeping it at home because the prices are so low. If the prices stay low, the business will fail. You can't open a factory to process ten bags.'[19] But she can't choose to do anything else with the mill but process coffee. So, for the moment, Mary chooses to keep the mill open, and the coffee is processed.

The coffee is bagged and, with a 2 cent per kilo freight cost, sent to Kampala, by which time the price has reached 26 cents. Yet the vast profits aren't being made here either. Hannington Karuhanga, a manager with Ugacof, one of the larger Ugandan coffee exporters, is happy to be making a profit of US$10 a ton, or 1 cent on the kilo. And that's on the quality coffee – 'Some of these grades we have are not worth transporting. It would be cheaper to destroy them.' Yet transport them he does, as part of the complex dance of sorting, grading, insuring and shipping the coffee to a roaster. By the time this kilo of coffee lands up in, say, West London, where Nestlé has a coffee-processing facility, it'll cost US$1.64 per kilo. Already, at the gates of the Nescafé factory, the cost per bag is well over ten times what the Kafuluzis or the Seguyas received for it. But here comes the big jump. By the time the coffee rolls out of the other side, the price is US$26.40 per kilo, or nearly 200 times the cost of a kilo in Uganda.

While coffee farmers there are living off their savings, Nestlé's profits seem unstoppable. In 2005, they sold over US$70 billion in food and beverages. With high levels of brand loyalty, and with such market dominance, Nestlé is in a position to raise the price that its growers receive. But why would it choose to do that? Nestlé isn't a charity – it's a corporation in a world of other corporations, guided by the cardinal rule of market capitalism: 'buy cheap, sell dear'. By virtue of its size, Nestlé can dictate the terms of supply to its growers, millers, exporters and importers, and each is being squeezed dry. If the coffee industry in Uganda goes belly up, that's OK. Vietnam has been brought into the world market by the World Bank, and they're turning out bags of coffee cheaper than anyone else. So wherever coffee is grown, farmers are struggling, pitted against one another across vast distances by the international market in coffee, with few if any choices about the future. Meanwhile, farmers who try to increase their share of the price find themselves facing the might of the food industry. Ethiopian farmers recently applied to turn their signature coffee bean names – Sidamo, Harar and Yirgacheffe – into trademarks, a move that might increase their share of the revenue by 25 per cent. They were opposed almost instantly by Starbucks, a company with an annual turnover equal to three-quarters that of Ethiopia.[20]

Large corporations are very reluctant to cede their control over the food system. Yet, Nestlé, Starbucks and every other food system corporation have a rock-solid alibi: us. In the name of consumers, and 'consumer freedom', wages are kept low and opportunities for farmers to increase their income are stymied. And, the thing is, it works. At my local Pick and Pay Supermarket in Durban, South Africa, there are 107 different kinds of coffee on sale, from a chicory blend to the freshest dark roast, across 15 feet of shelf space dominated by Nestlé. It's a very dark plenitude.

An Hourglass Figure

There is a superabundance of coffee farmers and coffee drinkers, there are many millers, and a good few exporters. But there's a bottleneck in the distribution chain, and what is true for coffee also holds for a range of other foods. At some stages in the chain that links field to plate, power is concentrated in very few hands. If there had to be a picture or two showing where power is concentrated in the way food is grown and sold, figure 1.1 would do the trick. The first figure shows aggregated data from the Netherlands, Germany, France, UK, Austria and Belgium. The second shows similar but not entirely comparable data from the United States. The numbers need to be taken with a pinch of salt. For

instance, the total number of farmers who grow food for Europeans and North Americans is far higher than indicated here. After all, millions of farmers and farmworkers, growing all kinds of
tropical fruits and vegetables for export, live *outside* the wealthi-
est countries in the world.

As far as power is concerned, the bottleneck is the central clue.
Somehow, we've ended up at a world with a few corporate buyers
and sellers. The process of shipping, processing and trucking food
across distances demands a great deal of capital – you need to be
rich to play this game. It is also a game that has economies of scale.
This means that the bigger a company is, and the more transport
and logistics it does, the cheaper it is for that company to be in the
business. There are, after all, no mom-and-pop international food
distribution companies. The small fish have been devoured by the
Leviathans of distribution and supply. And when the number of
companies controlling the gateways from farmers to consumers
is small, this gives them market power both over the people who
grow the food *and* the people who eat it.

One measure of the power wielded by these 'bottleneck corporations' is the size of the industry, and of the biggest players
in it. The retailers turned over US$4 trillion in 2009,[21] the seed-
sellers US$31 billion a year, the agrochemical industry in 2007
sold US$38.6 billion,[22] food-processors' revenue was US$1.3 trillion in 2007.[23] (Just for comparison's sake, the total GDP of Mexico
in 2007 was US$1.02 trillion.)[24] If the output of these industries
feels a little rich, the US$390.3 billion a year global weight loss
industry is happy to help.[25] And for those countries unable to find
enough to eat, well, the US$2 billion food aid industry can step in
there too.[26] (And that doesn't factor in the oil industry that stands
behind them.[14]) Meanwhile, those who can afford to consume are
left with calories too cheap to meter.[27]

The giants in the corporate food system are big enough that
they don't have to play by the rules. They can tilt the playing
field. At home and at venues such as the World Trade Organization, these corporations lobby governments for an economic

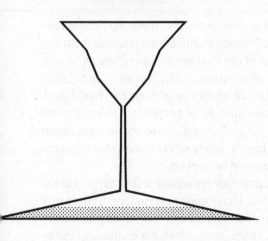

United States

People employed in agriculture and migrant and seasonal labor: 4,711,509

Farm operators: 3,337,450

Number of farms: 2,204,792

Farm product raw wholesalers: 6,628

Food manufacturers: 27,915

Grocery and related products wholesalers: 33,794

Food and beverage stores: 146,084

Consumers: 302,200,000

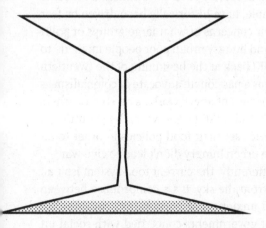

European Union

People working in agriculture: 26,669,000

Farm holdings: 13,700,400

Number of farm holders: 50,400

Agricultural wholesale enterprises: 46,300

Food and beverage manufacturers: 308,300

Wholesaling food and beverage enterprises: 210,300

Food and beverage retail locations: 914,500

Consumers: 499,800,000

Figure 1.1 Hourglasses: the concentration of power and players in the food system. (Source for 'United States': Passel, 2009; Population Reference Bureau, 2007; US Census Bureau, 2007; USDA, 2007. Source for 'European Union': EU, 2010; Eurostat, 2009; Marcu, 2009)

environment conducive to their activities. Trade agreements are one among many routes through which governments help the corporations at the waist of the food system hourglass. Other support is available too. If an overseas investment seems a bit risky, a public-funded export credit agency or perhaps the World Bank can help shoulder the risk directly, or persuade a country to underwrite the risk itself. If a country refuses to accept a particular product on grounds of health, safety or environmental concerns, direct diplomatic pressure can be applied.[28]

Against accusations that they are merely selling favours to the highest bidder, governments have gone to great lengths to ensure that interventions in the food system can be seen as functioning in the national interest. Often, these views are genuinely held by the people who provide governmental support, and the public undoubtedly benefited from initiatives such as the US New Deal, the European welfare state and the Indian Public Distribution system. Yet governments' motives are rarely pure. Governmental concerns about poverty, for example, have historically been driven by fear, not least because of their concerns of what large groups of politically organized, angry and hungry urban poor people might do to the urban rich. In the UK, back at the beginning of the twentieth century, Cecil Rhodes was a passionate advocate of colonialism as a means to hush the speeches of angry workers on street corners who wanted for bread.[29] And, in different ways, the countries of Europe and North America set their food policies in order to ensure that the cries of the urban hungry didn't lead to civil war.

To put it slightly differently, the current food system isn't an arrangement dropped from the sky. It's a compromise between different demands and anxieties, of corporations pushing for higher profit in food, of governments concerned with social unrest or, occasionally, a drubbing at the polls, and of urban consumers. Written out of this story are the rural communities, who seem to be suffering silently. And yet it is they who are leading the way in forging a new and different food system. They do it out of necessity, for they are dying.

Ways of Being Free

To none do countryside hymns sound flatter than to people in dying rural communities. As lands have fallen before the banks, repossessed and repurposed, suicide rates for farmers across the world have soared. Yet farmers and the dispossessed are not going quietly. There have always been, and continue to be, rebels. The food system is a battlefield, though few realize quite how many casualties there have been. While consumers have been only recently wrestling with the problems of how to eat well, farmers have long been fighting against the vanishing of their freedoms, and their battle continues today. From the ten-million-strong Karnataka State Farmers' Association (Karnataka Rajya Raitha Sangha or KRRS) in India, to the *campesinos* (translated as 'peasant' but without the pejorative association in English) in and from Mexico – there's a fistful of organizations not only fighting against this food system, and sometimes dying in protest, but building alternatives to it, and living in dignity.

Farmers' groups in the US, India and Mexico, for example, have taken their grievances about low prices from their fields to the barricades outside the World Trade Organization, or to the offices of companies that end up buying the fruits of their labour, like Taco Bell, or to the offices of the corporations who profit from the sale of seeds and pesticides, like the Monsanto Company, or to the governments which have abetted rural privation.

In Brazil, over one million landless people have organized and occupied disused farmland. As a result, they are living healthier, longer and better-educated lives than those in comparable schemes elsewhere. The members of this movement, the Brazilian Landless Rural Workers Movement, are part of arguably the world's largest independent social movement organization – La Via Campesina (The Peasant Way),[30] claiming a membership of 200 million people worldwide.[31] Incorporating groups from the KRRS, with an estimated membership of twenty million in India, to the National Farmers Union in Canada, the Korean Women

Farmers Association, the Confédération Paysanne in France and
the União Nacional de Camponeses in Mozambique, it's nearly as
globalized as the forces against which it ranges itself. It's a mixed
bag of movements. Some of its members are landless, some own
land and hire the landless; some are small producers, some are
medium-sized; what counts as a small farm in Canada is an estate
in India. Clearly not all farmers are equal, and neither are their
social organizations.[32] Even within countries, there are important
differences. In the US, for example, black farmers have consistently had it harder than white. One of the largest anti-discrimi-
nation lawsuits was settled in 1999 by the US Department of Agriculture, in restitution for consistent and ongoing discrimination
against black farmers in the distribution of federal funding.[33]

In the places where they fight, each movement confronts specific conditions, constraints, opposition and arms. Yet they are
able to unite around a common understanding of the international food system – the view that informs this book. These movements don't restrict themselves to joint analytical work. They are
also able to come together in action, in complex and sophisticated
ways. When the 2004 Indian Ocean tsunami struck farmers and
fishing communities in Indonesia and Sri Lanka, the movement
was there helping them to rebuild.[34]

As the hourglass shows, though, the food system doesn't just
put farmers at the blunt end of abuses of power. Consumers are
also subject to the market power of corporations. Of course, as
consumers our position is slightly different – as consumers we
can shape the market, however slightly, by taking our wallets elsewhere. But the choice between Coke and Pepsi is a pop freedom –
it's choice lite. Community organizations are fighting back for a
deeper kind of choice. The ways such organizations have tried to
reimagine our choices range from the creation of alternative food
distribution mechanisms for people of colour, such as the Peoples'
Grocery in Oakland, California, to the struggle to redefine what
food means, as the gastronomic grammarians at the Slow Food
movement are trying to do. Groups around the world have been

trying to broaden the food system to give back the choices that have been taken away from the people who grow, and the people who eat.

Of course, no group is without contradiction. There is no pure ideology made flesh, no holier-than-thou land in which resistance is perfect and untrammelled. We all make our politics with the tools we have at hand, in the places we find them. And I've made choices in presenting the politics I have in this book. There are social movements that want to turn back the clock – that are ready to funnel rural discontent towards conservative chauvinism and xenophobia. So, no mention in this book of the traditions of rural radicalism that have, for instance, generated the Ku Klux Klan.[35] The history of movements for 'pure food' aren't unsullied either. The British Soil Association, for example, provided agricultural advice to the British Union of Fascists in the 1930s, both being keen on the purity of blood and soil.[36] The wish of environmentalists to imagine a pristine environment and pure food, without any farmers or immigrants on the land, isn't only a European failing. The Sierra Club in the US has also been riven by worries over whether immigrants belong on the horizon, or beneath it.[37]

Instead, this book examines the fights over the food system that have a bent towards a politics of internationalism, ones with vistas as wide as the corporate globalization that they fight and shape and supplant, movements that can embrace migrants rather than lynch them. Despite the despair in the fields, such movements exist, and are binding themselves to one another through gifts of seeds, of culture and of practical successes. These movements aren't just the 'alternative' at the end of the desolate story. They're the constant reminder, throughout, that choices are there to be made, and to be imagined. Not just choices to turn back the clock, but to imagine something new. This can only happen after a cold look at where we are now, and at what has failed.

The Menu of Chapters

This book travels the length of the world food system, beginning with choices made in the fields and ending with the choices that are made for our palates. In the course of this book, I look at some of the ways the food system is shaped by farming communities, corporations, governments, consumers, activists and movements. The sum of these choices has left many stuffed and many starved, with people at both ends of the food system obese and impoverished, and with a handful of the system's architects extremely wealthy. Sometimes, the choices produce new ways of being free, and of connecting with one another, and the world around us. Sometimes, the choices are desolate. The next chapter examines farmer suicides, and the forces that are destroying rural communities across the planet. From the city, it is hard to see the violence in the countryside, both physical and economic, to which rural communities have been subjected. In the city, we see the effects of rural devastation through migration, both domestic and international. Chapter 3 takes stock of this migration, and situates it in a discussion of one of the most powerful instruments of modern rural change – the trade treaty.

The history of trade agreements is bound up with that of food aid, development and insurrection, and chapter 4 discusses the evolution of the global food system in the aftermath of the Second World War. The food system was designed to redistribute just enough to keep it stable, but the needs of the world's poorest have never been foremost in its design. Chapter 5 scrutinizes the food system's major winners, agribusiness corporations, and chapter 6 shows how their rise to power has used ideas of race, science and development to further their control over the very source of life: seed. On the way, national histories have been rewritten, to suggest that no other choice could have been made. Chapter 7 gives a concrete example of how all these forces have come together in one of the most important crops on the planet's surface: soybeans. An increasing number of us, however, meet the food system not in its fields or factories, but in its emporia of choice, and chapter 8 discusses the supermarket, the newest and now most powerful agribusiness. Chapter 9 asks how our tastes are sculpted, and how the food system constrains us not as consumers, but as people living in the world. The final chapter suggests that there are ways to reclaim our sovereignty, to become more than just consumers, by reconfiguring the food system and rewriting the relations of power that exploit people both in growing, and in eating. There are no guarantees that the hard tasks of living differently will succeed. But unless we choose to try, we are certain to fail.

2

A Rural Autopsy

See-Saw, Margery Daw,
Jack shall have a new master;
And he shall have but a penny a day,
Because he can't work any faster.

See-saw, Margery Daw,
Sold her bed and lay on straw;
Was not she a dirty slut
To sell her bed and lie in the dirt?

Traditional[1]

And on That Farm He Had a Wife

In a playground near you, children playing on the see-saw are
singing a song. It lilts from fifth to major third, as the frame tips up
and down: *See-Saw, Margery Daw*. They'll only sing the first verse,
and they'll sing the words like a mantra, devoid of meaning but
full of pleasant mouthy sounds, as they push one another off the
ground. The second verse of their song has been expunged from
memory. It's not unlike the way most children, and most of us living in cities, come to understand the countryside. If ever we think
of fields, our thoughts about the countryside are benign, passive
and vapid. To become and remain an idyll, the rural is forgotten,
sanitized and shorn of meaning to fit the view from the city. For
our purposes, airbrushing the countryside serves us badly. To understand the constraints on how food gets to us, we need to see

agriculture's collateral damage, and the ways in which the food system is already being imagined and built differently.

The city, now home of the majority of the world's people, writes the country.[2] But the country writes back, and always has. Let's take an example, one of many that we could choose, but one we might pick for its pervasiveness, its grip on the collective imagination. Consider India.[3] India fought for, and won, independence from colonial rule in 1947, and since then has been busy trying to write its own rags-to-riches story. At one level, it has succeeded. Today, India is, in the imagination of many outside the country, the place where all the jobs have flown, a Neverland of highly skilled workers willing to toil for very little. The new maharajahs of the IT industry routinely trumpet the industry's growth rate (19 per cent per year between 2004 and 2008)[4] and hail the pool of talent created by the government's investment in education. Much has been banked on this myth. India's ruling Bharatiya Janata Party (BJP) government even marched into the 2004 elections, with campaign literature depicting smiling fair-skinned Indians, triumphing over adversity, under the slogan 'Shining India'. The BJP lost the elections.

Yet, in parts, there's some truth to the 'Shining India' rhetoric. Go for a stroll anywhere within a couple of miles of the major city airports in Hyderabad and Bangalore, and you'll see a great deal of shining. Hewlett-Packard, Infosys, IBM, Dell, Intel, Microsoft, Acer, and Oracle all have sparkling new office blocks, glinting in the smogged sun. Hyderabad, the capital of the Indian state of Andhra Pradesh, is a town on the move. The corridors through which money flows – from airport to business park to government headquarters – have been polished so brightly they are unrecognizable to the city's older residents. At night, the young people from the back offices come out to unwind in a parade of tight jeans and scooters, women with boyishly short hair driving their 200cc scooters from call centre to coffee bar. This is progress of a kind. Yet even within the city, it doesn't hold true everywhere: hundreds of thousands of the city's eight million residents live in slums,[4] drawn to the city in hope of a better life, and with vanishingly little hope of ever joining the ranks of the tertiary-educated elite.[5]

If the narratives of urban progress camouflage poverty in the city, the tales told of rural India obliterate the very idea that suffering might be possible (unless it's the redemptive kind). Just as the United States has its heart-warming tales from 'the heartland', and England's Albion is always rural, India has sentimental stories of 'Mother India'. In these tales, the nation was born in the fields, and the proud modern state, now more urban than rural, is the offspring of the countryside. Reality is rather at odds with these homely national fictions of bucolic bliss. To take some scattered examples: in the US, more drug-related killings happen in rural America than in its cities; in the UK, more young people kill themselves in rural areas than in the cities. And India's stories of progress and homeliness come undone in the fields too.

Five hours out of Hyderabad, far from the money and the glitter and the bandwidth, in India's fields, it's still possible to find women with short hair. Shaven-headed children too. Parvathi Masaya[6] has a cropped cut quite different from the hair of other women in the village when I meet her on a hot, late monsoon day. I've pulled her away from her job making disposable plates from leaves. The younger of her two sons, a six-year-old, scrunches and unscrunches her sari in his hands while she talks. The eight-year-old is in a nearby classroom – joining in a chorus of reading from a blackboard.

Parvathi's day is long. It begins at 5 a.m., when she prepares food for her sons and does some housework – washing, cleaning clothes, fetching water. The children need to be in school by 8.30, and she drops them off before heading to the plate 'workshop', outside a neighbour's house. At 6.30 p.m. she returns, picks up her children from a neighbour, and goes to bed between 10 and 11. The plate-making pays badly – 25 rupees (US$0.56, GB£ 0.35) per day. It's not enough for her to bring her children up on. 'I used to put chillies in the rice to make it last longer, but then the boys fell sick. Now, my parents help me with a little money.' Parvathi has her own land, four acres of it. It lies fallow at the moment. 'I'm waiting for my boys to finish school. In maybe four years [when her eldest son, Chandramouli, reaches twelve], he'll be able to work in the field. I can't go into the city by myself [where wages might be higher]. Who would look after the children? So I'll make plates. And we'll survive.'

She doesn't blame anyone for what happened: 'I am not angry – what would be the point? If I were angry, I would not come back.'

At its peak, her family earned 12,000 rupees per year – less than US$0.74 (GB£0.46) per day – through farming. That's when her husband, Kistaiah, was alive. On 11 August 2004, Kistaiah looked up at the cloudless sky and despaired. He had been sinking deeper and deeper in debt since 2000. He'd borrowed money because the rains had become erratic, and the groundwater had disappeared. Trying to grow rice, he had taken out loans to drill for water, initially borrowing Rs8,000 (US$181, GB£110) from a local bank, and then borrowing Rs90,000 (US$2,031, GB£1,236) from what Parvathi calls 'a neighbour' – the local money-lender. He'd sunk three holes across his land, and none had struck groundwater. And, by the second week in August, the rains still hadn't come. His crops were dying in the fields.

That night, after everyone had gone to bed, Kistaiah got up and pulled down a small plastic packet from the shelf, a cheery green and white print bag, a little like the Indian flag, but with a band of pictures of perfect vegetables at the bottom of the packet and, instead of the cartwheel in the middle, a red and white diamond marked 'poison'. He filled a cup with the granules, dissolved as much as he was able into the water, and drank it. Then he lay down next to Parvathi.

The pesticide was an organophosphate called 'phorate', classified as highly hazardous by the World Health Organization and so toxic that the Food and Agriculture Organization sees no way it can safely be used.[7] It is, however, widely available in India[8], with farmers in Andhra Pradesh consuming 35 per cent of the national total.[9] It entered Kistaiah's body while he was still mixing it, passing through his skin and lungs even before it reached his lips. It jammed the receptors in his nerves. His respiratory muscles became paralysed. He likely slipped into a coma before succumbing to asphyxia. He can't have convulsed very hard. He died without waking his wife or two sons.

Parvathi shaved her hair off on 12 August 2004 in a ritual of grief.

Kistaiah was well liked by everyone in the village. 'He was a bit quiet, a good farmer, and a good man,' says Narasimha Venkatesh, the village representative. Kistaiah is mourned. But he was not alone. Authoritative figures are difficult to come by at a national level, but the state of Andhra Pradesh, with a population of seventy-five million, has been recording rural suicide rates in the thousands per year.[10] Nor is this a problem limited to Andhra Pradesh. The hinterland of Mumbai, where the city finds its food,[11] has experienced rocketing rates of farmer suicide. It's a problem that has even hit India's breadbasket. In Punjab, the epicentre of the country's high-tech agricultural 'Green Revolution', the United Nations scandalized the government when it announced that, in 1995–6, over a third of farmers faced 'ruin and a crisis of existence ... This phenomenon started during the second half of the 1980s and gathered momentum during the 1990s.'[12] It has been getting worse.[13] According to the most recent figures, suicide rates in Punjab are soaring.[14] As one newspaper put it, this sad end to the farmers who were meant to have thrived under India's brave new agricultural future is a 'Green Revocation'.[15] In 2009, 18 of India's 28 states reported increased farmer suicide rates.[16] During that year alone there were 17,638 recorded farmer suicides, one every 30 minutes for an entire year.[17]

Not all poor farmers kill themselves in India, of course. Rather than suicide, some farmers have sold their kidneys. In Shingnapur, a village in the Amravati district of Maharashtra, farmers have gone one step further, setting up a 'Kidney Sale Centre'. 'We ...

invited the Prime Minister and the President to inaugurate this kidney shop ... Our kidneys are all we have left to sell,' said one farmer.[18]

Shingnapur isn't alone. Many villagers have simply put themselves up for sale – bodies and all. Within villages, too, there is inequality. Beyond the pervasive inequality between men and women, there is a key difference between those who still own farm land and those who have nothing left to sell but their labour. While farmers are more likely to die by their own hands, landless families systematically face the threat of starvation.

One might want to explain the despair that precipitates suicide as part of some idiosyncrasy, as a failure of the Indian government. Yet across the sea, in Sri Lanka, there's a similar story. Averaged out over the country, pesticide poisoning was the sixth biggest cause of death in Sri Lankan hospitals, but within six rural districts, with a population of 2.7 million people, it was the leading cause of death in hospitals.[16]

East Asia is experiencing similar trauma. In China, '58 per cent of suicides were caused by ingesting pesticide', and there are two million attempts per year.[19] Of a sample of 882 suicides in China from 1996 to 2000, wage-earners and students comprised 16.9 per cent, homemakers, retirees and the unemployed comprised a quarter, but agricultural labourers made up over half of the dead. They were also the people most likely to die by other injuries.[20] And rural suicide rates are two to five times[21] those in urban areas, with women slightly more likely to kill themselves than men.[22]

We can also see an increase in some of these suicides in rich countries, not just poor ones. In Australia, the most acute rises in rates have happened in rural areas[23], and recent droughts have increased the risk of suicide in agricultural regions. A spokesperson for the National Farmers Union in the UK put it this way: 'There is not a farmer in the country that cannot name at least one friend, associate or colleague from within the industry who has taken his life because of the concerns they have for the future.'[24] Since 1982 in England and Wales, male farmers have had the highest rate of suicide of any profession. The date is no accident – it is in tragic synchrony with farmers across the Atlantic.[25]

In the US, during the 1980s farm crisis, the Midwest suffered a spate of suicides. Commenting at the time, Glenn Wallace, regional programme manager for the Oklahoma Department of Mental Health, spoke of feelings that would be all too familiar to farmers in the Global South today: 'the loss of a farm or the impending failure is worse for many farmers than the death of a loved one. The feeling of guilt that a family has when the sheriff's-sale sign goes up on the place a great-grandfather homesteaded is more than they can bear.'[26] National statistics are hard to come by and, strikingly, conclusive studies are yet to be conducted.[27] But although Midwestern suicides seem to have peaked between 1982 and 1984, a number of other features have remained constant.[28] Women, for instance, bear a triple burden, working both on and off the farm to supplement low incomes, as well as returning from paid work to take care of the home and participate in community activities. At least 25 per cent of US farmwomen find themselves in this position.[29] At the same time, rural America continues to become disproportionately poorer. In 2003, only eleven of the two hundred poorest counties in the US were metropolitan,[30] and while the drug-related homicide rate fell in urban areas in the 1990s, it tripled in rural areas.[31] In 2009 almost one in six people living in rural areas in the US fell below the poverty line.[32] While the acute symptoms of rural distress may have been dulled, its chronic features continue to plague the world's richest country.

Crooked Fictions

When suicides are recounted – and they seldom are – the death finishes the tale with the finality of the full stop at the end of this sentence. But the lives of families continue, and communities survive. These are not only individual tragedies, but social ones. If we

look at them from the perspective of society, farmer suicides cease
to be full stops at the end of a life. They become tragic ellipses in
the struggle of a community. Within rural areas, there's mounting
evidence to suggest that the burden of this tragedy is borne un-
equally. Women carry its brunt. In one district in Southern India,
for instance, a study found that the suicide rate for young men
was 58 per 100,000. For young women it was 148 per 100,000.[28] As
a yardstick, the rate in the UK is less than 5 per 100,000.[29] Rather
than understanding farmer suicides as a series of awful vignettes,
then, it makes more sense to see them within a more complex and
tragic tapestry. They're an acute symptom of a chronic malaise in
India's rural areas.

Mangana Chander, a strong and outspoken woman classed in
the Indian government's typology as 'tribal', lives in the village of
Nerellakol Tanda ('place where water always flows').[33] Two hours
out of Hyderabad, its twenty-seven households have unusually
small amounts of land, their tenure at the whim of the local land-
lord. They don't earn enough from their land to eat. So they do
what increasing numbers of rural families do – they migrate. 'We
women, fifteen of us, go to Hyderabad at a time, to do construction,' says Mangana. 'Women get Rs80 per day, men get Rs90–100
per day. There's a place where you sit waiting for work. If there's
a big house being built, then they come and get you. If there's no
work, we don't eat. It doesn't happen often that we work continuously. So each month is ten days in the city, fifteen in the fields,
and five days' rest.' Mangana is lucky. She borrowed just a little –
Rs2,000 (US$45, GB£27) a year ago, which has been compounded
by the moneylender to a debt closer to Rs3,000 (US$68, GB£41)
now. Her children are in school. She thinks they might have a
chance for a better life than her. But she's not certain. 'The people
in the city need to understand how hard we fight to survive.'

Women surviving under these conditions, especially after the
death of a partner, are fighting hard. Sometimes, the extended
family can help out, as in Parvathi's case, by sending along a few
extra rupees to keep the children fed. In some cases, they can

compound the disaster, handing the family land over to the dead husband's brother, treating the wife and children like slaves. In some states, the government offers compensation if it can be proved that certain conditions are met – forty criteria in some provinces.[34] In some cases, the village headman refuses to certify the death as a suicide unless he gets a taste of the compensation. When families get debt relief, creditors are paid off. But the debt is never forgiven. Even after the government hand-out, rarely is there enough money to put the family back onto any sort of secure long-term footing. So mothers are pushed by many prongs to the cities, to become domestic workers, construction worker and sometimes sex workers.

If the suicides and women's struggles have been written out of the story it is in part because their existence has also been whittled away. Officially, they can't possibly be suffering because, according to the government, the number of poor people in India has been falling. Farmers, and women farmers above all, are India's poorest people. Part of the telling of the fairy tale of 'Shining India' demands that the poor disappear. In India, this has been achieved through the waving of a magical, statistical wand.

A tireless scholar and award-winning journalist of rural India, P. Sainath, has tracked how the rural poor in India have become works of creative fiction. In the early 1990s, for instance, the Indian government commissioned a team of experts to put together a method of finding out the country's exact total of poor people. After a methodological review, investigation, debate and deliberation, the panel announced that two in five Indians were poor. The Indian government reacted as most governments, North and South, have tended to do: they found a panel of experts willing to certify that the number was substantially lower. Using outmoded methods, the government announced not that two in five Indians were poor, but rather that the number was less than one in five. That said, 'less than nine months before it found a fall in poverty in the country [the Indian government] . . . presented a document [at an international donor conference in Copenhagen] saying

39.9 per cent of Indians were below the poverty line. It was, after all, begging for money from donors. The more the poor, the more the money.'[35]

Economist Utsa Patnaik has followed the statistical sleights of hand that have enabled India's poor to vanish since the 1970s, and she has calibrated her observations by going back to one of the central features we associate with poverty – hunger. At the beginning of the 1970s, over half the population was classed as poor. Two decades later, in 1993–4, the number of poor people had fallen to just over one-third. This progress was achieved in no small part because the official threshold for poverty had been lowered. In the 1970s, being on the poverty line afforded you 2,400 calories per day – in the early 1990s, you were afforded only 1,970 calories per day. By 1999–2000, just over a quarter were poor – an impressive reduction. But the threshold for poverty meant consuming fewer than 1,890 calories per day. Patnaik anticipated, 'by the 60th Round, 2004–05 [the poverty line] is likely to be below 1,800 calories and correspond to less than one-fifth of rural population'.[36] Her predictions came true. By 2004-05, the official poverty line was at 1795 calories per day.[37] In 2007, when the official figure for poverty in India is around 28 per cent, a more accurate calculation based on the implied calorie norm of 2,400 per day puts 87 per cent of the population under the poverty line.[38][39] To put it slightly differently, around half a *billion* people have been written out of poverty, by the simple expedient of shifting the goalposts and the diligent advertising of present and future prosperity. This is how the story of 'Shining India' is told – with an official narrative about poverty that directly contradicts the facts. Jobs have been created for the educated middle class, but for those without access to education the story has been rather different.

Debtward Ho

A man can hold land if he can just eat and pay taxes; he
can do that. Yes, he can do that until his crops fail one
day and he has to borrow money from the bank. But –
you see, a bank or a company can't do that, because those
creatures don't breathe air, don't eat side-meat. They
breathe profits; they eat the interest on the money. If they
don't get it, they die the way you die without air, without
side-meat. It is a sad thing, but it is so. It is just so.

John Steinbeck, *The Grapes of Wrath*[40]

A rule, as true in the United States as in India, is this: farmers
who kill themselves have been scythed by debt. S. S. Gill, a professor of economics at Punjabi University who has studied the
phenomenon in India, even has a prediction: 'Show me a farmer
with five acres, and 150,000 rupees (US$3,386, GB£2,061) in
debt; I will say to you he is sure to commit suicide in the future.' In
Andhra Pradesh, for instance, 82 per cent of farmers are in debt,
and in Punjab, Kerala, and Maharashtra, the number looms over
50 per cent.[41] One study shows that in Maharashtra, 86 per cent
of farmer suicides studied were a result of indebtedness.[42] The
main reason they take their first loan is to invest in the land and
crops (although, like everyone else, they also borrow for other
reasons, like paying for weddings or health care). Debt has its origins in the entrepreneurial impulse. Urged towards cash crops by
the government (and, as we shall see, the large seed companies),
farmers adopt plants that they can buy and sell in the market:
cotton and groundnut, and to a lesser extent rice and sugar cane.

In India, before free market reforms, the government offered
a minimum support price for crops so that farmers could know
in advance what sort of returns they'd get, all being well in the
fields. If all was not well in the fields, there was a system of support payments, and a Public Distribution System for produce that
would provide cheap and wholesome food for all who needed it.

Although the free market was allowed to operate to some degree, the government would provide support for infrastructure, and the irrigation that the new crops needed, and outreach services in order to provide research for farmers, and information for them on new seeds, techniques and crops. It was a blend of free market and government assistance.

At the beginning of the 1990s, this bundle of supports for the rural poor started to be untied. Under the banners of reform and liberalization, the government began to dismantle its imperfect but vital public assistance systems for farmers, so that they could be exposed to the harsh but improving, and now untrammelled, disciplines of the free market.[43] Unfortunately, the free market neither supported nor redistributed to farmers who fell on hard times. Offering lower prices and fewer supports than the previous social arrangement, the freer market in agricultural goods presided over a split between rural and urban incomes. Every support that farmers had come to rely upon was systematically pulled away, and the farmers fell. At the same time, as the state of Andhra Pradesh's own *Commission on Farmers' Welfare* noted, urban areas attracted foreign investment and glass towers.[44] The result was that the rural hinterland's income was unhitched from the city, and in the decade after 1993, rural income fell by about 20 per cent while urban income increased by 40 per cent.

Indian farmers responded by organizing and protesting. Responding to rural unrest and the prospect of a drubbing in upcoming polls, the government launched an ambitious loan waiver program in 2008, forgiving Rs.710 billion ($US16 billion, GB£9.75 billion) in debt. But to be eligible for debt forgiveness, farmers needed to have taken out formal bank loans – the roughly 85 per cent of farmers with informal loans were excluded.[45]

Despite the government's failure and the farmers' understandable anger, there's an important point to consider here. Perhaps all is going to be well in the long run. Perhaps the divergence between urban and rural income, unfortunate though it may be, is just a bump in the road. Perhaps the increasing levels of inequality that we see around the world are transient. There's an economic thought experiment that predicts this, and which is important to understand. Imagine you've got two places and a population spread between them. Let's call these places the country and the city. In the city, wages are high, but at the start of our thought experiment, there are very few people living there. By contrast, in the country, wages are low, and the majority of people are there. Inequality is low, because almost everyone's earning the same low wage.

Now imagine that people drift to the city. When half the population is in the city and half in the country, as we have in the world at the moment, you'd expect inequality to soar, as it has over the past few decades. That's just a mathematical fact. If the wages in one place are low and in another place are high, and if there's an even split between the two, then of course there's going to be inequality. In the future, we might imagine that everyone will move to the city, and live on high wages. Inequality will be low and, what's more, wages will be high for everyone. There are, in other words, reasons to think that we don't have to worry about inequality because, in the long run, it'll come out in the wash. This is a logic which postpones worries about inequality, as levels of inequality increase worldwide.[46]

Two problems, though. First, the data in Andhra Pradesh show not just rising inequality, but *increasing* rural poverty. Rural communities are worse off in both relative and *absolute* terms. And, second, it's far from clear that the people from rural areas are actually the ones benefiting from higher wages. Although the pull of the city may involve the promise of a higher standard of living, no-one is there to make sure the promise is kept. But, as Utsa Patnaik cautions us,

> Let no-one imagine that unemployed rural workers are
> migrating and finding employment in industry: there
> have also been massive job losses in manufacturing dur-
> ing the reform period and the share of the secondary

sector in GDP has fallen from 29 to around 22 per cent
during the nineties, in short India has seen de-industrial-
ization.[47]

In other words, the vaunted 'Shining India' has seen not only rural
decimation, but also a progressive fall in the level of blue-collar
jobs. These are jobs in which one might have expected India to
excel, with its low wage rates. But no. India has skipped past industrial development, to become a software giant, a knowledge
economy in which one third of the population is illiterate.

After Despair

I was speaking to Sheshar Reddy, a leader of a farmer movement
in Karnataka, about crop prices, when he learned I was interested
in farmer suicides. 'My son committed suicide,' he said. 'He was
good-natured fellow. He was always helping other people with
our tractor. But I think he was worried about not being able to
get married. I'm not sure. One day he went to the clinic because
he had some sickness. I don't know why he killed himself. But he
committed suicide that day.' You'd have to listen very hard to pick
up the very faintest wobble in Reddy's voice. 'I myself have often
thought of killing myself,' he continued. 'If it wasn't for the farmers' movement, I think I would.'

Reddy is chair of the Karnataka State Farmers' Association
(KRRS), one of the largest movements in the world. Founded in
the early 1980s, and based on principles of self-reliance, it has already brought together millions of peasants within Karnataka. It
has also, according to Reddy, dramatically reduced suicide rates.
This may be true, and there are good reasons to imagine why it
would be. Social movements provide tangible support and help to
communities in need. But they also provide hope, and the promise of change. In India, the KRRS has been working with farmers
movements elsewhere in India and around the world to meet the

challenges facing their members, through protest, self-help, new farming schemes and rural education, including a programme which translated and distributed a draft of the World Trade Organization's charter document to the fields. The debate and discussion of texts by peasants in Karnatakan fields happened in 1992, seven years before the WTO's 1999 Seattle meeting, which is when most of the rest of the world caught on to the WTO's dangers.

Membership of a movement does not, however, confer immunity from despair. One of the most important descriptions of farmer suicide has come from a South Korean farmer, a former leader of a Korean producer's movement, who killed himself in 2003. These are his words, from a pamphlet he distributed on the day he died.[48]

> Once I ran to a house where a farmer with uncontrollable debts had abandoned his life by drinking a toxic chemical. Again, I could do nothing except listen to the wailing of his wife. If you were me, how would you feel? ... Wide and well-paved roads, and big apartment blocks and factories, cover the paddy fields that were built by generations over thousands of years. These paddies provided all the daily necessities – both food and materials – in the past. This is happening even though the ecological and hydrological functions of the paddies are even more crucial today than they were before. In this situation, who will take care of our rural vitality, community traditions, amenities and environment?

On 10 September 2003 at the World Trade Organization Ministerial meeting in Cancún, Lee Kyung Hae, a Korean farmer and peasant organizer, climbed a fence near the barricades behind which the trade meetings where happening. He flipped open his red penknife, shouted 'the WTO kills farmers'[49] and stabbed himself high in his chest. He died within hours. Within days, from

Bangladesh, to Chile, to South Africa, to Mexico, tens of thousands of peasants mourned[50] and marched in solidarity, peppering their own calls for national support for agriculture with the chant: 'Todos Somos Lee' ('We Are Lee').

Lee's was an activist life. In 1987, he was a leader in the founding of the Korean Advanced Agriculture association. His Seoul Farm, in Jangsu, South Korea was built on unforgiving country, not the sort of land on which Lee's neighbours thought he'd be able to realize his modest cattle-farming ambitions. Lee went to agricultural college, where he met his wife, and then returned to start farming. He installed a mini cable-car to pull hay up the hill in winter. He started a trend in electric fencing. He poured himself into the land, and into farming. Seoul Farm became a training college, and, in 1988, the United Nations recognized him with an award for rural leadership. It might have ended happily ever after. Except that the Korean government decided to lift restrictions on the import of Australian beef. The Australian government has been a strong supporter of the cattle export industry – Australia is the largest beef exporter in the world – and the concession to increase sales to Korea was a victory not only for Australian corporations like Stanbroke and AustAg, but for the large distribution companies like Cargill Australia and Nippon Meat Packers, owned by US and Japanese interests respectively.

The Korean government knew that the price for cattle would fall with the entry of the cheap Australian beef and so encouraged Korean farmers to make ends meet by upping the size of their herds, the extra cattle being paid for with loans. Following government advice, this is what the Lees did. But the price of beef stayed low and flat, and in order to pay off the interest on the loans, they had to sell cattle. Even shrinking their herd by a few head per month, using the cash to pay the loans, the Lees were unable to keep their land. In the end, Lee Kyung Hae lost his farm. It was the first time that anyone had seen him cry. His family found him in a cinema, in tears, ashamed to be seen in his grief.[51]

Did the WTO Kill Lee Kyung Hae?

I went to Korea to find out more about why Lee died. At the time of his death, Lee Ji Hye, one of his three daughters, said, 'He didn't die to be a hero or to draw attention to himself. He died to show the plight of Korean farmers – something he knew from personal experience.'[52] She was halfway around the world when she heard of her father's death. Kang Ki Kap was there at the time. Also a farmer, he is now a member of South Korea's National Legislature. Kang used to be a footsoldier with the Korean Peasants Association – he has his finger on the pulse of farmer politics and is a smallholding rice farmer. He, like Lee, knows the plight of Korean farmers first hand. And he sets it into context with the patience of a poet:

> The most essential things for human beings are the elements – sun, air, water and food. These are the essential resources for people's lives. God decided that these things would be the enjoyment of all, so that all might live. He does not intend that we monopolize the elements – yet because they're so abundant, people treat them as trivial, they do not take them seriously. The trend, the wind behind the WTO, is the globalization of the capitalist system. The fundamental contradiction is the polarization of the rich and poor, with the poor getting poorer and the rich getting richer. Some might say that this is the natural logic of competition. But if you're a human being with reason and conscience, then the WTO should be eliminated. Especially the agricultural sector and market pressures. Agricultural products should be saved as a human right. To live, people need to eat. You cannot commercialize this. It's such an anti-human behaviour, not just anti-social, but anti-people.
>
> And what has this to do with Lee Kung Hae's suicide at the WTO?

The reason I've told you all this is because I wanted
you to understand the impact that the trade system has
had on Korean farmers. The WTO policy is like a bomb to
peasants. They can't even live with agricultural products.
Before, a year's salary was the equivalent of eleven bags
of rice. Now eleven bags is US$700, which is one month's
salary. In most of the farming towns, 60–70 per cent of
people are seventy years old. Since it's not so profitable,
they're all in debt. They cannot pay back.

Among the local conditions into which the WTO plays, debt is
foremost. The problem of farmer debt is global, and I heard tell
of its contours from farmers around the world. The first loan isn't
the problem – it is, indeed, the promise, the hope of a better life.
The dream begins to crack when it can't be repaid. In South Korea,
since 1996 a member of the rich country club, the OECD, entire
villages have collapsed under debt. With the constant need to find
new sources of income, farmers have invented borrowing clubs,
guaranteeing loans for one another. They've remortgaged their
land so often that nobody else will lend to them except each other.
So they've drawn on Korean tradition, and made use of a social-
ized pyramid banking scheme. The system involves loans, remort-
gaging and refinancing to continue to bankroll the loss-making
farm operations for as long as they can. It's as ingenious as it is
desperate. It postpones the repossession of land. But it's utterly
precarious. When a single farmer defaults on payment, an entire
group is affected. When one goes under, another can't repay in
time, and therefore yet another goes into receivership, triggering
an avalanche of bankruptcy.

It's a reality that farmers in the US also face. George Naylor, a farmer and leader of the National Family Farm Coalition in
the United States,[53] puts it this way: 'The truth is obvious to most
farmers that commodity prices lower than the early 1970 prices
together with prices for things a consumer buys to farm and support a family at year 2000 levels means that it is almost impossible
to earn a living on the farm.'[54]

In any other business, perhaps the owner would have walked away, given up, tried something else. But the land that farmers work is often the land that was given them by their fathers and has been in the family for as far back as anyone can remember. To be the generation responsible for ending that legacy is too much to bear. This was certainly the story with the wave of farmer bankruptcies in the US in the 1980s. And it's not as if the trends hadn't been in place for a while. There had been a lengthy process of expulsion from the land beginning in the Dust Bowl years.

The number of US farms had been falling for decades, while the size of farms had been increasing. Debt had been the singular motor both of the increase in farm sizes and for the destruction of farming families. In a bid to make the farms more profitable, and then in a bid to repay the original loans when the economy turned sour, farmers borrowed heavily, mortgaging the soil on which they worked. When the banks came to repossess the land, some chose death over the dishonour of losing land that had been in the family for generations. The men who died in the US, as would those who would die in India two decades later, fit a strikingly similar profile: middle-aged, devout, well liked, a little introverted and dedicated to their families.[55]

So why can't farmers pay their debt? Part of the reason, clearly, is that the prices of most agricultural goods have been falling. Yet low prices aren't the end of the world, at least in the short term. There are ways around low prices. If you know that you're going to get low prices, you can plan – you can switch to grow something else, for example. Yet one of the greatest ironies in the shift towards markets in food is that by joining the world market, farmers have lost the very thing that justifies faith in the market's efficiency – price signals.

Suppose you're a farmer recently cast into the pool of the free market in, say, South Africa. You look for the return on a crop that will cover your expenses. Maybe you decide to stop growing food crops, and devote your entire land to cotton – between 1993 and 1996, prices for cotton were high. But for six years after that, the prices fell, as the former Soviet Union's textile industry, one of the

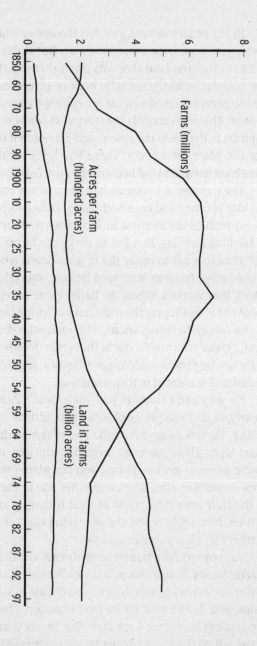

Fig. 2.1 Farm size and concentration in the United States 1850–2000
(Source: Hoppe and Wiebe 2003)

world's largest, imploded. With food crops for consumption in a local market, you know that if there's a generally good harvest, then your prices will be low, but because you've produced enough, you'll do okay. If everyone produces little, prices go up, and you'll be okay. But if you're growing cotton for the international market, you're hostage to a number of forces far beyond your control or ken. Is the US subsidizing its cotton farmers to produce at lower rates than you could ever produce? Is the slump in the former Soviet Union going to be offset by increasing Chinese demand? And even if the cotton market picks up, is the exchange rate going to be low enough for you to be able to export? Without an effective minimum price system in place, you've absolutely no guarantees at all. In other words, globalizing the market has effectively transferred control of farming away from the farmer, and into the hands of those who can shape that market.

Some Farmers Are Pushed

The market isn't always shaped through market forces. Or, better, market forces aren't just supply and demand. 'The hidden hand of the market will never work without a hidden fist ... McDonald's cannot flourish without McDonnell Douglas,' observes *New York Times* columnist Thomas Friedman.[56] What Friedman forgets is that the guns are invariably pointed not at terrorists (or people who look like them). The guns are trained on civilian populations most of all. Particularly in the Global South, poor people are under threat of direct physical harm, never more so than when they try to exercise their rights. In taking a stand against the illegal appropriation of their land, or even in merely raising their voices against the injustices they face, peasant groups across the world are targeted, often with impunity, by local and national forces, both public and private.

The catalogue of violations bruises the imagination.

In South Korea, farmers took to the streets on 15 November

2005 to protest the liberalization of rice imports. Kang Ki Kap had gone on hunger strike for twenty-eight days to try to prevent it, but in the end, the liberalization bill passed by 139 to 66. The Seoul Metropolitan Police, notorious for their liberal use of violence, clashed with the farmers. Many were injured, including Jeon Yong-Cheol, a 43-year-old farmer, whom the police beat over the head. When he returned home that evening, he collapsed. Nine days later, he died of cerebral haemorrhaging.

In Brazil, the targeting of peasant leaders has been an ongoing government and private-sector project. Over the past two decades, and according only to official sources, at least 1,425 rural workers, leaders and activists have been assassinated there. And yet only 79 cases have ever been brought to trial. In 2005 alone, there were 1,881 recorded conflicts in the countryside, with over 160,000 families experiencing some sort of disruption to their security. Further, three workers were worked to death on plantations, and over 7,000 were effectively enslaved.[57]

Similar stories of oppression can be told about about many other countries, from the Philippines to Honduras, from Colombia to Haiti, from South Africa to Guatemala.[58] In all these countries, when farming groups and workers try to assert their rights collectively, they face the wrath of local police, hired guns and, at best, judicial apathy.[59] For some, joining a movement can be a death sentence. Yet despite the repression, farmers' movements are expanding.

Collectively farmers have been fighting back. From the US farmer and writer Wendell Berry, to 'Prof' Nanjundaswamy, founder of the KRRS farmers movement in Karnataka, India, there are dissenting voices and visions. Chukki Nanjundaswamy, daughter of the late leader, and now an international emissary in her own right, explains her father's vision: 'All we want is a fair price. We're not asking for anything more. My father called it a "scientific" price – a price that includes the cost of growing, the cost of labour, the cost of land. Nothing more.'

One of the other KRRS farmers, Versatanarayanam, says, 'Our

message is this to the world: we the farmers need to stand on our own two legs. We don't want financial assistance, we know how to do this with our own resources. We don't want to be dependent on the WTO, the IMF (International Monetary Fund), the World Bank,' he says, naming the other international organizations that have shaped a great deal of economic reform in India (and that are discussed more in chapter 4). 'What they give, they give to spoil us. We're not beggars, we're creators. We have self-respect and we can be self-reliant. We can control our own resources.' For that to happen, though, the forces that currently control the resources will need to be confronted and dismantled.

But Where Does It Stop?

'It's not me. There's nothing I can do. I'll lose my job if I don't do it. And look – suppose you kill me? They'll just hang you, but long before you're hung there'll be an-other guy on the tractor, and he'll bump the house down. You're not killing the right guy.'

'That's so,' the tenant said. 'Who gave you orders? I'll go after him. He's the one to kill.' 'You're wrong. He got his orders from the bank. The bank told him, "Clear those people out or it's your job."'

'Well, there's a president of the bank. There's a board of directors. I'll fill up the magazine of the rifle and go into the bank.'

The driver said, 'Fellow was telling me the bank gets orders from the East. The orders were, "Make the land show profit or we'll close you up."'

'But where does it stop? Who can we shoot? I don't aim to starve to death before I kill the man that's starving me.'

John Steinbeck, *The Grapes of Wrath*[60]

Like millions of farmers at the top of the food system hourglass, Lee Kyung Hae was subject to the choices of others. The price he received for his cattle was beyond his control. The forces that shaped the market staked him at their mercy. He and his farming movement were brushed aside by their elected representatives. He chose to end his life. Even then, the venue was chosen for him. At the invitation of the Mexican government, the World Trade Organization had chosen to hold its 2003 Ministerial Meeting in Cancún. But Lee could pick the time. On Chuksok, the day of the Korean harvest festival and ancestral remembrance, Lee stabbed himself in his chest with his knife.

But what killed Lee Kyung Hae? Lee had used his body as a canvas of pain before – slashing himself across the stomach outside the building of the WTO's predecessor, in protest at its impending demands on farmers. He had regretted it afterwards, calling it an 'impulsive and uncontrolled action'. We might simply want to ascribe his suicide to an unstable personality. And yet. Although Lee flipped open the blade, we're not above asking for reasons that exist outside him. The question is how far we're prepared to look. The young man who started the Korean labour movement, Chun Tae Il, died by his own hand in 1970. After his death, it was said that 'his mother killed him'.[61] Yet today, we can read his decision to die for the movement as a mixture of romanticism and an assertion of his self in the face of circumstances designed to crush it. The same might be said of Lee Kyung Hae. The words of his last pamphlet weren't a conventional economic analysis, though they certainly called on economic fact. His analysis was a humanizing paean – one that put a face on globalization by counting the human costs. His statement wasn't of the 'goodbye, cruel world' variety, but a serious and honed critique of the forces that have long been at work on him, and other farmers. If one looks at Lee's words, engages with them, criticizes them,[62] it's possible to understand his actions as a way of his reclaiming control of his body in defiance of a system that wouldn't let him. And it's a system that stretches far beyond the WTO.

Although India served as our point of departure, I've argued here that there's a global crisis facing small farmers, one that's harder still for the landless and, above all, for poor women. As we'll see in the next chapter, although the WTO might get the blame for trade liberalization, it isn't the only, nor the most significant, fund of trouble for farmers. The food system has a web of different treaties and organizations that help to shape it. In Mexico, NAFTA, a prototype for the WTO, was extended to cover agriculture by the Mexican government, against the advice of the US government. In India, the decision to liberalize agriculture was a cocktail of local and imported ideology. Certainly, the WTO gets blamed by national governments, who sigh and explain that they would very much like to support farmers, but are prevented by the WTO from doing so. These governments neglect to mention that they have chosen to tie their own hands, chosen not to be able to help. Why governments would choose to do this, and how trade fits into a broader vision of national development, is the subject of the next chapter.

3

You Have Become Mexican

Within hours of Lee Kyung Hae's death, word had spread through a global network of small farmers, through phone calls, faxes, the Internet and word of mouth. Peasants on protest marches against the WTO in India, Thailand, Brazil and dozens of other countries observed silence in his memory. In Mexico, at the epicentre of grief, the chants from *campesinos* were the loudest. Half the chants for Lee were in English, half in Spanish: 'Todos somos Lee' ('We are Lee') and 'Lee no murió OMC lo mató' ('Lee didn't die, the WTO killed him').

The hardest chant to understand is this: 'Lee, hermano, te has hecho Mexicano' ('Lee, Brother, you have become Mexican'). It's worth trying to make sense of this shared identification, and to understand its power. Lee's becoming Mexican in the eyes of *campesinos* points to a shared kind of rural experience, a way of living, a way of dying. His struggles with free trade, his lack of freedom under the market and his despair after bankruptcy were so familiar to the *campesinos* in Mexico that he might as well have been Mexican. As the home of NAFTA – the North American Free Trade Agreement – Mexico has long been a pioneer in experiments with free trade, and trade in food in particular. Understanding how Mexico became a laboratory for certain kinds of trade experiments, and society's subsequent actions and reactions, gives us a model for understanding why farmers in vastly different countries – South Korea, Mexico, India and even the United States – find much in common in each other's lives, and deaths.

NAFTA and After

The North American Free Trade Agreement, an economic union between Mexico, the United States and Canada, was the mother of all free trade agreements. Although not the first such agreement (the European Union had long been a free trade area), NAFTA was the first to mesh two rich countries with a significantly poorer one. Not only that, NAFTA specifically included trade in agriculture, pitting the livelihood of Mexico's poorest against the most productive and highly subsidized agricultural sectors in the world. The rationale behind the trade agreement was this: the spark of wealth would, it was argued, jump across the border, bringing freedom, enterprise and the Good Life from a country of high potential to one a little less charged.[1] For some Mexican farmers, the spark has indeed ignited the gentle burn of wealth.[2] Those with larger landholdings, and living near the US border, have been brought closer to rich consumers. With access to funding and expertise, richer farmers have survived, and some have even thrived off NAFTA.[3] In the main, they have been farmers who've been able to access the lucrative US horticulture market, using the cheaper labour and land to grow fruits and vegetables for consumers across the border. But supplying fruits and vegetables is a tough game – Mexico supplied only around 2 per cent of the total consumed in the United States.[4] Only the minority of famers, 16 per cent, have the abundance of resources and support that allow them to compete.[5]

Further away from the border, and further away from wealth, small farms, which make up 85 percent of farmers in Mexico,[6] have been faring badly.[7] Indeed, for the majority of poor farmers, NAFTA hit hard. And that's because the crop they grew was treated with a mixture of contempt, ignorance and incompetence during the negotiations. Responsible for 60 per cent of the land cultivated in Mexico at the time the treaty was concluded, a source of livelihood for three million producers, and 8 per cent of the population, that crop was corn. Mexico is the centre for the world's corn biodiversity. It is where corn began, and today, forty distinct domesticated varieties are commonly grown, with hundreds of others still in existence. It remains a key staple food, not to mention a source of identity and community.

It was clear from the outset that corn farming would be hard hit by trade liberalization. The price at which US farmers sold their corn was much lower than the cost to produce it. In 2002, for instance, US corn cost US$1.74 per bushel to buy but US$2.66 for US farmers to produce.[8] This, because the United States had long supported its farmers and had made a range of subsidies available to them for machinery, fertilizer, credit and transport.[9] With the advent of trade liberalization, it was clear that US corn, subsidized by the US government, would destroy the livelihoods of the poorest in the Mexican rural economy. The cost of producing corn in Mexico was far higher than the subsidized US level. And yet NAFTA was approved by governments on both sides of the border.

The signs weren't good. Almost as soon as NAFTA began, on 1 January 1994, the Mexican Peso crashed, with a 42 per cent devaluation of the peso against the dollar.[10] Notwithstanding an initial spike, the real price of corn for Mexican farmers has fallen continuously since NAFTA began. But farmers didn't respond by growing less corn. In fact, the amount of corn that farmers grew *increased*. If one believes in laws of supply and demand, this might seem odd. Price is meant to be society's Great Communicator – a means for announcing, clearly and unequivocally, that society wants less or more of something. When prices go down, it's usually a sign that there's too much of it around to warrant producers' efforts to make more. The one thing they shouldn't do, then, is produce tons of it.

Microeconomic theory *does*, however, predict the panic. It does this by noticing that the world can't be rearranged in a day. It takes time for market signals to cause resources to be reallocated. So, when prices change, we can split up time into three blocks – an instantaneous period, the short run and the long run. In the 'instantaneous' period, when the price signals change suddenly, surprised producers find themselves unable to do anything but continue to produce. In the short run, producers switch away from production and, in the long run, supply and demand equalize.[11]

In Mexico, when the price of corn fell, the message many farmers received was that they were on their own, that the government was shuffling off its commitment to them, and that farmers had better think of some other way of feeding themselves and their families. The method farmers chose to face the falling price of corn was to grow more of it, to generate an income to meet the rising prices of all the things they couldn't provide for themselves.[12] Although free market thinking assumes that farmers can invest in other crops, the reality was that few had the necessary resources in order to be able to switch. Lacking money, technology and access to distribution networks, already relegated to the poorest-quality soil, without irrigation, and with indigenous corn so well suited to these conditions, there was little else farmers could do. As a result, after NAFTA, the farmers that could increase their production did so.[13]

Some, farmers, however, despaired. As in India, farmer suicide rates are rising. In 1990, rural suicide rates for men were 3.9 per 100,000, and for women 0.6 per 100,000.[14] By 2001, the rate had jumped to 6.1 per 100,000 for men and 1.2 per 100,000 for women. These are the rates for the entire population. Studies suggest that the rate for farmers is likely higher, and the number of deaths related to suicide almost certainly under-reported, given the particular stigma of suicide in a Catholic country.[15] We shouldn't use suicide as our *only* compass of social distress, not just because it is a blunt and unhappy metric of poverty and despair, but because it diminishes us to think like this. To reduce suffering to a grim body count is to erase the daily travails of those still living, fighting to survive. That suicide rates have soared in agricultural states (Campeche and Tabasco had rates of 9.14 and 9.85 per 100,000 in 2005, almost three times the national average)[16], is the beginning of our understanding, not a substitute for it.[17]

Yet perhaps farmers' distress ought not to come as a surprise. Producers aren't meant to be the winners from trade liberalization. Indeed, there's a radical kernel at the heart of the free trade competitive rhetoric which precisely targets producers. By forcing what is assumed to be a small number of producers to compete with one another, the price of what they produce falls. The few (producers) profit less, and the market redistributes the gains to the many (consumers) who can now buy goods just a little bit more cheaply.

The power of this model comes from assuming that the market looks like a pyramid, with a few on top scalping the many at the bottom. The trouble is that agriculture doesn't look like this. In agriculture, there are many at the top, and they are often substantially *poorer* than their customers. The consequence of slashing prices to the poorest farmers and farm workers is that, as producers, their income drops. As a result, they're able to consume very little at all.[18]

All this was predictable in advance. It is, after all, the way one expects economic change to work: it's the 'creative destruction' of capitalism at work,[19] with the inefficient being shucked away, and the efficient being given room to create. And what of the 'inefficient', of the poor rural farmers with few options? It is argued that the aggregate social benefits from trade make the pie bigger, and that with a bigger pie, those most hurt by the change can be given a slice of resources to cushion the blow of change, and to train them for their new and uncertain future. Particularly in the Global South, trade liberalization has rarely been accompanied by working mechanisms to redistribute its gains to the poor, or to provide meaningful work or retraining for those left unemployed by the consequences of market shifts.[20] This is because liberalization is part of a bigger political philosophy – one in which government intervention (even to provide a basic protection for rights) is considered meddlesome and inefficient. This is why, with few exceptions, the era of trade agreements has also been the era of increasing inequality.[21] Even as the world as a whole becomes wealthy, most poor people are being left behind.[22] The creative destruction of modern capital, almost by definition, crushes those least able to protect themselves, and whose contribution to society is priced low. And as part of this, the trade treaties that represent the zenith of our economic and political age signal a weakening, rather than a renewed, commitment to social redistribution. It's unsurprising, then, that Mexico's farmers have had it tough.

With the fall in the price of corn, and the subsequent glut, one might think those in urban areas with some income would be able to buy it more cheaply. It is they, the many consumers, who are intended to benefit from the magic of free market competition. Very few people, however, eat raw corn. It's usually processed in some way. In Mexico, the key Mexican staple is the tortilla. Traditionally, tortillas are made by hand, and by women, in a labour-intensive process that begins with boiling raw corn in lime water.[23] The process not only makes it easier for the corn hulls to be removed, but the alkalinity of the water releases niacin and other nutrients.[24] After thoroughly washing the limewater out of the corn, it's ground down into a dough known as *masa*, from which the final tortillas are then made.

When the price of corn fell, one would have thought the price of tortillas would also have dropped. But it didn't. It actually saw a price *rise* as NAFTA began. In January 1994, the average price for a kilo of tortillas was around 0.50 pesos. By 1999 the price was seven times higher.[25] This, again, makes no sense if we read the price of tortillas merely as an indication of society's costs and wants. There are many reasons why free trade failed to deliver on its promise of cheaper goods to consumers. Partly, the problem lay in the inflation that followed the peso collapse, when prices began to increase overall. But that wasn't the only reason, and it doesn't explain why tortillas should have been particularly subject to inflationary pressures.

Recall the waist in the hourglass food system. The many producers are not directly feeding a mass of urban consumers, but selling to a few food processors. It is *the intermediaries*, and not consumers directly, who benefited from the initial fall in the price of corn. In Mexico, the primary use of corn is tortillas. And in the tortilla market, the number of food processors is very small indeed: two. The players, GIMSA and MINSA, together control 97 per cent of the industrial corn flour market. GIMSA is owned by Gruma SA, which alone controlled 75 per cent of the corn flour market in Mexico, and 85 per cent of the corn flour market in the US.[26] It's a Mexican multinational with US$3.8 billion (GB£2.3 billion) turnover in 2010[27], best known in the US, where it dominates the tortilla market, as Mission Foods.[28] The Mexican government changed the mechanism through which it gave subsidies to its flour millers, switching to a system that allowed the subsidies given to the two largest producers to grow from US$2 billion (GB£1 billion) pesos in 1994 to US$5 billion (GB£2.5 billion) in 1998.[29] On top of this, the Mexican government decided to scale back the state-run social security system for the poor, which made cheap tortillas and basic food items available in government stores.

With the reduced income support, poor families were spending increasingly large parts of their income on food – and with prices going through the roof, the poor were hit hardest.[30] As a result of NAFTA, 1.3 million Mexicans were forced off their land. The flood of labour into the cities caused a 10 per cent fall in industrial wages. Female headed households have seen their poverty rate increase by 50 per cent.[31]

NAFTA was brought into Mexico in the name of cheaper goods for consumers, and under the banner of the efficiency that the market can bring. If it substantially failed in doing this, and this had been predicted to have dire consequences for the poor, the question then becomes 'why did the government let NAFTA go ahead?' To answer this, we need to take a step back, and look at NAFTA's context, and Mexico's history.

Corn for the Rich Men Only

> They said they were an-hungry; sigh'd forth proverbs,
> That hunger broke stone walls, that dogs must eat,
> That meat was made for mouths, that the gods sent not
> Corn for the rich men only: with these shreds
> They vented their complainings.
>
> Shakespeare, *Coriolanus*, Act I, scene I

We can begin our story in the 1970s and 1980s, when a new breed of economists, trained in the United States at a handful of elite institutions, began to find their way into Mexican government.[32] Foremost among these educational institutions was the University of Chicago, the birthplace of 'neoclassical' economics and free market libertarianism. Schooled in this economics, and its attendant political philosophy, these technocrats displaced the domestically educated, and usually legally trained, officials who had owned the business of government in the decades after the Second World War. The graduates from the new guard were able to advance themselves in large part because they had developed connections with key officials and organizations abroad, institutions to which an increasingly globalised and indebted Mexican economy needed access in order to survive. This generation of economists was able to out-manoeuvre, and wield greater resources than, their domestically educated counterparts. With their rise came the triumph of a certain kind of thinking about how 'development' might occur, what was thinkable and what was not.

The leading producers of knowledge about development supported and assured Mexico's young Turks. As the *Financial Times* reported in 1992, these producers included the World Bank. The Bank is an organization discussed in a little more depth in the next chapter. Suffice it to say, for the time being, that as the world's foremost source of loans for and opinion about economic growth, it was a powerful actor in the world of indebted developing countries, and an important ally for those Mexican governmental functionaries who spoke its language:

> When President Carlos Salinas decided to overhaul Mexico's antiquated agrarian laws, officials from the agriculture ministry called their friends in the World Bank to ask them for advice ... The World Bank wrote issue papers; the Mexicans responded in kind. Draft laws were written and rewritten. Eventually a constitutional amendment was drawn up, and passed ... Such intimate collaboration hardly raises an eyebrow in Mexico these days. The World Bank has closely advised Mexico on most of its economic reforms in the past decade – on trade opening in 1985, on the debt deal in 1989, and now on education, agriculture and the environment. In the last fiscal year ... the World Bank approved more non-poverty loans for Mexico than any other country. Approvals totalled $1.882 billion, an impressive $927 million more than Brazil, for instance.[33]

This access to the World Bank, simultaneously its finance and its knowledge about what to do *with* that finance, is an example of the kinds of resources which US-trained economists were able to bring to Mexico. But it wasn't only through access to a surfeit of dollars that the economists were able to entrench themselves in the Mexican policy establishment. Crises are opportunities, and Mexico's financial crises, particularly that of the early 1980s, were a central moment of triumph for 'new thinking' in Mexico.

After having devalued the peso in 1976, Mexico was trying to relaunch its economy, exporting oil and using the revenue to borrow heavily on the international capital markets. When oil prices dropped but international interest rates rose, and the US economy entered a recession, the peso collapsed in 1982. The 1982 debt crisis inaugurated Mexico's 'austerity' period – a policy authored, again, by US and US-trained Mexican technocrats.

Public spending was slashed. Government spending on agriculture plummeted, and programmes to support poorer farmers
were cut to the bone. By 1988, for example, over 10,000 irrigation
projects stood rusting in the fields.[34] Farmers' access to credit was
cut by two-thirds, with its administration shifting from the public
to the private sector. The result was that poorer farmers found
their low profits and high risks to be unacceptable to the market –
and they were unable to borrow.

The government argued that anti-poverty programmes would
help to cushion the blows. But the social programmes themselves
were undergoing 'austerity', and spending on them fell by 6 per
cent per year. In 1988 the National Solidarity Programme (PRO-
NASOL) was introduced, which in its turn sought to provide support for poor communities, but exhibited a strong bias towards
urban areas, where families could benefit from food subsidies of
up to US$145 annually, compared to US$10 in rural areas.[35]

Yet not all agriculture suffered under 'austerity'. Export agriculture, with the dollars it would bring in, became a way for
the economy to emerge quickly from the Mexican crisis. In the
recovery from the disaster of the peso crisis, agricultural export
businesses grew quickly, faster than the rest of the economy, at
the same time as hunger and poverty increased. Indeed, under
the debt negotiations, Mexico cut its tariffs from around 40 per
cent to 10 per cent.[36] For the right kind of agriculture, the kind
that required high levels of mechanization, inputs, credit, access
to markets and, of course, intermediary corporations to trade the
grain internationally, the crisis wasn't a disaster.[37] Yet for poorer
farmers, by the time NAFTA began in 1994, extreme rural poverty
was higher than it had been in 1984.[38]

NAFTA proved a godsend to those associated with the New
Thinking in the Mexican establishment. As sociologist Sarah Babb
observes:

by the time of the Salinas administration (1988–94),
organized popular interests were not playing a major role

in the negotiation and formulation of government policy. Similarly, the demands of small- and medium-sized Mexican businesses were effectively prevented from interfering with the negotiations leading up to the North American Free Trade Agreement – an agreement that run directly counter to the interests of many such businesses. In contrast, the eight most elite, powerful sectors of Mexican business did play an important part in negotiating the terms of liberalizing reforms in Mexico – particularly (although not exclusively) around the terms of the North American Free Trade Agreement (NAFTA). However, the impetus for NAFTA and other liberalizing reforms did not originate from domestic big business. Rather, actors within the Mexican state first chose to implement liberalizing reforms and *later* successfully mobilized big businesses as their allies in pursuing a course of free-market reforms.[39]

In other words, the government itself pushed for international trade in food, motivated primarily by ideology. Indeed, their US counterparts were surprised that this was an area in which the Mexican government was prepared to negotiate. The US was concerned that the economic impacts of free trade on farmers would cause such poverty that it might destabilize the Mexican countryside. The Mexican negotiators reassured them that all would be well.[40]

The negotiation of NAFTA represented a shift away from a commitment, however fragile, to poor people's livelihoods and towards a technocratic arrangement designed to benefit the extremely wealthy.[41] It was a result achieved only with the patina of democracy.[42] And it was one for which the Mexican government was happy to pay. As part of the liberalization of the corn trade, the Mexican government was allowed to 'transition' the price difference between local and international prices over a period of fifteen years, and to impose a limit on the amount of corn imported into the country. Any amount above this limit was subject to an import duty.[43] Between 1994 and 1998, when US corn imports to Mexico regularly exceeded this limit, the Mexican government chose not to charge the duty, arguing that allowing the corn in was keeping inflation down. The sum they decided to forgo? Two billion dollars.[44]

Once Were Farmers

> Little one, little one
> I can lift you to the sky
> I can cut your legs away
> I can remember your first kiss,
> your first goosepimple,
> your first crush
> I can bring the rain
> Ten pesos, ten pesos.
>
> Overheard on the Mexico City Metro

Mexico City, the fifth-largest city in the world, is home to over 20 million people. Its streets are a riot of sound and smells. Whichever part of Mexico you left to come to the city, you'll find its distinctive cuisine on sale by the side of the road. The rich, chocolate Mole Oaxaqueño, *cemitas* (a kind of omnibus bread roll) from Puebla, *salbutes* from Yucatán: all is there. At the centre of the city is the Zócalo, the City's central plaza. On one side is the Palacio Nacional, inside which is a staircase with a mural by Diego Rivera, a dense tapestry of Mexican history. At the top left is Karl Marx, holding *The Communist Manifesto*, pointing to the future.[45] In that crimson dawn, as far as it can be glimpsed, there will be industry and electricity and observatories and, at the tip of Marx's outstretched finger, a large-scale monoculture, with trees laid out like shopping aisles.

One version of this sterile, unpopulated and soulless vision of the future of agriculture has come to pass – under NAFTA. And it was the reason that on 31 January 2003 more than 100,000 peasants took to the streets of Mexico City in the largest protest against the government in living memory. Organized by the *El Campo No Aguanta Más* (The Countryside Can't Take Any More) coalition, the Zócalo was filled with more protesters than it had ever seen before. 'We are people of the corn, survivors who refuse to disappear,' said one slogan, 'Countryside yes, trade no!' another.[46] The coalition of peasant movements, some with historically close ties to the state, some with deeply oppositional ones, came together to demand that the government remember them. Demanding not merely recognition, but equality. The *campesinos* mobilized themselves, their families and their memories of Mexico's history: from the 1910 Revolution, with its promise of land for all; to the early 1980s, when, in certain areas and with the benefit of autonomous peasant mobilizing, the state had actually supported poor farming communities;[47] to the most recent betrayals of the latest Mexican administration. In the words of Luis Sánchez y González, a farmer from San Luis Potosí, 'When [the President] was on the campaign trail, he promised many things. And they have come to nothing. I gave my vote to Mr Vincente Fox, but I say no more . . .'[48]

In travelling to the city, the market's inequities became painfully clear. Sara de los Reyes Pérez, a farmer from Chiapas, noticed the disparities between the rural and the urban markets, and the price inflation along the way – 'the price of the products we sell every day has fallen. When we arrived here and wanted a cup of coffee, they charged us seven pesos. [In Chiapas] we sell it for two pesos per kilo . . . We have marched to change things.'[49] International inequities were also on the agenda. It was announced, to awe and insult, that the subsidy for every head of EU cattle was more, per day, than the income of three Mexican farmers. Also shared was the lament that, with soils and communities dying, children were heading to the cities, or 'to the north', leaving behind ghost towns of parents and grandparents as if the Pied Piper himself had twirled away an entire generation of Mexican youth.

NAFTA has encouraged migration from the country to the city (often then to live in the growing shanty towns).[50] Others have taken greater risks, dodging the border police, to find a better life up north. This trajectory, from country to city to border crossing, is one that has been imposed on them. Yet *campesinos want* a better life, and they want it in rural areas, in the communities where they live. The organizers of the *El Campo No Aguanta Más* events went so far as to apologize to the residents of Mexico City for the disruption of the protest, noting 'better one day with 100,000 peasants than a lifetime of 500,000 migrants, exiled by the governments of Carlos Salinas, Ernesto Zedillo and Vincente Fox.'[51] *Campesino* movements in Mexico were fighting not to have to move, to emigrate, if they could avoid it. They wanted employment, support, security and equality between the countryside and the city. To achieve this, they demanded redistribution. With government policy tilted firmly against them, Mexican migrants found themselves not only pushed off their land, but pulled forcefully to the United States. And they redistribute the money home from there: in 2010, US$22.1 billion (GB£13.5 billion) was sent, through official banking channels, back to Mexico.[52]

This is part of a global trend in migration, from the country to the city, and from the South to the North. In 2002, when NAFTA was being concieved,[53] the billionaire Texan presidential candidate Ross Perot projected that there would be a 'giant sucking sound' as the last US jobs drained into Mexico's lower-wage economy.[54] Globally, the biggest sucking sound comes from the slewing out of people from rural areas and into cities. The present countryside population is 3.2 billion, and will start to fall from 2020, while cities are becoming the engines of population growth.[55] More people now live in cities than in rural areas. For those in the Global South who can make it, though, the pull of richer countries can be more powerful, and in some cases more lucrative, than leaving the country for the city. Those who are able to migrate across international borders are profoundly important in keeping their home countries, their families and their communities alive.

In 2010, the global total of funds sent by immigrants to their home countries exceeded US$325 billion (GB£198 billion). And those are just the officially traceable figures.[56] Unofficial remittances are estimated at 50 per cent higher. These funds far outstrip the meagre development aid given by rich countries to poor, and many countries in the Global South are dependent on the monies which these circuits of migration have brought.

Protest is one way that people in rural communities choose to respond to poverty – fighting to make governments pay attention to their plight, indeed, to stop governments causing their plight in the first place. The uprisings in Oaxaca and Chiapas, for example, have come from rural communities consistently overlooked by the government, consistently the poorest, and the first to cultivate corn: Mexico's indigenous people. Indigenous people have a systematically higher chance of being poor, less well educated and in worse health in Mexico, and in Latin America generally, than any other group.[57] In Mexico, as elsewhere, the government is largely unresponsive to their demands, leaving communities of the poor with few other options. And under these constraints, migration is a choice that such communities make.

Patterns of migration vary, but a constant theme is that people, usually young, from rural communities leave their homes, and their countries, sometimes at great risk, to come to richer countries. It comes at a cost to families. As one Mexican woman reported, 'the kids miss him [their father], but he has a secure job there [in the United States], they pay him every week. Even if it's not much, I am certain that this money will arrive every two months.'[58] The certainty of a domestically earned monthly wage is one that NAFTA took away. And migration is a global response to the rural insecurity that economic liberalization in agriculture has fostered. From Korea to Mexico to South Africa, communities in rural areas have aged, while their youth have gone to the cities or, in some cases, overseas. From Mexico to the US, but also from Guatemala to Mexico, from Eastern Europe to the UK, from Zimbabwe to South Africa, from Morocco to Spain, agricultural labour is being done by people who once were farmers, with farms of their own.

Beyond a Border

> We're over here because you're over there.
>> Traditional immigrant anti-racist slogan

The border lands are the ones most drastically affected by NAFTA. If free trade agreements are meant to galvanize the spark of enterprise across nations, it is the border, the line of greatest potential difference between countries, which becomes most highly charged. For although money and goods are conducted across borders with ease, people are not. At the line where Mexico meets the US, the American Department of Homeland Security had awarded the Boeing defence company an initial US$67 million to create a 'virtual fence' along a 28-mile stretch of Arizona. After receiving $1.1 billion to spend on this 'Secure Border Initiative', the Department of Homeland Security cancelled it in early 2011, deeming it an ineffective waste of money.[59] Nonetheless, border patrol remains a US$800 million per year expense for the US.[60] On the Mexican side of this patrolled invisible divide, things have changed quite dramatically. At the interface of rich and poor countries, there certainly has been increased employment and job creation. But, again, it is those already in positions of relative power who have benefited at the border. The success of men with land and wealth in the horticulture industry stands in bleak contrast to the fates of hundreds of women, predominantly those working in the foreign-owned factories brought by NAFTA, who have been killed in Ciudad Juarez, in the Mexican state of Chihuahua, on the border with the United States.[61] It is through their bodies that the charge of the free market has been grounded.

Money and goods aren't the only thing that have managed to

jump borders. Culture has too. In Mexico, there have also been changes in the foods people eat as a result of NAFTA, particularly in the increased availability and consumption of high-calorie food.[62] This has led to a spike in levels of obesity with, as noted in the introduction, the observation that the closer a family lives to the border with United States, the more likely it is that its children are overweight.[63]

Not only are Mexicans now consuming more food, they're eating differently too. The consumption of wheat-based instant noodles is now higher than that of beans and rice.[64] Today, Mexicans drink more Coca-Cola than milk.[65] The consequences are more than cosmetic. With over one in seven Mexicans living with diabetes[66], the cost to the country is US$15 billion (GB£7.8 billion) a year.[67] The way Mexicans get their food has also changed. Supermarkets have taken the country by storm,[68] Walmart Mexico is booming, commanding half of all supermarket sales in the country.[69] Three out of every ten pesos spent in Mexico on food are spent in Wal-Mex,[70] with spending on diet foods rising by 20 per cent in 2003, and with spending levels forecast to rise.[71]

The wave of fat breaking from North to South in Mexico has been interpreted by many as an imposition from above – not just from the US, but from the country's elites. In recent protests against ballot rigging in the election between Felipe Calderón and López Obrador, voters vented their fury not only in public squares around the country but, on 24 September 2006, in every Wal-Mex in Mexico City. Wal-Mex's largest shareholder, Manuel Arango, had allegedly sponsored a smear campaign against left-leaning López Obrador. By aiming at the finances of the right-leaning Mexican elite, protesters made both a material and a symbolic statement.[72] Every Mexican Walmart was taken over and, as checkout staff looked on (and sometimes joined in), protesters, with carts filled with goods grabbed bags of Lay's chips and turned them into percussion instruments, shaking them and chanting 'They shall not pass', and 'Don't buy this shit'.[73]

On the other side of the border, in the US heartland, farmers have had their own struggles, deeply linked to those of their Mexican counterparts. It's no coincidence that at the same time that Mexico was going through its 1982 financial crisis, US farming was experiencing its own spate of suicides. Both can be traced back to the low interest rates of the 1970s, when the world was awash with petrodollars.[74] Petrodollars are dollars acquired through the sale of oil, in this case oil from the members of the Organization of the Petroleum Exporting Countries – OPEC. The oil price increases of the 1970s had generated a great deal of money for individuals and governments in these countries. They reinvested much of it back into the international banking system.[75] With piles of money to lend, banks dropped the interest rate to the floor. The US and the Global South borrowed heavily. On top of this, US farmers were pushed hard by their government to grow more to sell to what seemed an insatiable global market. The increase in output and the decision by other countries to compete with US farmers in some of the same markets led to an agricultural glut, which in turn led to falling prices. This led to farmers stepping on the 'productivity treadmill':[76] driven by the need to service existing debt and facing lower returns for their goods, farmers borrowed more to pay for farm machinery, pesticides and even land. It was a treadmill spun at increasingly frenetic speeds, with output never fully matching the costs of production.

The investment was unsustainable. By 1980, for every dollar US farmers spent on growing crops, they received only US$0.97 in sales. Between 1976 and 1983, US farmers increased the amount of land they farmed by 16 per cent for fifteen major crops. But the storm was too much to weather. While farmers had been able to borrow at an interest rate of 2.6 per cent in 1978, they had to repay in 1980 at 5 per cent and by 1982 at 6.2 per cent. Such was the scale of the financial failure, even banks declared bankruptcy, both rural banks and urban.[77] Between 1979 and 1986, over a million jobs were lost in the farming and allied industries, although food processing saw a boom: the number of people employed in making pasta, breakfast cereal, chocolate cookies, crackers and sausages increased, and urban food outlet employment increased at double the national job growth rate.[78] Farm poverty rates jumped from 12 to 20 per cent between 1978 and 1986.[79] Suicide rates jumped.[80] And most statistical indicators of welfare were, and remain, the lowest for communities in the rural United States.

The Wrong Explanation

The despair of US farmers in the 1980s would perhaps have seemed more familiar to Lee Kyung Hae than would that of his Mexican counterparts. But with rare exceptions, those who speak in the name of farming communities in the US tend not to find the related experiences of overseas farmers terribly compelling. Here's a commentator who has posed, and answered, the question 'who killed California?' He arrives at conclusions with which, in small part, Lee might have agreed. In the words of this analyst, what killed California was:

> global free trade and the trade deficits it produced ...
> This has killed millions of manufacturing jobs, as thou-
> sands of companies closed factories here and shifted
> plants to Mexico, Asia and China. The Third Worldization
> of California is now far advanced. Yet those responsible,
> Bush Republicans as well as Clinton Democrats, still can-
> not see what they have done to our country.
>   But what is happening in California is not confined to
> California. It is happening across America ... unless we
> find a Congress that will jettison the free-trade madness
> that is denuding America of her manufacturing, what has
> happened to California will happen here. President Bush
> appears oblivious to it all – but then, so did his father
> before him.[81]

The writer is Pat Buchanan. Buchanan, a US 'traditional

conservative'.[82] He attributes California's decline to the devaluation of California's debt status, a US$38 billion budget deficit, and
'unrestricted immigration from the Third World, an unrepelled
invasion from Mexico'.[83] There's much with which many in the US,
Democrat and Republican, would find themselves sympathetic.
For Democrats and Republicans with sympathies for workers,
there's little to distinguish the economic policies of Bush, *père et
fils*, from those of Clinton. And in his thoughts on immigration,
Buchanan was not alone – a Zogby poll conducted in early 2006
suggested that 66 per cent of Americans thought that rates of immigration were too high.[84]

Although many have observed that free trade has hurt American workers, particularly those without a college degree,[85] Buchanan might have overstated his case a little when it comes to
California. California, the sixth-largest economy in the world,
seems to be alive and well, at least if you look at how much people
are earning. A year after Buchanan wrote his lament, average income increased by US$1,500,[86] and between 1997 and 2003, Cali-
fornia's economic growth rate was the third-highest in the country,
after Arizona and Idaho.[87] After computers, transportation and
machinery, California's largest export is agriculture, responsible
for over a tenth of the state's US$120 billion (GB£73.2 billion) in
exports in 2009.[88] California produces over half of the fruits and
nuts consumed in the US, and one quarter of the vegetables.[89] The
statistics are remarkable. Almost 64 per cent of California's land
in farms is irrigated,[90] and its 25 million acres (almost a quarter
of the entire land mass of the state is in agriculture[91]) produced
over US$34.8 billion in sales in 2009[92], with just 868 farms (1 per
cent of all California farms) responsible for US$11 billion of total
sales.[93] California is the home of the small farm, but don't think of
the little house on the prairie. Think high-tech. Because the systems of flexible production, just-in-time delivery, small niche service provision and flexible financing that we normally associate
with the information technology industry were forged in the Californian fields.[94] California has pioneered the food system, from

finance to production to processing to retail and, even, internet home delivery. As in the IT sector, immigration has always been a central part of farming in California. Indigenous people, followed by Chinese, Japanese, Filipinos, Mexicans, Punjabis, and Oaxacans, have successively been brought into the country, together with their foods, skills, seeds and expertise. These communities have farmed and brought agricultural prosperity to the state, despite facing stiff racism and exclusion.[95]

Yet all is not well in the Great State of California. Not all are sharing the gains of the largest industry, and for those on whose backs the industry is carried, life itself is precarious. California has a higher number of people in poverty than any other US state.[96] Within agriculture, farm workers die on the job at rates five times higher than other comparable work.[97] To do this, they are paid US$8.99 an hour.[98] And that's the entry wage rate for a *legal* job. Illegal jobs pay considerably less. Migrant labourers' wages have been falling in real terms throughout the 1990s with, in some areas, three workers competing for every open job. If immigration has hurt anyone the most, and most directly, it's the poorest immigrants themselves. Over the past two decades, migration has pushed down the wage rate.[99] That US jobs in the agricultural sector are taken by migrant labourers is the other side of the equation in Mexico.

In the US, migrant workers have found work in low-paying, low-skill jobs behind the scenes in industry (with women targeted by the textile[100] and domestic work industries[101]), as well as in agriculture. It is a fact of which many US citizens were reminded when, on 1 May 2006, hundreds of thousands of immigrants, with or without papers, stayed away from work on a 'Day Without Immigrants' General Strike. Many companies most directly affected on that day came from the food and food service industry. Tyson Foods, the world's sixth-largest food and beverage company[102] had to close dozens of its plants in the US, cutting back staff in other plants, and joining firms and companies like Perdue Farms, Goya Foods, Gold Kist, Cargill Meat Solutions and McDonald's Corp. in seeing its profits dented through the political actions of its immigrant workers.[103]

The strike was a rare moment. Most immigrants have little choice about the conditions or terms of their employment. They have been targeted in their places of work by the US Immigration and Customs Enforcement (ICE) police. Under the banner of 'protecting US citizens from identity theft', ICE raided the Swift & Co. meatpacking plant in six cities across the US in one day, arresting over 1,200 workers. At the time, Swift was the US's second-largest meatpacking plant. And the 'identity theft' involved the declaration of a false social security number, with the result that workers had been paying a portion of their wages into a US citizen's social security account which they would have no chance of accessing in the future. For this offence, many have been deported, including US citizens, while other have been jailed and separated from their children, and removed from their jobs and communities. It took only five months for Swift & Co. to re-hire all of their old workers. The company then sold to a Brazilian meatpacking company for US$225 million,[104] and one human resources employee, one Union official, and another low-level employee were charged with "harboring aliens" and procuring false documents.[105] Upper-level management at Swift & Co. remained untouched by the raids, despite evidence that the company systematically hired workers it knew to be undocumented.

Workers entering the country in desperate circumstances are vulnerable to exploitation, and there has been no shortage of those willing to sink to the task. In California, rural workers have long fared poorly. In the 1930s, the journalist and public intellectual Carey McWilliams provided a typically compelling summary:

> [No-]one who has visited a rural county in California under these circumstances will deny the reality of the terror that exists. It is no exaggeration to describe this state of affairs as fascism in practice. Judges blindly deny constitutional rights to defendants and hand out vagrancy

sentences which approximate the harvest season. It is useless to appeal, for by the time the appeal is heard, the crop will be harvested.[106]

McWilliams' disgust was echoed by John Steinbeck:

> No one complains at the necessity of feeding a horse while he is not working. But we complain about feeding the men and women who work our lands. Is it possible that this state is so stupid, so vicious, and so greedy that it cannot clothe and feed the men and women who help to make it the richest area in the world? Must the hunger become anger and the anger fury before anything will be done?'[107]

They found a champion in Upton Sinclair, whose 'End Poverty in California' pledge in the 1934 Californian gubernatorial race, on a Democrat ticket, might have succeeded but for a systematic and virulent campaign against him not only by the state's wealthy Republicans, but by fellow Democrats.[108] Electoral politics was, of course, unlikely to provide support to those unable to vote. For migrant, non-citizen farm workers, the struggle would have to start with themselves. And the United Farm Workers of America set about doing precisely that.

In 1962, the United Farm Workers (UFW) movement struggled for the recognition of the dignity of farm workers as workers, and their right to bargain collectively. Almost immediately, they ran into opposition from farm owners, who fired organizers and intimidated workers. Having exhausted other means, the UFW called for a boycott on the key crop from which growers had made their fortunes: Californian grapes.

Grape growers responded by organizing 'freedom to work' committees. Heavies from the committees trailed the United Farm Workers' organizers, harassing, intimidating and sometimes beating them. In the media, growers spent two million dollars on public relations firm Whitaker & Baxter to persuade Californians to reject the boycott, and to eat 'Californian grapes, the forbidden fruit'. When thousands forbade themselves grapes, growers turned to mouths with little choice about what was put in them – soldiers. Growers, in their greatest coup, successfully petitioned the US Department of Defense to buy the grapes which consumers didn't want to eat, and feed them straight to the troops in Vietnam. In 1968, the military bought 6.9 million pounds of fresh grapes. By 1969, they bought 11 million pounds, with shipments to Vietnam increasing five-fold.[109]

The United Farm Workers continued to be undercut throughout the 1970s. The most effective foils to their organizing came not through the efforts of farm owners, but through other unions and, bitterly, through their own victories. From within the union movement itself, the UFW was hurt by a hostile deal between farm owners and the teamsters' union, based in no small part on a shared racism, who together undercut the bargains that had been struck by the UFW. A further, serious, demobilization followed the UFW's own success. They fought for, and won, a body that recognized farm workers as workers with their own rights. Thus was created the Agricultural Labor Relations Board in California. Designed to provide adequate support to migrant farm workers, the institution signalled that the power for change lay now not in the hands of farm workers, but in the hands of the body least inclined to take up the issue – the government.[110] In the waiting for it to work, the movement lost momentum. Today, the UFW still fights for the rights of farm workers – winning concessions like basic access to toilets and running water – in an economy in which farm workers remain exploited, if a little less than before.[111] For those living in California, like me, swept along by the 'eat local' craze, this is a grim reminder that local needn't mean ethical. But there is a place in California where local does mean ethical, in a garden made magical by immigration.[112]

Bringing Agriculture to the City of Angels

The California whose death Buchanan has mourned is an agricultural state. Its 'third-worldization' was also the source of the protection for workers in one of its largest industries. Workers' dignity had to be fought for, and still does. And the most vigorous defence of workers' rights was achieved by immigrants, without the help of political parties, against moneyed growers, and sometimes against the state's military resources. Migration hasn't only built workers' rights, though. It has built models for non-racialism and environmental community which stand as beacons to the rest of California and, indeed, the world.

Beneath the flightpath to Los Angeles' LAX airport lie the gridded streets of South Central Los Angeles. From the plane window, it's grey block after grey block after grey block. A flash of green. Then grey block and grey block. Two thousand feet in the air is about as close as most Angelinos come to South Central. Its reputation as the epicentre of racial tension and riots scare most of the middle class away. It's an odd place to find Darryl Hannah up a tree. But Hollywood's conscience has roused itself in defence of some 350 families, almost all immigrants, from South and Central America and Asia, who worked in one of the US's largest urban gardens.

The space, fourteen acres, sits at 41st and Alameda (which is Spanish for 'tree-lined avenue') in South Central, on the frontier of a zone of warehouses and light industry to the east and a low-rise residential area to the west, amid smog and trains. And just off Alameda, it's a haven of calm, and a riot of plants. The ones I could name were fairly basic: beans, strawberries, onions, corn, blackberries, industrial quantities of cilantro, Washington Apples, pomegranate. And then there are the ones that I couldn't. Alfredo Vaquero (translation: 'cowboy') had been there since the land was given to the community in the wake of the 1992 uprisings. Originally, the land had been expropriated by the City of Los Angeles for a rubbish incinerator, but the city was forced to back down by the community. Alfredo and his son José pointed to *papalo*, *pipicha*, *chipilin*, *overas*, *chayote* (plants for which translation, at least for me, is impossible). For Alfredo, it's important that José learn about the food. 'It's a way of reconnecting to nature, and to the past,' he says. 'Many people who don't have a space here have children who are just left to the streets. If not here, where are they supposed to go?'

'Here I can learn the names of things,' says José. 'A lot of the other kids, they don't have anywhere to go to. And there's gangs on the streets.' The streets, and the crime in South Central, are a concern to father and son, and both know of friends whose kids have drifted towards the gangs. But stronger than the push off the streets was the pull towards the garden. Alfredo again: 'It's important for the people who live here, for people who care about their food. It would cost a lot to buy the food we grow here in the market. And actually, most of the food you can't buy anywhere. Plus, it's a space to socialize, to meet people. It's rare space to find nature here [in Los Angeles]. It's beautiful to hear the sound of the leaves.'

There were between 100 and 150 species of plant on the farm. It was an oasis in an urban jungle. There's very little green space in South Central – 0.35 acres per 1,000 people, compared to an average of 1.5 acres per 1,000 elsewhere in the city. Within the garden were foods from around the world, a variety that owes everything to migration, to hybridity, to diversity. It was a lush, quiet and safe space in an urban zone left for dead by the city authorities. It was a place where parents and grandparents sat in the shade of their trees, exchanging banter, gossip and snacks, while their children play together. It is part of immigration's bounty.

And it, too, has been embattled. When the city expropriated the land, it was worth little. Now they plan to sell it back to the developers from whom they expropriated it, for US$5 million (though its market value is around US$15 million). The community that has been built through the garden has been responsible for pulling up the value of the land. Despite this, and despite attempts by the community to raise enough money to buy the land outright, to get the legal system to come to their defence, and even to use Hollywood stars to bring attention to their plight, they were once again to be turfed off.[113] In 2006 the farm was bulldozed. For eight hours, almost 250 LAPD officers surrounded the area while over 50 deputies came to arrest 40 protesters.[114] The farm was destroyed but its topsoil was saved, shared among a range of farming and urban agriculture centres around Los Angeles, places where newly Americanised plants can still put down roots.[115]

It's important to take a moment to remember, against the language of parasitism and sponging with which migrants are confronted, that we bring histories, cultures and ideas to our new homes. Food in Britain, for instance, would be deeply impoverished without generations of migration. And, of course, the United States is itself a country founded on migration, and the extermination of those there before. Yet even after bringing memories and cultures across vast distances, escaping the collapse of the rural economy, it seems that some migrants are destined to end up fighting exactly the same fights for land, equality and justice, even in their new homes.

Lee Again

So this is how Lee became Mexican. The effects of economic change, through the 1980s and 1990s in particular, transformed the lives of farming communities on both sides of the US/Mexico border. Although trade has promised much for the poorest, and although economic growth has happened, economies have grown and left the poorest behind. The resistance to being discarded has taken many forms – organized protest, increased self-exploitation and migration have been covered in this chapter. These were the predictable outcomes of the move towards trade liberalization in food. NAFTA was the focus of protest for hundreds of thousands of Mexicans. The WTO was the focus for Lee.

We have seen, though, that trade regards 'low-skill' producers, and agricultural producers in particular, as part of the detritus of economic dynamism in the move to a more rational and efficient economy. In the next chapter, we'll see how today's food system has been shaped by a range of forces – idiosyncratic, accidental and mercenary – and how the rural poor have long been the system's most disposable component.

4

'Just a Cry for Bread'

> And Hiram sent to Solomon, saying, I have considered
> the things which thou sentest to me for: and I will do all
> thy desire concerning timber of cedar, and concerning
> timber of fir. My servants shall bring them down from
> Lebanon unto the sea: and I will convey them by sea in
> floats unto the place that thou shalt appoint me, and will
> cause them to be discharged there, and thou shalt receive
> them: and thou shalt accomplish my desire, in giving
> food for my household. So Hiram gave Solomon cedar
> trees and fir trees according to all his desire. And Solo-
> mon gave Hiram twenty thousand measures of wheat for
> food to his household, and twenty measures of pure oil:
> thus gave Solomon to Hiram year by year. And the LORD
> gave Solomon wisdom, as he promised him: and there
> was peace between Hiram and Solomon; and they two
> made a league together.
>
> Kings V, 8–12

This Old Testament example, chronicling a transaction around
1000 BCE, is one of the first recorded instances of trade between
nations. In today's global food system, of course, the players in international trade aren't only kings, and more is traded than wheat,
lumber and oil, and those who do the heavy lifting aren't called
'servants'. But in its use of one part of the world to feed another,
and in its mix of national politics with economics, Solomon's bargain with Hiram strikes a contemporary note. In sourcing his food
from beyond his kingdom, Hiram demonstrated an early insight

into what trade can offer. Viewed one way, trade is a technology for reducing the price of food, and a way of increasing the total amount of goods produced.[1] Through the international truck and barter of food, new tastes and sensations have been brought to the world, and food has become cheaper. This chapter offers an explanation of why and how we've been able to get used to cheap food, and at whose expense.

A Secret History of Refreshment

> The law doth punish man or woman
> That steals the goose from off the common,
> But lets the greater felon loose
> That steals the common from the goose
>
> Anonymous[2]

The story of the modern world food system begins in Europe, and in Britain in particular. Although vast trading empires have flourished and died in the Middle and Far East over the past 2,000 years,[3] the invention of the world's first global food network has its origins in the colonial trade routes plied much more recently between Britain and its outposts. Britain's colonial adventures were linked, in turn, to domestic changes, particularly those in the British countryside. From the fifteenth century, rural England was undergoing Enclosure, the process by which the community rights of the poor to the land of the rich were transformed into what we understand today by 'private property'. The rural poor found themselves without access to common land, and had only their labour left to sell. It was an economic revolution, with profound social repercussions. For the landless, options were few. Peeled from traditional access to the land, many of the 'free' landless poor made their way to the cities to seek work. Those who remained on the land worked for a wage and only after-hours worked to feed themselves. On the other hand, for those who owned land, the shift from feudal to capitalist economics generated vast efficiencies, profits and hence the means to fund a growing national appetite to buy foreign food.[4]

Luxury foods were being brought to Britain so effectively that by 1733, George Cheyne – an eighteenth-century advocate of vegetarianism – was able to lament the rise of the systematic disease of affluence, which he termed 'the English Malady':

> Since our Wealth has increas'd, we have ransack'd all the parts of the Globe to bring together its whole Stock of Materials for Riot, Luxury, and to provoke Excess . . . Is it any Wonder, then, that the Diseases which proceed from Idleness and Fulness of Bread, should increase in Proportion, and keep equal Pace with those Improvements of the Matter and Cause of Disease?[5]

International trade in food did more, however, than add flab to the rich. As trade's net was cast ever wider, and with the industrial and national revolutions of the eighteenth and nineteenth centuries, agricultural commerce reshaped the entire planet. It's a strong claim to make, but international trade's effects have been so powerful that, two centuries later, eating and drinking would be unimaginable without it. Think, for example, of your last non-alcoholic beverage. In 2007, the world consumed 552 billion litres of such soft drinks, about 82.5 litres per person.[6] Chances are that the last drink you consumed contained caffeine and a sweetener, perhaps high-fructose corn syrup, perhaps aspartame, perhaps even sugar. Of the soft drinks consumed around the world today, the most popular is a caffeinated beverage, but it's not the one you'd expect. Although colas and coffees and bottled water are increasing their market share, the most widely quaffed drink is tea – with 57 litres per person drunk in 2005.[7] It is through tea and sugar that many of today's soft drinks trace their ancestry. Yet tea and sugar themselves are relatively new on the international scene, popular outside Asia for little over 200 years. In Britain,

it was (and remains) a drink usually taken with milk and sugar
added. But of the four things that go into a good cup of tea – water,
sugar, milk and tea leaves – only milk and water were to be found
in any quantity in Britain until the 1600s. Sugar was a non-Euro-
pean crop, and tea was new to the great diarist of London, Samuel
Pepys, in the 1660s.[8] As for sugar, Sidney Mintz, the grand master of food politics, sums up the transformation wrought through
sugar in his *Sweetness and Power*:

> In 1000 A.D., few Europeans knew of the existence of
> sucrose, or cane sugar. But soon afterward they learned
> about it; by 1650, in England the nobility and the wealthy
> had become inveterate sugar eaters, and sugar figured
> in their medicine, literary imagery, and displays of rank.
> By no later than 1800, sugar had become a necessity – al-
> beit a costly and rare one – in the diet of every English
> person; by 1900, it was supplying nearly one-fifth of the
> calories in the English diet.[9]

Sugar's high-end status fuelled its desirability, but it also mat-
tered that sugar was sweet, that it was calorie dense, even that it
was white. It became increasingly demanded by the new middle
and working classes and entrepreneurs found a ready market for
as much sugar they could lay their hands on. Most importantly,
sugar in combination with tea (whose bitter edge it took away
and whose mildly addictive caffeine[10] it complemented) together
with milk (to counter the drink's astringency) formed a beverage
to take on the world, and transform it.[11]

To grow tea and sugar required industrial agriculture's single
most bloody innovation – the plantation. The agricultural technology of advanced and permanent monoculture came bundled with
its own social technology, of soil tilled, cane hacked and leaves
plucked by an endless supply of almost disposable people from
the Global South. In 1645 (at the beginning of the two-centuries-
long era of slavery), records show the purchase of 1,000 slaves

for Barbadian cane sugar production. A commentator noted that more slaves would soon be on their way, for so lucrative was the sugar industry, and so low the value of human life, that within eighteen months, slaves had recouped their strike-price for their masters.[12]

Like sugar, tea leaves were acquired for consumption at home through empire abroad. The places where tea was grown – India and China – were inducted into international webs of trade for which the British government and the East India Company exacted heavy tribute (a fact to which North American colonists, notably in Boston, objected). These systems fuelled the growth of a drink which, in the United Kingdom, in barely 200 years, had become the iconic national drink. C. W. Denyer, a commentator writing at the end of the nineteenth century, writes on the increasing popularity of the beverage, taking the opportunity to decry the limited aesthetic sensibility of its principal consumers:

> It is to be feared that the average Englishman is a very bad judge of tea. His sole criterion of its quality is its colour and strength; its delicate flavour he drowns in sugar and milk. These latter are not to be despaired, for they constitute no considerable portion of his food; but they certainly help to put him at the mercy of the tea dealer.[13]

Crucially, the drink *had* become a central part of the working-class diet, particularly for women.[14] Tea with milk and sugar provides ready caffeine and carbohydrates to the drinker – it's good for stimulating and providing the calories for manual work.[15] Denyer again notes, corroborating the gendered consumption of tea, that:

> The factory girls have the teapot by the fire all day, and it is very common for the same girl to come in [to a teashop] five or six times a day for a 'pen'orth' of tea and a 'pen'orth' of sugar. They insist on having the strongest Indian tea, notwithstanding the serious nervous and

digestive evils which medical experience shows to result
from such excessive tea drinking.[16]

In the consumption of tea as a source of calories, exploited urban
workers in London mirrored nothing so much as the slaves at the
other end of the food system in the Caribbean, who chewed sugar
cane for energy enough to get through the working day. Tea was,
however, in competition with a beverage dear to English workers, far more nutritious, and one that could be made from local
ingredients: beer. For tea to become normal in Britain, a number of things were necessary. Sweet and hot drinks needed to be
something people were interested in. But through the increasing
availability of sugar from the colonies, the British had been developing a sweet tooth, and the British weather has always been
conducive to something warm.[17] The environmental and aesthetic
context was ready for a hot sweetened beverage.[18] Further, the
economics worked – supplies of tea were available. In order for
the companies to supply tea and sugar, imperial power was necessary, in India and China principally for tea, and in the Caribbean
for sugar. Britain had dominion over both regions. Religion also
played a part, with the Temperance movement and the Protestant
work ethic driving beer and gin out of the workplace.[19] And, for
the working poor, tea held an important advantage over a cold
glass of beer: 'Two ounces of tea a week ... made many a cold
supper seem like a hot meal.'[20] Beer, once available everywhere,
from factories to asylums,[21] was banished from the working day, to
be replaced by a beverage whose components were shipped from
halfway around the world.[22]

This is not to long for the days when workers were paid in
booze. To see why, one need only to look to South Africa, where
the practice known as the 'tot' system, outlawed in 1963 but still
continuing on a small number of vineyards today, has contributed
to apocalyptic levels of foetal alcohol syndrome, with 60 children
in 1,000 suffering it – the highest in the world.[23] The demise of
beer's place in everyday life does, however, show how traders in

tea and sugar were able to ride, and further cause, changes in centuries-old tastes, reduce levels of nutrition and get a more caffeinated workforce for the 'workshop of the world' as a result. This, then, is the genealogy of the can of Red Bull. Tea was the original Jolt. It was a drink high in basic stimulants and carbohydrates, sweet and perky. And, just as Dietrich Mateschitz, Red Bull's Austrian marketer, has made a cool billion dollars from his product, tea and sugar merchants earned equivalent fortunes before him, and off far bloodier trade.

International trade transformed the world and, in its high capitalist form, was premised on a great deal of exploitation, for a wide range of goods, across large parts of the planet. Slave labour was an integral part of the provision of cheap food to European cities. African slaves were an essential component, for instance, of the plantation economies of the United States, Caribbean and Brazil.[24] The mechanics of setting up a global food system involved the twin processes of colonization and the forced creation of markets. The long-standing provision of tropical foods from the colonies (sugar, tea, coffee, fruits, oils) was to be complemented with temperate foods (grains, meats) from the settler colonies, which would flow into the world market for foodstuffs, not just directly back to Britain.

Settler colonies were made possible because agricultural commercialization in Europe was driving smallholders off the land. Displaced settlers were sent from Europe *en masse* to populate newly conquered territories. From South Africa and then-Rhodesia-now-Zimbabwe,[25] from Argentina and Canada, all were hitched to the new system of agriculture, geared toward highly productive agricultural sectors to match growing industrial sectors.[26] For metropolitan cities to get their cheap food, the economies of settler colonies were also directed towards export agriculture. This is important to remember, because there tends to be a somewhat romanticized view of the 'family farm' in settler colonies.[27] Even the little house on the prairie was, by the end of the nineteenth century, an increasingly commercial operation,[28] governed by a sophisticated calculus of inputs balancing outputs, forecasts and foreign and domestic trade politics.[29]

In other (tropical) countries, settlement wasn't considered viable or desirable. In these cases, the British had pioneered the development of trade in grain, bringing the British system of free markets in land and labour to its colonies. Foremost among them was India. In India, the British systematically dismantled the existing feudal systems of duties of care for the hungry, in which landlords were expected to feed their hungry peasants in lean years. Instead, enabled by the technologies of telegraph and steam, village stores of grain (set aside for drought years) were linked to world grain markets. Indian grain was extracted and transported to England's grain markets. Peasants could no longer expect to receive free grain from the village lord if the harvests failed. Under modern British rule they were to work for food. The result was extreme rural hunger and poverty. And when adverse weather conditions struck, and harvests failed, millions died for want of being able to afford the grain exported to Britain. Mike Davis notes the contrast between the rationality being imposed and the facts on the ground:

> Although the British insisted that they had rescued India from 'timeless hunger', more than one official was jolted when Indian nationalists quoted from an 1878 study published in the prestigious *Journal of the Statistical Society* that contrasted thirty-one serious famines in 120 years of British rule against only seventeen recorded famines in the entire previous two millennia … Millions died, not outside the 'modern world system' but in the very process of being dynamically conscripted into its economic and political structures. They died in the golden age of Liberal Capitalism.[30]

Through directly extracting food resources from its tropical empire and a new commercial frontier of export agriculture in settler colonies, and with only a twinge of guilt at the human cost wrought, Britain was able to feed its working class. Joseph Chamberlain, who was at the time the British Secretary of State for the Colonies, put the competitive spirit behind the imperial agenda quite plainly in an 1896 speech to the Birmingham Chamber of Commerce:

> If we had remained passive . . . the largest part of the African continent would have been occupied by our commercial rivals . . . Through our colonial policy, as soon as we acquire and develop a territory, we develop it as agents of civilization, for the growth of world trade.[31]

Related to this was a second process, in which the internal balance of power within the colonial metropole was reconfigured. Britain's new imperial power was increasingly rooted in its industrial prowess, and its role as the workshop of the world. This strengthened the power of the owners of industry. As Britain became increasingly industrialized, the proportion of its food imported from elsewhere increased. Wheat, in particular, was available more cheaply outside the country than inside it. There were, however, high taxes on wheat. These so-called Corn Laws (the corn in Corn Law refers to the wheat kernel, not, as in the US or Mexico, to maize) benefited those most able to profit from the sale of high-priced domestically produced wheat – the landed aristocracy. By the same token, high prices directly hurt the workers, and indirectly harmed the new middle class for whom they worked in the cities. In 1848 the Corn Laws were repealed. It was a moment that signalled the reluctant abdication of the aristocracy and anointed the ascendance of the new middle class. It was a seismic shift in class politics. And it hinged on the availability of cheap food for the new working class.

Rhodes' Conundrum

The new-found national concern for the working class wasn't, however, based entirely on compassion or altruism. Cecil John Rhodes, the British mining magnate and plutocrat distilled (albeit decades after the end of the Corn Laws) the concerns of the times. His thinking on food had been widely shared by a number of his peers by the time he articulated it in 1895:

> I was in the East End of London yesterday and attended a meeting of the unemployed. I listened to the wild speeches, which were just a cry for 'bread', 'bread!' and on my way home I pondered over the scene and I became more than ever convinced of the importance of imperialism ... The Empire, as I have always said, is a bread and butter question. If you want to avoid civil war, you must become imperialists.[32]

The new and old elites were scared, terrified of what an increasingly organized working class might do to it.[33] To assuage the fear, men of business and government had a plan, one that lies close to the surface in Rhodes' worries. It's worth teasing out, for its basic lines remain with us today. We can understand Rhodes to be observing that:

1. The poor are many, and growing in number.
2. There isn't enough food to feed them all.
3. If there isn't enough food to feed them, they will go hungry.
4. If they go hungry, there will be civil war.
5. Other countries have enough food to feed them.

Therefore, supplying them with food from other countries will prevent civil war.

The first two steps of this argument belong to Thomas Malthus, the world's first paid economist. Malthus famously observed that, over time, the geometric increase in population would invariably outstrip the plodding arithmetic increase in food production, leading to starvation and a population crash.[34] His ideas, while both incorrect and misleading in their analysis of why famines actually happen (as we shall see in chapter 6), loiter in discussions today about population and hunger. From the solutions offered by eugenicists, to Lee Kyung Hae's worries about population, to anyone who has used the term 'welfare queen', whenever the threat of people breeding beyond their means is evoked, Malthus' ghost haunts.

Onto Malthus' ideas Rhodes bolted a second series of predictions based on his observations about class. He suggested that the poor, rather than waiting to die of hunger in a population crash, would organize and go after the rich. Through this logic, the poor were reduced to three basic organs: growling stomachs, clenched fists and insatiable genitalia. There is no need to ask why the poor are many, or why birth rates might be higher. Rhodes' argument for food-related imperialism becomes a *reductio* that argues for the prevention of hunger not on its own grounds, but because it will salt the earth for politically articulated discontent.

To the new middle classes at the end of the nineteenth century the first step in Rhodes' argument must have felt axiomatic – the poor were indeed many. The Industrial Revolution (from roughly the 1780s to the 1840s)[35] had transformed the country.[36] Through the late eighteenth and nineteenth centuries, the new working class were battered by the harsh living and working conditions in the new cities.[37] It is from this time that the word 'slum' derives, a new word to describe a new urban geography.[38] The mid-century misery of working-class London was well known by Charles Dickens, its chief chronicler. When Dickens was twelve, he was sent to work at a factory, where he pasted labels on jars of boot polish for ten hours a day. Young Charles' wages were his contribution to the rent, while his father languished in the Marshalsea debtors' jail. Although his biographical experiences of destitution only came to light after his death, Dickens' literature fully disclosed the venality and horror of the Industrial Revolution and the criminalization of the poor, which he himself had experienced. In *Oliver Twist*, Oliver's diet in the poor house consists of 'three meals of gruel a day, with an onion twice a week, and half a roll on Sundays'.[39] Although this might be something of an exaggeration[40] it is certainly no stretch to say that the diet of the working class was generally poor. From the beginning of the Industrial Revolution to the mid-1800s, working-class real wages increased by barely 15 per cent.[41] Diets reflected this, with bread the main staple, supplemented by potatoes. But Dickens had it comparatively easy. The deprivations of the Industrial Revolution were borne more by women than by men. If we look at records of English women's heights and literacy on convict ships leaving the UK, some painful trends become clear. Over the course of the Industrial Revolution,

> the average height of rural-born English women fell by more than 0.75 inches, and that of urban-born English women by 0.5 inches, between 1800 and 1815. The illiteracy of English women also increased. Only 10 per cent of transported women born in 1795 were unable to read, while over 20 per cent of those born in 1820 were totally illiterate.[42]

The new working class wasn't, however, passive to its fate. In this, Rhodes had observed history correctly. The first half of the nineteenth century was, after all, the apex of the Age of Revolution, and its legacy stretched beyond the century's end.[43] The second half of the nineteenth century saw the rise of workers' movements. *The Communist Manifesto* was first published in 1848,[44] a year which saw revolutions across Europe, from France to the Austrian Empire, to the areas that we know today as Italy and Germany. In Britain, the Chartists were demanding universal suffrage.[45] Europe even had, for a few weeks, its own commune, in Paris at the beginning of 1871. To the middle classes in Dickensian

Britain, especially those easily terrorized by the demagogues of their age, the world must have seemed rife with insurrection by the men and women who worked and lived in the dirtier, darker, denser parts of town.[46]

Workers in Europe weren't the only ones up in arms. Just as workers in Europe and the US resisted the poverty of life in new cities' slums, so did the slaves whose labour kept food prices low for the white working class. Slaves, too, had caught the winds of revolution, and never more than in the Haitian slave uprising. Inspired by the American Revolution, and after centuries of plunder by Europe, the Haitian slaves, led by Toussaint L'Ouverture, seized control of their country. After seeing off the French, British, Spanish and French again, the Haitian slaves fought their way to an independence that was, briefly, glorious.[47] The retribution was, however, uncommonly fierce and brutal.[48] Since its 1791–1804 revolution, Haiti has been reduced to the poorest country in the Western Hemisphere by the conscious action, over the subsequent 200 years, of the US, France and Germany. It is hard to understand the ferocity of the reprisals against Haiti unless we understand the fears of contagion that its revolution inspired among the elites of other countries.

The solution to worker dissatisfaction in Europe involved blunting the edge of discontent. It involved adhering to an unwritten social contract, keeping levels of hunger and deprivation within manageable limits by making sure enough quantities of cheap food were available. The cheap food demanded slaves and low-paid agricultural workers. By Mike Davis' estimates, tens of millions of such workers perished feeding Europe and North America, and through the development of the modern world food system, the poverty that would come to characterize the Global South in the twentieth century was created.[49] This is why slave uprisings were so fearsome to the architects of the new international food system. Without slaves, no sugar, and therefore no food to quiet the industrial worker. The slaves mistakenly thought that the words of the American or French Revolutions, which were led in large part by the middle classes against the aristocracy, might apply to them, that they too might qualify for life, liberty and the pursuit of happiness. They were not, however, the intended audience for this rhetoric, being too poor, too black and too indispensable to the production of food for Europe. The cheap sugar that they produced was intended to pacify the bodies of European workers. It served not at all to have slaves up in arms, bandying the slogans of European revolution, when they had been captured and brought to the Caribbean expressly to prevent it.

The Cold War for Food

Rhodes' potent combination of fears and national worries about losing ground in an increasingly international world economy were to characterize the next big iteration of the food system. This was to happen after the Second World War, as the locus of world power shifted from the United Kingdom to the United States. As it did, so did the way food was shunted across the world, reflecting US politics, economics and vast agricultural strength. But elite fears of worker organizing were to inform the new system of food distribution no less than the old.

For NATO governments at the beginning of the Cold War, Rhodes' worries felt very close to home. The end of the Second World War demobbed millions of men with high expectations of peace and a sense of entitlement, men who were disciplined, organized and weapons-trained. Domestic Communist parties, particularly in Europe but also in the US, were a potent political force. On top of this, two food crises, in Mexico in 1943 and then in Europe in 1946, focused the minds of cabinet-level policy makers. Critically, the crises had caught the US government by surprise. The US and Canada had, at war's end, enough food to feed their population to the tune of 3,000 calories per day. From that side of the Atlantic, the long lines outside shops in London, the first since the war had begun, suggested nothing more than post-bellum bureaucracy. The re-emergence of British food queues, while certainly inconvenient, affected the daily calorie intake only slightly: levels were at around 2,900 per day. But things in Continental Europe were much worse, with only enough food to feed the population at a level of 2,000 calories per day.[50]

The surprising re-emergence of hunger in Europe and the febrile climate of the Cold War turned food, not for the last time, into a weapon of class politics.[51] These politics were, however, to take a new form, one even more global in scope than its predecessor. In his 1949 inaugural address, US President Harry Truman announced that

> we must embark on a bold new program for making the
> benefits of our scientific advances and industrial progress
> available for the improvement and growth of underde-
> veloped areas. More than half the people of the world
> are living in conditions approaching misery. Their food is
> inadequate. They are victims of disease. Their economic
> life is primitive and stagnant. Their poverty is a handicap
> and a threat both to them and to more prosperous areas.
> For the first time in history, humanity possesses the
> knowledge and the skill to relieve the suffering of these
> people.[52]

This speech is generally considered the charter document for what today is called 'development'.[53] Less noted, however, is the extent to which development isn't an innocent process. It rested as a fourth point in a speech that began with an excursus on the evils of Communism, and then asserted:

> We must carry out our plans for reducing the barriers to
> world trade and increasing its volume. Economic recov-
> ery and peace itself depend on increased world trade . . .
> we will strengthen freedom-loving nations against the
> dangers of aggression. I hope soon to send to the Senate

a treaty respecting the North Atlantic security plan. In addition, we will provide military advice and equipment to free nations which will cooperate with us in the maintenance of peace and security.

Development was, in other words, part of a policy mindset that linked international trade, military power and a programme of redistribution. What was to be redistributed was, it turned out, food. The Marshall Plan – the US aid programme to Europe in the immediate aftermath of the Second World War – had instigated, among other initiatives, the transfer of food to the hungry and possibly querulous European population in response to the post-war food shortages. When European farmers were able once again to feed the continent, and even to turn a surplus, by the early 1950s, they wanted the aid to stop. Cheap US imports were, after all, preventing them from selling their crops to their own people.[54] From July 1954, US food aid was pointed at a new target, one where farmers were politically much less able to make the same demands of the United States – the Global South.

A number of international and domestic worries shaped the decision to send US food to the developing world. US farmers and rural voters were demanding their share of federal pork, and few politicians were inclined to cut off the supports that agriculture had been given to grow food for the war effort. At the same time, with the European market shrinking, the US was faced with the problem of disposing of its food surpluses. Domestic anti-Communist sentiment was just past its peak, this being the year in which Edward R. Murrow's *Report on Joseph R. McCarthy* aired. Countries in the Global South were, at the same time, perceived to be moving towards Communism. China instilled fear and incomprehension in US elites (no less than today). It was a context in which the logic of the Cold War joined the dots for policy makers, much as Rhodes' thoughts had fifty years before. The hungry might be rendered less troubled, more grateful and, in a new twist, more *dependent* if provided with cheap food. The logic presented an expedient solution to the constraints: take the US surplus to the hungry.

On 10 July 1954, President Eisenhower signed Public Law 480, the Agricultural Trade Development and Assistance Act of 1954, more commonly known as PL-480. While the language of the act ennobled its goals with terms of international camaraderie, PL-480 was a cunning and powerful foreign policy tool. Any US-aligned government that found itself battling worker-led organizing or, indeed, any plausibly left-wing political opposition could gain access to the US strategic grain reserve. Those countries abutted by socialist ones were bumped to the front of the queue.[55]

And so food aid became a central part of US foreign policy, accounting for more that half of all economic aid by 1956. Between 1956 and 1960 more than one-third of the world trade in wheat was accounted for by American aid. The world price of wheat was kept artificially low through food aid, hurting growers, but hooking countries of the Global South on US largesse. In 1968, the Global South's addiction for American goods peaked – 79 per cent of all US exports went to the 'Third World'.[56] It was an agenda fully subscribed to by the US. Earl Butz, Secretary of State for Agriculture under Nixon and Ford, observed: 'Hungry men listen only to those who have a piece of bread. Food is a tool. It is a weapon in the US negotiating kit.'[57] But it was not destined to be forever. Relationships between junkies and dealers never are.

After Food Aid

There's no tombstone for it, but the post-war food order died in 1973. There were many simultaneous causes of death. Principally, the old system halted because of a failure in circulation of the international economy's most important vital fluid: oil. The price of oil quadrupled from October 1973 to 1974.[58] The price shock stalled the global economy. In the light of the increased costs of buying and shipping grain to the Global South, the food aid system began to look like less of a bargain, particularly when the recipients of food aid seemed less than grateful. In May 1974, the United Nations, spurred by countries predominantly in the Global South that were tired of the endless application of carrots and sticks by the US and USSR, called for a New International Economic Order.[59] It was a call that, while relatively minor in its demands, was seismic in its insistence that rulers in the Global South, and not their Cold War patrons, call the shots in their own back yard.

The oil shock also forced a recalculation of the economics and politics of the Cold War. With drivers lining up for gasoline in the United States, securing the domestic supply of fuel became a strategic priority. It happened that one of the world's largest producers of oil needed to import wheat and was prepared to pay in oil. The supplier was the Soviet Union. Such were the constraints that the US government felt able to pinch its nose and sell its food aid wheat to the Communists.[60] With US food diverted to the Soviet Union, one might have expected rather dire consequences for countries in the Global South that had become used to the shipments. Gallantly, other countries in the Global North, notably European ones, used the opportunity to dispose of *their* agricultural surpluses.

At the same time, other technologies were being developed to resolve Rhodes' conundrum. Instead of feeding the hungry with overseas grain, yield-increasing Green Revolution technologies were being developed that allowed food to be grown domestically. These technologies – which ran from new seeds to economic measures to get farmers to grow more helped to shift the dependency of countries in the Global South away from food itself to a growing dependence on the agricultural technologies, such as fertilizer, necessary to grow enough to keep a lid on politicized hunger. Although ability to grow food was an improvement over the beggary to which many countries, especially India, had been reduced, the Green Revolution came at a high cost (as we see in chapter 6). And the Revolution's technologies were not the only ones developed to keep the masses quiet. The Gandhi dynasty in India, for instance, embarked on a programme of forced sterilization in its 'Emergency Period' in the mid 1970s, addressing the problem of a hungry population not by feeding the people, but by reducing their number. Rhodes' concerns were, indeed, alive and well.[61]

The donation of food as aid continues to be a strategic tool in the negotiating kits of rich and poor countries alike. But although the era of controlling foreign economies through growing their food supply ended in the 1970s other, more subtle, means of controlling the food system were being forged. The new political economy of food rested not on control through the United States' food surplus, but through the Global South's fiscal debt. Here's how.

At the same time that the US was scrambling for oil, most governments in the Global South were feeling the pinch too. They needed credit to pay for their oil imports. Oil-exporting countries, flush with cash, were happy to lend their new income. This was the era of the petrodollar. Cash was cheap, interest rates were at an unprecedented low, and the banks in which oil exporters had invested were lending money to anyone who'd take it. It was a system ready to collapse at the slightest breath of change. When that change came, with the high interest rates and global recession at the end of the 1970s, the accumulated debt set large parts of Latin America, Africa and eventually Asia on the route to bankruptcy.

All of a sudden, the spigots of cash flow turned tight. Loans became due, but because the international economy was in a recession, it wasn't clear how to earn the cash to pay off the loans. The alternative to defaulting was to borrow yet more, in order to pay the interest on the loans, to postpone the worry about the accumulated debt until brighter economic times. To do this, countries needed to borrow and, precisely because it was a time of recession, with high rates of inflation (and therefore high interest rates), money was much harder to come by. With the shrinking of other lending sources, a new series of actors were able to shape the destinies of the Global South: international financial institutions. This cluster of organizations is funded by taxpayer dollars and takes many forms – national export credit agencies,[62] loan guarantee organizations, national development agencies and the International Monetary Fund. But first among equals is the World Bank. To this day, when loans become due to international financial institutions, the World Bank is the first in line, a symbol of unity among its rich government sponsors. The Bank was a Cold War reconstruction organization whose mission had blossomed into a far broader, and now more powerful, campaign in the Global South. It was helmed by Robert S. McNamara (its president from 1968 to 1981), a man who was one of the principal architects of the US's war in Vietnam. At the end of the 1970s, because it was government funded, the World Bank was one of the few organizations that had both the means and the will to extend credit to governments in the Global South.

The Bank made loans available, but it did so only if certain conditions were met. At the Bank, these conditions were built into 'Structural Adjustment Programmes'. If Third World governments wanted money to pay off the debt that they'd incurred in the 1970s, then they'd have to accept the 'conditionalities' of a Structural Adjustment Programme. The programmes explained the crises of the 1970s as the result of 'unsound fundamentals', specifically finding blame in governments spending more than they generated in revenue, with overvalued exchange rates, bloated governmental apparatus and controls on the flow of capital in and out of the country. The conditions attached to loans involved a suite of sweeping changes in the economy – the government was not allowed to run a deficit, but needed to balance its books. The currency was to be allowed to float freely on the international market. In practice, this meant devaluing the currency with the result that home-made goods were cheaper for foreigners to buy, and foreign-produced goods were more expensive to buy at home. Trade would also be liberalized, and tariffs gradually reduced. Domestic supports for farmers, such as 'marketing boards' that provided a guaranteed market and minimum price for farmers, would be dismantled. And, usually, interest rates would be kicked up to keep inflation under control.

In a different context, each of these policies might have had the tang of merit about them. But they were rather different to the policies used by the countries in today's Global North in *their* quest for development. The US, UK, Japan, Germany and other industrialized countries had become rich by following courses diametrically opposed to the one they imposed on the Global South. When Europe, North America and Japan had industrialized in the nineteenth century (and as India and China have done in the twentieth) governments spent substantial amounts on industrial investment and sheltered those industries behind tariffs, while borrowing from the public and increasing the size of the public sector.[63] It was only by surrendering the possibility of doing the same thing that countries in the Global South were given a few years' grace on their debts. Under these conditions governments ceded large parts of their economic and social spending sovereignty to their donors. From this point on, choices over national development would be shaped not by national governments, but by their creditors.[64]

Food was, once more, to play a role in international politics. National debts still had to be paid, and paid in US dollars. Countries sought to find ways to get dollars. Those countries that could persuade tourists with dollars to part with them did. But the most direct way to get dollars was to produce and sell goods to countries with dollars. And one of the ways of applying their resources to the problem was through exporting agricultural goods. Through these mechanisms, it again became more lucrative for countries in the Global South with the right climate and soil to grow food for the North than food for themselves. And the Global North managed to replace the old colonial instruments of command and control with newer, and cheaper, mechanisms of 'self-imposed' market discipline. With currencies floating freely and trade barriers lower, the Global North found itself able to access cheap food from the Global South under the aspect of magnanimity – every bite of cheap food eaten in the North was helping the South to pay back its debt.

In barely a decade, the food system was rebuilt. Although food aid continued to be exported, the national economies and food systems in the South were now controlled not by assurances of the lifeline of food, but by threat of the noose of debt. Under this new regime, Rhodes' conundrum has been solved once again, reflecting the concerns of the times. With the blows dealt to worker organizing in the 1980s, and through the breaking of union power around the world,[65] fears of worker insurrection were set, temporarily, at bay. The new food order offered a way of maintaining cheap food supplies globally, but with an increased role not just for the US government, but for the private sector, in providing agricultural technologies and in international trade itself. And one institution above all was to frame this new agricultural order – the World Trade Organization.

The World Trade Organization

Through the post-Second World War era, the General Agreement on Tariffs and Trade had coordinated, more or less successfully, a downward trend in border taxes on industrial goods between its members. In the 1970s, with the global recession, countries were trying to shortcut those tariffs, protecting national industries from the worst effects of the recession. The organization was beginning to crumble. Through some hard bargaining, the US government persuaded GATT's members back to the negotiating table. The series of negotiations begun at Punta Del Este in 1984 came to be known as the Uruguay round, and lasted the better part of eight years. On December 1995, the World Trade Organization was officially launched. In addition to inheriting the core agreements of the GATT, the WTO had new domains of expertise – intellectual property, services, textiles, agriculture and, crucially, it had new mechanisms for the resolution of disputes that gave the WTO the teeth that the US found so sorely lacking in GATT.

The inclusion of agriculture in the WTO was a key addition,

and the point of sorest contention in the negotiation of the agreement. The European Union and the United States were loath to reduce their tariffs, both having developed sprawling systems of domestic farm support since the war (with the lion's share going not to poorer farmers, but to large agricultural businesses). Their aim was to keep their strategic reserves of food, while forcing countries in the Global South to cede sovereignty over their agricultural supplies. As the negotiations approached collapse in November 1992, the US and EU drew up an agreement which the rest of the world would sign. Through some tough negotiating, and some elaborate statistical footwork, the EU and US were able through their bilateral 'Blair House' agreement to develop a system of agricultural supports that, in essence, let them continue to subsidize their farmers, while countries in the Global South signed away precisely this right.[66] In the US and EU, the government and private sector were to work in tandem to keep domestic agriculture on an even keel. In the rest of the world, these same private sector companies were to be allowed to operate without impediment by other governments.

This was the architecture of the new global food order. In agriculture, the post-1970s world map was redrawn. Rather than using food aid to demonstrate its largesse, the US developed sophisticated new trading arrangements, while continuing to support its farming industry, and regulating the international domain through debt.[67] The post-oil-crisis world of development saw a new role for international financial institutions such as the World Bank and, later, the World Trade Organization. The then director-general of the World Trade Organization, Renato Ruggiero, put it well in 1996 when he said, 'We are no longer writing the rules of interaction among separate national economies. We are writing the constitution of a single global economy.'[68] The new constitution for global economic development wasn't designed to deliver wholesale improvements in the quality of life of the poorest.[69] It sits, rather, as the latest episode in the long history of the generation of supplies of cheap food to prevent insurrection. Lower trade

barriers in the countries of the Global South were introduced
not as a means to help the poor out of poverty, nor as a means to
agricultural development, but as an emergency measure to forestall bankruptcy. Rather than giving choices and opportunities to
the impoverished, international food politics has sought control
through intervention, patronage and, occasionally, violence. Yet
much of the language of these food system policies was suffused
with concerns for freedom and security. If the result of the food
system policies was that small farmers were denied both of these
(as we've also seen in chapter 2), it is not unreasonable to ask for
whom, then, the world was being made secure, and whose freedom was being expanded. That is a question for the next chapter.

5

The Customer Is Our Enemy: A Brief Introduction to Food System Business

> The competitor is our friend and the customer is our enemy ... There isn't one grain of anything in the world that is sold in a free market. Not one! The only place you see a free market is in the speeches of politicians. People who are not from the Midwest do not understand that this is a socialist country.
>
> Dwayne Andreas, then-Chairman, Archer Daniels Midland (slogan: 'Supermarket to the World'), in a 1995 interview.[1]

Permanent Banana Republic: The United Fruit Company

Trade treaties, like food aid, committed countries to the work of making the world safe for freedom. For poorer farmers this has led to catastrophe. Suicide, poverty and displacement have met many in rural areas who have been unable to survive the global market.[2] If trade agreements and liberalization did not buy their freedom, though, then whose did it buy? The answer lies in a group which, while making the occasional appearance, has thus far remained quietly in the background. Yet it's impossible to think about a 'global food system' without attending to the corporations that have controlled it for centuries, and who crack the supply chain like a whip.

Today, transnational agricultural corporations control 40 per cent of world trade in food, with twenty companies controlling the world coffee trade, six controlling 70 per cent of wheat trade, and one controlling 98 per cent of packaged tea.[3] The way this control is exercised varies. In the fields, companies offer advice, credit and, when foreclosure threatens, farming contracts. The result is that when farmers and corporations deal, the former submits fully to the will of the latter. Once secured for the company, the food is trucked nationally and internationally, with internal trade within the corporation used to minimize its tax burden. Food system corporations are also well versed in using the idea of national interest to demand subsidy, calling on the religious wonders of science to assure us of the sanctity of all these activities and even using the anxieties of race to justify their interventions. Wherever a profit might reasonably be speculated, they'll be there.[4]

Take, for example, one of the first products in the modern food system – bananas. Bananas themselves are biologically well suited to an international food system. Robust, with their own packaging built on, bananas are able to withstand shipment over long distances and still be a viable commodity at the other end. The United Fruit Company, founded in 1899, was the world's largest banana merchant. At its peak, the company controlled the trade not only in bananas, but also in freight, mail and money across an archipelago of Central American countries. It guarded its power jealously, and little stood in its way. When locally elected governments tried to curb the company's power, or when residents of the country organized to alleviate their exploitation, it struck back.

Most famously, the United Fruit Company used its connections in the Truman and Eisenhower administrations – especially through the Secretary of State John Foster Dulles, whose law firm had represented the company – to argue that Jacobo Arbenz Guzmán, the democratically elected president of Guatemala, was about to become a Communist. The reason? Arbenz Guzmán had in mind to buy unused land from the United Fruit Company to give to landless peasants, at the artificially low price at which the

Company had declared the land's value on its tax returns. In response, the president authorized in 1954 a CIA-backed invasion of Guatemala, Operation PBSUCCESS. The resulting war claimed 200,000 lives, over forty years. The land, however, remained in the Company's hands. Hence 'success'.

Incidentally, the CIA operation in Guatemala had a follow-up mission, to scour historical archives for evidence to prove that Guzmán was a Communist puppet. The mission was entitled 'PB-HISTORY'. Despite trawling through over 150,000 pages, no such evidence was found.[5] But the damage continued, for over forty bloody years, ending in 1996 with peace, of a kind. It was through acts such as these that the United Fruit Company earned the name 'el pulpo' – the octopus.

The complicity of the United Fruit Company in Central American poverty has rarely been acknowledged in the US. It is a history that has been erased. Indeed, the shorthand phrase through which most people come to know of banana-exporting countries in Central America and the Caribbean reflects not a history of rapacity and violence but the comically inept regimes installed by the export corporations. Such countries are known not as victims of empire, but as 'Banana Republics'. It's a taint which sullies the reputations of these countries' citizens, rather than reflecting back on the cause of their impoverishment. It is, in short, a textbook case of blaming the victim.

Today, the United Fruit Company has been rebranded as the warmer, fuzzier 'Chiquita Brands'. As a result of public relations exercises and 'fair trade' schemes, the company has worked hard to earn a slightly more favourable taste in our mouths. Not that it deserves it. The company recently paid a US$25 million fine as part of a guilty plea in its funding of paramilitary death squads in Colombia.[6] But beyond the tribulations of this particular corporation, the trajectory of the United Fruit Company presents, in microcosm, the story of today's agribusiness conglomerates. It's a story of colonialism,[7] control over channels of production, distribution, marketing and finance, mobilization of national interest, and a racialized repainting of the Third World.[8] Let's deal with the issue of consolidation of power first.

Varieties of Consolidation

> Put all your eggs into one basket and then watch that basket, do not scatter your shot. The great successes of life are made by concentration.
>
> Andrew Carnegie[9]

If Benjamin Braddock, the hero of *The Graduate*, were to attend a party today, it wouldn't matter what commodity he'd trade in. The money today is in one thing: consolidation.[10] Or, to expand a little, concentration of market power. Throughout the food system, concentration of market power has been a creeping trend. Market power, as the United Fruit Company reminds us, is nothing new. A century ago, four firms – Cargill, Continental, Bunge and Louis Dreyfus – ran the global grain trade.[11] But the shape and breadth of concentration today means that there are few corners of the food system untouched by agribusiness giants. Researchers at the University of Missouri have been tracking the rate of consolidation within a range of branches of the food business. They've measured this rate by calculating the total size of the US market in any given product or agricultural service and then working out how much of that is controlled by the top four related corporations. This is known as the concentration ratio of the top four – the CR4. The CR trends in the US market tell of the history, and future, of food.

Figure 5.1 shows the extent of concentration of the market in the hands of a few organizations, and its increase across a range of industries, from poultry to retail. It's a consolidation that spans the entire food system. The ten largest companies control half the world's seed supply.[12] The top ten companies control 63 per cent of the nearly US$20 billion veterinary drug market.[13] Ten

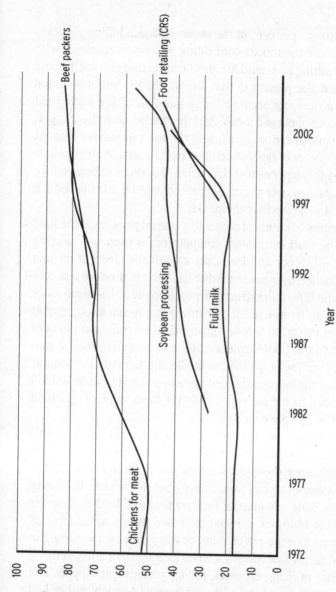

Fig. 5.0 Trends in concentration of the largest four companies within the United States in a range of different food system sectors. Source: (Mary Hendrickson, 2007; Shields, 2010; US GAO, 2009; US Census Bureau, 2007)

firms control 90 per cent of the nearly US$38.6 billion pesticide markets, while the top six controlling 75% of the market,[14] with analysts pointing to a trend in concentration that will see, by 2015, only three major players in that sector. The top ten in food and beverage processing account for 26 per cent of the US$1.3 trillion market in packaged foods. And the market with the sharpest trends in concentration, retail, sees the top 100 players accounting for 35 per cent of the US$4 trillion market, with Walmart alone accounting for 10 per cent of that share.[15] For those seeking refuge in their cups, just over 50 per cent of the world market for beer is controlled by the top four companies.[16]

This litany of numbers points to a central paradox in the food system. The market, through competition, is supposed to bring increased efficiency and lower prices. But the effect of turning food production over to the market has been to produce less competition, and offer more structural power to the largest companies. Consumers suffer as a result. According to a recent study, market concentration has led to food higher prices for consumers in 24 of 33 sectors in the US.[17] Farmers suffer too: as agricultural economist C. Robert Taylor testified to the Senate Agricultural Committee in 1999, 'Since 1984, the real price of a market basket of food has increased by 2.8 per cent, while the farm value of that food has fallen by 35.7 per cent.'[18]

In the decade since Taylor testified, little has changed. During the great food price spikes of 2007-8 and 2010-11, a casual observer might have thought that amid soaring hunger and food rebellions, at least farmers would have been doing well. To be sure, some large scale commercial farmers profited. In the US, farms earning over $500,000 per year increased their share of total US farm income from 66 per cent in 2006 to 73 per cent in 2009. But mid-sized farms saw lower incomes in 2007 than 2003, hit by a triple punch of rising expenses, falling government support, and the recession-induced end of the off-farm jobs on which they had long depended in order to keep their farms afloat.[19]

We might want to put our faith in various 'competition' or

'antitrust' commissions that exist in certain countries, in order to
prevent the formation of oligopolies that control the food system.
Such faith would be misplaced. When firms want to consolidate,
they approach these agencies with a range of justifications. The
foundational argument is Darwinian: the market is a mechanism
through which the fittest survive, and the government ought not
to interfere to save an entity doomed to extinction at the hands of
a rival. Mergers are justified on the grounds of efficiency, or that
there are economies of scale to be tapped by the 'synergy' of two
corporations. When mergers are being pitched to regulators, the
synergy may make an appeal to consumers' interests. Sometimes,
the problem is sidestepped entirely, by means of a revolving door
arrangement in which regulators, after a stint of good behaviour
as government officials, are given substantially better paying sine-
cures in industry.[20] Ultimately, though, the benefits must benefit
one group and one alone: shareholders.

A recent merger in the seed industry offers an object lesson. In
its acquisition of the vegetable seed company Seminis, chemical
giant Monsanto put together a presentation. The company noted
that 'technological capabilities are complementary: Monsanto's
research [is] now leveraged more broadly', the implication being
that with the combined expertise of Monsanto and Seminis, more
research and development would take place, and this would be
of final benefit to the consumer. The smart money wouldn't have
paid this too much attention. As the United States Department of
Agriculture's Economic Research Service has noted, concentration in the seed industry, and the privatization of seed research,
has resulted in *less*, not more, research and investment in research
and development.[21] Much more germane was Monsanto's observation that vegetable seed was a 'high value, high growth segment in agriculture', and that the merger would consolidate the
position of two market leaders, pushing Monsanto ahead of rival
DuPont.[22]

Perhaps, if we're looking for benefits to the public at large,
though, we're looking for the wrong sort of synergy. Corporations

are the first to admit that they're in business not for any wider social goal, but for profit. Although there's sometimes talk of 'wider social good', it's always done with a wink to the investors. News from the public relations department is to be trusted a great deal less than news from investor relations.[23]

A glance at what was until recently one of the world's largest food conglomerates, Altria, suggests the kinds of synergies being achieved. In 2007, Altria (previously known as Philip Morris) spun off its control of Kraft Foods, which in turn owns Nabisco (the National Biscuit Company which used to be part of the R. J. Reynolds tobacco group). Altria continues to own 27% per cent of SABMiller,[24] itself again a fusion of Miller and South African Breweries, as well as maintaining its core business – tobacco. The combination of tobacco and processed food seems an unlikely one. The tobacco industry had, for a while, watched its traditional markets slump, and the lawsuit bills mount, and Philip Morris had already purchased General Foods in a bid to diversify away from the tobacco business and provide an income stream independent of the liabilities it faced in tobacco. The tobacco industry was, however, buying more than a cash cow. With Philip Morris' purchase of Kraft in 1992 to create the largest consumer products company in the world, the Marlboro Man wasn't just buying himself the food that people eat. Philip Morris was also buying, through Kraft's distribution network, the means to make people eat it.

That a tobacco company should diversify into food seems odd. Yet it has precedent. In 1887, two brothers, Isidore and Montague Gluckstein, diversified away from their family-run, and reputedly ruthless, cut-price tobacco company to enter the catering business. Business was good, and by 1894, they'd bought a small factory at which they were mass-producing food and, in the same year, opened their first retail outlet, the J. Lyons and Co. teashop in London's Piccadilly. The tea houses, iconic in the UK, were the backbone for the company's food production, processing and distribution network throughout Britain. And they grew. As the company's biographer notes,[25] the company became the world's first food empire. The scale of the enterprise was vast. The company owned tea plantations in Nyasaland – now Malawi – and from leaf to tabletop, controlled every stage of the distribution. When the teashop's popularity began to fade, Lyons introduced the British public to fast food through the Wimpy chain in 1953 (and this was, through Lyons' imperial connections, India's first Western-style fast food too). The management of the company's assets required huge investments and innovations in technology, and it spawned the world's first business computer – the Lyons Electronic Office I, LEO I – to keep track of it all. Lyons also employed a range of food scientists to develop its food lines including, briefly, the young Oxford chemistry graduate Margaret Thatcher. The remains of the company are now owned in part by Nestlé, and in part by AlliedLyons, which in turn owns Dunkin Donuts – a rather ignominious end, perhaps, but entirely in keeping with its business.[26]

Like Lyons before it, Altria is a giant. Its net food revenues in 2005 were in excess of US$30 billion, when its products ran from Oreos to Starbucks Brand Coffee to Toblerone to Oscar Meyer meat-food to Marlboro to the Philip Morris Capital Corporation.[27] And, like Lyons, Altria's position in the market gave it both motive and means not only to play within the rules of the market, but actively to change and shape those rules.

As well as being a major player in the food market, Altria has access to the highest political circles in Washington, DC. It is, for example, a member of the US Trade Representatives' Agricultural Technical Advisory Committee. Rolling with the Washington set doesn't come cheap. Between 2005 and 2010, Altria spent US$120,679,496 on lobbying in Washington, DC, paying over forty lobbying companies to approach over a dozen federal agencies, from the USDA to the Federal Communications Commission, to entertain favourably Altria's point of view, and to write legislation and policy accordingly.[28]

This points to the deeper power gained by consolidation – the

ability to change the rules of the game. The processes through
which markets are created may reveal themselves most conspicuously at the World Trade Organization – and perhaps, given the
secrecy of the WTO's processes, conspicuous isn't the right word –
but the negotiating mandate for governments isn't written in Geneva. It is crafted in the conference rooms of hotels in Washington,
London and Beijing, where the refreshment and entertainment
of elected officials is paid for by the profits from candies and
cigarettes.

The Market for Political Favour

Altria isn't the only company in the business of buying governmental goodwill. Up and down the food system, from seed to
sachet, food system corporations lobby, threaten, plead and demand political favour. The consolidation of the control of the
food system finds a derivative in the structure of the markets for
political favours. As table 5.1 shows, if we look at the sums donated in the US political system (insofar as they are fully and accurately recorded) we see that the top four companies in many
sectors of the food system are responsible for more than half the
political contributions.[29] The mechanisms of political purchase
are used by different interests to push for concessions. Nothing
surprising in that. Nor, by consequence, should we be surprised
that, sometimes, different blocs of food producers demand con-
flicting things from the state. The outcome rests on a variety of
factors – the extent of contribution, certainly, but also the prevailing political climate, the extent to which external authority can
be used to justify a particular course of action, the guile of the
representations and, occasionally, popular opinion. For example,
in 1993, the US and Canadian governments announced that their
citizens should consume less animal fat in their diets. This advice
had been established by nutritionists for over a decade, but the
decision officially to adopt it marked the triumph, not of science,

Sector	Total recorded donations 2000-2010 (US$)	Largest contributor	Largest single contributor as % of industry total	% of largest four as % of industry total
Agricultural Services and Products	296,481,721	American Farm Bureau	22%	48%
Beer, Wine and Liquor Industries	167,445,512	Distilled Spirits	22%	55%
Miscellaneous Agricultural Interests	8,372,652	Agricultural Coalition for Immigration Reform	25%	70%
Food and Beverage Industry	214,244,928	American Beverage Association	15%	45%
Food Processing and Sales	176,088,238	Grocery Manufacturers Association	14%	39%
Retail Sales	232,747,159	Wal-Mart Stores	14%	39%
Crop Production & Basic Processing	164,022,223	American Sugar Alliance	10%	24%
Dairy Industry	48,525,407	Dean Foods	22%	60%
Livestock Industry	24,888,235	National Pork Producers Council	36%	58%
Poultry & Egg Industry	9,058,407	National Turkey Federation	17%	57%
Total food industry lobbying donations:	1,341,874,482			

Table 5.1 Food systems lobby spending
Source: (Center for Responsive Politics, 2011)

but of the vegetable oils industry over meat and dairy.[30] Political giving, then, might be considered an integral of the *status quo*, not a mirror. It's not just an indicator of who's on top now – it shows who's fighting hardest to be on top next.

Given the market for political influence, it isn't surprising that the line between legal and illegal activity in the food system gets blurred, and that the gulf between law and practice sometimes becomes so vast that some companies topple in. When cases are brought before the courts, they're not about stealing pencils from the stationery cupboard. Some of the largest legal cases in history have been won against companies in the food system. This includes the conspiracy to raise the price of sorbic acid (better known as E numbers 200–203) by chemicals companies Eastman Chemical Company, Hoechst AG, Nippon Gohsei and Daicel; the conspiracy to raise prices of vitamin food additives vitamins A, B2, B5, C, E, and beta carotene (added to breakfast cereals among other things) by BASF AG and F. Hoffmann-La Roche Ltd; and, most famously, the cartel that fixed the price of lysine and citric acid, raising the price by 70 per cent in a world market worth US$60 million, centring around Archer Daniels Midland, the supermarket to the world.

Before discussing the ADM case in more detail, a caution. It's important not to think about the domain of law exclusively as a domain of conflict between some putative interest of 'the people' on the one hand and corporations on the other. Justice wears a blindfold, and she is happy to provide a ring not only for The People's skirmishes with corporations, but also for bouts between contending blocs of companies. The law has, for instance, brought together the bitterest sweet-drinks rivals, Coca-Cola and Pepsico, in enmity against other giants of the food system. Although divided on most issues, Coke and Pepsi are united in their use of high fructose corn syrup (HFCS) as a base for their products (about which more in a moment). In the early 1990s, they united as members of a class action lawsuit against corn syrup processors, alleging that the producers had colluded to raise the price of their product. Pepsi and Coke said that the price-fixing actions of Archer Daniels Midland (ADM), Cargill and Staley cost them US$1.6 billion. Cargill settled the case for US$24 million, which wasn't a bad deal for them at all. Had the accused been found guilty, the jury would have been entitled to triple the damages, to a few hairs below US$5 billion. Rather than risk a guilty verdict, ADM settled for US$400 million. ADM in particular has been building expertise at this sort of thing for quite some time. In the mid-1990s, ADM were found guilty of price-fixing another vegetable by-product, lysine. The FBI mounted an extensive investigation against ADM, and the corporation was convicted in no small part because of a former vice-president who turned informant for the FBI, with the result that the company was fined a then-record US$100 million. Two executives who colluded to fix prices were sentenced to three years in jail. The vice-president who helped the FBI by wearing a wire for three years, Mark Whitacre, got nine years.[31]

Also, while different firms in the same business do compete against each other in the food system, they can still, legally, partner with other firms up- or down-stream of them. Cargill,[32] for instance, clusters its processing and logistics links in a partnership with Monsanto, which brings pesticides and seeds to the party. Novartis and ADM have a similar arrangement. ConAgra, one of the largest grain millers in North America, has arrangements with firms up and down the food chain from seed to plate.[33] It is through these economic joints that competition is squeezed out of the food system. But the business links wouldn't be possible without a great deal of political intervention. Although the food system is largely in the hands of the private sector, the markets in which they operate are allowed, and shaped by, societies and governments. Even if we might have forgotten this, agribusiness hasn't. And no firm remembers this better than ADM.

Dwayne Andreas and the Currying of National Interest

> But I make a profit of three and a quarter cents an egg
> by selling them at four and a quarter cents an egg to the
> people in Malta I buy them from for seven cents an egg.
> Of course, I don't make the profit. The syndicate makes
> the profit. And everybody has a share.
>   Milo Minderbinder in *Catch-22*[34]

A passionate attachment of one nation for another produces a variety of evils. Sympathy for the favorite nation,
facilitating the illusion of an imaginary common interest in cases where no real common interest exists, and
infusing into one nation the enmities of the other, betrays
the former into a participation in the quarrels and wars
of the latter without justification. It leads also to concessions to the favorite nation of privileges denied to others
which is apt doubly to injure the nation making the
concessions; by unnecessarily parting with what ought
to have been retained, and by exciting jealousy, ill-will,
and a disposition to retaliate, in the parties from whom
equal privileges are withheld. And it gives to ambitious,
corrupted, or deluded citizens who devote themselves
to the favorite nation, facility to betray or sacrifice the
interests of their own country, without odium, sometimes even with popularity; gilding, with the appearances of a virtuous sense of obligation, a commendable
deference for public opinion, or a laudable zeal for public
good, the foolish compliances of ambition, corruption,
or infatuation.

> George Washington, Farewell Address, 1796[35]

Archer Daniels Midland offers an object lesson in what the food
industry buys when it donates so handsomely to politicians' coffers. At the helm of ADM was Dwayne Andreas, CEO from 1971 to
1997. Born at the end of the First World War, he cut his commercial
teeth working for a food-processing company that was bought up
at the end of the Second World War by Cargill and, within seven
years, was able to resign from the company at the level of vice-
president.[36] In 1965 he was brought in, with his brother, to turn
around an ADM heading towards bankruptcy. Even then, he'd developed strong political ties, with large donations both to Democratic presidential hopeful Hubert Humphrey and his Republican
opponent Richard Nixon (indeed, by writing a cheque banked by

one of the Watergate burglars, Andreas was the first thread in the noose that hanged Nixon).

When agribusiness gives money to politicians, it sometimes buys politicians themselves. 'Dwayne Andreas just owns me,' confessed Robert Strauss, a board member of Archer Daniels Midland, and a former chairman of the Democratic National Committee in 1985.[37] 'But I mean that in a nice way.'

For his part, Andreas thinks of political donations as tithing: 'I consider politics to be just like the church,' he confessed.[38] It's a helpful analogy. If the benign, silent and ultimate authority in the Church is the Almighty, what is His analogue in politics? The analogue would need to be something that can't speak for itself, that breeds interpreters to speak and truck on its behalf and that, ultimately, commands absolute allegiance from all those concerned, to the extent that any criticism of the entity absolutely prohibits membership of the broader community of politics. Let us call it 'the national interest'. The national interest has no self-evident form or substance, but it has its high priests and oracles, to whom a tithe can secure a more favourable dispensation. And as with the medieval grace of the Almighty, the national interest has tended to bestow itself on the rich, rather than the poor.

The bales of cash that Andreas has been able to toss have attracted an awful lot of national interest from US legislators. Although he has occasionally been slapped on the wrist for skirting the bounds of propriety – ADM admitted criminal behaviour in a sale of grain for the Food for Peace programme's trade with the Soviet Union in 1976 – and although his influence hasn't been able to keep his son out of jail in connection with the lysine price fixing scandal, Andreas was able to shape the national interest at the height of the Cold War to a quite remarkable degree.

Take the example of corn. Just as chapter 3's story of Mexicans displaced by trade doesn't end in Mexico, neither does the story of corn. Despite the successful prying open of foreign markets, there's still a great deal of US corn to be disposed of. Much public coin has been spent developing other uses for it, and in

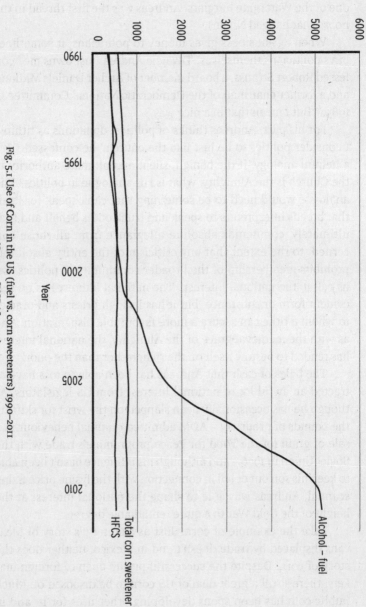

Fig. 5.1 Use of Corn in the US (fuel vs. corn sweeteners) 1990–2011 (Source: [USDA], 2011)

giving it away. At the outset, the corn surplus was part of a strategy against Communism. Since the end of the 1940s, food aid had featured in a logic of strategic defence in the Cold War, providing food to pacify hungry, fecund and possibly insurrectionary workers in the Global South.[39] Great quantities of food were shipped under the food aid rubric. In 1960–1, US food aid accounted for fully one in ten tons of corn, and one in four tons of wheat, flour, soy oil and dried milk, shipped around the world.[40] This orgy of self-interested largesse wasn't, however, sufficient to absorb the mountain of food produced within the US. Other uses needed to be found for the US food mountain.

In the 1970s came a breakthrough that would change the lives of millions: high fructose corn syrup (HFCS). It took a great deal of invention to figure out how to transform corn into one of the most ubiquitous sweet fluids on the planet. Through a process known as wet milling, corn is first dried, sorted and dipped in sulphurous acid; the germ of the seed is removed, washed, filtered, spun and then heated with weak hydrochloric acid to make corn syrup. At this point, the resulting mixture, once cleansed and treated, is about three-quarters as sweet as sugar. To raise the sweetness level, the amount of fructose is raised by reacting it with enzymes, and then it's made sweeter still by distilling and concentrating it. The resulting 80–90 per cent fructose is then diluted to get the industry standard 55 per cent high-fructose corn syrup.

Judging by figure 5.2, it has been in high demand. But HFCS has been a smash hit not so much for its intrinsic sweetness as for its two singular economic qualities. First, HFCS is not sugar, for which it has substituted since its introduction, and this makes HFCS attractive because the price of sugar in the United States is high. The average wholesale price for sugar in the US in 2010 was almost 36 cents per pound.[41] The world price was 22.5 cents per pound.[42] The protections enjoyed by the domestic sugar industry, which accrue to its processors, work by blocking sugar imports above a specific quota. This has the effect of keeping outside the

US a great deal of the cheaper sugar produced elsewhere – hence the higher price. This situation creates a funnel for cash not into the hands of poorer farmers, but to the processing industry at the waist of the food system. This is the intended result, and one which ADM lobbied hard to achieve. The justification? That the facility to produce sugar within the US is in the national interest.

Enter high-fructose corn syrup in 1969, and its second singular economic feature: the price of corn is low. Similar efforts at mobilizing the national interest around corn have resulted not in a quota system, but in a convoluted system of payments to US farmers for growing more corn than would have been reasonable, at the world price. The justification here? That the continued support of corn farmers, and the use of their output, lies in the national interest.

In the case of grain traders, the argument runs deeper, as we see below, but a corollary of this particular piece of national interest is that a conveniently cheap raw input is made available for the HFCS production process in which, as you might predict, ADM is a substantial player. Nearly 10 per cent of the total US corn crop is processed for HFCS, usually by one of three companies in the US that control the market – Archer Daniels Midland, Cargill and Staley, a Tate and Lyle subsidiary. As John Barnes observed in *The New Republic*, 'Since ADM can manufacture corn sweetener for between 9 and 12 cents a pound and sell it for between 18 and 19 cents a pound, they easily undercut the price of domestic refined sugar and make a killing.'[43]

And the stuff really is everywhere. In 1969, you couldn't buy it. In 2010, the average American consumed over 45 dry-weight pounds of it a year.[44] And all in the national interest. While production of corn for HCFS and other corn-based sweeteners has remained relatively steady since the mid 1990s, it is in fact corn for fuel production that has skyrocketed, from 707 million bushels in 2001/02 to 5 *billion* bushels in 2010/11 (40 per cent of all corn grown in the US).[45] And ADM is not missing out. In 2010, biofuels made up about 7.5% of ADM's US$61.7 billion in sales.[46]

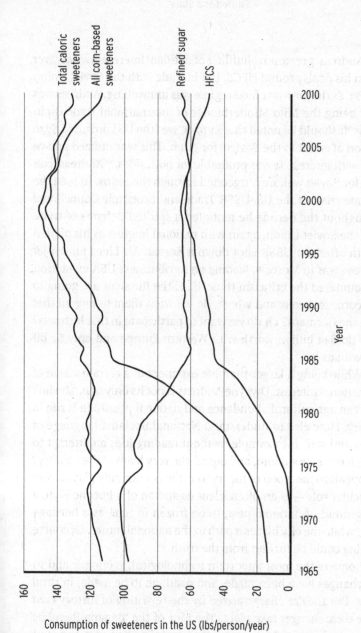

Fig. 5.2 Dry weight consumption of sweeteners in the US lbs/person/year
(Source: USDA/Economic Research Service, 2011)

Andreas' greatest reshuffling of national interest lay, however, not in his deals around HFCS, but in trade with the Soviet Union. In 1974, as the post-war food regime was unravelling, Andreas was busy being the Milo Minderbinder of international trade diplomacy: 'It should be noted that in 1973, we [the US] provided $750 million of credit to the Soviets for grain. This was utilized and repaid with interest. It was profitable for both sides.'[47] Andreas' concern for Soviet welfare burgeoned through the 1980s. In 1984, he became chair of the US–USSR Trade and Economic Council and throughout the decade he mounted a spirited defence of trade with the Soviet Union, again with national interest as his alibi. A month after the USSR shot down a Korean Air Lines jumbo jet, Andreas was in Moscow, leading an Agribusiness USA exhibition. He countered the criticism thus: 'If ... the Russians are going to buy corn, soybeans and wheat, do we want them to buy all that from the Germans? Or do we want to participate in that business? They do $44 billion worth with Western Europe and only $2 billion with us.'[48]

While being a larger-than-life exponent of a certain vision of the national interest, Dwayne Andreas is not its only one. The link between agricultural abundance and national plenitude is rife in history. How else to understand National Socialist language of 'blood and soil', for example, without reading it as an attempt to plough nationhood into, and out of, the very loam of the country? In appeals to the 'good of the nation', the countryside plays a very particular role – as an often silent custodian of a bucolic idyll, a playground of national past, to be frozen in time as a heritage park, while the city blazes a path to the national future. Of course, nothing could be further from the truth.

Some of the most important technological, economic and social changes have been made, and continue to be made, in rural areas. But they're characterized by the rewriting of history *even while these changes take place*. The idea of the 'Banana Republic' became current in the 1930s, at the same time as a vast and modern transformation was being forced onto the fields of Guatemala, for example. And it continues to happen today. Indeed, logically, it has to. If one of the singular features of the nation state is a narrative of inevitable progress and enlightenment,[49] then every generation must recraft its national past to suit the national present. We might expect to see history being rewritten, to show that corporate and national interests are aligned now, and have always been. As we shall see in the next chapter, President Bush's 2006 visit to India saw just such a rewriting.

6

Better Living through Chemistry

'Right you are,' says the man, 'and here they are, the very beans themselves,' he went on, pulling out of his pocket a number of strange-looking beans. 'As you are so sharp,' says he, 'I don't mind doing a swap with you – your cow for these beans.'

'Go along,' says Jack. 'Wouldn't you like it?'

'Ah! You don't know what these beans are,' said the man. 'If you plant them overnight, by morning they grow right up to the sky.'

Jack and the Beanstalk[1]

The fixation of nitrogen is a question of the not-far-distant future. Unless we can class it as among certainties to come, the great Caucasian race will cease to be foremost in the world, and will be squeezed out of existence by races to whom wheaten bread is not the staff of life.

William Crookes, 1898[2]

This chapter is about the central problem in the food system: hunger. For two decades after the Second World War, hunger was tackled directly through the export of the US food surplus. When the economics of that system began to falter, a new system was ready to take its place, one which broke the links between trade and aid, in which the private sector had an expanded role and, crucially, where breakthroughs in agricultural research made possible the vastly increased output of the staples of wheat, corn and rice in key areas in the Global South. This research created hybrid seed varieties that yielded more than traditional ones. In order to work, the seeds required almost laboratory-perfect growing conditions, which demanded irrigation, fertilizers and pesticides. These, in their turn, depended on fossil fuels for their production. And the entire enterprise required the expunging of native biodiversity, so that rows of the new seed might take its place. It was a transformation of agricultural practice that well deserved the title 'Green Revolution'. In some places, due in part to Green Revolution technologies, widespread hunger was kept in check. But the social and ecological costs were high. Recently, in places like India, hunger has returned. In response, the companies who were central to the first Green Revolution have proposed a second generation of crops, ones that depend on genetic modification to allow for increased production, under the banner of 'a new green revolution'.

The Knowledge and the Initiative

In 2005, Indian Prime Minister Manmohan Singh visited the United States and, with a version of history tucked into his back pocket, offered his vision of the future: 'We owe our Green Revolution to America. Now we can herald a second Green Revolution with American assistance.'[3] In his 2006 visit to India, President Bush reciprocated in kind:

America and India are . . . cooperating closely in agriculture. The United States worked with India to help meet its food needs in the 1960s, when pioneering American scientists like Norman Borlaug shared agriculture technology with Indian farmers. Thanks to your hard work, you have nearly tripled your food production over the past half-century. To build on this progress, Prime Minister Singh and I are launching a new Agricultural Knowledge Initiative. This initiative will invest US$100 million to encourage exchanges between American and Indian scientists and promote joint research to improve farming technology. By working together the United States and India will develop better ways to grow crops and get them to market, and lead a second Green Revolution. (Applause) ... to promote the ties between American and Indian scientists, we're establishing a new $30 million science and technology commission that will fund joint research in promising areas like biotechnology. (Applause) ... The great Indian poet Tagore once wrote, 'There's only one history – the history of man.' The United States and India go forward with faith in those words. There's only one history of man – and it leads to freedom.'[4]

This is something of a misremembering of the Green Revolution, and it's worth revisiting exactly why. India's trajectory of agricultural change had everything to do with policy choices made in the United States, but not quite the way the Premiers recall, and with considerably less freedom than President Bush might like to admit.

In the 1950s and 1960s, the US was tremendously keen not to see India fall to Communism. India was a major recipient of food aid as a result. But India's leaders were contemplating some profound changes to the country's agricultural production model by tampering with the central capitalist institution – private property. Prime Minister Nehru had observed that the Chinese had been able to boost agricultural yields through the land reform that followed the Chinese revolution.[5] He suggested that perhaps 'cooperative' land management between landowners and those working the land might increase food yields. It was a suggestion received coldly by the landowners and their representatives in the Indian parliament. A change in land ownership would pit the government (albeit with the majority of its people behind it) against the full political might of landlords and aristocracy. But something needed to be done. Poorer Indians in rural areas were suffering. The imports of cheap wheat put Indian farmers under tremendous strain. They couldn't compete with the subsidies granted in the US to its large producers (especially when Indian national interest was busy shifting local capital away from rural areas and into the development of urban industry and technical skill). So Indian farmers read the market signals correctly and didn't increase their output. Wheat production remained more or less static through the early and mid-1960s.[6] The effect of foreign food aid was to cause less food to be grown domestically. A food deficit began to loom, and as farmers refused to grow more, India became increasingly dependent on food aid imports, with imports increasing 10 per cent year on year through the 1960s.[7]

By the time food aid came to an end in the 1970s, the US owned over one-third of the Indian rupee money supply.[8] That leverage offered a means to transmit, and treat, anxieties in Washington over national security. It also provided an opportunity for US agribusiness to put down roots in the world's second most populous country. Fuelled by fears of Communism, there were concerns that the poor, seeing the obvious disparities between their income and that of the rich, would rise up and take their fair share. These concerns were presented as worries about 'security'. For example President Lyndon Johnson, in a January 1965 address to Congress, could not believe 'that our island of abundance will be finally secure in a sea of despair and unrest or in a world where even the oppressed may one day have access to the engines of modern destruction'.[9]

Nehru died of a heart attack in May 1964 and was succeeded by Lal Bahadur Shastri, who inherited a country on the brink of starvation. Food riots flared across the country in 1964 and 1965.[10] The protests were explained by the US press not as a symptom of increasing food aid dependency, but as a sign that India 'doggedly resists change', as *Time* magazine put it in 1964.[11] This behaviour was more than just stubborn – it could be downright dangerous. In the US, the link was clearly drawn, both in the press and in internal Johnson Administration thinking, between population, hunger, political instability and the spread of Communism. As Orville Freeman, Secretary of Agriculture from 1961 to 1969 in Kennedy's and Johnson's administrations, put it at a press club meeting, 'hopelessness breeds hostility, where the ever-growing gap between the haves and have-nots first provokes riots in the streets ... then the insurrection and toppling of governments [and then] the final desperate international aggression.'[12] When Shastri voiced his disapproval of the US bombing in Vietnam, the Johnson administration interpreted it as a sign linking India's intransigence and its slide towards Communism. Johnson sought to instil a little discipline and steer India away from its pro-Communist sympathies. He stalled on the July 1965 renewal of India's PL-480 food contract, shifting the approval of food aid away from an annual basis to a month-to-month system. By systematically withholding a guarantee of food aid supply, the US held a knife to the Indian government's throat.

But the US government also offered an inducement. If Shastri didn't pursue Nehru's thoughts of land redistribution, and if he proved more amenable to US foreign policy in Asia, the US government would help India out. Not only would the US resume food aid on a more predictable and long-term basis, it would sweeten the pot with new agricultural technologies. These technologies had been developed by a series of foundations, primarily Ford and Rockefeller, and applied with greater and lesser success in Mexico to increase crop yield.[13] The *New York Times* summarized the character of this inducement in 1965:

> To prod developing countries in the right direction ...
> India is already being told, for instance, that loans and
> grants from the Agency for International Development
> for economic development as well as for Food for Peace
> shipments will depend in part on the amount of foreign
> exchange she sets aside each year for fertilizer imports or
> the equivalent in new fertilizer plants.[14]

The Green Revolution was the solution that fit the constraints, offering a package of seeds, fertilizer and spatial organization that would allow the poor to eat, without suffering the rich to be parted from their land. Walter Mondale observed in 1966 that 'in this new concept of food for peace we are attaching strings to it to the recipient country. If they do not do what is best for them, aid can be chopped off overnight'.[15]

With Orville Freeman pushing the interests of the US fertilizer industry,[16] with India being held hostage by US food aid shipments, and with the choices for social reform effectively blocked by an Indian Congress unwilling to entertain them, India's Green Revolution began. To the extent that these are the circumstances under which it can be said that 'We owe our green revolution to America', Prime Minister Singh did not mis-speak. But the implication, that the Green Revolution was freely and willingly adopted by the government of India, let alone its people, is unwarranted. On the contrary, a good number of peasant movements were fighting for alternative ways of doing things.[17] It's just that the Green Revolution was perceived as the right solution at the right time. Increased yield put a lid on demands for redistribution. A technological solution muffled a political problem.[18] This is the history of freedom to which President Bush refers.

A simple assessment of the Green Revolution isn't easy. For those farmers with land able to access Green Revolution technologies in the north of India, to whom irrigation, assistance and price supports were provided, yield increased by as much as five times over twenty years.[19] This seems to argue for the spreading of these technologies elsewhere. It's indisputable that, with Green Revolution technologies, yields are higher than before. This fact of increased yields is appreciated even by those who speak out against the Green Revolution. Jagdish Papra is a farmer in Southern Punjab who has campaigned around the world against Green Revolution technology. Yet he recalls the moment, suffused with magic, when the first announcements of the Green Revolution wafted across the fields:

We had a broadcast from Punjab University. Someone turned up their radio very loud, and the whole village could hear it, even far away in the fields. Young people wouldn't believe it now, but things were quiet back then. We listened to the programme. We could hear the words of the Punjab Agricultural University, telling us about new seeds, fertilizer and machinery. And people tried it out slowly. The University used to come to our village and they gave out fertilizer. Together with the farmer, they would pick a corner. Many were against it, but they were won over by heavy propaganda. Now I think about it, with the poisons and everything else that they brought, now I realize. But ultimately, they increased profits, and they increased yield.

Despite this, Papra warns farmers against this kind of technology because, as he notes, the 'miracle seeds came at too high a cost'. The miracle of the seed was that they could, under the right circumstances, provide an unnatural abundance. When those circumstances were right, abundance was almost certain. The problem lay in the fact that circumstances were almost never right. The seeds required irrigation, leading to competition for water, which has resulted in groundwater levels dropping at over a foot a year in some areas.[20] Irrigation led to increased salt deposits in the soil, rendering increasing areas of the land unusable. Green Revolution monocultures also expunged indigenous biodiversity. The range of crops, developed over millennia to fit the ecological profile of Punjab, not only provided nutrients unavailable in wheat but also provided ecological harbour for non-Green Revolution varieties of wheat. Further, the cost of fertilizer could only be borne by those farmers who were able to access credit. Farmers who weren't able to muster the resources or technology to buy irrigation and fertilizer fell by the wayside: the number of small-holdings in the Punjab dropped by a quarter.[21] (This was another sign that the technology wasn't really designed to benefit farmers so much as to provide one crop, cheaply, to urban consumers.) Today, the Indian government's own data shows that the level of annual debt for Punjabi farmers is the highest in the country, at Rs 41,576 (US$ 918.30, GB£569.20) – far higher than the national average of Rs12,585 (US$ 277.97, GB£172.30).[22] The recent national debt waiver scheme is estimated to have reached only 7% of farmers in Pubjab.[23] The risks of defaulting are higher than ever, as are its costs. Within two decades, over a third of all farmers in the region were, according to the UN, driven to poverty by debt and the spiral of costs associated with needing increased levels of fertilizer to secure the same level of yield.[24]

Important to note, too, is that the vast state expenditures on the Green Revolution were concentrated in the part of the country with the greatest fertility – Punjab. Food grain production there increased from around 3 million tons over the 1965-1966 season to nearly 28 million tons in the 2010-2011 season.[25] Through Green Revolution technology, over 12 per cent of India's total food was produced by a state with 24 million people, about 2 per cent of the population.[26] But most Indian farmers, those without access to large areas of land and living in poorer states, were ignored by the government's Green Revolution policies. Three-quarters of all farmers, cultivating one-third of the country's landmass, continue to be marginalized by the government, despite being the backbone of India's food system.

By this account, at least, the only thing worse than having the Green Revolution was not having it. A more profound way to understand the Green Revolution, however, is to compare it not to its antecedent circumstances, nor to its absence, but to compare it to a different counterfactual, to what economists call its 'opportunity cost', the next best thing that might have been done. Perhaps the best case study is the Indian state of Kerala. Rather than engage in a technological fix, Kerala opted for a political solution, beginning with the 1957 Land Reform Ordinance and Education Bill. This legislation, as the title suggests, understood the dynamics of agrarian change to be bound to broader social concerns. Land redistribution was brought together as a policy package with public food distribution programmes, employment guarantees, education and healthcare systems, under the administration of the state-level Communist government. The package worked and has led today to the highest levels of literacy, health status and social development in the country, even though Kerala's population of 30 million is on average *poorer* than the average citizen elsewhere in India. Of course, Kerala isn't a zone of perfection – there remain tensions not only between left and right in Kerala, but also between, for instance, industrialists and fisherfolk. Yet the Keralan government has made a virtue of conflict, and with the return of the Communist Party to power in 1996 came the 'People's Campaign for Decentralized Planning', a plan which put 30–40 per cent of the state's budget into the hands of decentralized local committees, in which 2.5 million people are directly involved.[27] Through mechanisms of redistribution, integral to its broader political project, and despite the state's relative poverty, Kerala has literacy rates and life expectancy higher than parts of the United States.[28] It achieved this not through an individualizing, atomizing process, not through the politics of the farmer as a lone entrepreneur who lives or dies by the market, but through the social politics of change, by taking seriously the possibility that social problems might be addressed both comprehensively and *collectively*.

The Keralan solution seems to have had a more enduring impact than the Green Revolution. Twenty years after the Green Revolution, while Kerala's indicators of health and welfare remained high, an old spectre revisited almost everywhere else in India. Over the course of the 1990s, malnutrition *increased* in India, and during that period the average calorie intake declined among India's poorest. Today, 237.7 million Indians are undernourished, suffering from inadequate intake of calories and micro nutrients.[29] Of children under the age of five years, 48 per cent are malnourished.[30] (In China, by contrast, the figure is 8 per cent.[31]) Production of some of the most important staples has declined as

agricultural land is increasingly used for export crops. As table
6.1 shows, net availability of food grains per person plummeted
to levels unheard of since the 1930s economic depression under
British colonial rule.[32]

Period	Total food grains per capita output (kg/year)	Average population (millions)	Total food grains per capita availability (kg/year)
1921 to 1926	186.5	239.18	185.6
1927 to 1932	171.1	253.26	174.5
1933 to 1938	154.2	270.98	159.3
1989–90 to 91–2	175.6	850.70	173.5
1992–3 to 94–5	177.3	901.02	170.1
1995–6 to 97–8	171.5	953.07	169.3
1998–9 to 2000–1	171.9	1,008.14	159.9

Table 6.1 Food output and availability in India, selected periods
(Source: Patnaik 2001, 2004)

Why the decline? To a limited extent, there's just less food grain
around per person. But the decline in grain available per person
is much greater than the decline in the amount grown. Much
more of the mystery clears up when observing the simultaneous
dismantling, through the 1990s, of the national food lifeline, the
Public Distribution System (PDS). The PDS, like food system interventions in the Global North, was initially targeted not at the
rural poor but at providing cheap food in urban areas.[33] The system began in just seven cities in 1942 but, spurred by the Bengal
famine in 1943, grew to 711 cities and towns by 1946. The distribution network allowed the intermittent use of urban food rationing
through the 1950s. In the 1960s, the PDS was retooled to distrib-
ute US grain. Despite its uneven reach, the PDS, at its height, distributed 18.8 million tons of coarse cereals to more than 80 million people through a network of 40,000 fair-price shops.[34] Even
during the 1987 drought, one of India's harshest in the twentieth
century, public food stocks and redistribution measures managed
to contain the famine.

The period of the decline in welfare for India's poorest has coincided with the implementation of policies written by Prime Minister Manmohan Singh himself, drafted and brought into effect when he was Finance Minister under the previous Congress (I) government in 1991. The widely acknowledged need to fix the inefficiencies of the PDS became, under his policies, the rationale for systematically dismantling it. Under the Revamped Public Distribution System in 1992, and then under the Targeted Public Distribution System in 1997,[35] the amount of grain distributed through the government fell from 17.2 million tons in 1997 to 13.2 million tons in 2001.[36] If nothing else, we might wonder whether the drop in the tonnage of grain distributed by the government might not have something to do with the increase in the level of hunger. The amount spent by the government on rural development expenditure as a share of GDP also fell, from 14 per cent in the late 1980s to less than 6 per cent of total GDP in 2000.[37]

Let's just say, for a moment, that we're appalled by rural poverty and believe that efficient markets and new technology will solve hunger for both rural and urban poor. To think this, though, we would ignore one of history's most wretched lessons in economics. Recall that the Public Distribution System was expanded in the wake of the 1943 Bengal famine, in which over 3 million people died. The paradox is that, at the same time as people died of hunger, there was enough food in Bengal to be able to feed them. In his path-breaking research, economist Amartya Sen observed that modern famines weren't related so much to the absence of food as the inability to buy it. Looking at the 1943 famine, Sen found not that food had been lacking in Bengal. In fact, there was plenty of it around. It's just that those who owned it had hoarded it, knowing that less food meant higher food prices. Those who died in the street died because they simply weren't able to pay enough for the food locked up in the granaries.[38] This is a hugely important finding, because it breaks the link between the simple availability of food in the market and the question of whether the poor get to eat it. Merely having the food around doesn't guarantee that the poor will eat. In fact, if the only way that the poor can get food is through the market – as the British believed when they administered Bengal – then at times when food is perceived to be scarce, the hour-glass shape of the food system is almost certain to deliver not food, but hunger. Those who are in a position to control the distribution of grain will only do so if they're able to command a sufficiently high price. The only way that famine can be overcome is to guarantee rights to hungry people that trump those of grain-hoarders at the waist of the food system hourglass. And the only way that Sen sees this as possible is through, at a bare minimum, a functioning democracy.

Rather than acknowledge this, though, Manmohan Singh has turned his attention to the rise in malnutrition in quite a different way. His solution isn't to follow the trail blazed by the Keralans or to increase spending on rural development. As a short-term fix, he has proposed a relief system that will, in the words of journalist and analyst Devinder Sharma, benefit banks more than farmers.[39] And, as a longer-term strategy, he has introduced a second Green Revolution. As with the first time around, it's a means of patching an intractably social problem with technology that promises a surfeit of food, a solution to hunger that rules out of court other kinds of policy. For these other policies to be ruled out completely, however, requires that history be rewritten.

When George W. Bush waxes Hegelian and says 'there's only one history and it's the history of freedom', we ought to be concerned. The historical revision snuffs out the histories of power politics behind the first Green Revolution, and the alternative choices that were present then and remain today. The second Green Revolution can, however, be ushered in because the relations between India and the United States are more cordial now than they used to be. Gone are the days in which India under Nehru tried to carve a third way through the Cold War with the Non-Aligned Movement. Gone are the days in which the US held the entire state hostage with food aid, calling Prime Minister Indira Gandhi an 'old witch', as Nixon did in 1971. Nixon added that

Indians in general were 'slippery, treacherous people ... the Pakistanis are straightforward and sometimes extremely stupid ... the Indians are more devious', with Henry Kissinger chiming in that 'the Indians are bastards anyway'.[40] Today, the Indian government isn't buying Soviet MiGs so much as US Boeings. Today, as in Mexico, the elites of India and the United States share a broadly common set of assumptions about governance and the way the economy should be ordered. This alignment of interests allows India's economic door to be opened to a 'second Green Revolution' based not on fertilizers and improved seed but, this time, biotechnology.

Who Knows What

Human history, and its fairy-tale fantasies, are stuffed with ideas about how to get more out of the land. The first recorded version of Jack and the Beanstalk dates from the eighteenth century, but the myth has a longer history than that. Cornucopian fantasies express what farmers have been doing, successfully, since the beginning of cultivation. Farmers, and particularly women farmers,[41] are the first natural scientists; they are the custodians of biodiversity, they experiment, they save seed, they exchange and breed new varieties, with the aim of getting more out of the ground and making the plant resistant to pests, easier to harvest and yielding more to eat, burn, weave and build with than before. Until the late twentieth century, all this happened in most parts of the world without anyone owning any of the knowledge behind this breeding. A key feature of the World Trade Organization, however, was a provision for the enforcement of 'trade-related intellectual property rights'.[42] These rights allow for one individual or organization to own ideas, whether those ideas be software, music, trademarks, patents, processes or entertainment, and to charge anyone else for using them.[43]

Within India, the demands of intellectual property rights

have pitted agriculture, the occupation of India's poorest, against information technology, the domain of India's richest. Infosys, the first Indian company to be listed on Nasdaq, has a subsidiary that deals exclusively with 'business process outsourcing'.[44] Its CEO, Akshaya Bhargava, is keen on knowledge: 'The future lies in the knowledge-intensive processes,' he says. It's a view with which few scions of the Indian information technology industry would disagree. Their bullish prognoses for the future demand, however, that they be able to charge for the processes, and the ideas behind them. To ensure a revenue stream in this future, they want high-tech knowledge to be protected by law. But the same rules that protect software knowledge at the WTO also govern farming knowledge. The door is open for intellectual property rights to be claimed over virtually any agricultural knowledge. In one widely cited example, the W. R. Grace Company and the US Department of Agriculture (USDA) walked through precisely this door. In 1990, the public/private partnership tried to patent the Indian neem tree because they had discovered that neem was an effective pesticide. The trouble was that Indians had known this for centuries. So common was this knowledge, known within the farming community for over two millennia, that one Indian MP sneered that '[patenting] neem is like patenting cow dung'.[45] Yet it took fifteen years for the patent to be finally revoked.[46] While ultimately unsuccessful in the attempt to patent neem, companies domestic and international are using the cover provided by the WTO's intellectual property provisions to commit what has come to be known as 'biopiracy'.

The Indo-American Knowledge Initiative is a fruit from this tree. Its precise details at the time of writing, several months after it was announced, remain unavailable to the public. The secrecy has been justified in the national interest. But even if its exact terms aren't known, its broad thrust is. The USDA's senior advisor on biotechnology, Madelyn E. Spirnak, pulled no punches: 'The US goal is to make sure that the Indian biotechnology markets remain open.'[47] Suman Sahai, an Indian geneticist, has observed that: 'Earlier a private company like Monsanto only had the status of a business entity. Now they can ask the director-general of ICAR [Indian Council of Agricultural Research] to get our vast genetic wealth from any of its more than 200 research establishments. The private companies can develop gene patents and sell them at a much higher price.'[48] This access to genetic material is central to the future prosperity of the corporations behind the Knowledge Initiative. Access to Indian biodiversity, and to its DNA in particular, means that they've an unfathomable pool of information to mine, analyse, sequester and resell. As one Indian government official has put it, the Initiative will cost the Indian government over US$200 million, and the US won't have to pay a cent.[49] This is how the Indian IT industry and researchers (mainly men working over keyboards), with their deep need for intellectual property rights in the US, succeed in selling agricultural knowledge (mainly generated by women, working over centuries) down the river.

The companies behind the Knowledge Initiative, and in the forefront of the production of genetically modified seed, have a direct connection to the first Green Revolution. They're chemicals companies. The seeds that they have developed have come not from any deep desire to improve the lot of the rural poor, but as an extension of their pesticide product line. It is for this reason that pesticide companies are now the world's largest owners of seed companies.

In India, a key crop is Bt Cotton, which has an insecticide produced by a soil bacterium, *Bacillus thuringiensis*, engineered into the plant itself. Engineering pesticides into plants is one of many routes explored by the industry. Another key group of genetically modified crops, a product of the Monsanto Corporation, is known as 'RoundUp-ready'. These crops are not engineered to improve taste or nutrition or to grow taller or withstand drought; they're engineered to survive being sprayed by another product of the Monsanto Corporation – the RoundUp broad-spectrum herbicide. The idea is that farmers won't have to worry about weeding if they simply spray the soil with RoundUp and forget about it. This is the fire-and-forget school of farming. Of course, with chemical brand-names like Javelin, Bravo, Captain, Ammo and Warrior, the practice of pesticide application has long been portrayed as a military skirmish. It's just that now, as with the military weaponry, the business of killing undesirables has been reduced to a simple point-and-click.

When farmers buy this seed, which is a great deal more expensive than conventional varieties, they get a packet and a long, densely written legal tract, in a language that would be barely comprehensible to them even if it were written in their native tongue. This is where the money is. The closest that most of us come to an experience like this is when we buy computer software. The disks which contain software costs pennies. The reason we pay substantially more than the cost of a blank CD for it is because of the knowledge encoded onto the disks.

Like the software industry, the pesticide industry has gone to great lengths to prevent its property being stolen. Just as software has 'copy protection', the pesticide industry has developed 'terminator technology', a series of genetic modifications designed to make the seeds produced by one of its plants sterile. Like the software industry, the pesticide industry is also prepared to track down and sue people who don't comply with it. Microsoft developed the 'Windows Genuine Advantage' tool, which reports back to Microsoft headquarters if its operating system has been copied. The pesticide company equivalent, possibly under development at the moment, is far more futuristic. One informant told me of discussions at the Monsanto Corporation to engineer traits into its plants such that their leaves would reflect light in a characteristic way and be visible from an appropriately positioned low Earth orbit satellite. This wasn't a trait that would benefit farmers. It would simply make it easier for the company to survey its property rights from space, and chase up farmers who hadn't paid.

Ultimately, though, the software metaphor doesn't quite work. Unlike software, which can arguably be said to have been created out of nothing, the bulk of genetic information in the seeds isn't created by the pesticide company – it's the product of millennia of common usage. The fractional value added, however, allows the patenting of the entire seed.

It is pesticide companies who will benefit most directly from India's second Green Revolution, as they benefited from the first. They've got the policy architecture in place to make sure it succeeds, and a new history against which to measure their success and vouchsafe their credentials as the monopolists of violence in the 'war on hunger'. All they want for now is public support. Pesticide companies have come under heavy attack from social movements and civil society organizations around the world for the lack of concern they show to the world's poor, for the questionable science that supports the crops and for the alternatives that they stifle in bringing their products to market. Unlike the first Green Revolution, which was driven more by governmental concerns from which the private sector benefited, the second Green Revolution is spearheaded by the private sector, with governments acting as enablers. This flip in the control of the food system means that the private sector is more exposed to demands of public accountability. And this is why they have gone on an unusually strong offensive to promote their products.

Corporations Address the Needs of the Poor

In response to the range of criticisms laid at the door of pesticides companies, and given their need to secure public consent for their operations, a three-pronged strategy has emerged. The first has been to produce crops that do seem directed precisely at poor people. The second has been to increase the amount of science that justifies their current operations. And, third, corporations have tried to use and shape the 'culture wars' in order to make their case. It's worth examining each in turn, not just because the battles around each of these claims points to broader, and disturbing, social trends, but also because they stand in such contrast with the alternatives that might feed the world without the pesticide companies.

Let's look first at the attempts to develop crops that will help the poor. If it is true that the profit motive is unconcerned with the needs of the hungry, how can one business school academic assert that 'there are fortunes being made at the bottom of the pyramid'?[50] These are not inconsistent ideas. It is not inconceivable that businesses will invest a great deal in the marketing of goods and services to the poor and treat them as an important market without necessarily being concerned with their needs. [51] A good number of food system companies position themselves through a language of care for the world's hungry. The poster crop for the potential of the private sector to help the poor is 'Golden Rice'.

Around the world, between a quarter and half a million children go blind each year as a result of a deficiency in vitamin A and within twelve months, half of them die.[52] Golden Rice was created to tackle this problem, by genetically engineering vitamin A into the rice grain. It is golden because its vitamin A comes from beta carotene, which also puts the orange in carrots. One of the areas of the world where Golden Rice is designed to be consumed is Asia, where a high proportion of calories are derived from rice consumption, and where vitamin A deficiency is endemic. Unfortunately, in Asia, rice that isn't white is widely regarded as inferior. It might become acceptable to eat if there were an education programme aimed at wiping out centuries of habit. But children will have to eat an awful lot. Estimates of quite how much they'd have to eat range from the biotech industry's two bowls figure to independent assessments of nearer fifty bowls per day to get their daily allowance of vitamin A. And all this to 'save a million kids' as *Time Magazine* put it in 2000, the majority of whom live in countries that already have food *surpluses*. The technology presents itself as a feel-good solution for politicians who'd rather not face the more profound, persistent and difficult questions of politics and distribution. There's more than enough vitamin A to go around. Half a carrot contains the recommended dose of vitamin A. The plain fact is that the majority of children in the Global South suffer and die not because there is insufficient food, or because beta-carotene rice is nationally lacking. They are malnourished and undernourished because all their parents can afford to feed them is rice.[53]

The best that crops such as Golden Rice can do is provide a supplement in diets where nutrients are unavailable. And when a balanced diet is unavailable, the cause has more to do with poverty than with anything that can be engineered into the crop. It is absurd to ask a crop to solve the problems of income and food distribution, of course. But since this is precisely the root cause of vitamin A deficiency, the danger of crops such as Golden Rice is not merely that they are ineffective publicity stunts. They actively prevent the serious discussion of ways to tackle systemic poverty. This is why, secondarily, pesticide companies have taken to arguing that their crops will help farmers shake free of the yoke of poverty. And yet, even here, there's room for doubt.

In China, Bt crops were introduced in 1997, and farmers found themselves spending less on pesticides because the Bt in the plants fended off the bollworm. By 2004, however, farmers found themselves spraying three times as much as before, almost as much as with conventional seed, because a secondary pest unaffected by the Bt had found a new ecological niche, now that bollworm numbers had been temporarily depressed.[54] In India in 2005, the Indian state of Andhra Pradesh (population 75 million) banned Monsanto from licensing its genetically modified cotton seed on the grounds that they had been ineffective. Yields were lower, and more prone to disease, than non-genetically modified crops.[55] The experiment had a terrible human cost: 90 per cent of farmers who had committed suicide in Andhra Pradesh and Vidharba had been growing genetically modified cotton.[56] In the region of Vidharba in Maharashtra, there are 3.4 million cotton farmers, 95 per cent of whom are heavily indebted. The region also has a higher than average suicide rate – which has, on average, been going up during the past decade.[57]

The New Green Revolution has already brought revolt. Paramjit Singh, a farmer in Haryana state, was asked by Mahyco Monsanto to rent his land for a trial of what he was told were conventional seeds. When he found out that the company had planted genetically modified crops, his response was: 'It's not good for the farm, for the environment, for human life; I'm happy to see it burn.' Farmers, as one commentator has observed, are increasingly voting with their matches.[58] Word about the adverse effects of genetically modified crops is spreading, through farmers movements such as the ViaCampesina-affiliated Bhartiya Khisan Union (BKU). But because farmers are shunning genetically modified crops, they're increasingly the targets of large marketing campaigns to get them to adopt it. In one such advertisement, the monthly *Indraya Velaanmai* magazine carried a full-page spread entitled 'True Stories of Farmers Who Have Grown Bt Cotton' featuring a picture of a farmer in front of a tractor which, readers were told, the farmer was able to pay for as a result of his use of genetically modified seed. The farmer had, in fact, been told to stand in front of a tractor he'd purchased because of a bank loan, and that if he did he might win a trip to Mumbai.[59]

The problem is a little more serious than an individual farmer's travel plans. To be clear, the issue is not with the technology *per se*. There can be useful agricultural science that involves genetic modification (as we'll see below). The problem is one of power and control. When Monsanto's marketing department created a craze for its GM cotton seeds, it led not only led to farmers becoming 'deskilled' but, according to one senior anthropologist, who has studied the effects long after the pesticide companies' marketing departments leave, the collapse of an entire farming system.[60]

A further problem attends the claim that GM crops will lift farmers out of poverty. For crops designed for human consumption, the argument runs aground if consumers are unprepared to eat them. Consumer associations are worried about a number of things. First, they're concerned with the safety of the crops.

They have reason to be. Sometimes studies aren't carried out at all. In 2005, Monsanto agreed to pay a US$1.5 million fine to the US Securities and Exchange Commission after it emerged that between 1997 and 2002 Monsanto had paid over US$700,000 in bribes to try to repeal regulation that would have scrutinized its Bt cotton in Indonesia.[61] The only way that GM crops were allowed to be commercialized in the US was through the introduction in the early 1990s of red-tapecutting legislation drafted by US Vice President Dan Quayle (he of the grammatically modified 'potatoe'). In the US, the wording of the Food and Drug Administration's approval statement for new GM crops says that they believe that the corporations have performed all necessary tests to be in compliance with existing safety law. The government doesn't do any of the testing itself. The safety testing and evaluative science required to ensure the safety of the crop were part of the red tape Quayle cut.[62] And the company has yet to learn their lesson. In 2010 the EPA fined Monsanto US$2.5 million for selling Bt Cotton seeds in counties in Texas where it was restricted in order to prevent insencts from developing resistance to the Bt toxin. In 2007, the company had failed to label the restriction in a grower guide.[63]

In the UK, largely because of successful campaigning by activists, but also because of recent food scares around beef and mad cow disease, the government couldn't grant US-style indulgences to the pesticide manufacturers. The government was cajoled by public pressure instead to oversee a series of Farm Scale Evaluation field trials, the first of their kind in the world. These trials evaluated GM crops on the terrain on which the manufacturers felt they were strongest – the claim that GM crops are better for the environment. The last of these four trials has recently concluded. In only one of the trials, for GM maize, was there evidence that it was beneficial to wildlife. But this conclusion was the result of a comparison between GM maize and conventionally farmed maize sprayed with Atrazine, a pesticide that's soon to be banned because it's so toxic.[64] The real counter-factual – comparing GM crops with organic, let alone agroecological, farming – was never carried out.[65] The UK is lucky, however. In the US consumers eat GM crops without knowing that they are. Between 90 and 95 per cent of consumers in the US want food containing GM crops to be labelled.[66] The industry has fought tooth and claw to prevent that from happening. But in early July of 2011 they finally lost the battle to consumer demands. The US delegation to Codex, the commission which classifies and records the internationally recognized food safety standards, reversed opposition to GM labeling, meaning that countries that wish to label their food may do so without fear of being penalized by the US at the World Trade Organization.[67] Of course, this doesn't mean that the US is about to institute such labels within its own borders, but it's a start.

Consumer groups are also motivated, however, by worries about farming communities' ability to benefit from the crop. And these communities have voiced their displeasure in no uncertain terms. In India in 1998, for example, the Karnataka State Farmers' Association launched its Operation Cremate Monsanto. Following the announcement by the Indian Ministry of Agriculture that three fields in Karnataka were planted with genetically modified seed, the leader of the Karnataka State Farmers Association announced: 'Dear friends, Monsanto's field trials in Karnataka will be reduced to ashes, starting this Saturday.' Under this campaign, fields were burned, and Monsanto's offices in Bangalore were raided, with files torn up, by well-organized farmers. From Brazil to the UK, fields of GM crops have been torched. Reports of groups who do this often present them as unreconstructed Luddites – a mob fighting against the inevitability of progress. One can perhaps understand these tactics a little better if one sees that every other avenue for challenge and debate has been stitched up, from debate within a government that has already bet the farm on agricultural biotechnology to an academy that, increasingly, is run by the interests of the private sector.

I'd Like to Thank the Academy

> What makes all doctrines plain and clear?
> About two hundred pounds a year.
> And that which was prov'd true before
> Proved false again? Two hundred more.
> What makes the breaking of all oaths
> A holy duty? – Food and cloaths.
>
> Samuel Butler, *Hudibras*[68]

The second tactic in the industry's attempts to legitimize its practices lies in the control of knowledge itself. While advertising companies buff the image of the pesticides industry, a far more effective mechanism for preventing image tarnish has been to head straight for the place where its science might be put to the test – the academy. For those critical of the direction in which the food system is heading, particularly in the scientific community, the academy is a place of vanishing freedoms. Ignacio Chapela, a professor of soil science at UC Berkeley, ought to know. When he and a Berkeley graduate student, David Quist, published an article in the journal *Nature* in 2001 describing their finding that corn in Oaxaca showed traces of contamination from genetically modified maize (illegal in Mexico since 1998), the magazine did something that it had never done in its 133-year history. It retracted the article, saying that it no longer had faith in the original.[69] This was an unusual step. Normally, science proceeds on the basis that, after successfully passing a peer review, an article stands so that the community of scientists can either seek to build on it or tear strips off it or both. This, it is agreed, is the practice of scientific enquiry. Quist and Chapela's article cleared the hurdle of *Nature*'s peer review process and was published. Following a number of letters to the editor, the journal commissioned three independent reviews, after which the editor made the announcement to withdraw the article. The BBC show *Newsnight* obtained copies of the reviews. Although all contained criticisms, only one report dissented from the key finding of the paper. Yet it was pulled. 'The evidence available is not sufficient to justify the original paper', said *Nature*.

Chapela's luck didn't get any better. Soon after the publication of the article, he was subjected to a broad front of character assassination on the internet, by an 'Andura Smetacek' and a 'Mary Murphy', who carped that the paper hadn't been peer reviewed (it had) and that Ignacio Chapela was more an activist than a scientist (it is possible, as Einstein was, to be both). In the end, emails from these names were traced back to servers named 'gatekeeper2.monsanto.com' and 'bw6.bivwood.com', Bivwood belonging to the Bivings Group, Monsanto's digital PR firm. Emboldened, other pro-biotech researchers took up the smear campaign authored at Monsanto's headquarters.[70] They called for Chapela's resignation.

Chapela was scheduled to make the transition from assistant to associate professor, a rite of passage in the North American academy in which the university decides whether, on the basis of a person's scholarly work, teaching and conduct, they are fit to be tenured at the university. Given the resulting perks, and given the university, it's not surprising that, in the words of George A. Straight Jr, UC Berkeley's Assistant Vice-Chancellor for Public Affairs, Berkeley's tenure process 'is among the most strenuous, the most fair, and the toughest in the country ... No one person, no one institution, no one group has any undue influence.'[71]

Chapela was recommended for tenure unanimously by his department. An ad hoc committee was formed to evaluate his position which recommended, again, unanimously, that he be granted tenure. But then the Senate committee asked the ad hoc committee to review Chapela again, the chair of the ad hoc committee resigned without telling the other committee members, and the Senate then recommended to the Chancellor that Chapela be denied tenure, which he was.[72] It wasn't until a new Chancellor arrived, along with the threat of legal action, that Chapela finally got the position his peers felt he deserved. And even now, as an associate professor, he is paid at his former, assistant professor rate.

In both these cases, in the denial of tenure and the suppression of Chapela's article, we see similarities: the hijacking of due process, the machinations behind closed doors, the unusual fervour with which seemingly dispassionate organizations scramble to rid themselves of a single person. It warrants an explanation. It has one.

'One of the reasons I needed to be kicked out is that I opposed a $50 million donation to the university by Novartis.'[73] Chapela is a former employee of Sandoz, which merged with Ciba-Geigy to become Novartis. Novartis is a 90,000-employee 'life sciences' business with US$32 billion in sales in 2005.[74] They wanted to make a donation, reduced to US$25 million after the scandal, to Berkeley's Department of Plant and Microbial Biology. In exchange, they'd get a first look at all research papers published by scholars at the university, two seats on the five-person research committee and rights to negotiate licences on one-third of all the department's research output (whether funded by Novartis or through the public purse).[75] Given the falling public commitment to higher education, this might not seem such a bad deal for a cash-strapped university. Surrender some academic freedom, but get US$25 million.

There are two big reasons to worry, argues Chapela, because universities are in a position to provide resources unavailable elsewhere. The first is what might be called a demonstration effect. The amount of return that Novartis gets from its investment is much higher than its outlay. The effect comes not from direct spending on research, but through the competition to qualify for spending. Chapela again:

It might be that you're not directly getting the money from corporations. But you *wish* you did. If you can think of something that they might want to fund, you'll do it. If they don't fund it, they've lost nothing. And they've gained a huge pool of potential projects. All by dangling this little carrot. Think of the smallest community

college – all the people are looking for something that
will make them viable. They will put a huge amount of
their budget, they will go into debt, into something that
will make them attractive.

The hope of Novartis' money makes everyone's research Novar-
tisfriendly. The university also concentrates the pool of possible
projects. Chapela continues:

I remember a *viva* where I was the external examiner.
This woman was explaining what she'd discovered, and
she'd found something that was commercial. The people
from her department were sitting around the table and
they said, 'That's what you don't want to put in your
thesis, that's what you want for Novartis.' So you put in
your thesis everything that isn't commercially useful and
the company creams off the top, without any financial
exposure, the best thing.

A second resource that a university offers is, perhaps unexpect-
edly, liability protection. The university is an establishment that
in most countries has, through common usage, attracted a range
of exemptions from laws applied to other social institutions. They
are, for instance rarely answerable to elected officials, for the
good reason that academic freedom should not be conditioned
by the demands of the state. 'But today,' says Chapela, 'academic
freedom means "We should be free to sell ourselves to whoever
we want," and nobody can say: "What are you doing with our
public resources? You were chartered to do research in the public
interest for the betterment of society." The net outcome is that
there's a legal bubble around the university that protects everyone from litigation.'

Even legislators find it hard to disentangle the miasma of
clauses and codes around the university. A series of State Legislature hearings in Sacramento in May 2000 demonstrated the

length to which the University of California, a public institution, was prepared to go to avoid public disclosure around its dealings with biotech companies.[76] Senator Peace, chair of the finance committee, was quoted as saying, 'You have created a system of payment and transfer that is, basically, unauditable.' Senator Tom Hayden, at the end of an inconclusive and frustrating session of cross-examination, attempting to get to the bottom of the university's precise arrangements with the private sector, said, 'Let no-one think that today's session will change anything. All we're doing here is leaving fingernail marks on the wall, for future generations to know that at least we tried to do something.'

There's a wide discrepancy in the costs associated with what Chapela calls 'promotional' work – research that serves, across disciplines, to advance a particular research agenda – in this case, that of the biotechnology companies in the food system. The money to do promotional research is being scooped out of funding for other, more precautionary, science. 'People are asking, "How can I get this to be that?", "How do I change the flower to red?", not, "What would happen if I did?"' The questions that get asked are determined by the profit motive – a force that rarely meets the needs of the hungry. The questions are 'How do we get the vitamin A in the rice?' or 'How do we get the poor to stop breeding?' but never 'Why have the poor remained hungry?' And there is a mounting pile of questions that remain unasked. They could be both asked and answered, were there the will. Chapela's paper on the contamination of corn, since corroborated by Mexican researchers, cost US$2,000 for the initial research, and less than US$10,000 in total. Novartis gave the university US$25 million. 'That's an indicative figure of the proportion of promotional to precautionary research,' he notes.[77]

Chapela isn't the only scientist flayed by the biotechnology industry's PR firms: Tyrone Hayes and Arpad Pusztai are other names to note.[78] The tragedy is that, soon, the academy won't need to expose itself to the awkward spectacle of censorship. Today's successful graduate students are being forged in this environment.

Their success is guaranteed by the extent to which they're content to remain in an academy run along business lines. That means that Chapela, Pusztai, Hayes and others may be a breed on the verge of extinction; and that, soon, questions of academic freedom won't be an issue – those asking the industry's questions will have long forgotten how to ask anyone else's.

For Africa!

> For the sake of a continent threatened by famine, I urge the European governments to end their opposition to biotechnology. We should encourage the spread of safe, effective biotechnology to win the fight against global hunger.
>
> George W. Bush[79]

> How agonized we are about how people die.
> How untroubled we are by how they live.
>
> P. Sainath[80]

In their 1997 campaign, Monsanto tried to counter this perception with the slogan 'Let the Harvest Begin!' When a number of predominantly European campaigners took issue with Monsanto, successfully characterizing agricultural biotechnology as 'frankenfood', the biotech industry took a different tack. It mobilized racial politics. This is part of its third tactic in the industry's approach to legitimate its crops. The tactic involves the presentation of the needs of people in the Global South, who *want* GM crops, but who are being stopped by white middle-class environmentalists in the EU and US who scaremonger among consumer groups. There is no shortage of organizations in the South that campaign against GM crops.[81] That this is a tactic nonetheless speaks volumes about its audience. It is not an argument intended, in the first instance, to persuade farmers in the Global South at all, but people in the Global North. For it is in the North, and in Europe in particular, that consumers have put up the most effective resistance to GM food.

In 2003, the Congress of Racial Equality, a once-mighty organization that had marched with Martin Luther King[82] but had, through the 1980s and 1990s, found itself in difficulties with the Internal Revenue Service and drifting far from Martin Luther King's original politics,[83] burst back onto the stage. Roy Innis, its founder, and Niger Innis, Roy's son, Republican consultant and commentator on MSNBC, began to campaign for biotechnology. In a film entitled *Voices from Africa*, Roy Innis summoned the ghost of Thomas Malthus to declare:

> I am concerned that Africa will not be able to feed its rapidly growing population. Yet half the countries rely on food aid. Africa needs an agricultural revolution. Because of my concern, I came to Africa to see for myself. I came to see ... the potential for biotechnology.[84]

It's an odd thing for Innis to say because, first, 'Africa's rapidly growing population' is growing far less rapidly now than its peak in the early 1980s.[85] Second, it seems as if Africa has managed, however poorly, to increase the aggregate amount of food consumed by its population since the 1970s.[86] To Innis, the continent's ongoing need for food aid to be a straightforward failure of production, despite the fact that the continent's food production has been on an upward trajectory since the 1960s.[87] In offering this as an explanation for hunger in Africa, he and his corporate sponsors fly in the face of a great deal of thinking about the causes of hunger in Africa. In Africa, as table 6.2 suggests, recent starvation, mass-scale hunger and hunger-related deaths have not been triggered by an absence of appropriate crops. The truth is more complicated. Hunger is the result of a cluster of factors, including armed conflict, resource shortages, blood diamonds, recovery from the Cold War, and the dismantling of existing social mechanisms (so-called 'moral economies') designed to mitigate food emergencies, whether caused by the climate or by human factors.[88] Do we hear Innis coming to Africa proposing arms control, resource redistribution or political change? We do not. In many of the countries where food aid has been sent, just as in the Bengal famine of 1943, sufficient food to feed the population has been present. What have failed have been the channels of distribution. Does Innis or Monsanto propose to address these? They do not, because that is not what they sell.

Years	Location (Epicentre)	Excess Mortality	Causal Triggers
1903-6	Nigeria (Hausaland)	5,000	Drought
1906-7	Tanzania (South)	37,500	Conflict
1913-14	West Africa (Sahel)	125,000	Drought
1917-19	Tanzania (Central)	30,000	Conflict and Drought
1943-4	Rwanda	300,000	Conflict and Drought
1957-8	Ethiopia (Tigray)	100,000-397,000	Drought/Locusts
1966	Ethiopia (Wollo)	45,000-60,000	Drought
1968-70	Nigeria (Biafra)	1,000,000	Conflict
1969-74	West Africa (Sahel)	101,000	Drought
1972-3	Ethiopia (Wollo and Tigray)	200,000-500,000	Drought
1974-5	Somalia	20,000	Drought and Government Policy
1980-1	Uganda (Karamoja)	30,000	Conflict and Drought
1982-5	Mozambique	100,000	Conflict and Drought
1983-5	Ethiopia	590,000-1,000,000	Conflict and Drought
1984-5	Sudan (Darfur, Kordofan)	250,000	Drought
1988	Sudan (South)	250,000	Conflict
1991-3	Somalia	300,000-500,000	Conflict and Drought
1998	Sudan (Bhar el Ghazal)	70,000	Conflict and Drought

Table 6.2 Mortality from twentieth-century famines in Africa
(Source: Devereux 2000)

Yet this is the deeper story behind hunger on the continent. When flies buzz around the eyes of starving Africans on screens in the Global North, it is when they have officially been declared to be in a state of emergency. In 2002, for example, rampant Southern African hunger was tipped over the official 'famine' threshold by two years of bad harvests. What is rarely reported when the tragic pictures are beamed is that getting to the tipping point takes time. The reason that people in Southern Africa were starving in 2002 was that they had been starving for over a decade. The Southern African Development Community reported that, in Zambia in 1991, the chronic malnutrition (stunting) rate of children between the ages of six and fifty-nine months was 39 per cent. After then it increased to (and levelled off at) about 55 per cent. At the same time, acute malnutrition (wasting) rates remained stable at 4.4 per cent in Zambia. In Malawi, the rate of chronic malnutrition has remained at 49 per cent since 1990.[89] It is only acute malnutrition that has slightly increased over the same period, by 1 per cent for a total rate of 6 per cent. The United Nations Development Programme (UNDP) estimated in 2000 that 35 per cent of the people in the famine region were undernourished, with 54 per cent of Mozambique's population undernourished.[90] Among those most vulnerable to chronic hunger are women, children and the elderly. The UNDP reported in 2000 that 20 per cent of children in the region under the age of five were underweight.[91] And yet there were no shortages of food products in the markets in Lesotho. Two-thirds of the population live below the poverty line, and half are classified as destitute. Purchased cereals comprise three-quarters of annual food needs for Lesotho's poor, and over 70 per cent of the households classified 'very poor' in Lesotho have no cereal in reserve.[92] Again, the reason they are hungry is that many in Lesotho simply cannot afford to buy the food that is available.[93]

The situation is similar in Malawi where, in 2001, the International Monetary Fund told the government to slash its strategic grain reserve from 165,000 metric tons to between 30,000 and 60,000 metric tons. The IMF advocated this on cost grounds, and because erroneous data persuaded them that the coming year's harvest would increase stocks. A year later, when people were already beginning to die of starvation, the IMF denied disbursement of a US$47 million tranche of loans to the Malawian government, amid accusations of impropriety in the government's efforts to mitigate the famine.[94] The government accused the IMF of causing the famine, while the IMF blamed the government for corruption before admitting that it had, perhaps, behaved insensitively. Horst Koehler, managing director of the IMF, said at a British parliamentary hearing:

> [I]n the past we [the IMF] have not given enough attention to poverty and social safety nets when proposing structural changes. But structural changes are always accompanied by dislocation. We must live with permanent change in order to achieve economic growth in developing countries ... [developing countries] should be able to produce food for themselves – and we should help them strengthen capacity to produce food.[95]

Meanwhile, thousands were starving, and grain was being stockpiled by speculators betting that the famine would drive up maize prices – behaving, in short, precisely as they ought in a free market with high demand and a tight supply.

So how did it come to this? At the beginning of the 1980s, African states had a very clear idea of what their economies and societies needed in order to flourish. In the Lagos Plan of Action,[96] heads of state called for a type of economic growth disconnected from the vicissitudes of the world market, relying on import-substitution policies, food sovereignty and trade within Africa, and, critically, a reduction in the level of external indebtedness that was systematically siphoning value out of Africa. The World Bank disagreed, insisting in its 1981 Berg Report[97] that state interference in the smooth functioning of the market was precisely the cause of low levels of growth.[98] Most African governments were buried in debt, their futures mortgaged on declining commodity prices. The Bank had lent them money. The Bank's plan prevailed.[99]

The recent food crisis in Southern Africa, a product of these kinds of policies, was an opportunity for the pesticide industry. Promoting pro-GM African Americans like Innis *père et fils* to opine about the continent was one tactic. But there were others. Since 2000, when a Southern African Catholic Bishops' Conference had called for a moratorium of GM crops on the continent, the pro-GM lobby had tried unsuccessfully to persuade any country other than South Africa to accept the crops. The food crisis offered just such an opportunity, and the Church was once again to be a vector. At the end of September 2002, Colin Powell requested an altogether earthly intercession from Archbishop Jean-Louis Tauran, the Vatican foreign minister. The Secretary of State wanted the Vatican to persuade the Zambian government to accept US-supplied genetically modified (GM) food aid. 'Beggars can't be choosers' has been the response of one USAID official, in similar circumstances.[100] Despite howls from the US media,[101] Zambia refused to accept US GM corn because they hadn't been able to subject it to their own independent scientific scrutiny and were concerned that it might contaminate their own supplies. Instead, the country dealt with its famine by sourcing grain from within the region and weathering the storm, successfully, without US genetically modified food aid.

Again, these complexities have left the Congress of Racial Equality unmoved. Referring to Greenpeace's ongoing campaign against agricultural biotechnology, Niger Innis said, 'It's time to hold these zealots accountable for the misery and death they cause … because they serve their own ideological agenda, and want to keep the Third World permanently mired in poverty, disease and death. So far, it has succeeded.'[102] At the same WTO ministerial gathering in Mexico at which Lee Kyung Hae killed himself, Innis presented Green Power–Black Death awards to groups including Greenpeace, with an accompanying puff piece explaining that the award was being given to the organization

'[f]or leading million-dollar campaigns against energy,
pesticides, biotechnology, trade and economic development that could improve or save millions of lives,' . . . As
black-garbed Grim Reapers looked on, Innis presented
the first prize – Academy Awards style – to a colleague
co-ed [sic] representing Greenpeace. 'I want to thank
the mosquitoes for bringing malaria to less-developed
countries,' she bubbled. 'But most of all I'd like to thank
the millions of children who died to make this award
possible.'[103]

Again, these theatrics are aimed not at Africans, but at Europeans
and North Americans. The use of the Congress of Racial Equality
is part of a strategy aimed at delegitimizing organizations that
have successfully raised concerns about GM in Africa, Europe and
North America and have persuaded the majority of consumers
there that there are reasons to be suspicious of the pesticide industry. The strategy involves using the anxieties of race politics
in the Global North to have 'representatives' from Africa, whether
African-American or African, to present the authentic voice of
what people in Africa want, and to imply that any action to the
contrary is tainted with racism. But what actually happens in Africa? In his film, Roy Innis continues: 'In South Africa, transgenics
are already in growing the fields. These are the voices of Africa.'
What happens in the fields, however, has nothing to do with Innis' fantasies. In northern KwaZulu-Natal, a couple of thousand
South African farmers were introduced to Monsanto's genetically
modified cotton. It hasn't worked out as either Innis, Monsanto or
the South African government might think.

Making up Makhathini[104]

In the Makhathini Flats area of South Africa's northern KwaZulu-
Natal province is a hub of Monsanto's operations. Robert Horsch,

the Vice-President for Product and Technology Cooperation at Monsanto Inc., gave evidence about it at the US House Science Committee's Subcommittee on Research on 12 June 2003:

> T. J. Buthelezi, one of the first farmers to plant biotech cotton in South Africa, says higher yields from biotech cotton have helped him invest for the future in more land and better equipment. T. J. recently told me, 'For the first time I'm making money. I can pay my debts.' The success-ful adoption of biotech cotton clearly shows the power and relevance of biotechnology for Africa.[105]

Why is this small patch of land, with a handful of farmers, worthy of mention in a congressional briefing? Recall that the compa-nies behind genetically modified crops want for legitimacy, above all, from a Northern audience. With this in mind, we can put the pieces together. The innovation in genetically modified crops lies in 'making the seed an all-in-one' package – something so simple you need few skills in order to be able to grow it. Monsanto sells its crops worldwide, to large-scale farmers. But they can't sell their crops if countries refuse to accept them. Because of the place of Africa in the Northern imagination, if African farmers can do well with GM crops, anyone can.[106] And if African farmers want to do it with GM, who are white Europeans to stop them? Nobody wants to be accused of racism, after all.[107] For these reasons, Makhathini was a PR godsend.

Although some have access to irrigation, most in the Makha-thini Flats are dryland farmers. That the majority here own small plots of land, few more than ten hectares, also helps. They're not rich, and any intervention that promises to improve their lives will be well received. From its introduction in the 1998–9 grow-ing season it took only four years for nearly everyone to adopt the cotton.[108] The data, it seems, would speak for itself. Farmers had *chosen* to grow RoundUp-ready seed, and that, it would seem, is that. The market has decided, the environmentalists were wrong.

Except that the market has been a little distorted. In 2001–2, the company offering the genetically modified seed was offering loans to anyone who promised to use it to buy genetically modified cotton seed. People were queuing up at the gate, swearing blind that they were cotton farmers and could they have a loan please? As one might expect, as we would have ourselves done if we were in a similar position, the crop loans went to pay off existing debt, the 'cotton farmers' disappeared, and the cotton crop was significantly lower than the loan data would have led anyone to expect.

The local cotton firm dispensing the loans went out of business, replaced by a more prudent company, the Makhathini Cotton Company (MCC). Determined to clamp down on poor people asking for free money, the MCC instituted a new system. Rather than hand out money to all takers, the new cotton company stepped back from the loan market and instead offered concessions only to those people whom it knew to be farmers. It did this by providing free bags for farmers to put the cotton in, free transportation of those bags, and a guaranteed market for the cotton. In exchange for the bags, the company requires proof that the cotton seed has been bought legitimately, proof that the bag recipients are indeed the farmers they claim to be. The proof they demand to see is a valid Monsanto GM seed licence.

The net effect of this, of course, is to offer farmers the following choice: choose GM seed, or don't grow cotton at all. Since there are no other cash crops with a local market, farmers choose GM cotton.

Now, that said, it could be that GM seed is actually better if you want to grow cotton on dryland. The jury is still out on that: initial yield increases seem to have declined, and adoption rates can be explained for a range of reasons other than crop performance. Less money is spent on pesticides by people who buy GM seed, partly because the seed is much more expensive, and partly because farmers who buy the more expensive GM seed ignore Monsanto's instructions and choose not to spray at all. Given the history of the crop elsewhere in the world, though, it seems un-likely that GM cotton will prove a substantial improvement on its predecessor for small farmers. But there's a bigger picture here. Choices about choosing or not choosing what to grow happen in a context. What happens on that stage is shaped by its most pow-erful actors. And, in Makhathini, the most powerful actor is the Makhathini Cotton Company.

For cotton-ginning companies, there are economies of scale. The more cotton they receive, the greater their profit per unit of cotton. A cotton gin, even the mid-twentieth century model im-ported from the US that roars in Makhathini, is an expensive bit of kit. One look reveals why. It's a tangle of drums, saws and dryers, the size of several houses. Its job is to take seed cotton fresh from the fields, remove the impurities, clean it and draw the strands of cotton out. The economics of a cotton gin depend on receiving a bare minimum to keep the machine running. And in Makhathini, the gin doesn't receive enough. In an attempt to secure more cot-ton, the company has offered inducements to farmers in order to increase its supply. Farmers can choose to work as contractors for the company or even to accept a lump sum, while the company takes care of the cotton growing on their land. As a result of a se-ries of events – the location of the mill, the financial disaster of the previous company, the mechanisms of farmer verification – the consequence of the new seed experiment in Makhathini has been that some farmers don't even have to farm.

There's a further consequence of the cotton gin's hunger for cotton: the company's hunger for land on which to grow it. In order for large-scale farming operations to work, the land on which it happens needs to be contiguous. Small, disconnected plots aren't well suited to industrial farming machinery the length of several football fields. The Makhathini Cotton Company ap-proached local community leaders to ask them to sell their land. Local headmen agreed on behalf of 'their people', and the deal was signed. Except that not everyone wanted to move.

'They'll shoot me for talking to you.' Mrs X (her name for

herself) was terrified. 'Please speak to all the other women here otherwise they'll know it was me.' This was the response when our research team tried to start a conversation about the local cotton project. Mrs X didn't want to move from her land. She was forced out. Of course, the local cotton company didn't come around with the bailiffs. The company hadn't a clue that it had caused her to live in fear of her life. She was intimidated out of her home by the recipients of development, the local village headmen. Mrs X was evicted. The cotton company got its land. The seed was planted. But problems remain.

The seed itself is doing poorly. Without irrigation, and with increasingly unpredictable rain, it has been impossible to plant the cotton. In 2005 T. J. Buthelezi, the man whose progress was hymned by Monsanto's vice-president not three years before, had this to say: 'My head is full – I don't know what I'm going to do. I haven't planted a single seed this season. I have paid Rand 6,000 (US$820, GB£420) for ploughing, and I'm now in deep debt.'

T. J. is one of the faces trucked around the world by Monsanto to prove that African farmers are benefiting from GM technology. He's in a difficult position – he has twenty-seven children and needs to support them. He lives in a small house without electricity, and although he's one of the larger landowners in the Makhathini Flats area of northern Zululand, with over 30 hectares, and although he's doing much better than the workers on his fields, he's not a rich man. I'm not in a position to blame him for being Monsanto's Man in Africa. When the seasons turn against him, he suffers along with everyone else in Makhathini, albeit a little less.

Under scrutiny here, though, is Monsanto's use of T. J., and farmers like him. Africa has been a particular zone of engagement over GM crops. Although it's never officially admitted, it's hard not to think that the racially tainted images of permanent hunger, bestial violence and or prelapsarian incompetence with which most people outside the continent associate Africa don't play a role in its choice as the place in the world primed to benefit from biotechnology.

If we're taking the idea of choice seriously, then what would

these selfsame, allegedly lousy African farmers choose? In a range
of conversations with men and women in Makhathini, one thing
becomes abundantly clear. No-one, it turns out, would choose cotton if there were anything else to farm. This is a problem that the
Makhathini Cotton Company can't do anything about, for it too
is hostage to forces larger than itself. An official from CottonSA,
the South African cotton industry's own federation, sums it up:
'Yes, Bt cotton is a technology for a crop that's on the way out. It'll
help postpone the problem for a little while.' The problem is that
cotton is itself not an economically viable crop in South Africa.
The South African Rand is strong, and cotton produced elsewhere
in the world is cheaper. The South African cotton industry is in
terminal decline, and it will take much more than magic seeds to
make it better. The structural problems facing rural communities
can only be addressed by concerted public action. The intervention of genetically modified seed, however, postpones the need for
this action, delaying the imagination and creation of more robust
alternatives.

The farmers in Makhathini are desperate to grow something
else, whether sugar cane – which has a local market – or pref-
erably food. There isn't, however, a market for food. The local
Spar supermarket doesn't buy locally, but trucks its food in from
hundreds of kilometres away. Farmers in Makhathini aren't being
given the choices they really want. Just the ones that are most
profitable to those who control the food system.[109]

And this is something that the Congress of Racial Equality
doesn't seem to want to acknowledge. Of course, CORE isn't a major player on the international scene. But the questions they fail
to ask, the interests that they represent, the solutions they peddle
and the strategies through which CORE are used demonstrate the
forces prevalent within the food system.

Better Through Living Chemistry

That there are different ways of doing things, ways that might be better for the people concerned, though less profitable for the GM industry, is rarely noted. Bill and Melinda Gates' Gates Foundation has stuck itself in this rut, with a total as of mid-2011 of US$329.4 million to fund a 'new Green Revolution for Africa', and a massive US$1.12 billion for agricultural development in Africa.[110][111] They even hired Robert Horsch, the man from Monsanto who championed, and then dumped, T. J. Buthelezi in South Africa.[112] The Foundation believed in the Monsanto's future sufficiently in 2010 to add US$23.1 million of its stock to the Gates Foundation nest egg.[113] Yet there are alternatives to the pesticide industry. The Via Campesina farmers movement in Africa has its own set of solutions, developed by farmers, the landless and the rural poor themselves.[114] And, less than a hundred miles from the United States, a technologically sophisticated, environmentally and socially sustainable farming system is gathering momentum.

Consider the country that in 1988 used one of the highest levels of chemicals on its soil, with one of the highest rates of mechanization. That country was Cuba. Its economy used to be based on trade with the Soviet Union, with nearly 90 per cent of its goods going to the Warsaw Pact. In exchange for sugar, Cuba received oil at vastly below-market rates. The subsidy from the Soviet Union helped Cuba's economy to grow. It also made it deeply vulnerable. When the Soviet Union imploded, the price of almost everything which Cuba had previously received from the socialist bloc, and on which it depended, soared. Indeed, prices were higher than its Caribbean neighbours because of the US embargo. Goods that might have been bought 200 miles away had to be sourced and shipped from halfway around the world. Cuba's economy collapsed. There was acute hunger, as the economy grappled with the need to refoot itself. From a time in the 1980s when the country was so overrun with tractors that they were left unclaimed at the docks, the 1990s saw tractors rusting in the fields, for want of oil. Between 1990 and 1994, the average Cuban lost 20 lbs.[115] The 'special period', a euphemism for the trials of this harsh adjustment, spawned a great deal of dissatisfaction, hunger and dark comedy.[116]

The Cuban government found its industrial agricultural model unsustainable. In 1994, in the teeth of broad-based hunger, the government announced a comprehensive agrarian reform, once again in the national interest. The state had previously owned and run 79 per cent of all land. Through its reform, it decentralized this management to a range of privately run cooperatives. Today, 75 per cent of all land in Cuba is run privately, but 79 per cent is still *owned* by the government. The land can be passed on to the owners' children, but the rights to use it cannot be sold to a third party. It can only be returned to the state. The state still has a major hand in the distribution of goods, guaranteeing food packages for all and ensuring that markets and prices are set fairly. It has also supported urban food-gardens, which began as a local movement within Havana, to provide for the capital city's needs and reduce the distance food has to travel to sate those needs.[117]

There is also room in Cuba for agricultural biotechnology, and the human infrastructure to make it work too. Although Cuba has only 2 per cent of Latin America's population, it has 11 per cent of its scientists.[118] Technophobia isn't on the cards – there's plenty of science and technology. But the role that scientists play in the production of food in Cuba is shaped explicitly by public, rather than by private, ends. Genetic engineering has been severely restricted, allowed only if it can be proven that it is safe and, radically, that there is no other way of achieving the same goals through other means.[119] Such criteria force Cuban scientists, reluctantly it must be noted, to address the questions of context and need from which their counterparts elsewhere have been relieved.[120] And yet biotechnology there is. *Bacillus thuringiensis*, the very same active ingredient used in Monsanto's Bt cotton, along with a range of other biocontrol agents, is produced and distributed by the Cuban government.[121] The difference in this approach is that, instead of engineering pesticides directly into the seed (where it is available at doses sufficient to kill a few of its intended victims, and foster immunity in many others), the Cuban model uses it as a selective and high-dose insecticide applied if and only if required. The onus on the farmer is to become an expert in the use of the chemical not as a matter of course, but as a matter of last resort.

Cuban pesticides are produced to a limited extent by central government, but also by a range of almost artisanal cooperatively owned labs, which the government help to set up around the country, and which place scientists next to the consequences of their actions in the fields. The restrictions on energy available for farming have also pushed farmers, and the scientists who support them, to embrace ecosystemic levels of complexity. The problem with industrial agricultural methods of pest control is that they're based on a scorched-earth philosophy. Pesticides wipe out not only the insects that eat into plants, but also the insects that prey on the pests. It's a treadmill that, once embarked upon, is hard to step off, because each new invasion of unwanted insects prompts a further spraying. The solution, one Cuban soil scientist has observed, is this: 'to control insects, you have to give up controlling them'.[122] In other words, acknowledge that there are insects, learn ways to live with them, and minimize their negative impacts. Sophisticated systems of pest management have been developed in Cuba with this in mind, ranging from the cultivation of Bt insecticide to patterns of intercropping where, for instance, maize and sweet potato are grown together, and where the harmful insects attracted to one crop are driven away by those attracted to another.

Its strides in agro-ecology notwithstanding, Cuba isn't by any means an ecological paradise. Much of its rice is still grown using intensive agricultural methods.[123] Beef and milk production haven't recovered since the end of the Soviet Union. The energy-intensive feedlot systems that produce milk and beef aren't an environmentally viable form of agriculture: they produce waste and consume inputs at extraordinarily unsustainable levels.[124] The Cuban government has made choices, in the national interest, about what suits the country, and the needs of the people, best. They are choices that seem to be paying off, at least in terms of education and health indicators, which match or exceed countries with many more times the level of income.[125]

It's instructive to revisit the play of 'national interest' in the Cuban and US models. Within the US model, under which most of us live no matter where we are, decisions over the food system have been turned over, in one way or another, from the state to the private sector. This is not to say that there is no central planning under capitalism – there's plenty. State funding, which in the US goes under the misleading moniker of the 'Farm Bill', demonstrates this amply. Large sums are redistributed, largely to the rich, under the aegis of legislation directed at the farmers of 'the heartland'. The private sector, as Dwayne Andreas observes, has learned this well and profited from it enormously. Under the dominant system, then, decisions of national interest are either hidden in pork-barrels or presented as scientific fact, authorized by men and women in white coats. Cuba's model is perhaps more honest – the national interest remains, in profound ways, part of a communal project, its contours decided by functionaries rather than entrepreneurs. The role of the scientist in Cuba is a developer of public rather than private knowledge. The spread of this knowledge spills over Cuba's borders. Cuban expertise in alternative agriculture is being applied across a range of countries in Latin American, Africa and even as far away as Laos.[126]

Crucially, the main engine of change hasn't been the Cuban government – it has been the Cuban people demanding change from their government.[127] Governments are far more sluggish innovators than peasants and farmers at the edge of despair. In India, the Centre for Sustainable Agriculture, under the banner of 'no pesticides, no pests', is working with farmers' movements to develop alternative means of building and sustaining livelihoods. Japan's Masanobu Fukuoka systematized a philosophy of organic and scientific farming which has spread worldwide.[128] In Latin America, the *Campesino a Campesino* – farmer to farmer – movement offers perhaps the most profound example of decentralized learning and sharing, involving farmers travelling and sharing their ideas, seed, culture and history across countries and across the continent, circumventing the state and building their own independent networks as a result.[129] Eric Holt-Gimenez, director of Food First and a long-time scholar of the *Campesino a Campesino* movement explains how farmers themselves describe the movement: 'They say it "walks" on the legs of innovation and solidarity and "works" with one hand for food production and one for environmental protection. It "sees" a sustainable, rural future based on a vibrant *campesino* culture.' Indeed, the rise of agro-ecological approaches in Cuba were driven not by the state, but through *Campesino a Campesino* exchanges. In rejecting the privatization of knowledge, of land, of space, of memory, of expertise, the *Campesino a Campesino* movement shows the ongoing possibilities and lived experience of alternative agricultural systems, in particular places. It relies on precisely the opposite of the Indo-US knowledge initiative. Instead of the privatization of knowledge, its publication. Instead of wisdom handed down by experts, knowledge shared by peers. Instead of adapting the land to the crops, the farming is adapted to the land. Instead of a public told about it after the fact, the development project is the public's own knowledge initiative.

At the moment, the alternatives to industrial agriculture, whether state or non-state directed, are in the minority. But they have always been part of the agricultural landscape, and have survived even as the sucking weeds of industrial agriculture have blossomed. They offer hope, the seeds for a better agricultural system. Of course, what works in one part of Latin America needn't work elsewhere. Systems, like seeds, flourish in a context, and future agricultural systems will surely fail if they are insensitive to the biology, geography, history and democracy into which they are introduced. The urgency of these systems couldn't, however, be greater. To see why, it's important to look at the country that has, in many ways, not only fallen most for the seductions of agribusiness, but also offers one of the greatest hopes against it – Brazil.

7

Glycine Rex

All we'll have to do is give him a triple dosage of my wonderful Supervitamin Chocolate. Supervitamin Chocolate contains huge amounts of vitamin A and vitamin B. It also contains vitamin C, vitamin D, vitamin E, vitamin F, vitamin G, vitamin I, vitamin J, vitamin K, vitamin L, vitamin M, vitamin N, vitamin O, vitamin P, vitamin Q, vitamin R, vitamin T, vitamin U, vitamin V, vitamin W, vitamin X, vitamin Y, *and*, believe it or not, vitamin Z! The only two vitamins it doesn't have in it are vitamin S, because it makes you sick, and vitamin H, because it makes you grow horns on the top of your head, like a bull. But it *does* have a very small amount of the rarest and most magical vitamin of them all . . .

Roald Dahl, *Charlie and the Chocolate Factory*[1]

Secret Ingredient

Confectionery isn't all chocolate waterfalls and oompa-loompas.[2] One glance at the back of the wrapper of your last chocolate bar will give a clue. Beneath the cocoa is a cascade of unguents and potions that'd make even the quirkiest candy impresario blush. Most of the ingredients in a modern chocolate bar aren't really there for the taste. They've been added to make it easier to manufacture the bar, store it, ship it and keep it on the shelves: ingredients designed to raise the melting point of the chocolate, stabilize the flavours, prevent the ingredients from rotting for months, stop the bar absorbing water or bind together the ingredients so that they don't separate in the packet before you open it.

Among these ingredients is one you might have wondered about before: lecithin (pronounced lessy-thin). It's an emulsifier, an additive that makes fats and water mix. It means that milk chocolate can get very milky. Its main role, however, is industrial. Chocolate slurry containing lecithin is better suited to the rigours of mass production: as it's poured through the different machines in the factory, it won't separate back out into fat and water. Lecithin was first added to the industrial chocolate-making process in 1929; it has recently been abandoned by some of the world's boutique makers as an unnecessary additive. Since most of us won't be able to afford the chocolates that make do without lecithin, we're stuck with it for the time being.

Lecithin used to come from egg whites, but since the 1920s, it has increasingly come from another source – soybeans. Soy, it turns out, is not only a secret ingredient in chocolate. It is a component in nearly three-quarters of products on supermarket shelves, and in most products sold by the fast food industry.[3] It's also a key animal feed, responsible for a thick slab of the protein in meat. It's the main ingredient in a number of vegetable oils and margarines, which in turn are used at some stage in most processed food. You'd have to be diligent to spend a day without coming into contact with it. Yet, with rare exception, it's not an ingredient that advertises itself. It has come to occupy a key place in the world food system not because of its taste or flavour, but because of its utility to everyone *except* the consumer. At best, this means surrendering control over something ingested every day. But the darker story, involving environmental destruction, murder and slavery, is this: through the modern food system, through its monoculture and industrial production methods, one of the finest plants on the Earth has come to be a tyranny to those who grow it, and a mystery to those who eat it.

How did this happen? Let's start with the name of the bean. The European name 'soya' comes from the Japanese *shoyu*, the name of the salty sauce produced from the fermented bean.[4] The bean was named, in other words, for its processed product.[5] The first Europeans who ate soybeans never even made the connection between the range of foods it produced– tofu, soy sauce, miso, etc. – and the bean itself. Of course, the soybean was domesticated long before Europeans knew of it. Claims for the beginning of its cultivation begin in 3000 BC, but while proof for a five-millennium history is tenuous, the soybean has certainly been domesticated for at least 3,000 years.[6] It wasn't until 1712, however, when the physician, scholar and botanist Engelbert Kaempfer published his *Amoenitatum exoticarum politico-physico-medicarum*, that Europeans recorded the method for turning soybeans into tofu and miso. Today, soy still spawns exotic pleasures, physical and medical. But most exotic of all, and thousand of miles away from the origins of soya, are the political satisfactions.

Soybean plants are rather dull looking. They don't dangle little pulpy pods of tofu – just beans in pods on a shrub. Yet despite outward appearances, they are wondrous plants. Linneaus named them *Glycine max*, 'glycine' for sweet, 'max' referring to the large nodules on the roots through which they convert atmospheric nitrogen into compounds that help to fertilize the soil. They are exceptionally hardy, able to lose almost half their leaves without a serious yield loss. Perhaps most important for our purposes, the beans are rich in protein; not just one protein, but a broad range of amino acids, in a balance more akin to animal than vegetable. A range of benefits has been attributed to soy, from a reduced incidence of heart disease to lower rates of respiratory problems.[7] The American Heart Association recommends eating 35–50 grams of soy protein every day. Soy is a functional food. But in order for it to function, it needs to be processed. Little of its protein is digestible when the bean is eaten raw. Unprocessed, it just shoots through our bodies with little effect except, I noticed, some flatulence.

While the human digestive system fumbles raw soy, farm animals cope with it very well indeed. It is for this reason that the large majority of the soy consumed by people has first been eaten by animals – 80 per cent of soya produced worldwide is fed to the livestock industry.[8] But even animals don't eat raw soybeans – they take their soymeal ground. Indeed, a little over 10 per cent of soy is spared from processing, either for reuse as seeds or as raw beans. Most of the rest of the world's soy production is crushed, though 'crushing' doesn't really begin to describe the arcane processes through which soy is squeezed. Soy-processing factories are immense, sprawling and thunderous agricultural engines. The beans themselves arrive and are stored in cavernous, temperature-controlled warehouses. At dusk, a warehouse filled with 55,000 tons of grain piled four storeys high is deeply intimidating. It's a sight made more ominous by a constant pattering, like a thousand rattlesnakes in socks, as the soy mound slowly topples over itself. People have died in avalanches of earthy but sour little dried beans. You're advised not to step in the puddles of water and soy slurry around the factory – if you get it on your clothes, the smell will never come off. From the warehouse, the soy is taken by mile-long conveyor belts to the processing facility, where it is dried, ground into flakes and dried again; a solvent called hexane is then passed through the flakes, to pull out the oils, which are further refined and bleached to remove the noxious, sour smell and to produce, among other things, lysine, lecithin, vegetable oil and the residue, meal. Once crushed, then, soy yields two very different products – four-fifths meal and one-fifth oil. The meal is largely used as a protein-rich animal feed, while the oil is the world's most widely consumed vegetable oil, responsible for 28 per cent of the world's vegetable oil market, and 69 per cent of oils and fats produced and consumed in the US.[9]

A Whole Hill of Beans

It's important to recall, and there are plenty of contemporary examples to which we might turn to jog our memory, that not every part of the economy takes a turn for the worse when the world is at war. With the right connections, the right product and the right kinds of economic context, combat can be extremely lucrative. Soy was a war baby. In the First World War, the cutting of traditional supply lines for vegetable oil from Europe to America necessitated the import of 336 million pounds of low-grade soy oil from Manchuria, North-east China. Yet with the end of the war, and the restoration of European supplies of crops, US agriculture faced a glut.[10] Farms had responded to the war by increasing production to meet domestic market requirements and government demands, borrowing in order to be able to do so and bringing new land into production. Once the Europeans were back in the agricultural export business, US farms found themselves with too much soy and too few markets. To pacify a restive rural population and to support an increasingly powerful agricultural business lobby, the domestic vegetable oil industry in the US was protected by a series of tariff barriers after the First World War, including the 1922 Fordney-McCumber Act and, after the start of the Great Depression, the 1930 Smoot-Hawley Tariff Act.[11]

The Great Depression, and the Dust Bowl years, provided a further source of support for growers and processors through the coffers of the federal government. For growers, the soil conservation programme of the Agricultural Adjustment Administration of the United States Department of Agriculture provided a reason to grow soybeans. The Dust Bowl clouded the skies of the Southern Great Plains with the remains of the topsoil, desiccated and rendered infertile by ploughing and poor farm practices. Anything that could bind and regenerate the soil was prized. Soy fitted the bill. Because of its nitrogen-fixing properties, it was classified as a crop that could improve the soil, and therefore one that the government was prepared to subsidize. And subsidize they did, with big investments in rural infrastructure, support for the tractor and agrochemicals industry and funding for research into improved soy productivity. These trends buoyed both US soybean acreage and productivity.

The link between big business and soy is also long. Just over a decade after it was commercialized in the US as a feed crop, a number of industrialists were beginning to dream new and unusual uses for the miracle bean, among them Henry Ford. In 1935, he held a conference and gala dinner at his factory in Dearborn, Michigan.[12] At the dinner, at which only soy-based food was served, he wore a sharply tailored suit. 'Feel the cloth', he urged the conference delegates. Obediently, they caressed his sleeves. The material was soft as down. And it had been made entirely from soybeans. Their admiration became awe, as word of the suit's price began to circulate. The research cost behind Ford's clothes was rumoured to have been US$40,000 – over half a million dollars at today's prices.[13] The sticker price was a sign of Ford's deep interest in soybeans.[14] As one Ford engineer put it, 'Mr Ford hoped to meld farm and factory, to turn farm produce into Ford products ... He predicted back then that the day would come when automobiles would "grow" on farms. When he turned his attention to the simple soybean, he found his bumper crop.'[15]

Ford's romance with the soybean was poorly consummated. While it was possible to build a car chassis out of soy, it had to be coated with a pungent organic lacquer. Sitting inside smelled like waiting in a morgue. Still, by 1935 every Ford car had a bushel of soy involved in its manufacture.[16] And while Henry Ford's visions sound like space-cadetery, soy has found a number of new and unusual uses. Soy can now be found everywhere, from biodiesel to the ink on your morning newspaper.

But while Ford was busy trying to turn soy into a machine, others were turning machines to soy.[17] The Archer Daniels Midland Company, for example, had brought over some next-generation industrial processing technology from Europe – extraction units that used hexane to get the oil out of the crushed seeds, in 1934. In 1939, ADM opened the world's largest soy extraction facility in Decatur, Illinois – home of the soy industry today.

And then the war began. With it came the next big break for the soy industry. There was a peak in production in 1939–40 because of the expectation of a massive increase in soy oil exports (as figure 7.1 shows). The expansion of soy was helped in 1942 by the US government's decision to pay producers US$1.60 per bushel – double the pre-war price.[18] The Second World War had a different political economy to the first, though no less important for farmers in general, and for soy in particular. In the First World War, agricultural output grew to cover a domestic deficit in key crops. In the Second World War, it grew not only to ensure sufficiency at home, but to provide sufficient food for Allied partners overseas. After the Second World War, the danger for the US soy industry wasn't that European soybeans would be imported into the United States, but that Europe, and other parts of the world, would cease to be a market for US-produced agricultural goods. It's a crucial difference – one made possible by technological intensification, industrial design, international politics, the biology of crops themselves and a domestic configuration of politics in which farmers, and the rural poor, played an important part in the interwar years.

These concerns would be managed by a suite of policies after the war, including the US's PL-480 food aid programme and, in the case of soy, through international trade policies. In the 1960–1 Dillon Round of the General Agreement on Tariffs and Trade (GATT), the US managed to secure tariff-free access for its soybeans into the European market.[19] This was cemented by a deal struck at the next GATT round, the Kennedy Round of 1964–7, named for the US president. The agreement was that the EU would concentrate on the production of cereals, while the US would maintain its domination of the oilseed market.[20] And domination is the word. By the end of the 1960s, the US exported in excess of 90 per cent of the world's soybeans and just under three-quarters of its oil and meal. These trade negotiations, elaborate and protracted as they were, certainly helped the US to secure temporary control of the world soy market. But it was quickly to come undone. Soon after the Kennedy Round, the bottom was to fall out of the market. Within a decade, the US would have ceded

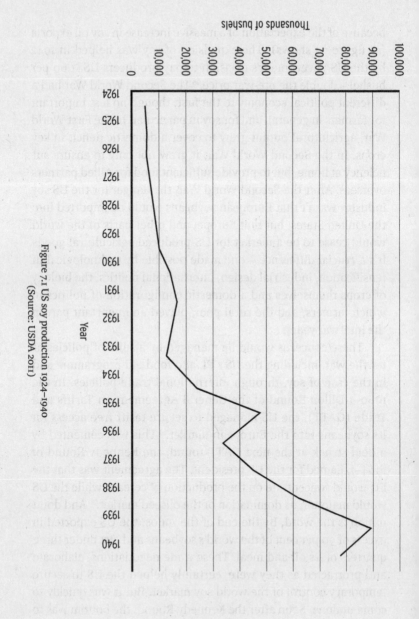

Figure 7.1 US soy production 1924–1940
(Source: USDA 2011)

its primacy of processed soy to a country with one of the highest concentrations of poverty on earth: Brazil.

Learning the Soy Samba

Every economic system has men and women behind it, people maintaining it, policing it, and proselytizing for it, fighting for it in some way or another. In the case of soy in the United States, its early exponents were mainly men, forming a cadre of crop scientists, businessmen, farmers, snake-oil vendors, members of the Department of Agriculture and entrepreneurs of various sorts. That's not to say that women weren't involved too. One of the key women behind the soy boom, a century before it happened, was Ellen G. White (née Harmon). Born in 1827, she became a Millerite in 1840, which committed her to a version of Christianity which believed that the world would come to an end on 22 October 1844. When it didn't, the sect split, and White began to have visions. Informed by these, she and her husband founded the Seventh Day Adventist Church in 1863. Her visions revealed much, from the exploits of tall people on Jupiter to, in a series of trances through the mid-1860s, the secret of longevity: stop eating meat or milk products. Rather portly at the time, Ellen White followed her own advice, quit meat, lost weight and ended up living to the age of eighty-seven. She also encouraged her brethren to follow a similarly abstemious diet. And they did.[21] Thus the Seventh Day Adventists became soy missionaries and the first white people in the United States to make tofu. Indeed, there has been a long religious history behind the soybean, always involving its suitability as a meat substitute. When soy arrived in Korea in the first century, it was brought by vegetarian Buddhist monks, who later took it to Japan in the sixth century.[22] But the power of religion in promoting soy pales in comparison to more modern faiths.

In Brazil, as elsewhere, the arguments for growing soy don't rest on its being, ultimately, a means to prevent the deaths of animals. After all, soy is grown in large part so that animals can be fed more efficiently, and thus more cheaply be sent to slaughter. The animus behind soy's cultivation in Brazil is a religious idea with origins at the beginning of the nineteenth century, one that has left its mark at the heart of the Brazilian flag.

The slogan on the Brazilian flag reads 'Order and Progress', and it has been the official national banner since 1889.[23] It was chosen by Brazil's national architects because it was the slogan of one of the most successful nineteenth-century religions – positivism. The new creed offered a path to the future, and the psychic tools to achieve a non-denominational, atheist and egalitarian order, through 'the great religion of humanity'. The founder of positivism, Auguste Comte, distilled his thoughts in the maelstrom of post-revolutionary France. He had come to accept that monarchy was a bad idea, and that it was for the best that there were to be no more French kings. The future, though, could be more than merely republican. One day, if people chose wisely, all religions would fade into altruism, private property would be abolished, and all would live in equality. This he derived from an epochal study of history from the earliest tribes to the pinnacle of contemporary civilization – early nineteenth-century France. He deduced that European society had passed through its 'theological' stage, in which gods were presumed to be the causes of all things, to its 'metaphysical stage' and could potentially reach its 'scientific' endpoint. Yet all was not well. Private property stunted the growth of pan-human bonhomie, promoting instead the vices of individualism, avarice and poverty. The solution, Comte argued, wasn't anything as revolutionary or precipitous as the dismantling of private property, but rather its stewardship in the hands of those in society most capable of its judicious and progressive use: bankers. Guided by positivist ideals, bankers could shape a society of the highest form, one in which altruism, equality and justice would reign. For progress to be true and unwavering, bankers would provide the requisite order. *Ordem e progresso*.[24]

This is more than historical trivia. It describes rather well the order of things in what is today known as the 'development' industry. Bankers, and their consultants, certainly provide order, with an unshakeable faith that their actions are, in the long term, to everyone's benefit, and with a strong stake in managing private property in the short term. The grammar of 'development' is also an important one to note, with its teleology and open invitation to intervene in those 'less developed' countries. It also describes rather well the mechanics of the Brazilian government's national development programme, the one that incubated the soy industry.

After the Second World War, Brazil followed something of an orthodox economic trajectory, piloted by prevailing ideas concerning the economic requirements of national development. In practice, this meant Import Substitution Industrialization, the creation of an economy that involved both funding the development of domestic industry as a replacement for dependence on overseas supplies, and a trade policy that protected local industry from international competition. It was a strategy that postcolonial countries around the world were adopting, in an effort quickly to build industries similar to those of their erstwhile masters in Europe and North America. Brazil saw itself in the vanguard of this strategy. In the words of Juscelino Kubitschek de Oliveira – the President of Brazil 1956–61 – the national development programme aimed to lift themselves out of the plantation economics that they had been wedded to by the Europeans, and claiming as their own the more lucrative engines of development that Europe and the US had so jealously guarded.

As the name suggests, Import Substitution Industrialization was primarily an urban strategy, directed by governments and financiers in the cities. Emblematic of this was the development of Brasília, the modernist capital of what was then 'the United States of Brazil', built in forty-one months on the sparsely populated Planalto Central.

The city made concrete the words of the Brazilian flag, with 'barren' land reclaimed for the nation, and the ordered, modern, stamp of the state put on it. The picture in rural Brazil was rather different. In the immediate post-war years, Brazil's rural areas were left to languish in barely reconstructed versions of slavery, with workers either chained by debt or 'free' but bonded to the land by traditions of patronage. This was of great service to Brazil's huge agricultural plantations, which needed both large pools of labour and large areas of land. By 1950, 62 per cent of those in the agricultural economy were landless.[25]

But in the post-war years, all was not going well with the import substitution strategy. Juscelino Kubitschek – popularly known as JK – was doodling on the positivist blueprint. His promise to the electorate had been 'fifty years of progress in five'. But instead of paying for progress with earned income, redistributed wealth or other sustainable bases from which to draw funds, JK had instructed the national bank to pay for the country's development by simply printing more money, leading to rampant inflation. JK's hyperinflation – fifty years of inflation in five, charged his critics – was unappreciated by the electorate. He was soundly beaten at the next election, with voters turning to Jânio da Silva Quadros and, soon after, to JK's former deputy, João Goulart, in 1961. A centre-left president, Goulart was mistrusted by the military and Brazil's wealthy elites. He also inherited a fundamentally untenable economy.

The inflation, and cumulative neglect of the food system in favour of urban industry, boiled over with food riots in 1962.[26] In rural areas, inflation was hurting the poor. Land rents soared, and wages failed to keep up. Workers, even those poorer rural workers who had access to some land, were squeezed. The big *latifundia* (large land-holding) estates mopped up the peasant insolvency, growing the estate size on the back of bankruptcy. In response, throughout the early 1960s, there was extensive, if fragmented, peasant organizing, involving unions, peasant leagues and the Church.[27] This radicalism, with the threat of insurgent Communism in both rural and urban areas, included a strike that won concessions for 200,000 workers. Although initially successful only at the margins, and doing little to change the fundamental direction of Brazilian agricultural policy, it worried the elites who owned and ran Brazil's expanding latifundia.[28]

A rural uprising in Paraná in 1961, against land speculation and the eviction of peasants from their land, offered what Goulart saw to be a way of boosting his popular base. He announced a Rural Labour Statute, which provided a means to increase wages for workers. At best, it offered little beyond improved conditions of peonage. The majority of rural people viewed it as an important but ultimately slim victory. The urban elites saw it as the harbinger of more dangerous kinds of redistribution. Both were right. Goulart moved to build a populist base for what was turning out to be an increasingly precarious presidency, announcing in 1964 the expropriation of a range of 'under-utilized' properties near major communication routes and federal projects.[29] But Brazil's elites were about to retaliate. In 1964, the regime was overthrown in a CIA-sponsored coup. A military dictatorship, in partnership with the anti-Goulart elite, seized power. The junta, ruling without the backing of Goulart's poor constituency, inherited many of his problems. And it just so happened that the domestic soy industry was able to fix a number of them.

Until the mid-1960s, the Brazilian soy industry was a smallish homespun affair, with the oil being used in the domestic food industry, and soymeal feed mainly used to fatten chickens. Although it had first been introduced into Brazil in 1822,[30] the soy industry was still finding its feet in the post-war context. Soy was considered a vastly inferior good. As a cooking fat, it was abjured. Coconut fat, lard or, in a pinch, tallow was used instead. Indeed, the first human consumers of soy in Brazil only consumed it under medical advice – understandable given that the refining techniques couldn't yet remove the pungent, gag-inducing beany flavour. The arrival of foreign companies, notably the Argentinean *Bunge y Born*, predecessor of today's agribusiness giant Bunge, promoted feed uses for soy but, again, the applications were small-scale and domestic. The first Brazilian soy exports

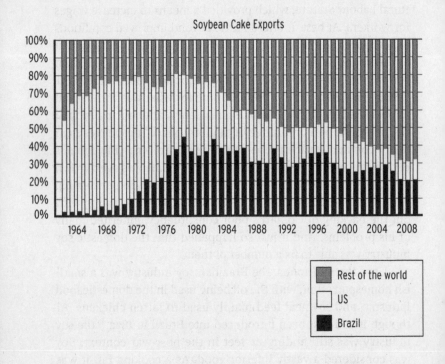

Soybean Cake Exports

Rest of the world
US
Brazil

Fig.7.2 US, Brazilian, and rest of world soybean exports
(Source: FAO, 2011)

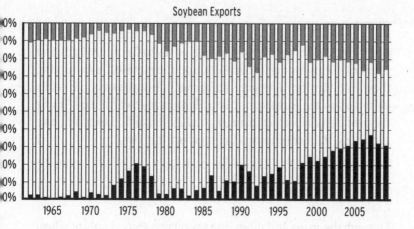

Soybean Exports

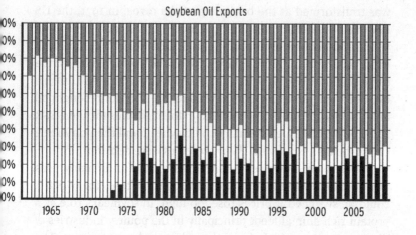

Soybean Oil Exports

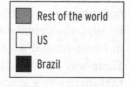

Rest of the world
US
Brazil

were, reputedly, in 1938, when a Brazilian entrepreneur in Rio Grande do Sul shipped 3,000 bushels of soy to Germany.[31] The war shut down this avenue for exports, and they revived, slowly, after the Allied victory.[32] As figure 7.2 shows, the soybean boom really kicked off in the early 1970s particularly in soymeal and oil. It was the product of a perfect storm, a combination of the weather, market forces, political choices, Communism and fish.

The Perfect Storm

Through the 1950s and 1960s, the soy oil was second only to wheat in terms of products shipped from the United States under the PL-480 food aid laws.[33] As with the rest of the food system, this was transformed at the beginning of the 1970s. In 1971, the US devalued the dollar, meaning that more dollars could be bought with any other unit of currency. This in turn meant that American exports became far more competitive on the world market. At the same time, the Soviet Union, driven by its own domestic deficits, decided to increase its crude oil production. The world bought oil and paid in dollars. This generated a dollar surplus for the USSR, some of which it spent initially on US wheat, and then on American soybeans. As a result, US soy reserves were depleted.

There were, however, alternatives to soy for its many uses. Soy oil had any number of vegetable oil substitutes for which it could be switched if prices rose too high. In soymeal's role as a protein-rich animal feed, principally in the poultry industries of Western Europe and Japan, fishmeal was a key substitute. The major source of this fishmeal was from anchovies caught in Peru. By 1971, the demand for cheap fishmeal had led to over-fishing in Peru's coastal waters. In 1972–3, the weather put the boot in. There was a strong El Niño Southern Oscillation, which means that there was a sustained temperature change in the surface of the central tropical Pacific Ocean. Specifically, that change was a temperature increase, when warm and nutrient-poor tropical currents displaced the nutrient-rich and colder Humboldt currents. So, new currents, low in nutrients, meant fewer fish.[34]

El Niño was causing trouble a little further away too. The change in Pacific coast sea temperatures also brought devastation to central Africa, in the form of a change in weather patterns. Specifically, the El Niño Southern Oscillation brought a widespread drought. As a result, West Africa's peanut crop failed. Why did this matter? Because the peanut industry was a source of high-protein cake that ordinarily would have substituted for either soy or fishmeal as a high-protein animal feed.[35]

It was a perfect disaster. Fewer fish, less fishmeal. Fewer peanuts, less high-protein cake. Less cake and meal, reduced availability of substitutes for soy. Fewer substitutes, higher prices for soy. This, combined with poor harvests in the previous two years, meant that stocks were already depressed. There was concern in the US that the country would run out of soybeans and have nothing to replace them with, especially with the price spiking at unprecedented levels. Figure 7.3 shows the price trend.[36]

In response to these circumstances, and the accompanying domestic clamour for soy security, President Nixon imposed embargoes on the exports of soy and soymeal from the US in June 1973. The embargoes were rescinded after a few days, but their lifting didn't end the story. The rest of the world, notably Europe – which had been persuaded in lengthy trade negotiations that its interests were best served by allowing the US to produce soy – and Japan, were concerned that the US couldn't be depended upon to provide protein for feed. The market lives on expectations, and when the US appeared to betray them, the market was ready to pay for certainty. The world was ready for a new soy producer. And Brazil was ready to produce.

The first foreigners to bankroll the burgeoning Brazilian soy market were Japanese. Seeding money for infrastructure, exporting and processing facilities, the Japanese intervention coincided with a domestic agenda for which soy was well shaped. Brazil's military government had been looking for ways to keep the lid on rural dissent. Violent repression of the peasant leagues had achieved this to some extent, but the government was keenly aware of the need for a more constructive programme. At the same time, a range of other problems seemed ready to be addressed by increasing soy production. First was the need for cheap food for urban areas, to keep the bellies of industrial workers full. This meant a need for vegetable oils, but also bread. Soy was initially considered useful because it was a crop that could be grown in wheat's off-season, recharging the soil and simultaneously boosting urban nutrition.[37] Shifting to soy would also provide foreign exchange, badly needed to repay Brazil's mounting international debts. It would, further, provide an alternative to coffee as an export crop, which had been increasingly unreliable as a source of income.[38] It would also create jobs for people in rural areas, taking the heat off bubbling insurrection.

Another, peculiarly Brazilian, goal served by the soy industry would be territorial expansion. Brazil remains one of the least densely populated states in the world, despite a population of 175 million, simply because it is one of the world's biggest countries. Brazilian Progress has long been associated with the conquest of new land, of providing 'men without land for land without men'. The expansion of agriculture north from the traditional grain-baskets of Rio Grande do Sul into the central plains was an explicit aim of national development.

For a cluster of reasons – political, economic, social and biological – the military dictatorship and later the civilian government supported the soy industry, funding land expansion, processing capacity and an export corridor, and providing state support for producer prices.[39] Loans for processing plants were made available at a negative interest rate. By 1977, there was more capacity for industrial processing of soybeans than could be supplied domestically, a gap that was filled by importing beans from the surrounding countries, and even from the US. By 1979, Brazil accounted for 18 per cent of world production, compared to 2 per cent just fifteen years earlier (see figure 7.4). The volume

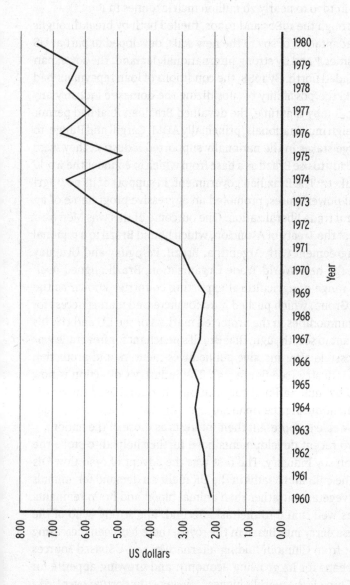

Fig. 7.3 Price for soybeans
(Source: United States Department of Agriculture, 1960–1980)

Year

US dollars

of soybeans crushed in Brazil went from less than 1,000 metric tonnes in 1970 to nearly 20 million metric tonnes in 1995.[40]

Through the 1980s and 1990s, fuelled both by breakthroughs in the adaptation of soy to the new soils, developed in part at US universities,[41] and by strong international demand, the soy expansion headed north. By 1988, the conditions of loan repayment had removed the possibility of subsidizing the domestic industry any further. But by that time, the devalued Brazilian Real had permitted foreign multinationals, principally ADM, Cargill and Bunge, to buy large stakes in the nationally supported industry. They were quite ready to use Brazil as a base from which to conquer the world soy market.[42] The Brazilian government, in support of its new agricultural powerhouses, promoted an aggressive programme of agricultural trade liberalization. One outcome of this was Mercosur, signed at the Treaty of Asunción, which bound Brazil to a regional trade agreement with Argentina, Brazil, Paraguay and Uruguay. Within the new World Trade Organization, Brazil aligned itself with a range of agricultural exporting countries known as the Cairns Group, which pushed hard for increased market access for their commodities in the protected markets of the EU and US. It's important to see, though, that Brazil's penchant for free trade was only possible after massive public investment in, and protection of, the industry (see figure 7.5). The industry's direction is now steered by multinational corporations that purchased the public investment during the financial crisis fire-sale. These companies are now able to represent their interests as those of the nation.

Two recent developments have further helped to stoke the Brazilian soy industry. The first was the advent of Mad Cow Disease. The culls and deaths in the UK fuelled a demand for animals fed on vegetables, rather than animal blood and brain remnants. Soy was well suited to the task. Second, in a strong echo of the Japanese entry into Brazil in the 1970s, there has been increasing interest from China in finding alternative, non-USbased sources of soybeans for its growing economy, and growing appetite for meat. China is the world's biggest soy buyer, importing over US$4

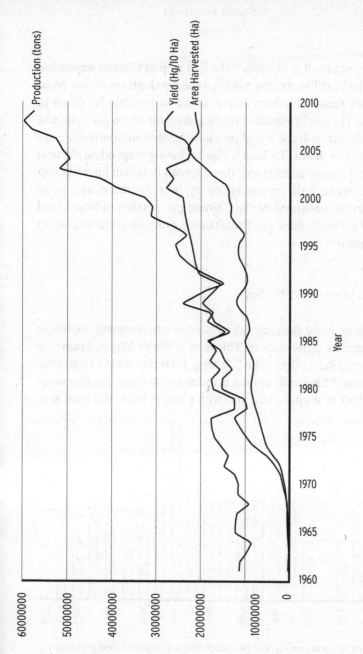

Fig. 7.4 Soybean production and area harvested in Brazil
(Source: FAO, 2011)

billion-worth of it in 2003.[43] The first step in Chinese expansion into the Brazilian market has been the development of, not physical, but financial infrastructure. It is now possible for China to bypass the world's leading trading floor for soybeans – the Chicago Board of Trade – and purchase hedges and derivatives for soy directly in Brazil. China is also beginning to spend on physical support for soy exports too, though, with Brazilian interests hoping to pay back the investment in soy, over the next twenty years. And in the vanguard of the Chinese partnership in Brazil, and indeed in any news about Brazilian soy, one name comes up again and again.[44]

Blairo Maggi – Poster Soy

One man, more than any other, has come to represent the future of Brazilian agribusiness. This man is Blairo Maggi, known locally as *O Rei da Soja* – the Soy King. He is the world's largest soy producer:[45] his family empire is estimated to cover 350,000 acres, with half of it under soy, and with plans to triple the total area

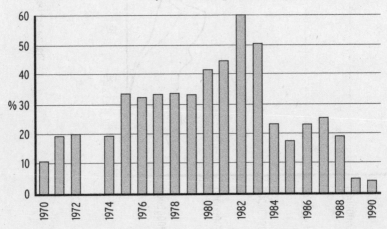

Fig.7.5 Percentage of soybean production financed by official marketing loans.
(Source: Warnken, 1999)

under cultivation by 2010.[46] Much of this land is in the state of Mato Grosso, the beating heart of Brazil's latter-day soy boom. Between 1995 and 2004, soy output increased by 77 per cent, and in that time, Mato Grosso became the largest single source of it.[47] Maggi is associated with a suite of companies that cover everything from the sale of soy seeds to water to transport to civil engineering.[48]

He became governor of Mato Grosso in 2003, elected not only because of his political clout, but because he is a farmer. Although he owns an estate that is orders of magnitude larger than other farmers, he is able to articulate the concerns of his fellow *ruralistas* against the urban biases of his competitors. A genial and affable man, he has been a tireless advocate of the Brazilian soy export industry; he has launched some particularly pointed attacks on its closest competitor, the US. 'The feeling here is that Americans depend on price supports . . . They keep producing for the market, even if the market is down. That hurts prices, but they don't suffer.'[49] His advice to US soy producers is fairly clear: 'Stop planting soybeans and grow other crops, like corn, for example. We can take care of world demand for soybeans.'[50]

Some US soy growers have taken him at his word, with US soy cooperatives coming down to Brazil to buy land and experiment with soy farming there.[51] There's good reason for them to do so. While the costs of pesticides are lower in the US, labour and land are considerably cheaper in Mato Grosso and, at the end of the day, the yield is higher in Brazil.

The calculus of labour, land and capital has had some important physical consequences. The low land price, for instance, has caused widespread expansion of soy plantations in Brazil.[52] Almost 60 per cent of the cultivated land in the *cerrados* is on farms larger than 1,000 hectares.[53] The land has to come from somewhere. Usually, it's the land that used to be the forest.

During the first year of Maggi's governorship, deforestation in Mato Grosso more than doubled. His response was this:

> To me, a 40 per cent increase in deforestation doesn't
> mean anything at all, and I don't feel the slightest guilt
> over what we are doing here. We are talking about an
> area larger than Europe that has barely been touched, so
> there is nothing at all to get worried about.[54]

Before we reach for the righteous indignation, let us consider
three points raised by the soy industry in Brazil. First, the image
that many will have in mind when reading this is of the apocalyptic landscapes left behind after the deforestation of the Amazon. Most of Mato Grosso isn't covered by this kind of vegetation
at all, but a far less dense and lush savannah called the *cerrado*.
Second, soybean farmers have tended not to be the first into the
cerrado. Trails into virgin territory have historically been blazed
first by lumber prospectors, and then by cattle ranchers, not by
pastoralists. Most soy farmers arrive only after the land has been
cleared by logging or livestock grazing. Third, it's important to
remember that North America and Europe have already done
their deforestation. What's left has been corralled into shrinking

Non-land costs	Cost per acre (US$)		Cost per bushel (US$)	
	Iowa	Mato Grosso	Iowa	Mato Grosso
Seed	21.00	11.00	0.42	0.20
Fertilizer and lime	25.00	70.00	0.50	1.27
Herbicides and insecticides	30.00	36.00	0.60	0.65
Labour	14.00	5.00	0.28	0.09
Machinery	34.00	29.00	0.68	0.53
Other	15.00	16.00	0.30	0.29
Total non-land costs	139.00	167.00	2.78	3.03
Land cost	140.00	23.00	2.80	0.42
Total cost	279.00	190.00	5.58	3.45
Yield per acre	50	55		

Table 7.1 Comparative costs of soy production, Brazil / US
(Source: Baumel et al. 2000)[55]

National Parks and wildlife reserves. From the perspective of national development, there's no moral high ground to be found in the Global North from which to criticize.

These three points do, however, have rebuttals. First, a concern about deforestation ought not to hang on a romanticized vision of what it is that is being destroyed. The *cerrado* may not be as pretty as rainforest, dry and unpromising as it looks, but remains an important ecosystem, and one which has been transformed into a monoculture by soy. It's also an ecosystem that sits atop one of the world's largest sweetwater aquifers, and the soy industry is sucking the water out of the ground unsustainably.[56] And, of course, the *cerrado* does border on the Amazon, and recent reports suggest increased, and substantial, encroachment over the *cerrado* into the Amazon proper.[57]

Second, while soy farmers may tend not to destroy forest cover directly, they're not merely mopping up the dregs of ranching – they're actively pushing ranchers into new forest cover. Not only do they move in swiftly after the ranchers arrive, they also bring in the transportation links that make it easier to push into virgin territory.[58] Increasingly, too, some soy farmers have found it sufficiently profitable to deforest virgin land themselves, rather than wait for ranchers or loggers to do it.

Finally, it's true that the Global North doesn't have a leg to stand on in terms of environmental policy, but this isn't an argument for further deforestation, but for the raising of environmental policy everywhere, and with a burden of restitution on the Global North. Furthermore, while the soy expansion towards the Amazon may look like a national development policy, it is far from clear that the entire nation benefits from the soy boom.[59] This is where it is important to disaggregate the benefits of the soy miracle. The national myth of order and progress works at a certain level of generalization. While the refrain 'Brazil has become an agricultural exporting giant' is true, the accompanying and tacit implication, that the majority of Brazilians have benefited from this new-found global status, is false. In a recent statement, a spokesperson for Brazil's Mehinaku indigenous people, living on soy's frontier, gave voice to the notion that only a few have benefited from the soy industy:

> The governor of Mato Grosso state, where we live, grows soya. He wants to grab half of our reserve, only to plant soya. I am beginning to understand things about the whites. What I see is that we, the Indians, respect them but they don't respect us. If you go to my land, all you will see is forest. It's unbroken. Now we have set up vigilance posts to protect it and the rivers. People come down the rivers in boats throwing out the rubbish and taking the fish. But I don't take things that belong to the whites. Funai (Foundation for the Protection of Indians) is responsible for our land. A long time ago, this was our land. Now everything is finished. All the trees are gone. There are no bees' nests full of honey and no eagles. There are no tapirs, no monkeys – they have all died or fled. There are no animals here at all. The Preto river is totally spoiled. There are no fish, and the river is all polluted. The ranchers are finishing everything, and this land has become ugly. We never knew that so many ranchers would arrive in our land. We didn't know that tractors existed and we didn't know about chain saws that cut down trees. Nor did we know about cattle. Then we saw that as the city people came on to our land, they brought diseases, they polluted the rivers and finished off the birds and animals. Five years ago, there was nobody here. Now many, many people keep arriving. It's one ranch after another. We are not interested in cows because we don't eat meat. So these cattle ranches are of no use to us, and we want nothing to do with them.[60][61]

While hit hardest, Brazil's indigenous people aren't soy's only victims. Indeed, the agricultural boom has been accompanied by persistent inequality, with people of colour[62] in rural areas suffering continued and acute poverty amid plenty.[63] Those lucky enough to own land, usually a lot of land, or those with the right political connections, have done well. But those in rural areas who work in the fields have not shared the prosperity. Compared to sugar cane, or even ranching (pernicious industries both), the number of people employed in the soy industry is small. As soy production becomes more mechanized, it absorbs fewer of the country's agricultural laborers.[64] And when they do have jobs, wages are low, with inequalities between seasonal workers in the fields and administrators increasing over the 1990s.[65]

Part of the reason for the increase has been the lack of other options in a context of few employment opportunities. But wages have also been kept low by a chronic problem, one that only recently has become as recognized for what it is: slavery. As figure 7.6 shows, the number of official farm inspections has increased only marginally, but a rapidly growing number of workers have been found in conditions of slavery. As Marcelo Campos, who heads the Brazilian Labour Department's anti-slavery campaigns puts it: 'Legal slaves were property, and watched over because they were an asset. They had food and shelter because the owner needed to make sure they stayed alive. Today's slave is not a concern (to the landowner). He uses them as an absolutely temporary item, like a disposable razor.'[66]

The International Labour Organization puts the number of people working under conditions of slavery in Brazil between 25,000 and 40,000 people, although some estimates suggest it might be as high as 50,000. It's hard to tell, because those charged with investigating slavery are themselves subject to violence. In 2004, for example, three labour ministry officials and their driver were killed while inspecting farms in the state of Minas Gerais. The farmer who paid US$17,000 for the murders owed the government US$700,000 as restitution for his use of slaves.[67] A law has been proposed whereby the land belonging to *fazendeiros* found guilty of slavery can be expropriated. It is being vigorously

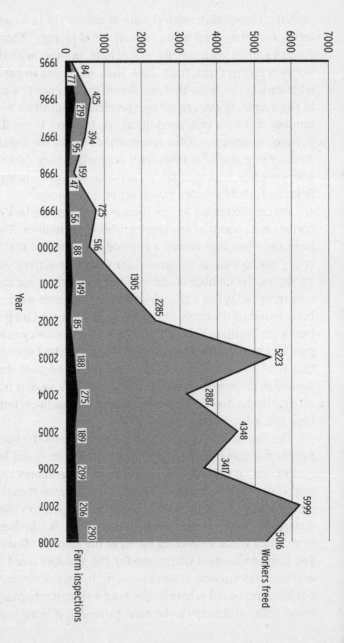

Fig. 7.6 Number of farm inspections and workers freed from slavery in Brazil. (Source: ILO, 2009)

opposed by the rural landowners lobby.[68] The use of slavery, while worse in industries such as sugarcane and biofuels than in the soy industry, has had widespread effects, including fuelling deforestation, keeping wages down and even tainting the governor. While Maggi claims to operate companies 'totally within the law',[69] the ILO discovered last year that Maggi had received soybeans from two farms on which slave labour had been used. Maggi claimed to be unaware of this at the time.[70] It's for this reason that a spokesperson for the Landless Rural Workers Movement in Brazil (about whom more in a moment) declared: 'Let it be known that Brazilian soybeans, which are exported in massive quantities, are produced by forced labour, unpaid labour. I hope the countries that buy Brazilian soy know this.'[71] Yet the fact remains not only that most people are clueless about slavery in soy plantations, but most of us don't even know we're eating soy at all.

The View from Afar

Depending on one's perspective, Maggi is either the brave new face of development or a cartoon villain, or possibly both. For neoliberals, he's the future of Brazil. For environmentalists, he has come to represent the very worst elements of agribusiness. And for US soy farmers, he's the new face of unfair competition. There's much at stake in the international representation of Blairo Maggi, and whatever your perspective, there are many willing to provide news that absolves your opinion. News about slavery, for instance, has raised levels of mistrust between US and Brazilian farmers. Much harder to find is a view that can make sense of the war of perception. One person in this business was Emelie Peine, a US soy farmer, graduate student and musician who worked with the National Family Farm Coalition. Emelie grew up in Tennessee, and farmed a 400 acre lot in upstate New York with her partner, where they raised organic soy, oats, spelt, peas, collard greens and the odd backyard chicken. She went to Brazil because 'as the biggest producer of soybeans, American farmers were worried about being out-competed'. She continued:

> In the imagination of the US farmer, Brazil is a Third
> World country, a place where there are no rules. It's a
> way of imagining farms like *maquiladoras*. And, sure,
> many farmers do exploit labour, no question. And, sure,
> there are certain farmers who don't care about deforesta-
> tion. Up in one of the most remote towns in Mato Grosso,
> I was driving on a tractor across a field in its first year of
> production, and the farmer waved his arm at a swathe of
> forest, and with an entrepreneurial gleam in his eye, said,
> 'In five years, that'll be soybeans.'

So it's true that the battle lines are drawn across national boundaries, and that Brazilian soybean farmers are, at best, cavalier
about the environment? Well, not quite.

> I've also been to meetings where they've been talking
> about the money that US farmers get, like we're in the
> land of milk and honey, where I have to stand up and
> tell them that we're facing a lot of the same pressures to
> drive down costs that they are. And when they find out
> where I'm from, the message I get from so many farm-
> ers is this – don't go back to the US and tell them we're
> chopping down the Amazon, because we're not. Many
> of the soy farmers I've spoken to are family farmers who
> care about their land, and realize that they have to leave
> something to their children, same as us.

The misperceptions of realities on both sides of the Panama Canal,
North and South, seem systematic. US farmers find it easy to believe that all Brazilians are socially and ecologically corrupt slave
drivers, and Brazilian farmers believe their US counterparts to be
suckled on taxpayer dollars. Examples can be found to support

the broad generalizations on both sides. We've seen the role that Maggi plays in the imagination of the environmental movement,[72] and there are countless articles in the farming periodicals of the US Midwest and Great Plains prophesying Brazilian-led doom. The view from Brazil is similarly fuelled. Brazilian farmers have grounds to think that some US farmers are getting very rich because of their government.

The US system of electoral politics, as in Brazil, is in the business of balancing the competing concerns of a number of interests. These interests have armies of lobbyists and, just as Maggi is a governor and soy exporter in Brazil, so the head of the US Department of Agriculture has traditionally tended to come from an agribusiness background. The Agriculture Secretary between 2001 and 2005, Ann Veneman, worked as a lawyer for Dole Foods and sat on the board of Calgene, the first company to get approval to run field trials for genetically modified crops, among other qualifications.[73] It was akin to inviting the CEO of Lockheed Martin to become the Secretary of Defence.[74]

Amid the more obvious corporate demands for trade liberalization and reduced taxation are further demands from agribusiness. Agribusiness as a lobby in both the US and Brazil can punch above its weight, largely because of the non-democratic architecture of US electoral politics. Agricultural states have a low population, yet are entitled to as many senators and votes in the electoral college as their more densely populated peers.[75] From Brazil, it's easy to see why a 2008 Farm Bill valued at US$288 billion would attract a great deal of scorn.[76]

Yet, beneath the surface of the farm bill, there's inequity.[77] Under the Federal Agricultural Improvement and Reform Act of 1996, the previous farm bill, rich farmers and corporations systematically received more than the majority of US farmers.[78] The trend has continued: from 1996 to 2010, the top 10 per cent of farms received 75 per cent of total farm subsidy payments. The average annual payment to the top 10 per cent is $30,751, while the bottom 80 per cent receive only $587 per year and nearly two thirds of American farmers collected no subsidy payments at all in 2010. 'Well, that's the main reason I came here', continued Emelie Peine:

> It's not just that there are some farmers who need to
> understand each other better. But farmers need to
> understand why they're competing against each other.
> The thing that made me realize this most is that Car-
> gill is not only the largest exporter of US soybeans but
> also the biggest exporter of *Brazilian* soybeans. So then
> what's the conflict of trade rules about? Farmers need to
> understand that every independent producer of tradable
> commodities in every country is being squeezed by the
> same companies – the big traders, processors, and retail-
> ers – and that the root of the problem is the corporate
> structure of the global agricultural economy, not one
> country's subsidies or another's environmental practices.

The corporate structure of the global agricultural economy certainly makes its presence felt along Brazil's soy trail, and between the different businesses there seems to be very little fight. There is, however, a great deal of freight. The roads of Mato Grosso run through the soy plains, covered in deeply rutted tar, and choked by the overloaded trucks that rumble over them, announcing the sounds and smell of Brazil's modern future. In the bigger soy cities such as Rondonopolis, surrounded as it is by agriculture, it's hard to find fresh fruit and vegetables. It turns out to be *much* harder to find fresh fruit at the smaller towns along soy transportation routes. All along the soy trails, things are burning by the roadside, with the occasional restaurant or hotels dangling the possibility of truck drivers getting lucky, of one-night stands, including a hotel offering itself as a refuge for cuckolds. The rail infrastructure is old and creaking, waiting for Chinese investment. So, for the time being, soy is transported by road, in trucks monitored by satellite, so that the drivers don't dally too long at roadside hotels on their way to the docks. This is the rural development prompted by the soy industry. At the end of the soy-trucked road, the situation is little better.

One of Brazil's premier soy ports is Paranaguá. It's a town with schizophrenia. On one side of the peninsula is the Baía de Paranaguá, a beautiful and languid stretch of water, surrounded by hills and bordered by fisherfolk. On the other side is a massive industrial agricultural export facility, bordered by state-of-the-art transfer hardware, behind which are strip-joints for the sailors and truckers who stop off there. The increase in sex-work, together with the violence against women, human trafficking and health risks that accompany it, is an almost constant accessory to the natural resources industry,[79] particularly an industry that pays quite so many men who travel across poor areas. The soy industry's touch can transform quiet towns into Barbary Coasts. And so it is with Paranaguá, where strip clubs are to be found four blocks from the offices of the major US agricultural exporters – Cargill, Bunge and ADM. These companies are the undisputed winners in the great soy boom. Between them, Cargill, ADM and Bunge finance 60 per cent of the soy produced in Brazil, and own three-quarters of all the processing facilities in Europe for the beans exported whole from Brazil.[80] Cargill has gone a stage further than its competitors, building an illegal port facility in the rainforest to make shipping that much easier. Its competitors aren't far behind, though. And, although they are meant to be rivals, there are occasions where competitors can overcome their differences and work in concert.

Normally, the wait time for a ship to arrive in the port at Paranaguá was forty-eight days. In the middle of 2005, the berths were all but empty. And that's because a few months before, the state of Paraná decided to uphold the laws banning the growing and transport of genetically modified soy. The exporters punished the state government for its enforcement by diverting their shipments, and thus their business, to Porto de Santos, the port facility for São Paulo, which has no such requirements. This move was a combined strategy of big agricultural exporters, the ones that normally would be competing against one another, as a way of putting pressure on the state of Paraná to rescind its ban.[81] This is a little unusual. When agribusinesses form alliances in Brazil, they tend to form allegiances across sectors. So, for instance, soy-trading Cargill will work with soy-seed-manufacturing Monsanto to ensure control over the entire chain of production and export, just as ConAgra and Novartis will work with ADM. That the exporters themselves are unified suggests the degree to which they feel their businesses are threatened by state-level bans on genetically modified crops. And it seems that corporations are able to go on 'strike' a little more easily, and with a great deal more impunity, than workers. When workers go on strike, they are accused of endangering development, society, the nation and the future. When ADM, Cargill and Bunge boycott Paraná, they're merely sending out a market signal.

This kind of collusion isn't technically illegal. But it gives a flavour of the kinds of power that agricultural industry can wield over governments. And if that's the degree of power they have over the state, it's not surprising that they're able to shape the economic climate facing farmers, paying them if needs be, and putting pressure on them if they can't be bought. Looking at the structure of the soy industry in Brazil, it's easy to see where the pressure points lie.

This is exactly the kind of thing that Emelie Peine's work addresses. She puts it like this:

> That's one of the things that farmers in Brazil and the
> US should understand. It's not about what makes you
> competitively advantageous in the food system – the
> parts of the system that never get criticized or taken up
> by the farm lobby are, for example, credit. That's because
> the leadership of the farm lobby is linked to agribusiness.
> The links aren't hard to find – just look at the funding
> of the American Soybean Association. It's a closed loop
> which farmers are outside of, and they don't have to be.

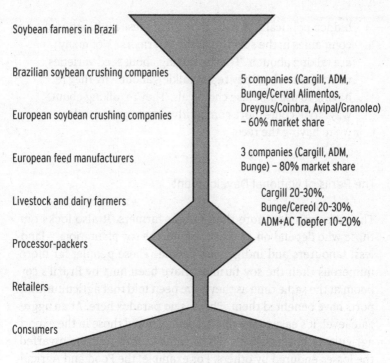

Soybean farmers in Brazil

Brazilian soybean crushing companies

European soybean crushing companies

5 companies (Cargill, ADM, Bunge/Cerval Alimentos, Dreygus/Coinbra, Avipal/Granoleo) – 60% market share

European feed manufacturers

3 companies (Cargill, ADM, Bunge) – 80% market share

Livestock and dairy farmers

Cargill 20–30%, Bunge/Cereol 20–30%, ADM+AC Toepfer 10–20%

Processor-packers

Retailers

Consumers

Fig. 7.7 Soybean feed 'bottleneck' from Brazil to Europe
(Source: Vorley, 2003)

The American Soybean Association (ASA) has close connections both with the government (it received most of its US$27 million budget in 2004 from the Federal Government) and agribusiness.[82] While it is certainly the best-funded organization representing soybean farmers' interests, it isn't the only one. Some farmers have organized independently of the ASA. The Soybean Producers of America is a much smaller outfit, one concerned that, across a range of policies, the ASA seems to be 'more worried about the profit margins of a few mega corporations than they are with negative impacts on U.S. farm families'.[83] Emelie was all too aware of this:

The link in the chain between agribusiness and farmers is

hidden politically. What's the role of these multinational
companies in the survival of these farmers? Not many
are talking about it. They're talking about seed varieties,
which is fine, but they're not talking about why they're
having to use all these chemicals. They're talking about
ways to become more competitive but not about why
we're having the race.

The Perils of National Development

The race excludes more than poorer farmers. It also locks out
those who depend on, or exist despite, the soy plantations – landless, labourers and indigenous people. These people, far more
numerous than the soy farmers, have been hurt by Brazil's soy
boom at the same time as they have been told that agricultural exports have benefited them. There is no paradox here. At an aggregate level, it's easy to see that trade has suited those in the export
agriculture business well. Their gains in fortune have dwarfed
the losses endured by others. For example, the Food and Agriculture Organization of the United Nations data suggests that food
consumption in Brazil fluctuated wildly during the 1990s, and
consumption of all staple food items fell for the poor during the
transitional period 1987–96, a trend that has continued with food
supply per capita of rice, maize and cassava falling in the periods
1980–91 and 1991–2001.[84] This fluctuation in food availability is
entirely compatible with noting that some people have made a
great deal of money out of the soy industry – so much, in fact, that
Brazil as a whole has benefited.

Brazil's growing inequalities have not gone unnoticed, or un-
contested. Increased international concern about deforestation in
the Amazon, for instance, has led to a certain modulation in the
approach of large soy farmers. Among these has been a business–
NGO partnership for 'sustainable soy'. It seeks to introduce 'best
practices' at the farm level, encouraging the Brazilian government

to stop the exploitation of the *cerrado*-Amazon border, and raise awareness of soy-related environmental problems. The initiative encourages Brazil both to specialize in higher-value products related to soy and to lobby for reduced tariffs on these higher-value products. The aim is to move Brazil away from its role as a mere producer of primary resources to one where it develops industries that produce goods made from soy.[85] While these goals might be laudable as a minimum point of departure, they are characterized by an almost desperate lack of ambition. This may be related to their being drafted with the acceptance of agribusiness in mind. One of the key stakeholders in the Sustainable Soy initiative, for instance, is simultaneously the president of the Argentinean FVSA (Foundation for the Life of the Forest – the Argentinean branch of the WorldWide Fund for Nature) and president of the Argentinean Agribusiness Association (AIMA) and the vice-president of Pioneer Overseas Corporation, part of DuPont.[86] Given such constraints, there are a number of problems that the authors of sustainable soy don't feel able to push too hard – particularly the social issues around land use, and advocating ecologically sustainable production methods that would, of necessity, move farmers away from their vast plantations and use of genetically modified seed. This analytical paralysis, it should be noted, is congenital. If the principal concern of the NGOs involved in the 'sustainable soy' initiative is the welfare of the rain forest, then this particular intervention is a reasonable one. But if the concern were more holistic, embracing the social causes of the ecological disaster, the remedy would necessarily be more profound.

The conservatism of 'sustainable soy' isn't only a product of the thinking behind it, or the power of its principle partners. There's an undeniable difficulty in moving industrial farmers to ecological production. This difficulty would be easier to explain if strictly ecological farming were to involve, as it does, an abandoning of monoculture in favour of more sophisticated and robust crop systems. But even at the margins, with small incremental steps that are demonstrably cheaper and more effective than the outdoor chemistry-set experiment that conventional farming has become, change is difficult to foster. Emelie Peine again:

> On our farm, we've been growing soy for four years.
> We're the only organic farmers in our neighbourhood.
> The reaction we get from our neighbours is interest-
> ing. They think we're nuts because, instead of using a
> herbicide to kill the weeds, we seed red clover together
> with the oats so that it grows up underneath the oats
> and takes over the field after the oats are harvested. It's
> cheaper and builds up soil fertility, and we can harvest
> the clover seed and sell it, certified organic, for $2 per
> pound. That's about $270 per acre! We tell our neigh-
> bours about it, but they're not interested. Hell, even Thor
> [Emelie's partner on the farm] said that organic farming
> never crossed his mind when he was first getting started.
> He was trained as a 'Nozzle Head' at Cornell. That's what
> he calls the farmers who use herbicides, pesticides and
> artificial fertilizers – Nozzle Heads. And they're not stu-
> pid. Quite the contrary. They see themselves on the cut-
> ting edge of technology. It's just that this is how they're
> trained. It's just the modern way.

This points to the second dimension that 'sustainable soy' doesn't address – the social relations behind farming that can keep it mov- ing along one particular trajectory or can vault it onto another. There is, after all, nothing natural about farming. It is a tangle of different social relations, of intervention and displacement in com- plex social and environmental webs. Just as in the United States, Brazil's dominance of the soy market was not a magic result of market forces, but the result of extended research and investment in the industry, in tandem with the private sector. This process has opportunity costs in terms of redirected funds and energy. For example, 90 per cent of research funding in Latin America used to be directed towards food crops in the 1980s. In the 1990s, 80 per cent went to research on export crops.[87] The rise of the soy society in Brazil also required the suppression of rural dissent.[88] Recall that this was one of the original goals of the soy programme, and while some of this was achieved through direct violence – the impunity of *pistoleiros*, hired guns, is well documented and ongoing[89] – it was also achieved through dispossession.

The World's Most Important Social Movement

The structure of land holdings in Brazil has long been unequal. In 1970, over 90 per cent of farms in Brazil were smaller than 100 hectares, while 0.7 per cent of holdings were greater than 1,000, covering just under 40 per cent of the country's land.[90] Liberalization has shored this up. By 1996, 1 per cent of farms were greater than 1,000 hectares, but they covered 45 per cent of the arable land.[91] In the soy industry, the crop's hunger for land has driven tenants off the land, displaced by the miracle bean. In 2002, there were 5 million landless families in Brazil, with 150,000 camped by the roadside.[92] The soy industry has, through the economic logic of its production, consolidated this inequity. The barriers to acquiring land in Brazil are, then, a product of sedimented social relations, choices and histories. The power to transform these is rare, but in Brazil, there is an organization that has cracked it.

Noam Chomsky has called it the world's most important social movement. It has succeeded in resettling over a million people since its inception in the 1970s in Southern Brazil, developing farms, livelihoods, healthcare, churches and, above all, education. Its agrarian policies have been demonstrated time and again to be superior to those of the government, though this hasn't prevented violent repression and denunciation of the organization by government forces, landlords, hired guns and the media. Born of the progressive wing of the Catholic Church, trades unions and the vestiges of the peasant leagues of the 1960s, the Landless Rural Workers Movement, in Portuguese 'Movimento dos Trabalhadores

Rurais Sem Terra' (MST), is in the business not only of producing new kinds of farming, but new kinds of people.[93]

With this kind of introduction, one expects its membership to constitute a frenzied gaggle of activists. This is certainly the rap that the MST gets in the mainstream Brazilian media, which has accused the organization of everything from brainwashing to fomenting insurrection to Stalinism. To find out, I travelled to a settlement in the middle of soy country, named 14 de Agosto, after the date of the first MST settlement in Mato Grosso. It's a settlement with slightly over 2,000 hectares of mostly degraded pasture, home to seventy families, a few kilometres away from the soy boom town of Campo Verde.[94] Most of the buildings in the town are less than a decade old, and even the church services are conducted in a contemporary style, blending High Church Catholicism with rock and roll. What's there is both banal and deeply beautiful.

Families on the 14 de Agosto settlement build their two-small-bedroom houses close together – close enough to hear arguments. Along the main street, there's a small bar, some big barns, a sports ground, where children play, a big water tank and a distillery, in which *cachaça*, the local firewater, is brewed. At the bar, people shoot pool like they do everywhere, the local radio station is blaring out of a tinny speaker, and folk are dressed in T-shirts and slacks. If these people are unusual, they are so on the inside.

And they are. Many of the residents of the settlement were veterans of other MST struggles. Before they were able to claim their land,[95] the prospective settlers formed *encampamentos* – encampments. This is a crucial part of the land occupation process. The encampments are harsh. They're characterized by extremely limited, if any, supplies of water and food, with poor-quality shelter and limited health and education facilities. These facilities have to be provided by the settlers themselves. And although it is meant to be temporary, a stage-post on the way to a proper settlement, families can spend years in *encampamentos* waiting for land. The time spent there is, however, an important part of the MST's political pedagogy. Here's Hannah Wittman, an activist and academic, describing how they do it in the '*nucleos*', the MST's basic organizing unit, made up of between two and three dozen families:

> Each *nucleo* is comprised of two coordinators (one man and one woman) and a representative to the sectors of production and of environment, health, security, political formation, education. This *organicidade* seeks to ensure that each individual person has a *tarefa,* a task or action that benefits the settlement as a whole, at the same time as awakening a process of self-education and responsibility in each person.[96]

There's a political logic behind this, and the MST is forthright about it: 'No one should represent anyone else, each man and woman represents him- or herself. We want to overcome the problem of representativity, of delegation of powers. It is in participating that everyone represents themselves.'[97] The result is what gives the MST bragging rights about building new people.

The MST encampments are schools. In the forge of poverty and adversity, the MST institutes a conscious project of political education. Lessons are taught about civil and social engagement, lessons that will allow the future settlers to live with each other, with other citizens, and with the government.[98] The experience is like boot camp, but more so. At boot camp, you tend not to think about where the food is coming from, or worry about the plumbing. On MST encampments, the physical environment matters a great deal, as do the relations between living systems. Finding water and growing food together is an integral part of the political education on an encampment. It's this integration of natural and social systems in its political education that qualifies the MST as an ecological movement. The movement has built a space for its members to think for themselves, to discuss democratically and to own their own mistakes. Nothing could be more anathema to the

expert-driven project of development, whose only slight concession to this is 'public participation' – a process in which 'the community' is called in to listen to, and thus validate, the plans that
experts have made for them.[99]

If these kinds of psychological reconstructions and 'speaking
truth' to government sound ominously like the rural re-education
camps of the Chinese Cultural Revolution, they shouldn't. Participation is, necessarily, voluntary in the MST. People are free
to leave at any time. In the case of the 14 de Agosto settlement, a
minority of people have left, with many farmers choosing not to
farm collectively after they have received their land, their parting
accepted without rancour or recrimination.

But the camps, and the settlements that follow them, lead to
important social changes. Consider this testimony:

> We tend to be sexist here; well, anyway, I have always
> been sexist. I never trusted the judgement of women. I
> always thought I knew better than a woman. Better than
> my wife. But in the camp, it was often the women who
> saved us, who kept us from being defeated. They were
> strong! Now that we have been farming for ourselves,
> well, I have learned to trust my wife's opinion in running
> the farm too. I am still kind of sexist, I guess, but I have
> learned.[100]

Then consider when you last heard this sort of statement volun-
teered by any man living in Europe or North America. A transfor-
mative education, one that changes who we are, and the way we
think about ourselves, is one of the goals of the MST. Few notions
of the self are as embedded and resistant to change as the way
men think about themselves in relation to women. By insisting
on women's rights to represent themselves, and by creating a language, space and examples for change, the men and women who
come out of the MST's educational programmes are very different
from the ones who go in.

The movement recently celebrated its first Ph.D., when Juvelino Strozake defended a dissertation entitled 'Access to Land and the Public Civil Action Law' at the Pontifícia Universidade Católica of São Paulo. He, too, once camped on the side of a road, in Paraná, occupying land with other landless families. But his rise up the ranks, through a seminary and then into the MST secretariat, isn't unique. The organization has forty partnerships with thirteen universities.[101] And these links aren't the most important educational interventions, nor are the qualifications received through them the hardest struggle. Life on the settlements is hard as a matter of course, especially when trying to maintain a progressive bent in a society geared towards high agricultural capitalism.

'Democracy isn't easy,' says Lydia, one of the founders of the 14 de Agosto settlement. When the cooperative on the settlement tries to sell its wares, it has a great deal of trouble with intermediaries. Supermarkets want standardized and bar-coded product, which is hard to produce on a farm that has embraced the diversity that accompanies organic farming. 'Also,' Lydia continues, 'when we sell a box of vegetables to the supermarket, they give us R20, and charge R40. If we sold it ourselves, we'd get R30.' There are plans for direct sales of food, though 'it's hard to make people so interested, because although people should know where their food comes from, many don't care. It's hard.'

And it's a shame. The settlement fields are lush, a riot of organic maize, beans, sugar cane, bananas, vegetables and pasture for the cows (whose milk is sold to a Nestlé subsidiary – because there's no other choice). The one crop conspicuously absent, because abundant in the neighbouring fields, is soy. Had they ever considered growing it? 'No, no, NO!' says Maria Luisa. 'Are you mad? We'd never grow it here. It's not right.' Nor, it turns out, is it sensible. Lydia points out that it's not a crop that's economically viable. The cooperative farm turns a profit with its existing crops, with the food, work and revenue shared equally among the farmers. But 'we don't have enough land or money for soy to work', says Lydia. The economies of scale, the consequences of monoculture and the fact that nobody particularly feels that it's a wise thing to grow all mean that there'll not be any soy on the MST settlement. It's a rational economic decision as well as an ideological one; 2005 is a bad year for even the biggest soy farmers because of the dollar's depreciation: 'The world soybean price isn't bad in dollars, but the amount of local currency we get has fallen to impossible levels.'[102] And that's Blairo Maggi's lament. Smaller soy farmers were feeling the squeeze in 2005. But not the MST settlement. Indeed, the dip in soy prices eased the pressure on land in Mato Grosso, making it a little easier for occupations to proceed without the militarized opprobrium that they usually bring down on the MST.

One problem that the settlements face, like every other community seeking to build a future for itself in a wider world in which it doesn't fit, is how to keep the community going. Children never experience the travails of encampment life unless they're taken there by their parents. If they're born in a settlement, they'll never experience the same kinds of socialization that their parents did. They'll certainly grow up close to MST values, especially if their parents are part of a cooperative, but they'll always be in contact with the rest of the world, whether at school, or through TV (every home in the settlement has an antenna on the roof) or by radio. It's not possible, as M. Night Shyamalan's underrated *The Village* shows, to seal off a community from the influences of the modern world. 'The settlements that have lasted the best are the ones far away from the towns,' says Zé, Maria Luisa's husband, his three small children clambering over his thick arms. The settlements find it easier to continue and reproduce themselves when the call of the cities is faint. But, as the cities multiply, so the challenge facing the settlements grows stronger. How are children of the settlements meant to choose, freely, to stay? As the Amish have long known, there isn't a solution to this other than to let children leave. 'They go to the cities,' says Maria Luisa. 'If they come back, we welcome them.' As the MST improves its education and quality of life, more and more children are returning. And Lydia, Maria Luisa and Zé wouldn't live anywhere else.

It's clear why. This isn't some sort of rural paradise – the physical work of farming is hard. But it is a very modern affair. There's a tractor. There's a range of crops being grown almost but not quite without pesticides. Most of all, there's a sense of choices being made, with a sophisticated taste for self-government. The gulf between this kind of democratic living and the ritual of voting every four years is the difference between wine and cola. It takes a place like this to remind us that, although most of us live under what's called democracy, we've never tasted the real thing. And by precisely this token, we've never owned the mistakes that have come of poor democratic decisions – we've merely had them thrust upon us.

Now, it would be a mistake to generalize on the basis of just one settlement. There are important regional differences in the way MST settlements have fared, and are experienced.[103] Yet, in key respects, the fundamental principles of democracy and collective social transformation obtain widely. The MST does seem, across the board, to have produced better development outcomes than the government's own meagre land-titling programmes, with better levels of long-term success.[104] And key to this, according to the movement, has been the political and social reconstruction and reeducation of its members.

The MST isn't infallible. No movement is. What makes this movement interesting is that, because it takes its democracy seriously, and takes seriously the thinking that such commitment involves, it is able to recover from mistakes. The lessons of reproducing the movement, of creating the conditions in which settlements succeed, and in creating robust mechanisms of direct and representative democracy, have been learned through hard trial and error. There was a time in the 1980s when the MST tried to enforce cooperatives. 'It was a disaster,' says Geraldo Fontes, an organizer at the MST offices in São Paulo. Through the 1980s and 1990s, the leadership learned to take a step back and, rather than insisting, offering the choice over whether to farm collectively or individually, with information circulated about both options. Some settlers went it alone, but increasing numbers, especially those from the cities, decided to go it together. Today, the MST is working to develop new ways of farming, based on agro-ecological techniques. And, rather than impose them on the membership, it has learned from its mistakes. It is developing a university, with support from the Cuban and Venezuelan governments, which will function as a research and training station in advanced agro-ecology, and as a training centre for those from the movement who want to learn. The first students walked through the doors of the university, soon after they constructed them, in 2006.

This isn't the only mistake from which the MST has recovered. It almost looked like the organization wouldn't survive a split in the early 1980s, amid fights about how it got its money, who held power and how the movement was to be run. But after tough discussions, much soul searching, and a decision to become financially independent, (even if that meant becoming drastically poorer) the movement made it through. Today, the movement is funded largely by the donations of the settlements, which pay for their members to be bought out of their work to train and work as 'militants', as well as providing around 5 per cent of sales from their produce to fund the broader movement. This way, the MST is able to pilot its own future, without needing or being able to point the finger at outside influence – at the Church, the government or international donors – because through their financial independence, the members of the MST are beholden only to themselves. It was through this, argues Fontes, that the MST has come to be what it is today: a beacon for organizations of landless people, the poor and the oppressed, fighting for equality, autonomy and a new kind of citizenship in the twenty-first century.[105]

Bringing It Home

> Against barbarism, study. Against individualism,
> solidarity.
>
> MST Communiqué[106]

If the MST is grounded, the soy against which it fights is ethereal. When it leaves Brazil, soy takes a number of forms. Flakes, oil, whole beans and chickens, which, as one activist pointed out, are merely 'soy with feathers'. And all along the way, a handful of agribusinesses reap the profit. Indeed, along some routes, it's only ever one agribusiness. Take the example of Cargill. The company grows its own soy on farms illegally established, crushes it, moves it within Brazil, ships it out through its illegally built port, imports it into Europe, say through the Netherlands, moves it within the EU to the UK, where it is either then crushed, again by Cargill, or sold forward to Cargill's Sun Valley division, which then feeds it to animals, which have seen neither sun nor valley, and which are then slaughtered and processed, again by Sun Valley, before being sold as McNuggets. It is a chain of total control.[107] And it's one McDonald's seems to appreciate. The golden arches awarded Cargill their 'supplier of the year' award in 2005,[108] and their 'sustainability' award in 2010.[109]

The MST has disrupted the beginning of the chain, resisting the take-over of their land by both government and soy industry, and building not only sustainable agriculture, but alternative economies and ways of living that, contradictory and flawed as they might sometimes be, are nonetheless experiments in ways of being free. They have, in short, carved out ways in which they might think for themselves. An abiding lesson from the MST's struggle is that the place where we live matters to the kinds of people we can be. For young people growing up in the MST settlements and encampments, the siren of the city can be overwhelming. And if children don't return to the settlement, parents can at least know that they were given, and made, a choice.

But what of us, the majority, who live in the cities? The odds are against us finding that freedom, for in the city our human connection to those who grow our food, or make our goods, is very remote indeed. By the time we dip them in barbeque sauce in the controlled environment of a McDonald's, we are as far removed from the fields as the McNuggets we crunch. Given that most of us won't be moving to Brazil any time soon, what are the alternatives? Well, perhaps we could choose not to go into a McDonald's. But we'd have to eat at some point. We'd eat the soy in chocolate. If not chocolate, ice cream. If not that, any number of packaged or processed foods. If we were sufficiently obsessive, we might become label vigilantes, expunging from our diets anything containing lecithin or an unmarked 'vegetable oil' as well, of course, as all meat. And we'd certainly choose to cook our own food (and fewer and fewer of us do even that – only 38 per cent of meals made at home, in one recent study, were homemade, and increasing numbers of us can't make a meal from basic ingredients).[110] So, off we'd go to the supermarket, armed with a shopping list of acceptable goods in order to get off the corporate grid, only to find ourselves at the food system's Ground Zero.

8

Checking out of Supermarkets

Little Jack Horner
Sat in a corner,
Eating a mincemeat pie.
He stuck in his thumb
And pulled out a plum,
And said, 'What a good boy am I!'

Traditional

Grace to Be Said at the Supermarket
That God of ours, the Great Geometer
Does something for us here, where He hath put
(If you want to put it that way) things in shape,
Compressing the little lambs in orderly cubes,
Making the roast a decent cylinder,
Faring the ellipsoid of a ham,
Getting the luncheon meat anonymous
In squares and oblongs with the edges beveled
Or rounded (streamlined, maybe, for greater speed).

Praise Him, He hath conferred aesthetic distance
Upon our appetites, and on the bloody
Mess of our birthright, our unseemly need,
Imposed significant form. Through Him the brutes
Enter the pure Euclidean kingdom of number,
Free of their bulging and blood-swollen lives
They come to us holy, in cellophane
Transparencies, in the mystical body,

That we may look unflinchingly on death
As the greatest good, like a philosopher should.

Howard Nemerov[1]

The Self-Serving Store

The highest temple of the modern food system is the supermarket.
The supermarket chain is an empire of logistics, one that governs
and regulates the smaller fiefdoms within the food industry, such
as the commission agent's rule over the grower, or the distribu-
tor's clutch on the agent. Through its decisions, and through its
close supervision of each step in a product chain, supermarket
buying desks can fire the poorest farm workers in South Africa,
flip the fates of coffee growers in Guatemala or tweak the output
of paddy terraces in Thailand.

Supermarkets are patented inventions and, like all innovations, they responded to a specific need at the time and place
of their conception. That place was the early twentieth-century
United States, a time and place of unrivalled plenty. The wheels
of American industry were turning fast, and manufactured goods
were being pumped out in ever-greater quantities, packaged and
stuck on shelves for the growing urban population. There was a
worry among manufacturers that, in fact, too much was being
produced and that consumers couldn't afford to make purchases
fast enough to soak up the flood of goods. There was a parallel
concern that even if consumers *could* afford to buy the goods on
the shelves, they wouldn't want to, because they didn't strictly
need them. The timeless technique for persuading consumers to
buy more of something was and remains this: reduce the price.
For the early twentieth-century grocery industry, cutting prices
was a challenge, particularly since profit margins were already
slim.

One way to manage the cost/price squeeze was to take advantage of economies of scale. The bigger the firm, the greater its

power to negotiate down the price it pays per unit. But there were no corporations dealing exclusively in food retailing that were large enough to do this. Size was the privilege of manufacturing and shipping corporations. The giants of the late nineteenth- and early twentieth-century agricultural corporate world were principally the processors and conveyors of food, not its retailers. One shipping company, the Atlantic and Pacific Tea Company (better known today as A&P), realized that there was money to be made not only in trading food, but it selling it to the consumer. It established an archipelago of grocery stores, which it supplied using the country's growing road and rail infrastructure, taking advantage of relatively low transport costs and the savings accrued from being able to sell its own products direct to the retailer. A&P's logistical feats laid the foundations for what we recognize today as the modern supermarket: a large company, able to bargain down supplier prices, able to ensure that shelves are never empty, specializing in logistics and marketing. Once goods reached the A&P grocery store, though, the retail experience was essentially the same. The clerk was the front line between the buyer and their purchases. Customers still had to ask for what they wanted, and they were kept well away from products until they'd committed to buy them. All this was about to change.

The whole business of agriculture was in flux in post-Civil War America, and nowhere was the boom louder than in California. The Gold Rush had given way to agriculture, and California's fortunes were being earned by landlords, horticulturalists, researchers, farmers, railroad magnates, the occasional immigrant with seeds and a dream, corporations with access to water, and banks with credit to fund it all. The food production industry was being turned on its head, and not only in the fields. Experiments with new ideas were being conducted at the retail end of the chain. Albert and Hugh Gerrard, for instance, had started tinkering with the notion that, rather than have grocery clerks do it for them, consumers themselves might pick their own groceries. This, certainly, would persuade people to buy more, and at less cost to the retailer. When encouraged to help ourselves, to graze *ad libitum*, people tend to consume more, to pick things off shelves with an abandon seldom felt if there's an intermediary. For this to work, though, consumers needed to know where to look for their groceries. So, primarily as a marketing gimmick, the Gerrards opened grocery stores that stocked items in the most logical way they could conceive – in alphabetical order. The Alpha Beta chain of stores had, by 1914, embraced a self-service format, allowing customers to pick food from open shelves. From their first store in Pomona, they had established a small chain in California, and were fairly successful.

While the self-service format was being pioneered in the west, it took a combination of a savvy Virginian working in Tennessee and a series of geopolitical events to usher in the real retail revolution. In 1916, a confluence of two events transformed the United States' grocery business. The first was when the US joined the First World War. With that entry, food prices climbed by 19 per cent. (In 1917, there were to be food riots in protest at the price rises in New York, Boston and Philadelphia.)[2] More than ever, grocers felt the pressure to cut costs, since food buyers were prepared to go to great lengths to find cheaper food. Cutting costs through scale was one option, but on 11 September 1916,[3] local retailer Clarence Saunders finally turned retailing on its head with a shock far more profound than the US entry into the War. Saunders opened the first 'King Piggly Wiggly' in Memphis, Tennessee. In it, he codified the key retail revolution that was to reverberate through the twentieth century. It all turns on transforming the relationship between the buyer and the seller in a way that cut retail costs to the bone. Here he is in his own words, as he used in US Patent 1,242,872 for the 'Self-Serving Store'.

> The object of my said invention is to provide a store
> equipment by which the customer will be enabled
> to serve himself and, in so doing, will be required to
> review the entire assortment of goods carried in stock,

conveniently and attractively displayed, and after select-
ing the list of goods desired, will be required to pass a
checking and paying station at which the goods selected
may be billed, packed, and settled for before retiring
from the store, thus relieving the store of a large proportion of the usual incidental expenses, or overhead
charges, required to operate it...[4]

The new store combined the idea of getting consumers to shop
for themselves (and so reducing staffing costs) with the means
for making sure that they were exposed to everything for sale
(thus maximizing potential revenue).[5] The plan view from Saunders' patent shows how the internal geography of the store balanced stock-control with the communicative architecture of what
was, ultimately, the first consumption factory. You begin at the
entrance, you walk through a turnstile, pick up your basket, follow the maze of products back and forth until you arrive at the till,
at which point you pay. There's only one path to follow, there's
no one to talk to, and the store is designed first and foremost to

Source: US Patent Office

get you to put as much as you can into your trolley in as little time and with as low a cost to the store as possible. In it, shoppers resembled nothing so much as rats in a maze.

That said, some consumers didn't quite understand the system. In Australia, supermarket promoters hired instructors, who taught adults and children, men and women, how to push carts down the aisles. And in US stores today, one can find child-sized carts with long poles attached. While intended to help parents better find their children in the aisles, the mini-carts serve an educational purpose. The flag proclaims it quite clearly: 'Customer in training'.[6]

For Saunders, the supermarket was both a logistical intervention and an educational one. Individual clerks, who in ordinary grocery stores would pick items from a shopping list provided by the customer, were banished. The very same employees who had been clerks in the old format stores were told in no uncertain terms that in the new King Piggly Wiggly self-serving store, they were not to assist the customer in choosing products at all. Customers were now 'free' to do this themselves. With store attendants reduced to Trappist silence, customers were to receive instructions on the location of goods from the physical architecture of the supermarket. The space of a supermarket was built around the owners' needs to shift stock, but was mindful of the need to recruit and train the customer as an integral part of the logistics of sale. It was an architecture that would inaugurate the sciences of impulse and pester purchasing[7] and provide active schooling in the ways of 'consumptionism'.[8]

This is the moment of conception of the institution we now consider the home of consumer sovereignty. The irony is this: shoppers' freedom of choice was born in a cage. What we have come to believe in as 'unfettered freedom to consume' was always intended to be guided by chickenwire. And while we might have received some basic information from clerks at a store, the supermarket changed that. Through a studied manipulation of space, geography and employee communication rights, the only possible

C. SAUNDERS.
SELF SERVING STORE.
APPLICATION FILED OCT. 21, 1916.

1,242,872.

Patented Oct. 9, 1917.
3 SHEETS—SHEET 2.

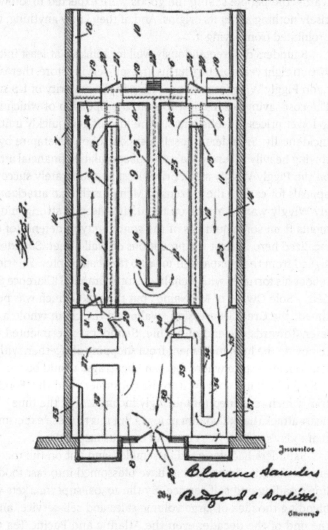

Inventor

Clarence Saunders

By Bradford & Doolittle

Attorneys

Source: US Patent Office

point of contact between the person eating the food and the person who grew it became the label on the tin. From this point onwards, the people selling the goods were expected to know precisely nothing about its origins. And, if they knew anything, were prohibited from saying it.

Saunders did tremendously well for himself, at least initially. Within eight years of starting his first self-serving store, there were 1,200 Piggly Wiggly stores operating in the majority of US states. The cost savings of his new format, a proportion of which went to lower prices for consumers, were instant and quickly imitated. Incidentally, Saunders himself lost control of his empire by borrowing heavily to fend off a series of speculative financial attacks on the Piggly Wiggly stock price. Despite moderately successful appeals for cash to the citizens of Memphis that an attack on Piggly Wiggly was an attack on them, and despite strong endorsements from some quarters of the community in defence of their localized hero against the predations of Wall Street, Saunders resigned from the company in 1924, to face bankruptcy. He tried to reboot his fortunes with a chain of stores branded 'Clarence Saunders – Sole Owner of My Name', but the 1928 launch was poorly timed: the Great Depression swallowed the chain whole a year later. Towards the end of his life, Saunders experimented with removing the human element from shopping altogether, with the Keedoozle (a store where food and beverages would be mechanically packed and conveyed to the consumer) and the 'Foodelectric', which remained tantalizingly incomplete at the time of the heart attack that killed him in 1953.[9] But it is to these experiments that today's self-service checkout owes its inspiration.

Saunders had designed, assembled and put on the road the engines of consumption that have blossomed into fast food, online retailing and self-service. By the 1930s, supermarkets were blending the idea of large volume sales and self-service, and by the end of the decade, even the Atlantic and Pacific Tea Company was switching to the branded supermarket format (a move that would make it the second-largest corporation in the US by revenue before the war – even by the end of the 1970s, A&P was second in retail sales only to Safeway).[10]

Consumers have, of course, changed since Saunders' day. We'd be appalled at the idea of a single route to follow in a shop, or that shop staff were not there to assist us. Today's modern grocery allows us to wheel our trolleys where we please,[11] and most supermarkets make the concession of having at least one person on duty who knows where things are, or knows who to phone to find out. Today's reign of service is only possible, however, because customers have successfully internalized the cost-saving measures of 'self service', so that cosmetic changes in supermarket architecture don't affect its logistical underpinnings. Supermarkets are constantly rearranging the layout of stores, adding and removing impulse purchases at the checkout, tinkering with the placement of beer and diapers. Yet no supermarket would dream of changing to anything other than a self-service format. And this is because consumerism today has constructed *us*, built consuming people at the same time as building consumer goods, in ways unthinkable to the first people who nudged their way through Saunders' turnstiles in 1916.

Almost Orwell

Outside an intensive care unit, there are few environments so obsessively monitored and reconfigured as supermarkets.[12] A great deal of money has been spent on ensuring that the supermarket shifts as much product as possible in as little time. This involves a complex balancing act. The space has to be both one that allows the fast refilling of shelves and just-in-time inventory control, but one that has an ambience that helps us to forget that we shop in brightly lit warehouses. A small academic industry has dedicated itself to the task of reconciling the facts of the retailing environment with their perception by shoppers. The name these academics give to their work is the study of 'atmospherics'. Under this rubric, much public and private money has been spent to discover, for example, that muzak matters. There's a lively debate in the literature about how musical tempo matters in our shopping patterns. At stake is the amount of time we spend in the store, and the extent to which we're annoyed when we queue. Some gurus suggest that the slower the music, the more leisurely will our promenade around the perimeter of the supermarket, the more languid our forays down the aisles. Others suggest that a familiar musical preference, rather than tempo, is the key to making our painful shopping experience pass quickly.[13] Classic rock can be the key to making babyboomers loosen their purse strings, though it has the disadvantage of sending those a generation older off in a huff of decades-old disapproval. And classical music lures everyone into buying items more expensive than we'd otherwise be inclined.[14] With similar depth of concern, researchers have also tackled the problem of colours within supermarkets, finding that colour affects simulated purchases,[15] purchasing rates, time spent in the store, pleasant feelings,[16] arousal, store and merchandise image,[17] and the ability to attract a consumer toward a retail display.[18] In fact, everything, including the smell of the air, the kind of lighting, the positioning of product and wall coverings, has been pored over and dissected. Some studies argue that stores should make things hard to find in order to increase sales. Sales floor planners are ever-aware of avoiding the "butt-brush effect", in which customers stop browsing for products if their rear is brushed more than once by another passing shopper (so advanced is the field of atmospherics, you'll note, that this phenomenon has its own name).[19] To appeal to those hoping to change the world through their wallets, the wizards of 'green atmospherics' advise stores to boasting of employee well-being, community service, and to use lots of cork, bamboo and straw for decoration and construction.[20] All this so that we feel sufficiently stimulated to part with our cash, though not so bombarded that we leave as soon as we've found the milk (which, incidentally, is placed at the back of the store because it's the item we're most often in there for, and therefore placed so that as many products pass our eyes as possible *en route* to it).[21]

While the environment is tweaked in a range of different ways, the subject most constantly manipulated and prodded is, of course, us. Within the space of the supermarket, we are subject to some fairly hefty experimentation, although the experience is made to feel as unobtrusive as possible. Take loyalty cards. The purchases that we associate with them give supermarkets an Orwellian fund of data with which to play. Through the cards, supermarkets are able to associate our name, address and other demographic information with our shopping habits. Our collective will is analysed (one of the more popular software packages is cheerfully known as VIPER), and marketing targeted accordingly. Marketing's resolution has, as a result, become increasingly sharp. In 1996, the British supermarket chain Tesco had identified twelve different market segments, each of which it targeted differently. By late 1996, 5,000 different versions of its direct marketing magazine were being mailed to different customer segments, and by mid-1998, that figure was 60,000. Today, each magazine is individually tailored to the information on your loyalty card. This is, of course, exactly what we think we want. We're all quite pleased that we're individual and unlike anyone else, with differing needs for security and comfort and new experiences and health. And the more a company can match itself to our own balance of preferences, the more of its product it will sell. The innovation that began with all products being displayed for consumers to take their pick finds its contemporary evolution in pinpoint precise marketing. The key to this has been improved data about consumer desires.

Yet the vast amounts of data with which we're tracked and analysed do not sit benignly. Brad Templeton, chair of the board of the Electronic Frontier Foundation, is concerned.[22] He tells the story of a firefighter whose house burned down in Tukwila, Washington. 'Once you get over the irony of that,' he says, 'there's a deeper story.' Police suspected that the fire, in which firefighter's

wife and child were in the house, was started intentionally. Fo-
rensics identified a particular type of firelighter used in starting
the fire. And a central piece of incriminating evidence was the
firefighter's Safeway card, which showed a purchase of those selfsame firelighters. Luckily, the real arsonist owned up before the
trial began. But the lesson is clear – the data was taken and used
in evidence against him.[23] 'There has never been a case where this
sort of surveillance is not abused,' says Templeton. 'Of course,
there may be benefits for us that come out of it – but at what
cost?' Templeton himself gets around supermarket surveillance
by swapping his Safeway card with his friends, so that the data
the company gets is corrupted, but he and his friends are still able
to pocket the loyalty card savings.

In a quest for more accurate data, however, supermarkets are
developing new ways to make sure their data remains uncontami-
nated.

666 and All That

The way that we give supermarkets their money-making information is through the checkout. As with the best inventions, though,
the data for desire's algebra have a dull origin: in this case, stock
control.[24] Think, for example, of the barcode. When it was first
introduced in the mid-1970s, consumers didn't like it. Punters
wanted their prices stamped onto the product as they always
had been. The barcode wasn't a technology for consumers, but
for retailers, so that they could gather information on inventory
far more accurately and cheaply than a daily shelf-count. Indeed,
barcodes began with a vision of supermarkets (Saunders' among
them) in which customers would select not the products they
wanted, but their punch-carded representations, to be inserted
into a slot at the checkout, where the customer would pay. Machines would read the punch cards, and giant engines of satisfac-
tion would pluck the stock off the shelves and present them to

the consumer. This, it seemed, would be the logical conclusion of the trend towards turning the grocery store into a factory.[25] The cost of automation was, however, far too high to make this viable when it was first mooted before the Second World War.

It took three decades for the technology to catch up with retailers' grand designs, or at least parts of them. By 1974, National Cash Register was experimenting with low-powered lasers, which could read a code printed by manufacturers on the side of their products. And on 26 June 1974, at Marsh's supermarket in Troy, Ohio, a pack of Wrigley's Juicy Fruit (now on display at the Smithsonian Institution in Washington, DC) was the first item to be scanned at a checkout.

The barcode needed to be on around 85 per cent of packages passing through the till for the investment in equipment to be outweighed by time and stock-taking information savings. When this happened in the late 1970s, the technology took off. In addition to the benefits of time (and hence labour) savings at the checkout, and reduced time spent on inventory control, the marketers found themselves sitting on top of something far more valuable: pliable data on what each consumer in the store was buying.[26]

Each barcode has two components: a unique manufacturer identifier and a product number, in the form 6-(Manufacturer ID)6-(Product ID)-6. Jokes about consumer culture being intimately bound up with the number of the beast are old. Soon, they'll be out of date: the beast is getting an upgrade. The latest generation of inventory control technology is called 'radio frequency identification', RFID, and it builds on the existing technology by adding an extra bit of information – a unique item code. Look out for a little stamp on products at a supermarket near you soon bearing the letters EPC.

EPC stands for 'electronic product code', and it takes the idea of barcoding a step further. Every item we buy with an EPC label will have a tiny passive radio built in. With the appropriate technology, you can get this radio to emit its three-part identifying number – one part for the manufacturer, one for the product, and one for the individual specimen of that product. With the appropriate software (Savants, they're called), and with appropriate databases, retailers can find out everything about the item you're holding in your hand. Where manufactured, how shipped, when about to expire, and when so many of them are in the same cart that they're probably being stolen (important, for example, with razor blades).[27]

As with barcodes, there are few advantages for consumers in the new technology. It will probably make checking out a little quicker, but the technology is more properly understood as the fusion of three retailing technologies: the anti-theft device, the barcode and the closed-circuit television. EPC doesn't only provide information about what's in your cart when you leave the store. It also provides information about what was in the cart but then you decided not to buy, and what route you took to get everything. The technology helps to paint pictures like the one in figure 8.1.

It is a picture of us, shopping. It is generated using RFID technology embedded in shopping trolleys which, every few seconds, pings back our location to a central computer. While the overall map looks a little messy, they've been able to pick apart our different shopping trajectories. We've surprised supermarket scholars by not following a lawnmower path up and down the aisles, but saving time by sweeping around the perimeter of supermarkets (the 'racetrack', they call it) and darting into aisles to pick up whatever it is we need before retreating once again.[28] This is surprising to the atmospherics wonks because they still assume the trace of Saunders' original floorplan, and the logic behind it. They oughtn't, however, be taken so aback. We don't need the single path of Saunders' original Piggly Wiggly – we've created our own paths through the slew of products and services on offer, we've broken free of the narrow paths scripted for us by faceless architects and we hew our way through the aisles with nothing but our desires for a compass, with time pressure as the wind in our sails. But we're no less rats in a maze for that.

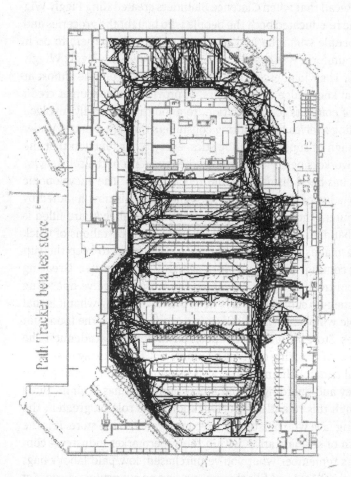

Fig. 8.1 Shopping carts tracked using RFID chips. (Source: Larson, Bradlow, and Fader, 2005 PathTracker by TNS Sovensen. Used with kind permission.)

Path Tracker beta test store

Discipline in the Aisles

Shoppers are not the only subjects of discipline in the supermarket. Recall that when Clarence Saunders created King Piggly Wiggly, he re-educated both the people who bought the groceries and the people whom he had previously paid to help them to do it. Their uniform was coordinated with the new King Piggly Wiggly livery. Their job description was downgraded from the almost artisanal knowledge of customers, of providers of consumer credit and of conduits of information, to a job that primarily involved stacking shelves and pointing consumers through a maze. Under the reign of supermarket logistics, every other function that the shopworkers performed prior to the invention of the self-service store has been dismantled and redistributed.[29] The encyclopedic knowledge of your personal shopping habits is now handled by computer. The logistics of ensuring that the shelves are filled is also handled by computer, which commands battalions of truckers, armadas of ships and squadrons of aircraft to keep the supplies coming. Setting up work schedules? Computer. Greasing the political machinery to allow the store to receive operating and start-up subsidies: that's head office. Choosing what it is that people will want – head office, in negotiation with the food companies. Store layout? Head office, consultants and academics. The process of checking out is also automated. The stocking of shelves is still a mainly human task, as is cleaning the store, taking your money and guarding it. And a new profession has been invented through this relentless specialization – the role of 'greeter', the smiling face who personally welcomes you into the store. It is the zenith of specialization within the supermarket industry – computers remember what you've purchased, low-paid labour bags your purchases and fills the shelves, and an avuncular retiree is at the door to administer a cheery welcome.

The effects of self-service in retail share much in common with Ford's introduction of mass production in industry. Employees in early supermarkets were subjected to the same kinds of time and motion studies as their counterparts in the motor industry, honing their skill at one particular task with the sole aim of increasing productivity and reducing costs. Just as at the Ford factory, though, the increase in productivity through specialization in the retail sector has led to a mind-numbed and unhappy workforce. A range of solutions have been tried to overcome this all too human problem – from sponsoring employee paintball games to locking workers in the store. To understand how successful these attempts have been, let's turn to the industry leader, to see how it's treating its employees.

Walmart

Walmart is the world's largest corporation, responsible for 2 per cent of US GDP[30] and owner of the second-most-powerful computer after the Pentagon. It has 80 per cent of the US as its customers and has made multi-billionaires of its founder's children.[31] It created over 22,000 jobs in 2009[32] – with dozens of people competing for each vacancy, with a management structure that promotes and rewards from within the company, and with prices lower than neighbourhood grocers can deliver. Its opponents claim it is a multibillion dollar succubus on the public purse. Undoubtedly it is, in the words of its CEO, 'the focus of one of the most organized, most sophisticated, most expensive corporate campaigns ever launched against a single company', and is currently subject to billions of dollars of class-action lawsuits for discrimination against female employees, anti-union actions and illegal hiring practices.[33] One could argue that there might be something pernicious about Walmart in particular that it should find itself subject to quite so much litigation and scrutiny by unions, women's rights advocates and anti-sweatshop campaigners. But convenience, low prices and a paradise of choice in supermarkets go hand in hand with price gouging, discrimination, exploitative labour practices, local community destruction, environmental degradation and shiftless profiteering. Despite its scale, Walmart isn't an exception – it just reminds us of the rules of supermarket convenience. It's hard to write about the global food system and not be transfixed by Walmart, though.

The way the founder, Sam Walton, tells it, Walmart was the product of hometown values, a great deal of hard work, dedication and getting the basics right. There's a ticker-tape parade of stories about the internal Walmart culture: executives instructed to bring back pens from conferences, Sam Walton flying economy class, sharing rooms to save money. But more than mere frugality and confraternity with work colleagues, the company defined new frontiers in managing consumers, employees and suppliers in the tightest and most expansive logistical net outside of the US military.

And the reason that all this came about was, according to Sam, 'Here we were in the boondocks, so we didn't have distributors falling over themselves to serve us like competitors in larger towns. Our only alternative was to build our own warehouse so we could buy in volume at attractive prices.'[34] Because Procter & Gamble wouldn't come to Benton, Arkansas, explains Sam, Walmart took on the business of logistics and supply in-house. More than any other retailer, Walmart was built on the back of a logistical empire. Within the world of information technology, they're known as an IT company that happens to do retail. They pioneered the development of a set of distribution and control standards known as EDI (Electronic Data Interchange), which has now become mandatory in order to do business with them. They're also at the forefront of using EPC technology, not least because it'll stop its employees from helping themselves to the stock. At 2 per cent, their level of theft is lower than the industry average of 3.5 per cent, but with worldwide sales last year of US$419 billion,[35] that's still a meaty chunk of inventory that makes its way home with the checkout staff. The firm's level of logistical control is something of which they're proud. They hail their information technology department, the nervous system of the entire enterprise, as a reason for faith in the firm. In their annual shareholder report, they tell us that their data warehouse has more storage capacity than the fixed pages of the internet. And then they offer this:

> We have a remarkable level of real-time visibility into our merchandise planning. So much so that when Hurricane Ivan was heading toward the Florida panhandle, we knew that there would be a rise in demand for Kellogg's® Strawberry Pop-Tart® toaster pastries.[36]

This claim is worth taking the time to chew over. Certainly, if you're running a chain of grocery stores and you're anticipating bad weather, you'll order in batteries for torches, send for extra bottled water and go heavy on the Spam. But the power of the Walmart data-mining algorithms is that they're able to point to region-specific and product-specific impacts of a particular kind of weather. Like a regional preference for a particular flavour of a particular long-life packaged breakfast food for emergencies. That's impressive data-mining.

No less awesome in the annals of Walmart are its employee relations. According to the firm, employees are content and possessed of an almost fanatical devotion to the company.[37] In its early years, Walmart instituted a profit-sharing arrangement that worked wonders for a few high-profile winners, like the truck driver who joined the company in 1972 and had US$707,000 in profit sharing paid out when he left in 1992.[38] But in the main, it doesn't look good for Walmart employees. And there are a great number of them. Walmart is the largest private employer not only in the US, but in Mexico, where it has recently reported record profits.[39] It employs 2.1 million people worldwide.[40] And their working conditions are so parlous that even a few US politicians have risked the wrath of the world's largest private employer to raise their concerns.

Representative George Miller cites a range of abuses, including a case in which a random audit of '25,000 employees in July

2000 found 1,371 instances of minors working too late, during school hours, or for too many hours in a day. There were 60,767 missed breaks and 15,705 lost meal times.'[41] These moments of reprieve in the working day were ones to which workers were legally entitled, but effectively prevented from using by management. 'Missed breaks', incidentally, means trips to the toilet. And at least one former Walmart cashier reports that because the breaks were skipped, the employees were forced to urinate at the tills where they sat. Indeed, sometimes the toilets are the only space of refuge and respite for Walmart employees. When the company first began its ultimately unsuccessful operations in Germany, employees hid in the restrooms rather than perform the morning Walmart cheer.[42] The cheer runs 'Gimme a W, Gimme an A, an L, a squiggly,[43] an M, an A, an R, a T. Whatdya get?' Yet the cheer, like the metered 'rest periods', are all designed in the name of increasing efficiency and provide those 'everyday low prices'. Indeed, it's a stated goal for Walmart managers to maintain everyday low wages, with penalties if payroll costs rise above a strict threshold as a percentage of sales.[44]

One of the ways it does this is by leaning back on traditional levers of power. And, despite the odd jibe from a lonely wanderer of a corridor of power, Walmart has a number of friends in high places. The Wage and Hour division of the US Department of Labor gives notice of raids on child labour law violations and allows Walmart to co-write the press releases afterwards.[45]

Sometimes, though, the levers of power on which Walmart rests are more traditional still – such as sexism. The most important case against the corporation is Dukes vs. Walmart, a case still being heard, but which has overcome the hurdle of achieving class-action status. It is named for its lead plaintiff, Betty Dukes, an African-American woman who still works at Walmart in Pittsburg, California. The case asserts that women, the majority of Walmart employees, are discriminated against in Walmart's management structures. Evidence for the plaintiffs comes from Walmart itself, from its head of human resources, Coleman

Peterson, who repeatedly complained that Walmart lagged behind its competitors in the promotion of women to management.
Peterson also dismissed the 'Resident Assistant' programme, designed for women who were unable to move from store to store
in the standard pattern required for management training by the
company, as a dead end.[46] There does seem to be ample data to
suggest that Walmart has systematically excluded women from
management positions, and that the culture of the organization's
management is profoundly misogynist. For years it seemed as if
they were on a losing case, and the number of women in the class
eligible to claim damages was 1.5 million former and current female employees since 1998. In 2011 with a 5 to 4 vote, the US Supreme Court dealt the case its final blow, largely on the grounds
that women managers were part of the class, and therefore made
a mockery of the case because they couldn't possibly have been
discriminated against if they made it to management.[47]

Business as usual for Walmart is cut-throat, but doesn't always mean 'Always Low Prices'. In cases where the store operates
near competitors, its prices are lower, certainly. But one example in Nebraska saw a shopper buying identical carts of goods in
two different Walmart stores, with a 17 per cent price difference.
The reason? In the neighbourhood of the more expensive store,
Walmart had already killed the competition off and was now free
once again to raise its prices.[48]

We might just want to put this down to the cut and thrust of
the free market. Although we may wince as workers, as consumers
we couldn't be happier with Walmart. This is the tongue-in-cheek
argument presented by former Clinton-cabinet member Robert
Reich.[49] Yet as Stacy Mitchell of the New Rules Project points out,
'Walmart is as much a product of public policy as it is of consumer
choice. Local and state governments have provided billions of dollars in tax breaks and subsidies to fund big-box development. Tax
policies in many states allow national retailers to escape paying
much of their income tax, while local businesses must shoulder
their full-share.'[50] At a minimum, over US$1 billion in US federal

public subsidy has gone directly to support Walmart – the figure increases when state-level and foreign subsidies are included – while the company has avoided paying at least US$1.2 billion in taxes..[51] This at the same time as evidence mounts that the arrival of a Walmart store signals the demise of the local economy and community.[52] And without an income, fewer and fewer can afford to be consumers anywhere else but Walmart.

Supply Chain-gangs

While employees at Walmart may have it tough, the most serious discipline is saved for the people outside the big box. Precisely because they're so big, and shift so much product, supermarkets are able to control supply lines. Again, Walmart is the biggest of-fender, simply because it's the largest corporation, but it's not the only one.

Let's look at the world's third-largest supermarket chain, the UK supermarket giant Tesco. The development group ActionAid recently traced back the apples on UK shelves to the orchards in Ceres in the Western Cape of South Africa. South Africa is, like New Zealand and Chile, in the position of being able to provide large quantities of counter-seasonal fruit to Europe and North America. With deregulations in global trade, the fruit growers in these countries compete directly against one another, at the mercy of the weather, the exchange rate, and the distributors and super-markets who deign to make a contract with them. The downward pressure on costs is one that is whipped through the supply chain. Just as Tesco or Asda (Walmart's UK subsidiary) play fruit supply firms in different continents against one another, so these firms treat their workers. The increased pressure to cut costs is trans-mitted from the international to the national economy, and then to the fields. This means that labour on farms is becoming increas-ingly casualized and precarious. The average wage for men in formal agricultural employment is R900 (about US$127, GB£77)[53]

per month, with women making less money than men and receiving less non-monetary compensation. Aruna Morrison, one of
the women working on Ceres Farm, puts it bluntly: 'The men get
everything – boots, uniforms – all free. Seasonal women workers
get nothing. Why must we pay, and the men not?'[54] This is harder
yet to bear when women are charged with raising children. 'What
hurts is when my child begs, "Mummy, mummy, please, please . . ."
but they don't understand.' Overall, the worst thing is the shame
she feels amongst her peers. 'I don't have the courage to lift my
head up high and look people in the eye.'

Aruna is a member of Women on Farms, an organization that
is currently fighting for the rights of farmworkers in the Western
Cape. Working collectively, they have confronted farm-owners in
the Cape and forced them to address the pervasive discrimination against women faced in agriculture. As elsewhere, agribusiness views women as a soft target, easier to control, requiring less
support and pay, than men.[55] It is only through organizing that
women have fought to be treated with the same dignity as men.
And that level of dignity, as with farmworkers in the US (see chapter 3), is minimal.

The Contradictions of Convenience

But while we're looking at the effect on those responsible for the
production of the foods that end up on Northern shelves, we ought
to think about the effects on those newly inducted into the world
of consumerism. We've already heard from Makhathini in chapter
6 about the genetic engineering miracle that wasn't. Of course,
there's more to be said about Makhathini than the story of genetically modified crops. The further away one lives from Makhathini,
the more it becomes a place viewed through one facet, a place
made through a single story – Makhathini becomes the place told
by genetically modified cotton. It's as if Cuba were told by cigars.

There are obviously more lives and histories to tell. Here's a group of eight women talking about nutrition, and about how things have changed since apartheid ended.[56]

> 'I don't think there has been any change since the end of apartheid.'
> 'Well, that's not true, we can sell our vegetables outside the supermarket without being chased away.'
> 'And there's the child grant.'
> 'And the shops.'
> 'Oh, the shops.'
> 'What about the shops?'

Beginning in the mid-1990s, as apartheid crumbled, there was an influx of small stores with the kinds of trinkets that we'd think cheap, but which were already more than most of the residents could afford. It was round about that time, the women said, that children started stealing from their parents so that they could buy the toy mobile phones and flashlights that they'd seen. And that wasn't the only change: 'The shops were coming in selling bread, smokes, sugar. The children didn't want to eat maize meal bread, they wanted Albany sliced bread ... and they wanted money to buy food for school rather than eating what they were given.'

This isn't, however, an unvarnished pining for apartheid. Far from it. The women we spoke to also reported that they were much happier buying ground maize meal from the supermarket than grinding their own. This is double-edged – 'people are lazy to go grind maize, and laziness kicked in among the people,' Thoko Dlamini said.

The women were also angry that the local Spar supermarket wasn't buying their fruit and vegetables, but trucking produce sourced from elsewhere into their neighbourhood, undercutting them and pushing them to grow other things, like cotton. All this has had an impact on community health, which the women, mothers all, were unhappy about. 'We're weaker now than we used to be. And it's not because we're growing old. Even our children don't have the same strength that they should', Zacharia Jobe, one of the area's leading cotton farmers, told me later. Women working in fields across the world have been quick to make the link between the food system's pesticides and declining health, as well as the lower nutritional quality of its finished products.[57] Yet, the women in Makhathini continue to buy their maize from there, because grinding it is tedious and unpleasant work.

In other words, supermarkets are convenient for the women as consumers, even if they're not necessarily good for women as producers. Supermarkets can bring with them extra demands on women's time that often make them less, not more, free.[58] It's a statement of the ambivalences of supermarkets, one that is as true in northern KwaZulu-Natal as it is in Los Angeles, Mexico City, or China, where recent riots started in the city of Xintang when a local official assaulted a pregnant woman selling her goods in front of a supermarket.[59] In the Makhathini Flats, the women we spoke to had already arrived at a solution to the ambivalence: ideally, they wanted their own machine for grinding maize, rather than having to grind by hand. This way they could be independent of the supermarket, but still profit from the technology that made it convenient. In other words, the women wanted control of the means of production.

The practical insight here is important. Supermarkets' convenience derives from their being able to control the use of certain kinds of technology, in this case, milling equipment, within a certain broader context. But that technology comes as a bundle with other things, in this case, the need to buy someone else's maize. For Makhathini women to have more freedom, and more real convenience, they don't want supermarkets to disappear *in toto* – they just want to be able to control both ends of the food system more democratically. There's no fear of technology here – the women in the community want to be able to grind their maize at the flick of a switch. But since they don't have the money to pay for a mill (many of them, especially those without children, have an official

annual income of zero), they want this technology to be provided
for free.

It's an argument that many others in Makhathini make in different ways. Supermarkets provide a channel for farmers to sell
their goods. But in Makhathini, supermarkets aren't buying from
small producers at all. Again, what farmers in Makhathini want is
the access to consumers that the supermarket's logistical network
can provide. This used to be done, to some extent and badly, by
the government. Now it's done by the private sector, and the poor
don't even get a look-in. In the space of a decade, Makhathini has
undergone the kind of retailing transformation that took generations in the Global North. But many of the women in Makhathini
had a clear-sighted understanding, not only of its effects, but also
of the alternatives they'd like to see.

Makhathini is not alone. In Zambia, the South African Shoprite supermarket chain was accused by farmers of 'stealing all the
market'. Tensions ran so high, farmers threatened to burn the supermarkets down – a move that brought Shoprite's representatives to the negotiating table.[60] But the expansion of supermarkets seems unstoppable. In Latin America, at the beginning of the
1990s, supermarkets controlled approximately 10 per cent of the
food market – by 2000, they'd achieved levels of around 50–60
per cent. They achieved in a decade what it took half a century
to do in the United States.[61] A similar story is spinning out in Asia.
In India, the Reliance group has begun a US$7 billion investment
in field-to-fork supermarket chains.[62] In this, they follow the trail
blazed by Carrefour, the French supermarket group, whose first-
quarter sales in 2010 were over E99.85 billion (US$141 billion), of
which only about one third came from France.[63] One of the key
reasons that Carrefour – the world's sixth largest employer – has
an international presence at all is because of all the damage it
was causing within France. In 1973, the French government acted
to stop the crippling effect that hypermarkets were having on
smaller businesses on the French high street.[64] Finding their expansion clamped down by domestic worries about social welfare,

Carrefour took its stores to countries with more malleable governments. From their initial 'everything under one roof' concept stores in Annecy and the suburbs of Paris in 1963 – for which the term 'hypermarket' was coined – Carrefour are now in control of 7,824 stores worldwide, including 1,308 hypermarkets. They have 1,151 in Latin America, pulling in over E13.9 billion (US\$19.9 billion) and 600 stores in Asia, grossing over E6.92 billion (US\$9.9 billion).[65]

The other central reason that supermarkets are able to sprout in the Global South has to do with the macroeconomic environment. Makhathini residents want the government to provide them with a market. It's a call that farmers around the world have made. And the government used to do it, through an elaborate array of marketing boards, which would purchase goods from farmers at guaranteed prices and provide enough of an income for rural communities to survive, and even flourish. But World Bank structural adjustment policies (SAPs), initiated in the late 1970s, changed that. Providing farmers with ready markets was, it was argued, a waste of public money. If the government wanted to increase the incomes of rural people, it could do it better by giving resources to them directly. So the marketing boards were eradicated.

Rural constituencies have very little political clout to press their needs, though. In India, for example, 70 per cent of the population live in rural areas,[66] but 80 per cent of government spending is urban. Governments used structural adjustment policies as a way of reneging on their commitments to the rural poor. The vacuum left by the end of government-run marketing boards in the Global South, boards which have mutated but survive in the North because of stronger political pressure, has increasingly been filled by supermarkets. Their logistical operations have moved in to take over the buying, selling and conveying of produce in poor countries once undertaken as a public commitment. Unlike governments, they have no incentive to spend a penny more than they have to in rural areas. And while the supermarkets may not directly cause the kind of distress that leads to the suicides described in chapter 2, they certainly profit from the low prices that accompany them, and indirectly create the precarious penury that drives farmers to death.

Supermarkets, and agribusiness corporations more generally, are doing well in the post-SAP economic environment. Growth in the Global South is turning out to be a cash cow for today's retail giants. There, the range of outlets for food range from the small 'full service' kiosks, usually catering to pavement traffic, through the public market and the self-service grocery store, to the supermarket.[67] In Latin America, the supermarket format dominates the food retail business, and since the 1990s, the full-service stores and markets have, just like their US counterparts eighty years before, been rendered obsolete. Within Latin America, there has been a great deal of consolidation within local firms. The Uruguayan/Argentine chain Disco battled for regional dominance by absorbing smaller Argentinean firms, together with a Chilean firm with regional interests, Santa Isabel, before itself being bought out by the Dutch company Ahold. In China, supermarkets have done even better– in 2004, the government allowed foreign retailers to operate and own grocery stores for the first time. By 2009 in urban areas, where the majority of supermarkets are located, 46 per cent of meat, 37 per cent of fresh fruits, 33 percent of fish, and 22 per cent of fresh vegetables came from supermarkets. With 48,907 stores already in 2010, many retailers are looking to move out of the city centers and into suburbia.[68] With Northern markets saturated, it's not surprising that in all three of the world's top retailers, the strongest growth has come from international divisions.

Every Cloud Has a Redlining

Before moving to discuss a thoroughgoing alternative, it's important to put supermarkets in their proper context. That context is sprawl, the strange new geography that, whether in the North or

South, has insinuated itself past our cities' limits. The manipulation of architecture inside supermarkets has been part of a wider overhaul in geography outside them. Towns have been getting bigger – even, in some cases, as fewer people live in them – stretched by an architecture that assumes that car ownership is natural, and that distance is nothing more than a chance to listen to the radio. Yet a third of the US population doesn't drive, and that proportion is much higher in the Global South.[69] The kind of 'big box' retailing that Walmart epitomizes, and into which most other grocery chains are trying to clamber in order to remain competitive, encourages a dependency on fossil fuel.

But there's another side to sprawl. While the geography of the 'big box' succeeds by stretching cities out, the stretch isn't even. Supermarkets are in the business of cream-skimming, of dropping their stores in areas that are able to afford them. Supercentres are predicated on access by car. In rural areas, large swathes of the countryside are underserved by supermarkets, and traditional markets are on the decline. This means that in the midst of food-growing rural areas it is possible to find places that have come, unhappily, to be called 'food deserts' – areas in which it is extremely hard to access fresh food without a car.[70] And in urban areas, particularly in the US, the people who are denied access to supermarkets are people of colour.

Now, having railed against supermarkets, it may seem a bit odd to complain that poor people don't have access to them. Yet, although the 'freedoms' experienced in supermarkets are few, the options in lower-income neighbourhoods are fewer. This is a turnaround. The first supermarkets targeted poor people, who were ready to sacrifice personal service for a discount in high food prices. Yet supermarkets have been increasingly reluctant to enter neighbourhoods of people of colour. From an economic perspective this is puzzling. Studies have shown that such neighbourhoods can be profitable for supermarkets. People need food and are willing to sacrifice other things in order to have it. And from the end of the Second World War on, the discrepancy between poor urban and middle-income suburban families' spending on food has persisted.[71] A 1991 study by the New York City's Department of Consumer Affairs found an 8.8 per cent discrepancy between the prices charged in low-income neighbourhoods and in richer areas.[72] The poor were paying more. One commentator had observed this trend in the 1980s, estimating that 'a family of four with an annual income of $9,999 was likely to pay $1,500 more for food than a suburban family'.[73] Not only are the prices higher, but because supermarkets have been so successful in shutting down neighbourhood channels for the distribution of fresh fruit and vegetables, the foods predominantly available in poor neighbourhoods are highly processed and fat-saturated. Yet this is the effect of 'supermarket redlining' – a term borrowed from the illegal banking practice of encircling neighbourhoods of people of colour in red and refusing to lend to anyone within them.

When supermarkets decide that they will not expand into areas of predominantly poor people of colour, and having by their very existence already restricted the possibilities of other fruit and vegetable distribution mechanisms, they consign the residents to a diet of 'frozen pizza, pork rinds, beef patties and corn dogs'.[74] It is perhaps unsurprising, then, that in one US study the presence of supermarkets was associated with lower levels of obesity.[75] Given this, it would seem that the only thing worse than having a supermarket in your neighbourhood is not having one. Except, of course, supermarkets don't make race disappear. Supermarkets in black neighbourhoods stock systematically less healthy food than in white neighbourhoods. Yet study after study shows that, when healthy food becomes available, there *are* increases in the amounts of fruit and vegetables consumed.[76]

Shelves of Love

In buying the goods on supermarket shelves, we forget the social relations that made them possible. Nothing demonstrates this amnesia better than recent debates around organic food. In the United States in 2000, the Secretary of Agriculture was Dan Glickman. The US Department of Agriculture had been through a period of unusually hard battering, having been sued by black farming organizations for the USDA's behaviour in distributing grants, and facing the largest racial discrimination settlement in history (with US$2.2 billion in damages). Under Glickman, the USDA was also being sued by women and elderly farmers for discrimination damages of US$3 billion. It was in this context that Glickman announced 'the strongest, most comprehensive organic standard in the world',[77] a standard for food growing that would make it easy for farmers across America to reap the rewards associated with higher prices associated with organic food.

The standards themselves had, however, been through the Congressional mill. They are stitched full of odd exemptions and kinks that owe more to the lobbying power of individual industries than any commonly accepted definition of 'organic'. The main beneficiaries of the standards haven't been the small-time farmers who might have shifted to organic production, but the large food corporations.

This might not seem a bad thing. People are eating organic food, of which we can all approve, and fewer pesticides are being used, of which we can also approve. Why get het up if the big companies are making money – surely they're precisely the vehicle to share organic food beyond a set of privileged people who can afford to buy the stuff? Surely the best way to democratize good food is to give dominion over it to the people who fill us with the less healthy versions?

It may well be true that more people will eat organic food than would without large corporations participating as organic farmers, but we've seen this sort of argument before. In the GM crop debate, field trials offer only two choices: GM crops and 'conventional crops', grown with standard pesticides. A third option, of agroecological farming guaranteed to produce food in a manner beneficial to wildlife and free of dangerous pesticides, wasn't on the table. There's a direct analogy with the debate around organic crops. To turn agribusinesses loose on organic food is to legitimate their rule, to concede that no kind of food system is possible without their participation, just as to choose between high-pesticide farming or GM farming is to admit that, either way, the pesticide companies are a part of our food system. But there have always been alternatives.

In the growing of food, there has always been sustainable, yield-rich, agro-ecological farming. In the buying of food, there have always been local markets, through which we were able to get to know the people who grow our food, talk to them about it, live with them through the seasons and eat according to the natural cycle of seasons. Today, the fastest-growing packaged food on the market is processed organic food.[78] Yet when the Heinz Corporation cans organic tomato sauce, it does nothing to support farmers, and precious little to encourage us to eat better. Corporations can only comprehend the potentially radical call for sustainable agriculture as customer demand for processed food grown with fewer pesticides. This sets at zero the importance of social relations through which the food is produced, and the politics that permits these relations.

So while there is an important environmental difference between industrially produced organic food and industrially produced non-organic food, and while it's a difference of which we can simultaneously approve and find wanting, the social difference between industrially produced organic and non-organic food at the supermarket is vanishingly small. We already have a colloquialism to describe the kind of choice that's no choice at all, the kind of choice that supermarkets are geared to provide – 'Coke or Pepsi?'

Think of it as a kind of culinary taxidermy, in which the living social relations are shot, stuffed and mounted on the shelves. Never having experienced a direct connection to the people who grow our food, we're tricked by the simulacrum, mistaking the dead green 'Certified Organic' packaging for a living connection.

It's a difference to which anyone can attest who has eaten fresh food picked locally and recently, as opposed to the organic that appears on supermarket shelves, trucked and shipped thousands of miles. It's a difference that can't get by our sense of taste. But if all we've got to go on is the label, we're often led astray.[79] And that would go for all food sold in a supermarket. Although the packaged organic food industry is booming, close behind (and with higher margins over a broader range of food and non-food goods) is a segment that pulls the logic of labelling in full reverse – the supermarket own-brand. Sold alongside brand-name products, at lower price, and with all trace of their provenance erased, these are products with no logo, for none is needed. In every way that matters, when you shop in a supermarket, you're already inside the label.

In the Garden of the Black Panthers

It becomes easier to understand the extent to which supermarkets sell us short by thinking of an alternative – a shift away from shopping at the supermarket to a relationship with producers that is more direct and engaged. Community Supported Agriculture (CSA) systems, for instance, involve a contract between the farm and the consumer, involving a weekly delivery of whatever happens to be in season. These are on the rise in the United States, where there were virtually no CSAs in the 1980s, over 500 by 1995 and now more than 1,000. Farmers' markets have had a similar renaissance, from a handful in the 1970s to 2500 at the end of the century. And they're ways of organizing production that don't involve the sprawl of an urban or peri-urban distribution centre. The food is dropped off directly to the consumer by the producer, ensuring not only that there are fewer miles travelled between the grower and the eater, but also that energy and resources used in refrigeration and transportation are saved too. Stores can successfully operate on the principles of CSAs – in Austria, one prototype was found to generate 75 per cent less waste and 63 per cent less air pollution, using 72 per cent less energy and 48 per cent less water.[80] Although the savings are significant, they're largely an indication of the resource profligacy of the way we expect to eat, with foods from around the world, on tap, all the time.[81]

Community Supported Agriculture initiatives offer a solid way to reconnect with producers, but even CSAs don't guarantee that workers in the food system receive a fair wage for their labour. To secure labour rights, a different model offers inspiration. In the San Francisco Bay Area is a group of shops inspired by Basque priest José María Arizmendiarrieta Madariaga, known to most as 'Arizmendi'. Working in post-Civil War Spain, Arizmendi helped to develop a system of cooperatives headquartered in Mondragón, with a number of characteristics we've seen elsewhere. The cooperative is open to all who agree with its basic principles, everyone is an equal member, and all workers make decisions equally, with a strong commitment to self-government, social transformation and education.[82] Arizmendi's thoughts on cooperatives are striking: 'To build cooperativism is not to do the opposite of capitalism as if this system did not have any useful features ... Cooperativism must surpass it, and for this purpose must assimilate its methods and dynamism.'[83] It's an insight common to all the social movements in this book that none wants to do away with markets, or innovation, or vigour.[84] They merely want to put markets under their control, rather than being controlled by them. And it can work in the food system.

Terry Baird is one of the founders of the Arizmendi Bakery in Oakland, where, across the Bay from San Francisco, he and his coworkers make and sell sublime bread, rolls and pizza. 'What makes our bread different is that it's sourdough. It uses a starter that just keeps growing,' says Baird. The starter itself is a fermented culture of lactobacilli, yeast, flour and water. 'Every day we dump out about 80 per cent of it [to make dough]. The living yeast makes the bread rise. And every night we mix more up and let it ferment with the old culture. We got ours from the Cheeseboard Collective [another Bay Area food coop], and they had theirs for about twenty years.' There's a characteristic sour tang in the loaves, and it's one peculiar to the area – so much so that the lactobacilli in the bread bears the stamp of the area: *Lactobacillus sanfranciscensis*. The culture of the workplace is no different. 'Our model is each one teach one,' says Baird. The teaching pays, and pays well. 'We pay $16.50/hour and we also have what works out to be a $4 patronage refund, a share of the profits that depends on how many hours you work. Plus we have decent healthcare, with a $5 prescription and copay. Most of all, though, we've got more flexibility around where and when we work.' This is in stark contrast to the conditions, pay and benefits of the supermarket giants. Walmart's average sales associate's wage is US$8.81,[85] and in 2010 only 54 per cent of Walmart associates were covered by the company's insurance.[86] 'Also, we pay everybody the same thing from day one. Even the trainees. In fact, because they're employees under state law, they're eligible for overtime, at time and a half. So they can end up making more than a member of the cooperative.'

Arizmendi isn't the only group that has risen to meet the challenge of finding food, and employment, in the city. Oakland itself is a community with a memory of struggle. The last struggle, fought against institutionalized racism within the police and the government, summoned the full fury of the state. The struggle was that of the Black Panthers. Most of the community leaders were imprisoned or killed, and the community was subsequently torn apart by urban development projects and transportation links. But from the ashes of the old struggle come important lessons for the new.

West Oakland is beset now by slightly different troubles, but people's bodies are still battlefields. Today, the leading cause of death isn't the police or firearms. It's heart disease. Given what we know about redlining, and the quality of food available to people of colour in the United States, this might not come as a surprise. West Oakland abuts the altogether plusher bit of Northern California's Bay Area in Northern California known as Emeryville (home

to Pixar Animation's campus, among others), and Emeryville has
more supermarkets and big-box retail space than you could swing
a trolley round. West Oakland, on the other hand, has 30,000
residents, thirty-six convenience and liquor stores and a single supermarket.[87] It's redline city. And it's the home of the People's Grocery. Founded by three young activists, Brahm Ahmadi, Malaika
Edwards and Leander Sellers, the People's Grocery resembles supermarkets insofar as it's in the business of education, logistics
and transformation. If you wanted to stretch a point, you could
also notice that it uses free labour and benefits ever-so-slightly
from state subsidy – the grocery operates a small vegetable garden, using volunteer labour, on a 200-square-metre (2,150-square-
feet) patch of unused land under permission from the city council.
But the similarity between the People's Grocery and ordinary supermarkets stops there. The grocery grows a great deal of its own
food on the donated land, and its orange truck putts around the
neighbourhood selling subsidized organic fresh fruits and vegetables, together with whatever processed organic food they buy at
a steep discount from Mountain People's Distributors, one of the
largest distributors of organic food in the United States.[88]

The grocery takes its educational activities seriously. At the
local YMCA, residents can attend nutritional classes organized by
the People's Grocery to learn what to do with locally grown food.
The People's Grocery is also in the education business, developing
a holistic understanding of community change, by providing the
services to the local community that no one else will. They are, in
some ways, walking in the footsteps of the Black Panthers. The
Panthers dealt with life-and-death issues facing the community,
saw access to food as a community concern (setting up food give-
aways and community breakfasts) and using the energy and savvy
within the community to do much better than people outside the
community feel they ought.

The danger in this kind of activism lies in the differences between the People's Grocery (and the many similar groups around
the world which direct their energies towards community hunger)

and the Panthers. Unlike the latter, the former tend to be popular with governments and donors. Suzi Leather, writing about the UK, puts her finger on it precisely: governments are keen to sponsor organizations that are founded on a 'self-help ethos, involv[ing] vanishingly small resources and [that] can be encouraged without at the same time having to admit to the existence of poverty'.[89]

The people at the People's Grocery are aware that theirs is a political project. The raised fist on their logo is more than a genuflection to the ghost of black power. It's an appreciation that there's important confrontational work ahead. Brahm talks of the incipient dangers facing West Oakland of 'Emeryvillification' – of the entry into West Oakland of the big-box stores from its northern neighbour. But the People's Grocery are pushing with Oakland City Council to try a new kind of development model that puts food at its centre, and that involves everything from a change in the council's accounting practices to allow derelict land to be turned into community gardens, to changes in school curricula to make space for education about food.

It would be naive to think that this plan is going to transform West Oakland. Or rather, naive to think that it'll happen without a fight, naive to think that, through the ordinary hand-over-fist of democracy, the needs of poor people will prevail over the needs of the corporations that increasingly pay for local government. So far, the People's Grocery has succeeded through wit, hard work, inspiration and a great deal of community goodwill. The moment it succeeds too far, and starts to change the environment for business, is the moment it can expect a bigger fight. And that's because what's at stake isn't only the dominion of the supermarket, but the stability of an entire matrix of living, working and consumption, one that shapes not only our choices but, as we'll see in the next chapter, our very selves.

9

Chosen by Bunnies

And the dish ran away with the spoon . . .

On Places and Taste and Food

The anthropologist Claude Lévi-Strauss observed that before food is nice to eat, it has to be nice to think about.[1] Every year, food corporations introduce 15–20,000 new food products to the market.[2] We certainly don't think consciously about them and yet we're unfazed when we see new items on the shelves. Clearly, there's some thinking going on, even if we're not conscious of it. This thinking about food is embedded deep into the structure of our lives. As a result, through the way we live, work and play, we don't really choose our food – our food chooses us. It isn't easy to think this through and take seriously. Doing so means unravelling more than a simple decision over whether we would like fries with that. It means questioning our most fundamental instincts about individual freedom.

Let's begin by looking at a contradiction in the heart of the world food system's nemesis. Back in the 14 de Agosto MST settlement in Brazil, supper is a shared meal of beans and rice: hearty, delicious and warm. It's a balmy evening, the sunset sky is pink-blue, and people are chatting in the recreation facility, a small shack and a corrugated iron roof, under which the settlement's teenagers are shooting pool on a fraying table. After dinner, from behind the counter at the shack, Lydia asks for a packet of crisps and a bottle of beer. I'm a little surprised. Isn't the MST settlement meant to be the cutting edge of resistance to corporate food? Shouldn't there be rules against industrially produced crisps, and beer bottled hundreds of miles away?

It's my mistake. The settlement isn't some zone of gastronomic purity. I've seen far more zealotry in an economics department than from the land-occupiers in Brazil. Think of a non-smoking actor whose character smokes. The actor is able to take up and then stop a habit that, for smokers, is profoundly debilitating, simply because smoking isn't something the actor normally does when out of character. Similarly, a packet of crisps in a settlement is a different thing from a packet of crisps outside. In the settlement, it's unusual, a treat, an allowable exception to the choices made about food, how to grow it, and how to eat it within the settlement. Within the settlement, these choices are made consciously and democratically. Outside it, many choices have already been made for us by our environment, our customs, our routine. Choice is the word we're left with to describe our plucking one box rather than another off the shelves, and it's the word we're taught to use. If we're asked why we use the word 'choice' to describe this, we might respond 'no one pointed a gun to our head, no one *coerced* us' as if this were the opposite to choice. But the opposite of choice isn't coercion. It's instinct. And our instincts have been so thoroughly captured by forces beyond our control that they're suspect to the core.

To suggest that humans might have developed instincts to navigate through the modern world of supermarkets is slightly silly. Yet there *are* ways of eating, and ways of choosing, that have become second nature. They have been measured not by the toll of natural selection, nor the rhythm of the seasons, but by the beat of more human drums – by war, by work, by architecture, by television, by food corporations, and only finally by ourselves. Most of what we consider our choices at the consumer end of the food system have been narrowed and shaped before we even begin to think consciously about them.

This chapter, then, looks behind our choices, arguing that the way we eat today is the result of forces that are hidden from us, and to which we almost never pay any attention, because their effects have become normal. Through a few examples, it becomes easier to see that the way we choose food today comes from distinctly abnormal roots, and that 'normal' can often be a thin veil that blinds us to poverty, racism and sexism. Many groups have attempted to uncover, change and redefine their food choices. The groups covered in this chapter have done so not as a way of generating a list of ideologically acceptable foods, or creating and mandating a radical diet. Rather, for them the collective attempt to eat differently is a process, a way of becoming more in control of, and of understanding better, what happens when we choose what to eat.

Food Is from Mars

Until recently, the greatest engine of change for human diet has been war. The most pointed military tactic involving food, practised from antiquity to Iraq, is the siege.[3] But it's not through sieges that many of the technologies and possibilities of our modern diet were invented. The connection between war and food has had deeper and more subtle effects on our everyday diets, for better or worse. Consider this story of food and the military, which provides not only a foundational moment in the science of nutrition, but also heralds the birth of the modern controlled experiment.

Scurvy dogged the British fleet. The bleeding gums, scabs and falling hair caused by what we now know to be vitamin C deficiency had been observed since antiquity. The perishability of sailors was an impediment to exploration, and the commerce that followed it. Chinese fleets in the Ming dynasty had, at least by the time Zheng He's armada set sail in 1405, cracked the problem before the Europeans by germinating soya seeds aboard their ships – soy sprouts are rich in vitamin C.[4] Although John Woodall, the Surgeon General for the British East India Company, had in

1614 prescribed a range of cures, from fresh food to sulphuric acid, it was unclear which worked most effectively. Aboard the HMS *Salisbury* in the Channel Fleet, to which he was appointed ship's surgeon in 1746, James Lind began a series of trials that would lead to his publication of *A Treatise on the Scurvy*. With the materials to hand, Lind began to experiment on the mariners afflicted with scurvy. To some he gave nutmeg; others were given water gruel or vinegar or *elixir vitriol* or an assembly of garlic, mustard-seed, balsam of Peru and gum-myrrh. The two worst hit were given a course of sea water. And two others were given daily two oranges and a lemon, which Lind reported 'they ate with great greediness, at different times, upon an empty stomach'.[5] Six days later, the citrified sailors were back on their feet, while the condition of the others had deteriorated. The results of the controlled experiment were unequivocal. The policy of providing such fruit on British Naval vessels was cemented, as was the method which arrived at this conclusion. Lime juice consumption was enforced aboard all Royal Navy vessels. And, in a demonstration of the connection between food, power and meaning, British sailors and their nation came to be known as lime-juicers, or Limeys.[6]

Lind's method of experimentation came to be used in the first industrial mechanism for storing food, again, via the military. On board British Naval ships, the food was for the most part good, if slightly stodgy. The 1785 weekly ration was seven pounds of biscuit, seven gallons of beer, six pounds of meat, two pints of peas, three pints of oatmeal, one-third of a pound of butter, and two-thirds of a pound of cheese.[7] Of course, with prolonged periods at sea, the Navy needed to take its food with it. The Army fared worse, with food provisioning out-sourced to a range of 'sutlers' who trailed the army and whose business it was to obtain, and then resell, local food. This, incidentally, was a key means through which new tastes were spread, and soldiers brought new tastes home with them. Today, though, we wouldn't expect troops to come back from Iraq with a fondness, say, for *sumac* or *Afkhadh al-Dijaj bil-Teen* (chicken drumsticks baked in fig sauce).[8] This is because the arrangements for military food procurement have changed, at least partly because sutlers couldn't be relied upon if the local population proved hostile. Concerned about the need for food to survive its distribution, the French *Directoire* offered a substantial, 12,000 franc, prize to the inventor of a method for keeping food in good nick.

Its winner, Nicolas Appert, provided one of the most crucial series of innovations in the transformation of the modern diet. His first invention was tested by sending the food across the equator, through high sea and humidity, and back to France, where it was consumed and found to be entirely preserved. His invention involved this: place food into a jar, boil it and stop the jar with a cork.[9] This paved the way for the invention of canning, for which Appert won a further prize from the *Directoire* in 1820, this time for preserving '8 to 10 kg of animal substance in the same vessel for one year'. This prize was aimed not just at military provisioning but also towards larger-scale manufacturing. Eight to ten kilos (22 lbs) of meat is, after all, more than the dainty morsels distributed and sold by artisanal manufacturing. That the military could commission such quantities was a sign of the co-development not of an industry to make the tin containers, but of a meat-processing industry to fill them. And, of course, there's an irony here: putting processed food in large slop-tins was, ultimately, the invention of the home of *haute gastronomie* – France.[10]

The invention of food processing that could maintain foods in edible condition, and allow them to be transported over vast distances, immediately stretched the possibilities of what could be eaten where, and by whom. New technologies of transportation and communication helped war to be conducted over ever-increasing distances. The success of these technologies in European theatres of war led to their adoption across the Atlantic, in the US Civil War. At conflict's end, these technologies found a new life in postbellum industry. The civil war ended in 1865, and by 1870, large quantities of tinned US meat were finding their way not only into the furthest reaches of US territory, but back across the Atlantic into the shops of London, Liverpool and Manchester.[11] The meat, it must be said, wasn't very nice. An 1874 description puts it like this: 'it was in a big, thick, clumsy red stain and was very cheap ... I have a vivid recollection of the unappetizing look of the contents – a large lump of course–grained lean meat inclined to separate into coarse fibres, a large lump of unpleasant looking fat on one side of it – and an irregular hollow partly filled with watery fluid.'[12] It is from the meat in this tin, and specifically through the technologies that made its long-distance distribution possible and its consumption normal, that the modern Big Mac can trace its genealogy.

The Big Mac isn't the only fast food with a military pedigree. The Second World War provided a prime example of the subtle ways through which military might changes our tastes, through aligning them directly with patriotism. If the British taste for tea was forged in the Industrial Revolution, the US taste for Coca-Cola was first chorused in the theatre of the Second World War. The drink itself wasn't given away during the conflict, but General Marshall went to great lengths to make sure that it was freely available to buy wherever US troops were stationed. The Coca-Cola Company was exempted from sugar rationing so that it might produce a drink that came, for US soldiers, to signify the very lifeblood of the country. In the words of one soldier, he fought 'as much to keep the custom of drinking Cokes as I am to preserve the millions of other benefits our country blesses its citizens with'.[13] Through its position in the Second World War, then, Coca-Cola came to signify, at home and abroad, the apogee of the American way.

Of course, this has its darker side, as Mark Prendergrast notes in a section from his 'For God, Country and Coca-Cola' that reads like *Catch-22*:

> War correspondent Howard Fast ... couldn't fathom why
> his transport plane landed at a remote Saudi Arabian
> Army outpost where the thermometer read 157 degrees
> Fahrenheit. They were there to pick up thousands of

empty Coca-Cola bottles. When the overloaded C46 lumbered off the desert runway, it failed to gain altitude, barely clearing the sand dunes. The writer logically suggested jettisoning bottles. That, he was told, was impossible. 'Guns they could dump, jeeps, ammo, even a howitzer ... but Coca-Cola bottles? No way. Not if you wanted to keep your points and not become a PFC again. The pilot summarized the well-learned moral: 'You don't fuck with Coca-Cola.'[14]

Even today, food corporations find themselves in the thick of war, jockeying for association with the meanings of patriotism. Burger King had already opened its first outlet in Iraq while aid trucks were still phutting at the border waiting for hostilities to be officially declared over. With one permanent location at the Baghdad International Airport, and three mobile units, plus free Whoppers to welcome home the troops who've not been killed, the Burger King empire has been able to ride the wave of 'home' food. So saturated in oils, sugar and meaning is the Burger King Hershey's pie that, in the words of one captain from the 1st Armored Division, the food 'speaks for itself'.[15]

Wheat is Murder

Spurred by martial needs, it's perhaps unsurprising that food science has itself been an arena for pitched battles. Nutritional science is a key tool in the armoury of those who would persuade us that one new food is better than another: we see the skirmishes whenever we read that margarine is better for you than butter (or vice versa). When industrial food companies engage in scientific debate, they do so in an attempt to change our tastes, even reversing what was previously considered good science. Take the example of one of the world's most important staples, and therefore one of the most lucrative: bread.

Nutritional science had, by the beginning of the Second
World War, established in the UK the nutritional superiority of
brown bread over white.[16] This was not a finding that pleased
flour-milling companies. They were keen to extract as much value
as possible from bread's raw ingredients. This could be done by
processing the whole grain that makes brown bread brown, using
the germ as a nutritional supplement, and the coarse bran to feed
animals. Further, the shelf-life of bread could be extended if some
of the essential fats were removed from it. Processing wheat into
a number of different products means that the resulting flour was
not brown, but white. Here, the flour millers faced a problem. Science had sanctioned the nation's original decision to hold brown
bread close to its bosom. Any change in the colour of the national
loaf would have to be similarly consecrated. So after the war, the
techniques spawned by James Lind on the HMS *Salisbury* were
deployed, cosmetically, to bleach the colour of the national loaf.

An experiment was carried out to discover which bread was
nutritionally best, white or brown. Sponsored by Britain's Medical
Research Council, its subjects were German foundlings in Wup-
pertal and Duisburg. The two groups of children were fed a diet
that varied only in the kind of bread they were given (white and
'fortified', or brown). Happily for the children, but unfortunately
for science, their diet was rich, nutritious and varied. Both groups
thrived equally. The experiment demonstrated that children do
well with good nutrition, but precisely because the high quality
of the children's diet prevented there being a control group – a
central feature of Lind's original experiment – there wasn't a way
of discerning whether the children's wellbeing was related to the
equal nutritional value of their overall meals or the smaller contribution of the different types of bread. Undaunted, the scientists
were pleased to report a scientifically unrelated but politically
important conclusion: that, for both white- and brown-bread eating groups, 'their heights and weights went up faster than those
of American children'.[17] On the basis of these ruddy-cheeked or-
phans, then, it was officially decided that white bread was no

worse than brown, and that the milling companies were therefore justified, on the grounds of national health, in being granted their more lucrative white bread production. After all, the new white British loaf had been proved not only every bit as good as brown, but was better than the Americans'.

The effort to build a taste for wheat was an international undertaking as well as a domestic one, made possible in part by the sanction bread had received at home. Following the end of the Second World War, the Cold War changed food habits throughout the Global South. No matter what existing staples were, as Harriet Friedmann notes, 'when previously self-provisioning countries began to import food in the 1950s and 1960s, the food they imported most was wheat because that was what was offered as food aid . . . As a result, when they became dependent on imports they were hooked on the most expensive grain.'[18] Wheat prices were sub*stantially* higher – more than five times more expensive than rice, six times pricier per ton than petroleum. In Korea, a country that continues to pride itself as the 'home of rice', schoolchildren needed to be taught how to consume bread. And this education came through the PL-480 programme's free school-lunch donation of bread, with the knowledge that today's aid recipients would be tomorrow's customers. It's the marketing idea of a free sample writ very large. At the same time, South Korean wheat production fell. Between 1966 and 1977, it declined 86 per cent, as the amount of wheat brought into the country increased fourfold.[19] Similar stories might be told of other recipients of PL-480 aid.[20] Wheat was US agriculture's battering ram. The food aid programme during the Cold War was as political and economic as it was aesthetic. It respins the adage 'Give a man a fish, and you'll feed him for a day; teach a man to fish, and you'll feed him for life.' Food aid shifted eating habits away from extant (and usually more nutritious) norms toward the single commodity which was in superabundance in the United States. 'Give a loaf, and you feed for a day. Inculcate a taste for loaves, and you've baked goods customers for life.'

In all these cases, what's being fought over is what food *means* to us, how we receive it, how we think about it. And it matters not least because in eating, food physiologically and semantically becomes part of us. How else, after all, to explain the theatrics of the 'Freedom Fry', the partly-tongue-in-cheek rebranding of French fries by some restaurants in the United States which followed the French refusal to join the war in Iraq. At the same time, the French earned themselves a food-related sobriquet in American popular culture too: they became 'cheese-eating surrender monkeys'.

Certainly, the example is a little flip. But it's a sign that a great deal of effort goes into linking together the meaning of foods. Foods are associated not just with nation, community and identity, but status, sex, destinations and desire. At its most successful, the attempt to change the way we think about food and its meanings becomes so normal, so much a daily part of our lives, that we don't have to think about it at all. And nothing demonstrates this better than the TV dinner.

Hooked on TV Dinners

Modern food tastes have been crafted by war, by the demands of national security, by technology, and corporations' attempts to profit from these by shaping the meaning of food. But while technologies such as canning allowed the storage of certain kinds of food for long periods of time, twentieth century diets and tastes were to be irrevocably altered by two new pieces of technology – the refrigerator and the television. At the end of the Second World War, the technologies of supplying and heating food accompanied the troops home. Companies that had created the gastronomic infrastructure and technology of the battlefield now competed for housewives' dollars by emphasizing, above all, how little time the modern woman would have to spend preparing frozen meals.[21] But while seeming to address the time-poverty of women in the Baby Boom, frozen meals were designed more for the convenience of their producers, rather than their consumers. Consider, for instance, the genesis of the original TV dinner.

In 1953, after the late-November Thanksgiving weekend, a 240 ton glut of Swanson frozen turkeys travelled the railroads of the United States in refrigerated carriages for want of storage, or consumers. Faced with the prospect of losing their investment, the turkeys' owners realized that, repackaged, yesterday's leftovers might become the food of tomorrow. With the purchase of metal trays and a small marketing spend, just in time for Christmas, TV Brand Frozen Dinners were invented. At less than a dollar per aluminium plate, they soon exhausted the original supply of turkey and went on to become a food marketing legend. It's important to note, though, that although TV Brand Frozen Dinners were packaged with a covering design to make them look like TVs, the marketing campaign didn't itself cause people to eat in front of the TV– they were what people ate while they dreamed of affording one. The meal could only actually be eaten in front of the TV after everyone had a set, and at the time of its launch, few did. In 1950, only 9 per cent of the US population had a television. By the 1960 census, the figure was nearer nine out of ten households.[22] Indeed, once everyone had a television (in 1963), the Swanson Corporation stopped calling its meals 'TV Dinners'.

TV dinners' packaging contained two significant design elements, beyond a representation of what was in the aluminium tray – first, a picture of a television and second, a beaming woman holding a TV dinners package (which had on it a picture of food, a TV and a woman with a TV dinners package, and so on). The marketing was aimed at making more convenient the lives of women who, after the war, found themselves working for a wage, but still found themselves expected to prepare food at home. The skills of preparing this new food had to be learned. Store managers often faced irate housewives, who'd boiled frozen peas for twenty-five minutes 'just to be sure' and laid the responsibility for the resulting sludge firmly at the door of the manufacturer. In the US, women's magazines had successfully been used by the Food

Administration to promote new nutritional ideas in the interwar years. They were used once more to spread information about TV and its foods. It was in women's magazines that television was promoted as an intervention in that most intractable of mothering tasks – persuading truculent children, usually sons, to eat as they're told. An Australian example gives a flavour of the sales pitch:

'Kitchen TV a Joy to Housewives. . . Junior can come home from school, raid the fridge, and stay in the kitchen watching TV. He doesn't mess up the living room, he's under mother's watchful eye, and if the kitchen extends to dining facilities he doesn't have to be cajoled into coming to eat – TV in front of his eyes is inducement enough.'[23]

The culmination of the marketing of television came through both the social content and context of the show. Prime time was the intersection of money and food. Initially, the TV Dinner Party was a self-conscious embrace of this novelty, when family and friends would gather around the new screen. Compelled by the TV schedule to have the food ready in time, and reluctant to miss the show, middle-class women found themselves needing food that required minimal preparation before consumption. Through fitting a novel social situation, in which the necessity of convenience was both created and sated, the TV Brand Frozen Dinner® became a TV dinner.[24] The television's interaction with food also cemented a modern way of eating. Today, six in ten US households watch TV while eating.[25] Yet barely fifty years ago, this would have been utterly inconceivable, for there were no TVs to own.

Eating while in front of the television is not, of course, an exclusively US enterprise. The history of how domestic eating habits changed with the advent of television, and how women were conscripted to the project, is one with broad global similarities. There's a further point to be made here, though. The transformations wrought by television have had consequences far beyond the way individual families eat. There have been systemic effects. The next example, which also involves television, comes from the UK. It shows how a large human population can be made to move and consume in sympathetic resonance with a schedule.

The British National Grid, the UK's electricity transmission system, distributes over 60 gigawatts of power at peak demand, between 5 and 7 p.m.[26] In order to make sure that there's enough on tap, they monitor consumer demand. The bane of the electricity companies are 'TV spikes'. These are surges in demand that happen in the advertisement breaks during, or after the end of,

Date	Actual pick up (MW)	Programme title
07.04.1990	2800	World Cup 1990 Semi Final – West Germany v. England (end of extra time)
01.22.1984	2600	*The Thornbirds*
06.21.2002	2570	World Cup 2002 Quarter Final – England v. Brazil (half time)
06.12.2002	2340	World Cup 2002 – Nigeria v. England (half time)
04.20.2001	2290	*EastEnders*
04.28.1991	2200	*The Darling Buds of May*
05.12.1991	2200	*The Darling Buds of May*
07.20.1989	2200	*The Thornbirds*
01.16.1984	2200	*The Thornbirds*
05.08.1985	2200	*Dallas*
11.22.2003	2110	Rugby World Cup 2003 Final – England v. Australia (half time)
04.18.1994	2100	*Coronation Street*
06.30.1998	2100	World Cup 1998 – England v. Argentina (half time)
02.19.1986	2100	*The Colbys*
04.07.2002	2010	*Coronation Street*
04.02.1984	2000	*Coronation Street / Film: Blue Thunder*
07.29.1981	1800	Royal Wedding: Charles and Diana

Table 9.1 Selected British TV pick ups 1980–2003
(Source: National Grid plc, 2006)

popular TV programmes. This is when the audience gets up to make a cup of tea, and the electricity needed to boil water causes a massive and synchronized increase in the demand for power. The TV spike is biological (people are thirsty), it's cultural (tea is, as we saw in chapter 4, a very British drink), it's about the space in peoples' homes (the TV is in the living room, the kettle in the kitchen) and, clearly, it's a social phenomenon, with large numbers of people watching the same thing at the same time.

This is odd, because we'd like to think of our choices more as individually spawned, as products of a kind of liberty. Yet this behaviour is nothing if not collective, as millions of people herd at the same instant from television to kettle and back.

Our collective viewing of TV demonstrates how our tastes, and even their timing, are synchronized and set by forces that we rarely acknowledge or even think about. And this makes the broader point that food always exists *somewhere*, in space and time. This matters more than one might suppose. *Where* we live and work shapes *what* and *how* we eat and drink. We need better to understand who controls space, and how this systematically shapes what we choose to eat, even in our homes, in the intimate places most directly under our control and influence. To see what this means, we ought to look at the most comprehensive systemic effort to control who gets to eat what and where. And that means looking at apartheid.

The Now of Chow

When they squeaked to victory in 1948, the South African National Party wasted little time in consolidating a racist project of separation and discrimination. The political philosophy of apartheid supported a raft of legislation, to give the government the last word in racial classification (the Population Registration Act 1950), to make it illegal for people from different races to have sex (the Immorality Act of 1950), to split the country up into black and white areas (the Group Areas Act of 1950) and to prevent whites and blacks from using the same beaches, toilets and other spaces (the Reservation of Separate Amenities Act of 1953). In so doing, South Africa not only inaugurated an official policy of state racism, they also spawned a new kind of food, and a new way to eat it.

In apartheid jails, of course, the apartheid regime regulated food, space and race with intricate precision. 'Coloureds and Asiatics', for example, were given different rations from 'Bantus' (Africans). The white government would, for example, provide no bread or jam to 'Bantus'. These processed foods were the privilege of white people. They were the sweet concessions given to coloureds and Asiatics for being more 'civilized' than Africans. But while apartheid's racial fantasies could be enforced and monitored every hour of the day inside the prison, it was outside the barbed wire, where apartheid tried to shape the diets of millions and where it was subverted, that we will find lessons on food and consumption for us today.

With the onset of apartheid, blacks and whites were prevented from eating together. Black caddies at Durban's Greyville Golf Course were, for instance, unable to use the same cutlery and washing facilities as the white golfers. Yet they needed to eat quickly and speedily, in order to be able to spend as little time away from their jobs at the golf course as possible. This called for some invention. The solution meshed together two culinary traditions, both of which themselves had been transplanted to Durban. The new apartheid-compatible food involved the ladling of curry (a food that came with indentured Indians, who'd been brought to South Africa's Natal province by the British to work on the sugar plantations)[27] into a hollowed-out loaf of white bread (a food enjoyed by the British themselves). White bread, never brown.[28] The enterprising Gujarati Hindus who first put the two ingredients together were of the Bunia caste. Thus was created Durban's signature food: 'bunny chow'. At its best, the curry is rich and warm. The pithed out bread can be dipped into the bunny itself, the corner of the loaf lending itself to scooping the larger pieces of potato or chicken in the stew. You eat it entirely with your hands, which soon develop a yellow stain from the turmeric in the curry. And it's thoroughly delicious.[29]

The key features of bunny chow were that it was hot, ready to eat, filling, appetizing and portable (though not too far, before the curry soaked into the bread, making a mess of both). It meant that caddies could, on the run, eat food that they enjoyed, that nourished them and that embodied and celebrated an identity, a meaning that fought against racial injustice.[30] In mixing black and white foods along the boundaries established by the apartheid state, the bunny was both an obeisance to existing law and a gastronomic fuck you.

Both the ruthlessness that made apartheid possible, and the inventiveness that fought back with bunnies, teach us a little about the geography of our tastes and our choices. At the same time as making it possible to open restaurants for whites only and catering differentially to its black prison inmates, the South African partition also made it necessary for thousands of caterers to develop a new, *quick* food to be developed to cater to the poor, who were only marginally able to control the tempo and compass of their lives. In this, apartheid foreshadowed today's metropolises, and the way we eat within them.

In the Global North, the country that carries a candle for apartheid South Africa, through the segregation of diet between rich and poor, black and white, is the United States.[31] Levels of obesity in the US and South Africa are, strikingly, about the same.[32] South Africa is one of the wealthier countries in the Global South, and the United States has the highest number of people below the poverty line (12.7 per cent) in the Global North.[33] In the US, people of colour and the poor have access to environments that are more likely to lead to obesity, while their richer and whiter counterparts are more likely to have access to foods that are fresh, nutritious and lower in salt and fat. Across a range of neighbourhoods in the US, the poor ones are not only likely to have four times fewer supermarkets than rich ones, they're three times more likely to have places to consume alcohol.[34] Even after adjusting for levels of commercial activity, the presence of highways and median home values, fast food restaurants are concentrated in neighbourhoods of poor people, and people of colour.[35]

But the environment is more than shops. It is the architecture within our homes, the spaces through which we move to work, eat, play, learn, rest and pray. To see this, it's worth looking at geography through the eyes of a child.[36] Within the home and state institutions, particularly within schools, children are forced through a mangle of TV advertising and educational co-branding. Pizza Hut has 'Book IT!', McDonald's has the All-American Reading Challenge, Minute Maid/Coca Cola has the Minute Maid Summer Reading Program and, in Durban, the Wimpy beefburger chain has even managed to sponsor a Hindu school.[37] These are topped off by a range of ingenious tie-ins and sponsorships, through which food corporations pitch for children's attention. The increased availability of food (especially sugary, snack food, or any other) targeted at children, together with an environment in which children are able effectively to howl for it, and in which this pester-power is leveraged by marketers, has led to explosions in children's ill-health. Over US$10 billion a year is spent marketing food to children in the United States alone. According to Richard Watts, Coordinator of the Children's Food Campaign at the UK group Sustain, for every dollar spent promoting healthy food globally, US$500 is spent on promoting junk food.[38]

The kinds of advertising that lead to paediatric disease aren't restricted to print or television. Advertising media, and the needs to which they cater, are woven into the fabric of children's lives, from textbooks to cyberspace to playgrounds to parks to packaging. This isn't to suggest the totalitarian grip of food corporations on every fibre of a child's being, but rather that their circumstances make choices for them, and that the food system fits into, and amplifies, the most profitable of these circumstances. This is why looking at the case of children is so revealing. We tend to think that children need shepherding in their choices, because the world not only shapes their choices, but shapes *them*. While we look at children as those least capable of independent choice, study after study (sometimes sponsored by the advertising industry, sometimes not) has found that children are often able to tell the difference between what is an advertisement and what isn't. The implication is that it's okay to expose children to advertising, because they'll figure it out. But these results can be interpreted differently. It's also possible to conclude that adult responses to the inducements to consume are, in a meaningful way, no more sophisticated than those of a three-year-old.

Certainly, the consequences of advertising food to children have blurred the diagnostic difference between kids and grown-ups. It has led to the renaming of 'adult onset' diabetes as 'type II', given the increasing numbers of children with the disease. In Chinese cities, the prevalence of childhood obesity increased from 1.5 per cent in 1989 to 12.6 per cent in 1997.[39] In Beijing, the combined overweight and obesity rates in 2004 have soared to 30.6 per cent for boys and 18.5 per cent for girls.[40] A 2001 study found that in China, 81.8 per cent of advertisements shown during Saturday morning television and children's hours are for food, and another study in 2010 found that children who pay attention to television marketing are twice as likely to request and buy what they have seen advertised.[41] And in Brazil, in a series of landmark studies, it becomes clear that poor children have it worst – nutritionally deprived while young, they're at higher risk of obesity as they grow older.[42] Now and in the future, the fates of children will be visited on adults. The argument, to put it differently, is that children are the canaries in the mineshaft, for adults are no less bombarded with inducements and signs to make poor consumption decisions. We consider children hostage to their impulses, and insufficiently responsible for their actions to be able to navigate a world of junk food and unhealthy snack temptations. Their bodies are already beginning to suffer from the poor confections with which they are bombarded every day. It is the price they pay for being profit centres for the food industry. Yet the food with which they are surrounded, and the nutritional messages they're supplied with, are little different from the ones facing adults. At the very least, we can conclude that the world around us is rife with potentially harmful and certainly unhealthy food.

The physical world, its meanings and our interactions with them all contribute to what Kelly Brownell calls 'toxic environments'.[43] High streets and highways have been transformed into commercial spaces offering easy, iconized access to quick calories. McDonald's Golden Arches are now more widely recognized, claims the *Guinness Book of Records*, than the Christian cross. Even in our places of work, the vending machine eats change and spits out sugar to accommodate the increasingly irregular hours we are required to work.[44] Away from work, at play, we find the environment shaping both how we acquire and how we expend calories.

Poor people in cities, whether in the US or elsewhere, have systematically less access to green space and recreational facilities, and this has a direct impact on health. Across cities in Europe, and controlling for income, the high availability of green space means that citizens are three times more likely to be active, and 40 per cent less likely to be obese, compared to those in areas with little green space and lots of graffiti, where people were 50 per cent more likely to be overweight, and 50 per cent less likely to exercise.[45]

In the US, it's clear that poor neighbourhoods lack recreation facilities, and just as with blacks in urban South Africa, areas in which African Americans live are substantially less likely to have access to green spaces, beaches and swimming facilities.[46] For parents taking a breather from the work of childcare in the home, for children playing, for families being together, green space is a vital daily resource.[47] And, increasingly, the enjoyment of green public space is a pleasure only the rich can afford.

Diets aren't only affected by space, but by time. For working people in the United States, time poverty is a serious issue. With housing markets being the way they are, commutes are longer for poor people.[48] A recent US report showed that for every dollar saved on cheaper housing, commuters spent 77 cents on transportation. The twenty-three cent saving on the dollar doesn't include the time spent commuting. And there's mounting evidence that the longer one spends commuting, the more likely the risk of being overweight. Yet, precisely because of the pressures to get to work (and, possibly, then to a second job) the working poor are substantially less likely to be able to eat well. In circumstances such as this, it shouldn't surprise us that fast food, with all its burdens up and down the food system, remains a meaningful choice to many of us. Just as tea nourished the Victorian English working classes, a $1 double cheeseburger and fries comes to be a welcome and warm meal in a day, and night, filled with work.[49]

The story of bunny chow points to an interesting anomaly in the way this is thought through.[50] Under apartheid, it was easy to see how space was legislated, how blacks were denied control of the rhythm and place of their lives. The statutes were in the books, the police forces would make damn sure that the spatial order was adhered to. The problem, everyone could easily and readily acknowledge, was a social one and it was to be addressed not through individual transformation but by social protest, subversion and widespread change. Today, when a growing number of working poor people are forced into similar conditions, the target is not the social and political substrate of the problem, but its most cosmetic and superficial effect: obesity. It's like suggesting that the reason blacks had it bad under apartheid was not because of apartheid, but because they were poor. And that the remedy was not to challenge apartheid, but to become rich.

War on the Obese

If the quality of food we eat is shaped by work and play, by the neighbourhoods we live in, the jobs we can get and the time we spend travelling between them, then we might want to consider poor diets as a symptom of a systemic lack of control over our spaces and lives. Yet in the media and in government, that diagnosis is ruled out of court. Instead, poor diet is understood to mean obesity, which in turn is considered an end in itself, simultaneously symptom and disease, a skin-deep ill without need of further clarification, because we have all become literate in the art of reading the individual body. The meaning not only of food, but of obesity, has already been suggested to us. We are encouraged to understand obesity to be, at the end of the day, an individual failing, an inability to deal with the farrago of choices offered to us, a deficit of impulse control. Conventional wisdom sees obesity as a symptom of an impoverished faculty of choice, never a result of an impoverished range of choices. And this is because, in large measure, the solution offered to the *social* problem of obesity has been an *individual* one.

Suggesting, for example, that obesity is a deficit of self-control on the part of the poor summons forth a set of social anxieties.[51] If at the beginning of the twentieth century those concerns were couched in worries over national security, and about what the poor might do to the rich if given cause to riot, at the beginning of the twenty-first, the same worries are articulated in concerns over social security, and about the claims that the disabled and poor will have on the young, rich and productive. In an influential 2005 article in the *New England Journal of Medicine*, a group of academics put it like this:

How much higher can life expectancy rise? This is not just an academic question. The answer formulated today will have substantial influence on the rate at which taxes are levied and on the potential solvency of age-entitlement programs... The Social Security Administration (SSA) arrived at a ... view that life expectancy in the United States will continue its steady increases, reaching the mid-80s later in this century... Dire predictions about the impending bankruptcy of Social Security based on the SSA's projections of large increases in survival past

65 years of age appear to be premature. However, this 'benefit' will occur at the expense of the economy in the form of lost productivity before citizens reach retirement and large increases in Medicare costs associated with obesity and its complications. Presently, annual health care costs attributable to obesity are conservatively estimated at $70 billion to $100 billion. With rapid increases in the prevalence of diabetes, and a decrease in mean age at the onset of diabetes, the cost of treating diabetes-related complications, such as heart disease, stroke, limb amputation, renal failure, and blindness, will increase substantially. A similar escalation of health care costs from other complications associated with obesity (e.g., cardiovascular disease, hypertension, asthma, cancer, and gastrointestinal problems) is inevitable. The US population may be inadvertently saving Social Security by becoming more obese . . .[52]

The worries of public-minded scientists in the US have their analogues elsewhere, and all of them are concerned with what has come to be known as 'the obesity epidemic'. Clearly, much is at stake. But national concerns with obesity aren't new. In 1952, Lester Breslow, a consultant to the US President's Commission on Health Needs of the Nation, had raised a flag, suggesting that

a substantial proportion of Americans are overweight. One out of 6 'well people' examined in the Boston Health Protection Clinic were 20 per cent or more overweight, and 2 out of 5 among a group of men employed in a physically arduous occupation in San Francisco were 20 per cent or more overweight. It is clear that weight control is a major public health problem today.[53]

If the handwringing about obesity is a more constant feature than we might think, it is wise to ask whether there is any reason to be concerned. Obesity increased in the US by 71 per cent from 1991 to 2001,[54] and similar data exists for developed and developing countries.[55] There seems little to dispute. Yet much rests on how we understand what obesity means. In terms of the crude figures, the rise in obesity levels in the US is equivalent to an increase in the average individual's weight of between 3 and 5 kg (6 to 11 lbs) over a generation. This has the effect of shifting the bell-curve of everyone's weight over to the right a little. This in turn leads to many more people being classified at or above the cut-off point for obesity.[56] In the words of biologist Jeffery Friedman:

> Imagine that the average IQ was 100 and that five per cent of the population had an IQ of 140 and were considered to be geniuses. Now let's say that education improves and the average IQ increases to 107 and 10 per cent of the population has an IQ of 140. You could present the data in two ways. You could say that average IQ is up seven points or you could say that because of improved education the number of geniuses has doubled. The whole obesity debate is equivalent to drawing conclusions about national education programmes by saying that the number of geniuses has doubled.[57]

Those who urge caution in interpreting obesity data do not deny that there are cases where concern is warranted. It is entirely appropriate to worry over the increasing number of people who suffer ill-health as a result of morbid obesity.[58] There is reason to be concerned that a mere 3–5 kg per generation still signifies an imbalance between the amount of food eaten and the amount of energy expended. There is little sign that the imbalance is 'self-correcting', to use the language of markets. Further, the causes of weight gain are also, it has been increasingly recognized, the causes of other kinds of ill-health, from heart disease to diabetes. But critics of the popular descriptions of the obesity epidemic point out that this isn't the sort of language or care that gets used in talking about obesity. Instead, they observe, when the obesity epidemic is discussed as a social problem, particular social groups become targeted as a result.[59] In other words, they argue, the obesity epidemic has become a 'moral panic'. In a recent study,[60] researchers examined 221 newspaper, medical and book sources. They found that two-thirds mentioned individual causes for obesity, while less than a third mentioned structural factors (such as the food industry, or geography). More striking:

> A full 73 per cent of articles that mention the poor, African Americans, or Latinos blame obesity on bad food choices, compared to only 29 per cent of articles that do not mention these groups. Similarly 80 per cent of articles that mention the poor, African Americans, or Latinos but only 29 per cent of articles that do not mention these groups blame obesity on sedentary lifestyles.[61]

Indeed, poor people (particularly poor mothers)[62] and people of colour (particularly immigrants) catch a great deal of the individualized blame for ill health. Take one widely circulated example, of Greg Critser in *Harper's Magazine*: 'Inside, Mami placates Miguelito with a giant apple fritter. Papi tells a joke and pours ounce upon ounce of sugar and cream into his 20ounce coffee. Viewed through the lens of obesity, as I am inclined to do, the scene is not *so feliz*.'[63] The obese children of immigrants have been blamed for not suiting the proper image of middle-class America.[64] Or we could take another example, a 13 January 2005 *New York Times* article on obesity in Brazil, accompanied by a picture of 'fat Brazilians', three large women in bikinis, turned out to be women from Europe.[65] We were encouraged, nonetheless, to find something rebarbative and unusual about their bodies.

This is not to argue that significant public health challenges do not face the poor. After all, 80 per cent of people with diabetes live in low income countries and, in rich countries, poor people are disproportionately affected by the disease.[66] The rise in cases of diabetes, especially type II, which has doubled over the past three decades, happens at the same time as funding for research into the disease is flatlining.[67] Diabetes is associated with obesity, which in turn is associated with lack of exercise, poor diet and smoking. Forty per cent of all people with diabetes are from India or China. Cardiovascular disease, related to the way people eat and exercise, is found in India and China at rates higher than all the countries in the Global North put together, though the rate of increasing prevalence of diabetes is nonetheless higher in the Global North.[68] It is clear that these diseases should be the subject of broad-based public concern. That's not what's at stake here. What's really up for grabs is the politics and economics of the analysis of causes, and its insidious by-product, the politics and economics of blame.

Feeling the Burn

The individualization of blame plays into the ways we're invited to fight obesity in society. The gym, the functional food and the diet are, more often than not, deeply secluded experiences. In gyms, collective management of fat involves running on the spot, alongside dozens of others, with the equipment ranged against mirrored walls – so that we all face the Mecca of our imperfect bodies. As with the industry behind food, there is an industry behind these individual responses to size. In the UK in 2011, the fitness industry employed over 200,000 people, turned over GB£3.81 billion (US$5.4 billion), and counted 12 per cent of the population as members of a gym.[69] In North America, 58 million people spent US$20.3 billion in 38,000 facilities. Nearly four million Japanese spent US$5.3 billion.[70] In Brazil, people spent US$1.1 billion at 15,551 facilities.[71] Across the world, there's an explosion of concern – and business – around the effects of obesity.

But as Robert Atkins notes in his eponymous Diet, it is clear that the forces shaping what we eat are collective and social:

> One lesson I learned is that many of my patients are ad-
> dicts. Not drug addicts, but addicts of a substance in the
> diet ... That substance is sugar ... Because so many of us
> consider our desserts and sweets to be the high spot of
> our day's eating enjoyment, we are all more than willing
> to listen to the sugar industry' s propaganda and believe
> such misleading statements as 'our brains can't function
> without sugar.' These are the same voices who during
> the next decade will be telling us, 'it has not been proven
> that sugar is a cause of heart disease, or of diabetes, or of
> hypoglycemia.'[72]

Certainly, the sugar industry has much to answer for and continues to undermine public health initiatives, like the World Health
Organization's 2004 global strategy on diet, physical activity and
health, which seeks to rein it in.[73] But by using arguments against
the sugar industry, by playing off fashions for thinness, the diet
industry has been able to invent itself as the righteous opposition.
And a lucrative one too. Although figures aren't hard and fast,[74] the
world's diet industry easily runs to annual sales of over US$100
billion. It's a big bandwagon. On it you can find the pharmaceutical industry, and its search for ways of medicalizing obesity and
for a drug to suppress appetite. The food-processing industry is
on board too, attempting to engineer virtues into food vices, such
as Olestra – the indigestible and therefore zero-calorie cooking
oil, also used for making paint and lubricants[75] (which has the
disadvantage, as the fine print on foods containing it warns, of
occasional 'anal seepage,' and which has recently been associated
with weight *gain*[76]). One fusion of food and pharmaceuticals is
the nutraceutical – the food product with medical benefits thrown
in.[77] It will soon be joined by the cosmeceutical – a blend of nutritional science, food marketing and the cosmetics industry – when
Coca Cola and L'Oréal release their collaborative beverage named
'Lumaé', which will allegedly improve skin tone.[78] It will add to
Coca-Cola's product line already on sale in Japan, which includes

'Love Body', a drink sold, allegedly, to help women increase their breast size.[79] And, of course, alongside the food and drug industries are those magazines selling diets (among the best-selling food magazines in the US are *Eating Light* and *Shape*) and the fitness industry.

Although there are more individual diets than social responses to the way we live in our skins, the latter do exist and have a strong history. The National Association to Aid Fat Americans (now the National Association to Advance Fat Acceptance),[80] for example, held a Fat-In in New York in 1967.[81] The tyranny of a particular body shape, and the neuroses about physical appearance, about how we ought to look starved,[82] or indeed what we should wear, has always been a way to fight back.[83] 'Acceptance' of fat is, however, only one side of the equation. The 'healthy at any weight' approach, found in increasing numbers of scientific publications,[84] balances the rejection of conventional ideas of beauty with an adoption of healthy behaviours. It promotes a blend of sound diet and exercise, at the same time as it gives the finger to socially sanctioned bodytypes.[85] It is possible to choose to be healthy, and to reject the tyranny of what is considered a 'normal', and 'normally desirable', body. Through interventions such as these it is possible to broaden the imagination of beauty, by invoking sensuousness, and inviting us to consider a range of ways of being gorgeous. If this seems like a fringe idea, it's worth recalling that there are many societies, including those in India, the Middle East and the South Pacific, where ideals of beauty have until recently fallen far from the standard of tall and skinny. But it has only taken generation for the tyranny of a particular beauty standard to sweep the globe. In 1990, anorexia and bulimia nervosa were almost non-existent in the Fiji Islands. In 1995, television began to be beamed in. Within three years of the arrival of predominantly US terrestrial television, 11.9 per cent of teenage Fijian girls were bulimic.[86]

By understanding the politics of diet and obesity, we've looked at the causes and repercussions of one of the ways the food system is structured. Further, these politics are outcomes of a complex system that, if left to its own devices, is far from self-correcting. To best see this, one need only look at who's profiting from both stuffing us, and then solving the resulting weight gain. In 2006, Swiss chocolate manufacturer Nestlé acquired the Jenny Craig weight-loss brand. And it's not even the first merger of its kind. In 2000 Unilever, the owner of Ben and Jerry's ice-cream, purchased Slimfast.

The increasingly centralized control of both the source of our modern food and the amelioration of its attendant ailments mirrors another system effect. Recall that Monsanto sells RoundUp Ready soybeans as a pair with RoundUp herbicide. It's a seduction that traps farmers, who buy GMOs and then commit to paying for matching pesticides. In both cases, consumers are sold products that are attractive in the short term, but which in the long term offer only a cycle of addiction.

To get out of these unhealthy cycles we need a reset and a fresh start. That's why the most interesting social responses to the food system – flawed and contradictory though they may be – don't attack symptoms, individual responses or products. Instead, they attempt to think about food anew, to short circuit their way out to a fresh – and more independent – way to fix our relationship with our food and our bodies.

Your Pace or Mine?[87]

One of the foremost movements addressing the questions of who makes food, where it comes from, and how we might enjoy it better, is the Slow Food Movement. The Movement fights for the right to choose food differently, and savour it fully. It has triumphed in Italy and, increasingly, around the world. Today, the Slow Food Movement has chapters in over 100 countries, with 100,000 members and 1300 'convivia' – branches where food is tasted and exalted.[88]

The food is – need it be said? – magnificent. The metric for most of us seems to be tomatoes. I'm not sure why, but nearly everyone can remember that tomatoes used to taste much better than they now do. Slow Food tomatoes, in Florence, are very good indeed. And they are merely the garnish to a brace of rare cheeses, which did things to my mouth I've not been able to replicate since – a tingle on every taste-bud, a wash of tastes, a high of slow pleasure. The food is all produced regionally. It's important for the movement that food is grown, and eaten, in a particular *place*. Eating food that has been locally grown makes it easier to nurture a social connection with the producer, to know how and where and why things are grown the way they are. It's a kind of eating that is transparent and socially embedded in a way that industrially-produced food can't be. It's a movement that has adhered to the tenets of its elegant manifesto, one signed by, among others, Nobel laureate Dario Fo:

> Our century, which began and has developed under the insignia of industrial civilization, first invented the machine and then took it as its life model.
>
> We are enslaved by speed and have all succumbed to the same insidious virus: Fast Life, which disrupts our habits, pervades the privacy of our homes and forces us to eat Fast Foods.
>
> To be worthy of the name, Homo Sapiens should rid himself of speed before it reduces him to a species in danger of extinction.
>
> A firm defence of quiet material pleasure is the only way to oppose the universal folly of Fast Life.
>
> May suitable doses of guaranteed sensual pleasure and slow, long-lasting enjoyment preserve us from the contagion of the multitude who mistake frenzy for efficiency.
>
> Our defence should begin at the table with Slow Food. Let us rediscover the flavours and savours of

regional cooking and banish the degrading effects of Fast
Food.

In the name of productivity, Fast Life has changed
our way of being and threatens our environment and our
landscapes. So Slow Food is now the only truly progressive answer.

That is what real culture is all about: developing
taste rather than demeaning it. And what better way to
set about this than an international exchange of experiences, knowledge, projects?

Slow Food guarantees a better future. Slow Food is
an idea that needs plenty of qualified supporters who can
help turn this (slow) motion into an international movement, with the little snail as its symbol.[89]

It's quite a call. And it's one that has been embraced by increasing
numbers of food aficionados. But the movement cares not just
about enjoying food, but about making it. The movement directs
a great deal of support to producers. In its *Presidia*, the Slow Food
movement links together producers of different foods. Harriet
Friedman describes the dairy-related aspects of North American
presidia like this:

Now that industrial dairying and cheesemaking have
become standardized on a continental scale, innovative
farmers, mainly women, have revived old cheeses and
are inventing new ones. These are usually made on the
farm from its own milk and sold locally. The presidium
links cheesemakers across many regions who use raw
milk and are in danger of violating myriad sanitary regulations which favour industrial methods. This is a battle
that has been fought longer within the European Union.[90]

In Europe, among the its other features, Slow Food is a bulwark
of tradition and of self-conscious enjoyment of taste and flavour,

against not only the industrial and mechanical foods of modern capitalism, but also of imported foods and cuisines. The presidia in North America are, however, havens for foods that have been forged over innumerable migrations and globalizations.[91] As Harriet Friedman elaborates, there are differences in the way consumers relate to their food in the US and Canada:

> In North America there is less traditional loyalty of consumers to local products. The *presidium* links 'over 30 producers, connected not by historical or geographic links but by common aims: the improvement of quality of American raw milk cheeses and the creation of links between cheesemakers. A group of tasters, comprising Slow Food and cheesemaking experts, select the best raw milk farmstead cheeses each year from among participating producers. Because cheeses have always been introduced to North America from Europe, there is no *terroir* – the French word for the ineffable qualities of a particular region, referring to its soil and climate, but invariably expressed in products reflecting knowledge and skill of farmers and artisans who are inextricable parts of the farming system. American cheeses are based on European originals: e.g., Dry Jack on Parmesan, Teleme on Taleggio, and Brick on Limberger.

Indeed, when Slow Food is transplanted to the New World, the resulting organization sharpens a contradiction that's everywhere. There's a deep tension between preserving a tradition of food and admitting that culinary traditions are changing all the time. It's a problem that matters for a movement that has come, in some of its chapters, to be a guardian for a certain purity of tradition, to the exclusion of novelty. Yet precisely because of this dynamism, we might, several generations from now, have presidia for American chop suey, or British chicken tikka masala. And if we will, why should we wait? Even the tomato, the *sine qua non* of Italian food, comes from the Americas. Tomatoes were unknown in Italy until Europe discovered the New World. In the UK, the late British Foreign Secretary Robin Cook celebrated chicken tikka masala as a quintessentially British food. And it is: the 'masala sauce', absent in the original North Indian dish, was added to make it palatable to a British public who wanted food with gravy.[92] If Mr Cook could celebrate it, why should the Slow Food Movement rule it out? Because it isn't traditional? Traditions, and their power in shoring up the interests of some in 'the community' over others, are inherently suspect. Tradition is the first refuge of scoundrels, before they are shaken out, and have to scurry to patriotism.

While it is important to remember how labour has been embodied in food, with care and with the wisdom of ages, it's also important to remember that cuisines aren't static. As a movement, Slow Food is aware of these tensions. Gianluca Brunori, a professor at the University of Pisa with strong ties to the movement says, 'With immigrants, local Slow Food groups prefer to develop involvement based on interchange of food cultures and food identities,' he notes. In evidence, he cites that at the Terra Madre in Turin in 2006, people from 150 countries shared food and their visions of change around the food system under the Slow Food umbrella. In 2010, the Turin meeting had record attendance, with over 200,000 people, a third of whom came from outside of Italy.[93] Gianluca argues that change does need to be embraced, and the movement has begun to explore this.

It is inevitable that any attempt to find a radically new way of eating that starts from the situation we have today will run into contradictions. One of the biggest that Slow Food faces, beyond the insoluble difficulties of defining authentic and pure traditional food, is the question of affordability. It's a tension that becomes more apparent after appreciating the roots of the movement. Founded in 1989, the Slow Food Movement began life as an insert in the Italian Communist Party newspaper (*Manifesto*), entitled 'Gambero Rosso'. The title in fact means 'red shrimp', a play on words, not least because of its allusion to the rallying song of the Communist movement, 'Bandiera Rossa' – the red flag.[94] The Movement was originally an attempt, among other things, by the left to reclaim the idea of pleasure, showing that enjoyment could and needed to be linked to a rigorous support of workers rights. Outside Italy though, it has been a little easier for subscribers to Slow Food to shrug off the movement's Communist history. Indeed, in Australia, the Slow Food Movement seems to have been happy to behave as if there were no history at all. One of its puff pieces turns Slow Food into a rather upmarket food and wine club: discussing Barossa Valley, South Australia, the Slow Food Magazine claims that 'the combination of this rich European heritage and the fresh vitality of Australia is embodied in its lifestyle and landscape'. As if Barossa Valley really *were* a *terra nullius* into which European heritage was poured, rather than an enclave of middle-class food aficionados and wine-growers.[95]

Not everyone is part of the community, of course. There's something about the imagined community of taste, of some rural idyll, an Albion, which remains deeply embedded in the national imagination, and which is the natural home of conservative politics. Even Slow Food Italy is susceptible to it. In Slow Food shops in Rome, at the time of the mayoral elections for instance, candidates endorsed in the shops were either from the Green Party (a member of the left coalition) or from the Forza Italia rightist party.

Beyond this, the most pressing problem for most of us as consumers is, of course, that to be able to go on a culinary odyssey in the first place and, even more, to be truly at liberty to savour food, to have the time to quaff and roll, the majority of people need that passport to all other freedoms – money. Admittedly (and Slow Food admits this, not me), the prices make the eyes water as readily as the food does the mouth. But the Movement also points out that we've become too used to cheap food bought off the backs of workers in rural areas. Explaining this, Carlo Petrini, a founder of Slow Food, pulled his mobile phone from his pocket and said, 'Food *should* be more expensive. We spend so much on *this*, yet we can't even spend the money for a proper cheese.' Yet in a view widely shared, one shopper in Rome put it like this, in describing a butcher who'd recently been tapped by Slow Food: 'it was expensive enough before, but now for a single vertebra of oxtail, he'll ask for 60 (GB£52.37, US$86.24)! Who can afford to eat like that?'[96] It's a criticism that Slow Food takes on the chin. The response is that both cuisines offer a beacon for change, a kind of gastronomic utopia to aspire to and, on occasions when we can save up enough, to enter.

But are the rest of us, the multitude in Slow Food's manifesto whose pace of life is beyond our pocket's ability to control, condemned to eat at McDonald's? Not if one man can help it.

Anti-Malbouffe

On 12 August 1999 French sheep farmer and Roquefort producer José Bové and a few of his friends were involved in an engagement with an under-construction McDonald's in Millau, in the south of France. Depending on your sympathies, he either 'dismantled' the store or destroyed it. His action, precipitated by an EU–US trade dispute at the WTO in which French Roquefort had been slapped with a punitive tariff, was a family affair:

> everybody, including the kids, helped dismantle the
> interior of the building: partitions, some doors, electri-
> cal outlets, and sheet metal on the roof that was nailed
> down but which came up easily, because it was part of a
> kit, decorative stuff. It was really a lightweight piece of
> construction, the whole place.[97]

While some have accused Bové of chauvinism, and of crude nation-bashing, Bové himself was clear that his target, like that of Slow Food, was not the national origin of the restaurant. Rather, it was the quality of what was served inside:

This was not an anti-American action; it was *anti-mal-bouffe* [against-bad grub]. We were determined never to be trapped by the logic of being anti-American. This is a fight against free trade global capitalism. It's about the logic of a certain economic system, not an American system. It can be a struggle against any country, this one or that one. It's not against those who have an American passport.

The context of the struggle was explicitly international. In a later infraction, when Bové was detained after setting fire to a field of genetically modified crops, several hundred Indian farmers, from a range of peasant movements, were touring Europe as part of an international caravan. After Bové was cuffed, the farmers petitioned the French police to arrest them too, for the meaning of McDonald's for them was just as objectionable as for Bové. His fight against the golden arches was theirs too.[98]

Bové is part of an international movement, but one that is very far from knee-jerk. It's a movement that, literally, wants to turn back the clock – specifically the clocks in figure 9.1.

The amount of time spent cooking and eating in UK homes, as elsewhere, has fallen dramatically. This has happened as a function of women's changing roles in the home, the availability of refrigeration, longer working and commuting hours, the availability of food that's quicker to prepare, and the strong sense that there are better things to be doing than making food.[99] The movement of which Bové is part aims to change the meaning of food, from a requirement to a celebration. On this, Bové makes the following observation:

> When people no longer want to eat at home or cook for themselves, the family begins to disintegrate. Those citizens who resign themselves to this fate are condoning the failure of a system and hardly preparing a bright future for their children. They are complicit in a sort of

doctrine of universal alienation. They must realize this, and soon.[100]

That children tend to do better when they eat with adults isn't rocket science.[101] Children who eat regular meals with nutritional role models tend to choose better food when out on their own.[102] But Bové is making a deeper point – that *adults* do better when taking time to eat, to appreciate the ingredients and labour that transforms ingredients into dinner.

And still, we face the problem – who has the time and money to do this?

One way to try and understand how to work around this challenge is to look at the movements that have started to make the links between rural and urban poverty. If farm work is to be better paid, workers off the farm need jobs with living wages, so that everyone can afford to eat well. Such movements are turning the politics of the food system on its head in the process. In South Africa, Peter Dwyer is an organizer with the Right to Work Campaign. His call is not to demand cheap food for poor people – the solution to urban hunger over the past two centuries. Rather, his movement demands that poverty be eradicated, so that every person can access healthy food:

> What's the point of even having cheap food if you can't afford it? Unless you've got a decent wage and a regular stable income, you can't afford decent healthy food. That's why we're organizing. Business and government aren't going to want to pay this, but that's what we fight for. These are literally bread and butter union issues. Here in South Africa, the gains that unions make are, in most cases, won for all employees. And for people without work, the Right to Work and other similar campaigns to mobilize to provide an income to survive. We're looking for government to massively expand the public sector to provide jobs – more hospitals, more schools, more

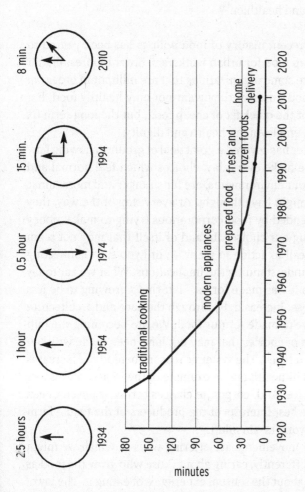

Fig. 9.1 Home cooking times 1934–2010
(Source: Professor David Hughes, personal communication)

teachers – all these things have multiplier effects. And
so you end up not only with better-fed people, but more
educated and healthier.[103]

So, while the recent history of food politics has been geared to
providing cheap food for urban workers in order to forestall mili-
tancy, there are some organizations that are militant in order *not*
to have fast food. Instead, they want not only healthy food, but
fuller lives. Not the quick fix of cheap food, but the long-term fix
of high wages, employment, health and dignity.

This chapter has covered a great deal of ground, showing how
the choices we make every day, choices which feel normal and
well suited to our environments, are far stranger and more unnatural than we might have thought. At every step of the way, they
have been attended by food corporations trying to make money
out of changing our choices. In and of itself that may not seem
like a clarion call to action to many – until you start connecting
the dots and understanding the implications. What we eat today
may seem like it was made for us – but that's growing to be less
and less the case. Increasingly, through the pace and architecture
of our lives, we're made for our food. We are becoming the puppet consumers of choices that may not have been made with our
best interests at heart. The systemic reasons behind the increases
in diet-related ill-health are an example of the impact of this loss
of explicit choice. And, corporate choices certainly haven't been
made with the best interests of the producers of the food – farmers and farm workers – in mind.

But social movements are offering ways in which we might
choose diets differently, caring about those who grow the food as
well as caring about the sensual experience of eating it. The joy of
food isn't one that ought to be restricted to those who can afford it.
All should be able to have the time and money to eat well, rather
than being pushed towards 'malbouffe'. And, in order to secure
this, the political project is a collective and social one, rather than
one driven by individual purchasing choices. This is precisely the

political programme advanced by La Via Campesina, the international farmers' movement, of which the Brazilian MST is a member. They've a democratic framework within which they're fighting for it, called 'food sovereignty'. It broadens the imagination of possible politics by putting the idea of equality right back into the heart of food politics. It is to this that we, in conclusion, turn.

10

Conclusion

Inside the Hourglass

> So off went the Emperor in procession under his splendid
> canopy. Everyone in the streets and the windows said,
> 'Oh, how fine are the Emperor's new clothes! Don't they
> fit him to perfection? And see his long train!' Nobody
> would confess that he couldn't see anything, for that
> would prove him either unfit for his position, or a fool.
> No costume the Emperor had worn before was ever such
> a complete success.
>
> 'But he hasn't got anything on,' a little child said.
>
> Hans Christian Andersen, *The Emperor's New Clothes*[1]

Unless you're a corporate food executive, the food system isn't working for you. Around the world, farmers and farmworkers are dying, with the connivance of elected officials, and at the whim of the market. Through processed food, consumers are engorged and intoxicated. The agribusiness's food and marketing have contributed to record levels of diet-related disease, harming us today and planting a time-bomb in the bodies of children around the world. Supermarket shelves offer an abundance of cheap calories, even as they bleed local economies. We are increasingly disconnected both from the production of our food and from the joy of eating it. Most of this happens with consumers ignorant to the suffering that precedes every mouthful of food. And the architecture of our neighbourhoods and working lives makes it impossible to imagine anything better.

Yet there is more than hope. One of this book's guiding themes is that wherever and whenever the wounds of the current food order have been inflicted, people have organized and fought back. The ideas nurtured through shared and public deliberation point the way to a new and better food system. No one person, no one group, has all the answers, but this chapter brings together some of the lessons of the past, that we might better shape the future. Before getting to that wisdom, though, a reminder of the urgent need for change. There are reasons to be optimistic that things will improve, not least because there are so many reasons to be pessimistic that the current food system can continue.

There are many more arguments than I've been able to present for why we might want a radically new food system. In choosing the cases in this book, I have cleaved to ideas and principles in which people from across the political spectrum might believe; in terms of justice, fairness and equality of opportunity, our current food system fails. But these aren't the only ways that it falls flat. Most of us care about more than a set of political assumptions. We care about the environment, about sustainability, about other living things, about enjoying ourselves, about being better than we are. In these broader terms, the current food system is a wasteland. The case against it extends beyond the harm it causes to people and communities caught up in it. The way we eat today also engenders systematic cruelty to animals. It demands unsustainable levels of energy and water use. It contributes to global warming and provides fertile ground for disease.[2] It limits our sensuousness and compassion. Perhaps most ironic, although it is controlled by some of the most powerful people on the planet, the food system itself is inherently weak.[3]

It is fragile because of the size of its ecological footprint, the resources needed to sustain it and the exploitation it requires. Just like any logistical network with bottlenecks, it has systemic and structural vulnerabilities. Those vulnerabilities lie close to the surface of our daily lives. All it takes to expose them is a gentle jolt to the system. Something like an oil shortage. Activist and scholar

Laura Davis was living in London in a squat in the 1970s when the first oil crisis hit. She remembers the effects: 'There was panic buying in the shops. And I wondered, well, what'd happen if all the food disappeared. That's when I first got into organic farming.' But what *would* have happened had all the food on the shelves run out? At the beginning of the new millennium, sixty million people came close to finding out. In the year 2000, Britain saw a wave of protests, headed by the UK haulage industry, which blocked access to six of the eight major oil refining facilities. Fuel stations closed. Traffic on motorways was cut by 40 per cent. Freight and logistics operations ran dry, with the consequence that the country was within hours of running out of food. The precision of 'just in time' supermarket logistics, together with Britain's century-old dependence on food grown elsewhere, meshed. The shelves almost emptied.[4]

It's unsurprising that UK stomachs became hostage to its fuel supply. A quarter of all trucks on UK roads are carrying food, and the average British family drives 136 miles a year to buy it.[5] Figures for elsewhere in the world vary, depending on the specific product, local climate and measurement, but one study in the US measured the difference in distance travelled by locally grown food versus its conventionally sourced equivalent. For a basket of local produce, the average distance from farm to market was 56 miles. For conventionally sourced food, the distance was 1494 miles.[6] And these transport costs are just the most visible sign that the modern food system is utterly dependent on fossil fuel. 'Green Revolution' technologies such as chemical fertilizer need large amounts of energy to produce. As writer Richard Manning has noticed, today's food system requires just as much energy as it generates.[7] Without the energy available to manufacture and ship pesticides and fertilizers, the conventional food system would grind to a halt.

Laura Davis has tried to raise this while carrying out research into local public sector procurement for the British government. 'We were talking about developing a healthy food economy, and we were mapping out the supply chains. But I wasn't allowed to use the food miles argument, because it seemed to be anti-competitive, because it discriminates against foreign goods. I wasn't allowed to refer to the fuel economy as a justification for the development of a local food economy.'

Laura might equally well have been talking about water. The modern food system demands access to unsustainable amounts of fresh water in order for its 'high-yielding varieties' to have the laboratory-perfect growing conditions in which they were designed. In Brazil, the one message that I was charged with delivering from activists in Mato Grosso was this: 'Tell the people that we're running out of water, and that it's the soy industry draining the Guaraní [the world's largest underground source of water].' It can take a ton of water to produce a kilo of grain. Much of that grain goes to feed animals. When it takes seven kilos of grain for each kilo of beef, it becomes easy to see how the industrial meat system exploits Brazil's groundwater.[8] Multiply that across the planet, and it's easy to see how water and energy have brought about wars, and not only in the Middle East. We can expect more resource conflicts as this century continues. That's not my prognosis, by the way. It comes from John Reid, Britain's former Secretary of State for Defence.[9]

Depleted reserves of fossil fuels, soil fertility and water are the sinking foundation of today's food system. Yet activists trying to point this out are quickly muffled. Christine Dann, an activist with the Green Party in New Zealand, has had a similar experience, with her calls for food sustainability falling on deaf ears in governmental meetings, despite an unarguable array of facts. 'That's what we're up against, the emperor has no clothes, but we're not allowed to say he's nude.'

The Green Party in New Zealand has been running a 'food revolution' campaign for SAFE food for the past five years.[10] The Greens define SAFE food as sustainably produced, accurately labelled, free from drugs, disease and contamination and ethically marketed since 2002. Christine Dann reports that results of the campaign have been mixed. There have been successes in getting some limited state funding for organics research, organizational development and grower support. The drive to shift schools away from selling junk food and towards providing healthy food and drinks has been well supported by health campaigners and the general public.

'Ordinary citizens take a more holistic view of the food system than the government does', says Dann. 'They want to know where their food comes from, how it was grown and processed and exactly what is in it. But when consumer freedom of choice comes up against corporate welfare in the form of 'free' trade – trade free of ethical, health and environmental considerations – the NZ government consistently sides with the corporations.'

Governments have gone to great lengths not to hear the demands of both consumers and producers. Sometimes, it's just a case of clamping their hands firmly around their ears. We've already seen that in the US, for instance, over 90 per cent of consumers want labels on food if it is genetically modified. The US government won't entertain the idea. In February 2006, the US went a step further, proving that, while content to ignore consumer demands, governments are prepared to gag them if need be. José Bové was scheduled to attend a conference at Cornell University. Because of his actions against McDonald's, and the conviction he accrued thereby, he was prevented from entering the country. The US government isn't alone in muffling the voices of agricultural activists. Later in 2006, eighty representatives of farmers' movements attending a World Bank/IMF meeting in Singapore were detained, and many were deported, because their views of rural development were not concordant with those of the international financial community.[11] At the World Trade Organization meetings in Hong Kong in 2005, farmers who were there to speak their truths to power were similarly criminalized. Such international events are only the most visible of the daily persecution of the rural poor, with the poorest always the most vulnerable to police brutality.

Yet governments haven't been entirely immune to concerns about food. Cold War fears that linked food with national security have now been updated to suit the tenor of our times. Today, governments are paying increasing attention to the food system, not primarily to pacify workers' discontent, but because it might be vulnerable to terrorist attack.[12] As reporter Stan Cox has eloquently pointed out, though, the damage to the US agricultural economy has been largely self-inflicted. Were agroterrorists to poison the food supply, they'd find it hard to make their attacks stand out against background levels of 76 million cases of illness, 300,000 hospitalizations and 5,000 deaths every year from 'ordinary' food-borne disease in the United States.[13] If they wanted to poison the wells, they'd have to compete against levels of pesticide-related poisoning of up to one in four wells contaminated with nitrites above a safe level.

For many communities, nitrite pollution comes from the livestock industry. Concentrated Animal Feeding Operations (CAFOs) are the brutal flesh pits that produce an increasing amount of the meat consumed around the world. The feedlots are cauldrons of blood, antibiotics (70 per cent of antibiotics produced in the US are used in the livestock industry) and grain (60 per cent of US grain is fed to animals). And, of course, shit. In the US, feedlots produce 300 million tons of manure a year, and animal runoff has caused a dead zone the size of New Jersey in the Gulf of Mexico.[14] As agribusinesses, CAFOs are exempt from many of the environmental regulations that would attend other businesses. Because the average pig produces four times more manure than a person, a modest CAFO with 5,000 swine will deal with as much shit as a city of 20,000 people. Except that it doesn't have a sewage system.[15] The waste produced by CAFOs is solid, liquid and gas, and it damages the land, water and, perhaps most of all, the atmosphere. The livestock industry produces 18 per cent of all CO_2-equivalent emissions on the planet and contributes more to climate change than driving cars.[16]

As well as destroying the physical world, the food system

has proved itself exceedingly good at generating its own biological horrors. Mad Cow Disease, and its human form, variant Creutzfeldt-Jakob Disease, were products of the industrial food system. In a bid to boost the protein content of animal food (the better to fatten cows quickly), meat and bonemeal was added to cattle feed. The infectious proteins that cause Mad Cow Disease survive long after the animal is butchered. It may have all started with one sick cow. When its nervous system entered the food chain, its infectious body parts were recycled back into the animal feed. The cycle continued, with more animals eating more infected beef-based food, until the epidemic was spotted. By then, it was too late to stop its effects in either cows or humans. Some estimates suggest that the active agent behind the human vCJD can be carried in humans for up to forty years, and that nearly 4,000 Britons may harbour the disease still.[17]

Across the Atlantic, the US seems to have escaped the worst of the BSE epidemic. The US Department of Agriculture (USDA) attributes this to its high standards of inspection and hygiene. Dave Louthan, who used to work in a meat plant, offers a different reason:

> The USDA had told the world that the mad cow had been slaughtered here, but it was not in the food chain. A blatant lie. I walked out with the news crew at lunch time because I can't stand a government cover-up. They asked me 'was the cow in the food chain?' I told them of course it was, it's meat. Where else would it be? When the USDA said no more downers [cattle that cannot walk] would be slaughtered, they essentially said no more BSE testing would be done. The minute the USDA found the contaminated cow, they stopped the brain stem collection and testing. Why? Kaching! It's the money. Billions.[18]

Louthan, predictably, doesn't work in that meat plant any more, and his whistle-blowing doesn't seem to have lessened the food system's dangers. After all, the problem isn't confined to beef. The latest threat to emerge from the food system is the H5N1 virus, better known as avian influenza – bird flu. In the press, the cause has largely been laid at the door of migratory birds. Yet H5N1 is, overwhelmingly, a poultry disease. And in every case where there has been an outbreak, the cause can be traced in the first instance not to migrating birds, but a connection with large-scale poultry industry in the vicinity.[19] It is little surprise that the world's most recent spurt of H5N1 activity as this book goes to press comes from Europe's largest turkey farming operation, Bernard Matthews' UK-based outfit.

The outlook for industrial agriculture isn't rosy. When the food system is merely working normally, it is centrally responsible for climate change, ecosystem degradation and fatal levels of pollution. When it goes wrong, it incubates new and lethal diseases in the Petri dishes of animal feedlots. The food system is a machine gun that generates new threats as part of its routine operation. And this doesn't begin to cover the human, let alone animal, harm caused in the food system through low wages, exploitation and even slavery. Those looking to fix the crisis on land by going to the sea are out of luck. Current research suggests that, at current rates of industrial overfishing and consumption, there won't be any fish left by 2048.[20]

It's Just We, Ourselves and Us

All my life, I have been driven by one dream, one goal, one vision: To overthrow a farm labor system in this nation which treats farm workers as if they were not important human beings.

Farm workers are not agricultural implements. They are not beasts of burden – to be used and discarded. How could we progress as a people, even if we lived in the cities, while the farm workers – men and women of our color – were condemned to a life without pride?

Those who attack our union often say, 'It's not really a union. It's something else: A social movement. A civil rights movement. It's something dangerous.'

They're half right.

We were fighting for our dignity, that we were challenging and overcoming injustice, that we were empowering the least educated among us – the poorest among us.

The message was clear: If it could happen in the fields, it could happen anywhere – in the cities, in the courts, in the city councils, in the state legislatures.

Once social change begins, it cannot be reversed. You cannot uneducate the person who has learned to read. You cannot humiliate the person who feels pride. You cannot oppress the people who are not afraid anymore.

Cesar Chavez[21]

The food system can't carry on as it is. Nor need it. There are ways that every person can affect the food system and can reshape it for the better. There are ways of getting back what the food system has taken from us: dignity in refusing to accept what we are told we must want, and how we must work and live; control over our lives, bodies and self-image; the knowledge that no matter where a child is born, she will be able to eat healthy, nutritious food and grow up free of poverty in a world that today's generations have ceased to destroy; and, perhaps most of all, a rediscovery of the pleasure of eating good food.

One of the most vital and comprehensive responses to the parlous state of the world's food system can trace its origins to Via Campesina. The vision is known as 'food sovereignty'. It's important not only because it has been authored by those most directly hurt by the way contemporary agriculture is set up, but also because it offers a profound agenda for change for everyone. It has

a lengthy and sometimes cumbersome definition,[22] but here's a
snippet:

> Food sovereignty is the peoples', Countries', or State
> Unions' *right* to define their agricultural and food policy,
> without any dumping ... [of food from other coun-
> tries. It includes] the right of farmers and peasants to
> produce food, and the right of consumers to be able to
> decide what they consume, and how and by whom it is
> produced ... And with the recognition of the rights of
> women, who play a major role in agricultural production
> and in food.[23]

Food sovereignty is a vision that aims to redress the abuse of
the powerless by the powerful, wherever in the food system that
abuse may happen. It is very far from a call to return to some bucolic past, bound by tradition. By laying particular emphasis on
the rights of women farmers, for instance, food sovereignty goes
for the jugular in many rural societies, opening the door to a profound social change, starting in the home. While women in the
Global South grow 60–80 per cent of the food, they own less than
2 per cent of the land.[24] The commitment to women's rights, and
the acknowledgement that the food system depends on women's
work, from seed development to harvest to cooking to serving, is
one of the clearest signals that some farmers' movements aren't
pining for some rustic past, but want to shape a radically different
future.

What does it mean, though, to say that *peoples* have rights?
It's odd to jumble the rights of women, consumers and producers
all under one umbrella term when rights are normally considered
to be the sort of thing that belong only to individuals. This apparent weakness is, on deeper reflection, a masterstroke in the definition. It becomes clearer when looking through the lens of 'sovereignty'. The shape and content of today's food system is defined
not by the many, but by the few. Most people are left experiencing

the consequences of others' choices, whether that be in the home, in the fields or along the aisles. Across a range of places and circumstances, we are not sovereign. Reclaiming control of the food system requires both an individual and a collective effort, and requires both individual and collective rights. It demands tough democratic deliberation about where the boundaries between the two should be. It's a discussion that ought not to be pre-empted by its definition so much as broached by it.[25]

The span of these actions ranges from the individual to the global. Some will require international cooperation for change. Some will be up to us as individuals. Together, these actions and rights form a cycle – to change ourselves, we need to change our world. To change our world, we need to change ourselves. Both are necessary. Both are difficult.

Listing those changes is hard, because they vary according to circumstance. There are some broad outlines, though. Starting at the individual level, one of the most difficult, because fundamental, changes that many of us will face is to:

1. *Transform our tastes*. Much of the damage done by the food system is carried out under the alibi of 'consumer demand'. Food system corporations are merely providing the sugar, salt, fat and flesh that everybody wants to eat – or so they claim. The most obvious way to choke the supply is to douse the demand. This is easier said than done, of course. It isn't easy to override our body's hard-wiring for processed and energy-dense foods, especially when we have come to accept them as normal. But why would we expect it to be easy to wean ourselves from these foods? Since birth, we've been stewed in the food industry's broth. Their aesthetics are embedded in our taste-buds. To spit them out means to distrust our desires. Born of the food system, our food instincts are unreliable guides to eating better. There is a reason, after all, why the snacks and nibbles that are central to today's unhealthy diets are called *impulse* purchases.[26] The food industry sank billions into the cultivation and misdirection of our physiological needs. Becoming sovereign involves re-examining our urges and

putting our corrupted instincts on probation. In reclaiming ourselves from the choices made for us by the food system, 'I like it'
temporarily becomes an object of suspicion, not a prelude to a
purchase.

Food sovereignty isn't, however, a call to asceticism. Learning
to eat with the seasons can be joyful. Changing our palates is a
cultural invitation to the deeper and subtler pleasures of food that
can't be transported, can't be processed, can only be eaten in a
short season every year. It's a celebration of sensuousness. We eat
with five senses, and part of the joy of reclaiming sovereignty over
our tastes is the ability to savour food far more richly and deeply
than we had. The best way to do this is to reconnect with the art
and sensuality of preparing our own food.

I've learned a great deal about culinary sensuousness from a
dear friend, Marco Flavio Marinucci. He is a San Francisco-based
artist and long-time lover of good food. He recently decided to
get online and share his passions. He organized a walking tour of
a local food market. Then he posted a note on his blog asking if
anyone was interested in preparing seasonal, local food together.
After only a handful of cook-togethers, his 'Cook Here and Now'
meals are instantly oversubscribed, always joyful, never preten-
tious events. Marco has written wonderfully about his own philosophy:

> Evolution gave us the gift of having to eat frequently:
> Let's not treat it as a chore. I believe that when we devote
> attention to what we do, we feel more satisfied and sati-
> ated by it. Each meal gets my full and undivided atten-
> tion. Choosing the best ingredients from what's in season
> locally, preparing the dishes from scratch as often as time
> allows, and keeping in mind who's sharing them – it's all
> gastronomical foreplay that creates the emotional build-
> up released in a delightful meal.[27]

Marco's right to draw the link between food and sex. Compared to a meal savoured to the full, the food industry's stock in trade is an adolescent and fumbling moment of onanism. And he's right, too, to link the quality of ingredients so emphatically with the pleasure of the outcome. Few people who've experienced good, seasonal, home-cooked food would favour its industrially produced counterpart. It's an important part of food sovereignty that changing our tastes means changing what we eat, according to where and when it is grown. It means trying to:

2. *Eat locally and seasonally.* Food that doesn't have to be grown or treated for long-distance travel tastes better, costs less to make and has a smaller carbon footprint. It is dependent on the seasons. Eating this way means fewer fresh tomatoes in winter, for instance. But as part of the drive to re-educate the palate, it compensates by offering a far broader range of food than one might expect. Food grown for local consumption doesn't have to be bred for haulage. Changing our tastes means rejecting the food industry's pabulum, and seeking out food produced with care. It means that if we want to eat any meat, fish or animal products at all, we ought to be prepared to pay a great deal more for their sustainably raised versions.[28] Changing our taste demands a shift not only in what is eaten, and where it comes from, but how it is produced. A third rule of thumb, then, is to:

3. *Eat agroecologically.* In the Global North, the virtues of organic food are increasingly recognized. 'Organic' is now, however, an industry. Today's food system can easily bend its industrial production methods to accommodate the reduced-pesticide food. If the only criterion at the shops is to buy 'mass organic', we might dent the profits of pesticide companies, but do little else to change the way food is farmed.[29] Above all, organic farming remains compatible with monoculture. As the dean of food writers, Michael Pollan, has observed, 'monoculture is at the root of virtually every problem that bedevils the modern farmer.'[30] Even if farmers' dependency on pesticides were severed, they would still be hooked on the rest of the food system's apparatus. A more profound challenge is offered by a set of farming principles that abide both by

the letter and the spirit of 'organic': agroecological farming. It's a method of farming we saw developing in Cuba, and which has its local versions around the world, from Masanobu Fukuoka's *One Straw Revolution* in Japan – which farms without tilling the soil at all – to the United Nations Development Programme-sponsored Sustainable Agriculture Networking and Extension (SANE) project in Asia, Africa, Latin American and the Caribbean.[31] It's a farming philosophy that farms with nature, developing and maintaining soil fertility, producing a wide range of crops, and matching the farming to the needs, climate, geography, biodiversity and aspirations of a particular place and community. It's an approach that develops deep local expertise, and means that farmers aren't disposable and substitutable resources, as they are under the reign of 'industrial organic'. It promises to be able to feed the planet.[32] And it is an approach that, above all, sees agriculture as embedded within society.

The best way to ensure that food is produced in harmony with one's local environment is to learn about the local environment, and then grow the food oneself. Growing your own food shares many virtues with cooking your own. It's deeply empowering, cheap, a way of building community and, better yet, a great way to get exercise, as The Peoples' Grocery and the South Central farmers can attest. You don't even need to own any land to do it. Britain's Guerrilla Gardeners turn public space into sources of organic food, changing our appreciation of places and architecture in the process.[33] If it's hard to find the time or space to grow your own agroecological food, it shouldn't be difficult to find other people's. And this points to a fourth rule of thumb in transforming the food system:

4. *Support locally owned business*. Although supermarkets portray themselves as zones of choice and variety, the opposite is often the case. Supermarkets, while offering shelves of plenty, employ fewer people and charge more for less fresh food than local growers and businesses. The food in street markets is about a third cheaper than in supermarkets, and more often sourced

locally.[34] London's Queens Market offers a haven of cheaper goods and *more* choice than supermarkets and is about 50 per cent cheaper than the local Walmart/Asda supermarket, while being more racially diverse and a lot less sterile.[35] The food in street markets, because it's less processed, also tends to be healthier. But markets such as these are struggling against the higher level of resources that supermarkets can deploy.

The destruction of local businesses by supermarkets is global. I visited a street market in Durban, South Africa that was about to be decimated by the opening of a large supermarket complex a few miles away. A local shopper, Mrs Perumal, expressed sentiments that would have been familiar to any small-town resident in the wake of a Walmart opening. 'Why must we go to the supermarket? Will the Megacity have dhanya [coriander] this cheap? Marigolds like this? I can't get there if I walk. So must I buy a Toyota so that I can eat?'[36]

We have seen one solution to the problem of transportation in chapter 8: Community Supported Agriculture initiatives (CSAs) are growing in number across the world.[37] Supporting locally owned CSA arrangements can reduce the amount of time spent in cars driving to supermarkets and offer a way to connect with farmers directly.[38] They're also better for the local economy. When money is spent at a local market, it tends to get recycled within the community, and spent on local goods over and over again. This is called a community multiplier effect. At one CSA in Britain, the multiplier effect was found to be around 2.59 per £1 spent. Compare this rate with a supermarket, where store revenues are sent back to head office and to shareholders, rather than spent again in the local economy.

So, for every £1 spent at the local supermarket in the same town, the community saw a rate of only 1.4.[39] CSA members in the US can, according to the government, save 60–150 per cent on the prices of comparable goods in the supermarket, though it remains difficult for poor families to afford the subscription fees.[40] And in the US, CSAs have also brought communities together. One woman, in a study about CSAs and gender, said 'I'm empowered by my commitment to this organization, and just to hear about it, even if I couldn't participate, I'd still be empowered – that it exists, that I know about it, and I have learned from it.'[41] Few have said this about a supermarket.

The wave of alternatives has already prompted agribusiness to make concessions. Like a vacuum cleaner salesman who has just dumped a pile of dirt (or transfats or corn syrup or salt or aspartame) into our homes, the food industry is now making a great show of removing its effluent from its processed foods. Some food companies are investigating ties with pharmaceutical companies in order to develop nutraceuticals – foods that are almost as good for you as having a balanced diet. Retailers are responding too. Walmart is currently positioning itself to be the largest retailer of organic food on the planet. Tesco is investigating 'carbon labels', so that it can declare the amount of CO_2 used in the production of some the goods on its shelves. Supermarkets can also home-deliver like CSAs. Some supermarkets have even courted outdoor farmers' markets, or tried to create a simulacrum of them, under their corrugated roofs.

Some retail giants are not just aiming to stock goods that are ethical, they're trying to wrap their entire operations in a sheath of corporate responsibility. Take, for example, the British supermarket chain, Waitrose. The firm recently announced that it had 'ploughed back' over GB£330,000 (US$660,000) for educational projects in South Africa, for communities whose labour grows the fruit sold in its shops. It's the new, caring face of supermarkets. Waitrose Managing Director Steven Esom visited the projects and 'came away with a terrific sense of pride in what they are doing out there. I was 100 per cent convinced this is the right thing to do before I went; now I'm 110 per cent convinced. It is absolutely clear that it's trade not aid that will work.' Customers, he says with equal conviction, feel a 'strong link' with people growing their food. This, he admits, before he has actually brought over any South African growers to the UK.[42]

We oughtn't to be surprised about Mr Esom's discovery that 'trade, not aid' works, though. He'd be in the wrong business if he thought otherwise. Before casting aspersions on Waitrose's efforts, we must observe, of course, that it's a good thing that South African children are educated. It remains a scar on the conscience of the South African government that their efforts to transform the apartheid education system have been so modest, and that Northern countries' debt continues to hobble development efforts in South Africa and elsewhere.[43]

But aspersions must be cast. When Waitrose talks of 'ploughing back in', they neglect to mention that their largesse is funded by what they've siphoned out. Not only is the basis of their generosity deeply suspect, but the resources from which they reap their profits are illegitimately owned. The farm land on which South Africa's most lucrative export farming happens is land that was stolen under colonialism and apartheid, and for which the South African Landless People's Movement (also a member of Via Campesina) is still fighting to reclaim. Since the end of apartheid, less than 6 per cent of it has been given back.

The fight for land, and for justice in the food system, is real, and worldwide.[44] As this book was nearing completion, I phoned Mangaliso Kubheka, an organizer for the Landless People's Movement for his thoughts on Waitrose's largesse. He couldn't talk. He'd just been teargassed and bundled into the back of a police van (with his mobile phone), for protesting outside the provincial land commissioner's office. And, on the same day, on the other side of the world, the bulldozers moved in to the South Central Farm, in Los Angeles, levelling fourteen years of crops, community and hope.

It is the cardinal condition of corporate social responsibility that good works are constrained by profitability. When supermarket giant Tesco touts its Computers for Schools programme, it neglects to mention that a parent would have to spend over GB£100,000 to earn enough vouchers to buy a single computer.[45] From Whole Foods to Walmart, retail giant ethics can only be paid from their excess profits and, no matter what the public relations department says, it is the shareholders who pay the piper. Supermarkets, like all corporations at the waist of the food system hourglass, oblige consumer desires only so far as they are profitable. They operate on the strict market principle of one dollar, one vote. They won't, therefore, address needs where there are no dollars to be found. (One need only to look at the salaries of those employed in supermarkets to see the truth of this.) And this is where a retail vision of ethical shopping falls short of the vision of food sovereignty. In the US, the supermarket chain that has put itself at the forefront of corporate social responsibility has been Whole Foods. The company's executives tout their mission as 'No. 1, to change the way the world eats, and No. 2, to create a workplace based on love and respect'.[46] It's certainly true that more and more of the world finds its foods in supermarkets – and that Whole Foods is contributing to this global transformation. But to change the way the world eats requires not just a commitment to providing local foods,[47] but also the empowerment of society's poorest members to be able to afford to eat differently. Whole Foods, otherwise known as 'Whole Pay Check', certainly encourages us to pay more for our food, but it's far from clear that the extra charge makes its way to those who need it most. For this to happen would demand a profound and political change all along the food system. And supermarkets simply aren't the venues through which this kind of change can be enacted, no matter how much they claim to be. Few novelties on the shelves demonstrate this better than Fair Trade-branded products.

Fair Trade labels promise that, at a minimum, some farmers get paid a little more than market rates for the produce they grow. Such certification offers a far from guaranteed way for farmers to claw back a margin of dignity and income from a food system that holds them in contempt. This is my view, and the reason that I buy Fair Trade. For others, though, Fair Trade can be much more: a gateway to a new post-capitalist future, in which chains of exploitation have been replaced by bonds of solidarity. It is a future much to be desired. But Fair Trade is unlikely to get us there. Indeed, mounting evidence suggests that Fair Trade is a thin patch on an unsustainable system. Fair Trade turns out to be a way for farmers, hanging on by their fingernails, to be able to hang on a little longer.[48]

In part, the problem lies in the under-representation of farmers on the Fair Trade certification bodies. It is in farmers' names, after all, that Fair Trade exists. Yet they often find themselves outnumbered on the bodies by those who profit most from the labels: distributors and retailers. This might be fixed, and Fair Trade prices might be raised by the orders of magnitude necessary to fund decent wages for all.[49] The problem runs deeper, though, than a systematic flaw in the certification process. The basic price of agricultural goods is low. While Fair Trade raises it slightly, the price is not nearly high enough to sustain, much less develop, communities in the Global South. The process of Fair Trade commodities also encourages monoculture – it sucks farmers and rural economies into a single crop. It hitches the fortunes of vast parts of the world to desires in the Global North. If you can afford it, you can throw a penny or two to the people who grow your brew or the beans for your chocolate bar. But it's still consumer desires, consumer charity and consumer pity that govern the lives, and plantations, of lands far away, with the choices, aspirations, dignity and demands of the Global South still counting for very little. Supermarkets are, after all, the classrooms of modern consumerism. They are the high temples where we learn to forget how things are produced and learn the guilty and addictive pleasures of purchase. They can at best only offer social change as a bauble, dangled in front of the consumer, far from the engines of profit, and exploitation.

The honey trap of ethical consumerism is to think that the only means of communication we have with producers is through the market, and that the only way we can take collective action is to persuade everyone else to shop like us. It alters our relationship to the possibility of social change. It makes us think we are consumers in the great halls of democracy, which we can pluck off the shelves in the shops. But we are not consumers of democracy. We are its proprietors. And democracy happens not merely when we shop, but throughout our lives. The connection between those who eat and those who grow food cannot be measured in terms of brand loyalty points or dollars spent. To short-cut the food system, and to know the people who grow our food, is more than to broker a relationship between buyer and seller. It is to build a human contact that goes beyond a simple transaction and that recognizes certain kinds of commonality, certain kinds of subjugation, and struggles, fights, for an end to the systemic inequalities in power which shape the way rich and poor live today. The food system, as we've seen, creates poverty at the same time as it produces an abundance of food. It fosters hunger and disease through its mechanisms of production and distribution. And it was forged in large measure because of the fear that urban workers and rural peasants would jump out of their social positions. That they would demand equality. The system was designed to siphon wealth from rural areas, with just enough redistributed to keep people quiet. But people acting, en masse, for equality has been the only force that has changed the world.[50] This is what makes food sovereignty far richer, and more enriching, than an ethical form of hedonism for those able to afford it.

It invites us to become fuller and more politically responsible people. It invites us to take specific actions, and to develop compassion for, and solidarity with, a world of people. It invites, for instance a commitment that:

5. *All workers have the right to dignity*. Today's certification systems offer little in the way of worker protection. The best guarantee that workers are being treated as they would like is if they own the company themselves – worker-owned cooperatives are on the rise and offer a fine model of economic democracy.[51] In any event, the history of labour relations suggests that workers' lives have only improved after a great deal of struggle, and after widespread unionization. Concessions have rarely been given

freely. United they have bargained, divided they have begged. To strengthen the bargaining position of farm workers, even in Fair Trade agreements, requires that they be allowed to organize freely and without persecution. Unions have been increasingly broken over the past twenty years, with governments systematically undermining them, in the global North and South, and with free trade agreements locking in their demise. The struggle of workers also points to the need for:

6. *Profound and comprehensive rural change*. Although the poorest people in the world live in rural areas, they get disproportionately less development assistance and investment than the rest of the economy.[52] The nature of that assistance is also tilted in favour of the rich, whether the landlords or the agribusinesses that profit from farmers. The redistribution of resources for the poorest of the poor, including land, has rarely been brokered. The countries that have had recent and systematic land reform (like Japan, South Korea and China) have populations that are significantly better off than similar countries that have concentrated land ownership.[53] But without transformations in education, healthcare, infrastructure and opportunities, land reform on its own will simply result in people selling their land and moving to the city. Comprehensive rural transformation will mean building the kinds of rural areas with economic opportunities and a quality of life to which families will want to move and commit. As the principles of food sovereignty insist, this process is one that should be driven not by technocrats or agribusiness, but by every person equally, with their rights guaranteed. No matter where we choose to live, though, a prerequisite for a more equitable and sustainable food system are:

7. *Living wages for all*. At the moment, good food (not to mention Fair Trade food) is the domain of those able to afford it. It consigns those without income or time to the domain of poor-quality, non-nutritious and unethical food choices. Moving towards a just food system means a commitment to income redistribution so that everyone, and everyone's children, can access good, healthy

food, and have the time, space and resources for all to savour it. This means supporting campaigns for living wages, decent working conditions and dignified work for all. And it means:

8. *Support for a sustainable architecture of food.* Local markets, currencies and CSAs are an important and practical way of wrenching back control of the food system from corporations. But our tastes are driven by the architecture around us, the pace and rhythm of a world of work and leisure that cannot be sustained. One of the deepest and long-term projects of food sovereignty involves addressing our built world. Challenging a local food architecture means rethinking open space, and sprawl. Houses, schools, hospitals, offices and prisons would all have to change.[54] But these would all be ways of:

9. *Snapping the food system's bottleneck.* The companies that benefit most from the food system's inequities are also the companies that are most resistant to its fundamental transformation. The subsidies to agribusiness must, however, end. It doesn't only mean an end to the hand-outs to corporations offered as part of the Farm Bill in the US and Common Agricultural Policy in Europe. It also means cutting off industrial farming from the subsidized carbon that it receives from fossil and biofuels.[55]It means aggressive policing of the monopolies that exploit consumers and producers, and far more aggressive anti-trust legislation. The full costs of the food system's environmental and public health costs ought to be reflected in the price of its output. That means taxing processed food to a level where it reflects the harm it does us and the planet. Some districts and cities are as matters of public health, restricting the ambit of food system corporations. Whether it's a case of removing their products from schools, or banning the harmful additives (as New York has done with transfats), people are succeeding in putting pressure on their governments to curb the power of the agribusiness giants. There is, however, much further to go. For residents of the Global North in particular, that means:

10. *Owning and providing restitution for the injustices of the*

past and present. Few in the Global North have not profited from the exploitation of rural people in the Global South. The British Empire was fed, for instance, by forced international trade in wheat. The plantations that brought sugar and tobacco were engines of slavery. Today, many of those economies send tribute to the Global North in terms of debt repayment. It is time those debts were cancelled, and reparations from the Global North paid to the South. The debt owed by the Global North to the South will need to be paid for quite some time to come. As a result of the North's industrial activity, climate change will affect the planet and it is agriculture in the Global South that will be hardest hit.[56] Further, the lives of farmers in the Global South are made significantly harder by the political manipulation of the food system, with excess crops produced in the Global North dumped at below the cost of production into the economies of the Global South. This, too, must cease. For food sovereignty demands that the rights of people in the Global South be respected no less than those in the North, that those of the poor be respected no less than those of the rich, people of colour no less than whites, women no less than men.

Follow the Leader

> *Brian*: Look, you've got it all wrong! You don't *need* to follow *me*, you don't *need* to follow *anybody*! You've got to think for yourselves! You're all individuals!
> *The Crowd*: Yes! We're all individuals!
> *Brian*: You're all different!
> *The Crowd*: Yes, we *are* all different!
> *Man in crowd*: I'm not ...
> *The Crowd: Shhhh!*
> *Monty Python's Life of Brian*

What's striking about *campesinos'* proposals for food sovereignty is that they mesh so well with what increasing numbers of consumers today want. Everyone wants to be able to eat well, and few want it to happen at the expense of the poor. Via Campesina, turning around the language of the World Trade Organization, says, 'Access to markets? Yes, we want access to our own markets.' One of the members of Via Campesina is the Karnataka State Farmers Association (KRRS). Chukki Nanjundaswamy of the KRRS states their vision simply: 'We have been trying to cut out the middlemen. Our motto is "one rupee more to the producers, one less to the consumer".' The call for food sovereignty pushes for political action to fight the poverty caused by the food system at both ends, rural and urban, in poor neighbourhoods across the planet. For what happens in the fields and in the cities is intimately connected and is, at the end of the day, part of the same problem. One that requires a political solution.

Quite what these politics will look like depends entirely on local conditions and forces, and that *because* it depends on everyone having a say. Food sovereignty implies a diversity of solutions, not a monoculture, not an approach owned and patented by a single corporation. It does not involve a single size fitting all. It is a set of ideas, policies and ways of eating that are sensitive to history, ecology and culture, and that respect human rights. The website for this book, www.stuffedandstarved.org, has suggestions of hundreds of organizations doing great work near you, as well as guides to what's in season and good at your local market. There's no easy answer, but its one of thousands of places to start.

At least now we know what questions to ask not only about the provenance of our food, but about our relationship to it, from the top of the food system hourglass to the bottom. In order to become food sovereign, we can't surrender our thoughts about food to nursery rhymes and fairy tales, nor rely on knee-jerk reasoning to explain hunger and obesity. A commitment to food sovereignty demands we ask about the food system, about seed and the context in which it was grown – was it genetically modified, who owned the land, how are workers treated? We can ask about the resources that made its production possible – where did it come from, how did it get here, how much water was needed to grow it, how much fossil fuel was used in its growing and transport? But we can also ask about our ability to access the food we want – how much time do we have to eat with our families, to cook, how much income would we like to spend on food, what foods would we like to eat but are prevented from eating? And we can ask questions about the international context – what are the conditions in the countries where our food is grown, how much illegitimate debt do they have to service,[57] how free are local people to set their own life courses, how entitled, how do the actions of consumers support or hamper them? These are questions to pose when hearing the news, when challenging elected leaders, when building our own democracies. But whatever the questions, hope for improving the food system lies in the kinds of collective action for alternatives with which the food system is already strewn.

Groups like the Peoples' Grocery and the MST are, at one level, deeply remarkable. They bring together an understanding of injustice in the food system with a deep respect for education, ecology and the politics of the possible. Yet organizations like the MST are a smattering of the myriad organizations that already exist, almost certainly near where you live, remarkable and yet familiar and ordinary organizations, struggling to create a more democratic, sustainable and joyful food system. None of this is easy. But what it has at its core is an understanding of the importance not only of freedom and fraternity, but the third French revolutionary pillar: *equality*.

Struggles are a permanent feature of the food system. There is no epic battle, no final defeat or victory – merely different kinds of skirmish. Movements of the landless and land poor are already imagining and building different ways of eating and being, near and far away. Right beneath our noses, urban gardens are supplying food to the poor, and guerrilla gardeners are expanding our imaginations about what can be grown where.[58] What characterizes all of these fights is that they're fights for space not only to grow and to exchange, but to think independently, and then to act for equality. They are organized collectively. Throughout the food system, everyday heroines and heroes are taking the vital but limited individual choices of conscience or ethical shopping and moving beyond them. And their movements are open to anyone to join.

Terry Baird from the Arizmendi Bakery co-op sees the problem of responsibility and leadership from the retail end: 'The style of baking we do is not that complex – you could pretty much teach it in a day. What we can't teach people is how to be responsible for themselves. People come here because they say, "I don't want a boss." What they don't get is that no one wants to be their boss either.' In the struggle for food sovereignty, there can be no bosses. Just hard, argued, engaged democratic decisions, sometimes right, sometimes wrong. But never lorded over by a leadership, always owned by us, in the social spaces we carve out for ourselves. Social movements have faced this challenge too. The working-class slogan 'Neither God nor Master' has in Millau, the home of José Bové, been embellished: 'Ni Dieu, ni Maître, ni José Bové' – Neither God, nor Master, nor José Bové.[59] No prophets or leaders or supermarket offers can make us own the choices and system to which we are party. We either own it by action or are implicated by indifference. Either way, we're part of it.

Organizing, of the kind demonstrated by these movements, offers the road to a deeper choice than we have known. Reclaiming the food system, reclaiming our choices, isn't something to be done individually. The way we become singular is plural.[60] That means coming together locally, regionally and internationally, to better understand the choices we make and the food we eat in the places we make them. As the MST put it, 'Against barbarism, education. Against individualism, solidarity'. It is time to organize, educate, savour, reclaim and build anew.

Notes

Preface to the Second Edition

1   FAO, 2006a.
2   Estimates vary between 1.3 billion Brinkman et al., 2010. and 925 billion FAO, 2011a.
3   Latest data at http://faostat.fao.org
4   Lobell, Schlenker, and Costa-Roberts, 2011.
5   United States Bureau of Labor Statistics. [accessed October 20 2011] http://www.bls.gov
6   Ghosh, 2010.
7   Tang and Xiong, 2011.
8   Masters, 2009.
9   UNCTAD, 2011.
10 Bush, 2008b.
11 Mitchell, 2008.
12 Angus and Butler, 2011.
13 Bush, 2008a.
14 Farrell and Beinhocker, 2007.
15 WorldWatch Institute data.
16 Prabhu, 2007.
17 Childs and Kiawu, 2009.
18 http://www.fao.org/economic/est/est-commodities/rice/en/
19 Lex, 2011.
20 Patel, 2010.
21 World Summit on Food Security, 2009.
22 Navdanya and Navdanya International, International Commission on the Future of Food and Agriculture, and The Center for Food Safety, 2011.
23 Vidal, 2011.
24 World Bank, 2010a.
25 LaSalle and Hepperly, 2008.
26 See the work of the current UN Special Rapporteur on the Right to Food, Olivier de Schutter, for more. www.srfood.org
27 WHO, 2011.

28   IAASTD, 2008.
29   Pretty, Morison, and Hine, 2003.
30   Holt-Giménez and Patel, 2009.

Introduction

1   The Food and Agricultural Organization of the United Nations put the global number of malnourished people at around 925 billion in September 2010 FAO, 2010. Since then, the recession has deepened and food prices have increased, and the World Bank has increased its estimates of the number of hungry people, and as this edition goes to press, there are few reasons to contradict the World Bank's view that both high food prices and high levels of hunger will be with us for "years to come" FAO, 2010.

2   WHO, 2011.
3   Patnaik, 2007b.
4   Gale, 2010.
5   Nord et al., 2010.
6   World Bank, 2011b.
7   Following the global recession, World Bank data show a rise in the number of people living at or below $1.25/day from 2006 to 2008, the latest available year.
8   Bonvecchio et al., 2009.
9   Sawaya et al. 1995; Hoffman et al. 2000.
10   Olshansky et al. 2005 – though see Oliver 2005, and discussion in chapter 9
11   Wang et al., 2008.
12   WHO, 2011.
13   *Which?*, 2006.
14   Harvard School of Public Health, 2011.
15   Centre, 2010.
16   This is a term much to be preferred to 'Third World' or to the depoliticized 'developing countries', and certainly better than the increasingly out of date division of the world into 'the West' and everyone else.
17   Gresser and Tickell 2002: 6.
18   Gresser and Tickell 2002: 22.
19   Gresser and Tickell 2002: 23
20   Seager 2006. Klein 2000 has made public the ruthlessness of their marketing practices.
21   USDA, 2009b.
22   ETC Group, 2008.

23 ETC Group, 2008.
24 World Bank, 2011a.
25 Markets and Markets, 2011.
26 Salzman, 2009.
27 Marion Nestle's 2002 guide to food politics is an indispensable introduction to capital and the food industry. For more on the myth of food scarcity, see Lappé and Collins 1977.
28 On export credit agencies, see, e.g., Goldzimmer 2003.
29 Lenin 1970: 75.
30 I'm grateful to Kolya Abramsky for reminding me that Via Campesina isn't the first international farmers' movement. The Krestintern was created by the Communist International in 1923.
31 Rosset and Martinez 2005, http://www.viacampesina.org/en/index. php?Itemid=44 accessed 28 August 2011.
32 These are important differences, but this isn't a book that can cover them. See, though, Bundy 1979; Chari 2004; Brass 2000; Agarwal 1994 for four very different examinations of the consequences of these differences, in Asia, Latin America and South Africa.
33 *Cincinnati Enquirer* 2005. See also Flanagan and Inoyue 2006. Note that it took more than a decade – and the election of an African American president – for many farmers in the class action to see any restitution at all.
34 Unlike other international reconstruction efforts, which effectively took over the shoreline and deployed international military force to prevent the poor from returning to their homes as the coast was transformed into a tourist resort, La Via Campesina's efforts, funded by movements around the world, actually supported the communities hardest hit. Also Via Campesina 2005; Kar 2005; Rosset and Martinez 2005.
35 Catherine Stock's fine 1996 book presents a good treatment of the contradictions in US rural organizing.
36 Reed 2001.
37 Hall 2005.

Chapter 2

1 Anonymous 2004.
2 Williams 1973
3 There is, of course, a fair history to the writing and rewriting of myths of progress in India. The British Empire, for example, had a well-thumbed anthology of tales about India, and about rural India in particular. These legends were told in the Victorian Parliament and in the press, lauding Britain's

civilizing mission in the colonies, weaving together myths of progress, of technology and of a stable future. These were bundled in a firm compassion that enabled the Queen's envoys to enforce these gifts on a backward country, whether it was ready for them or not. The romances spun by the government, its writers, its civil servants, and – new on the scene – its economists, were rather at odds with the reality of colonialism, and the battles being fought against it.

When the Indian Prime Minister, Manmohan Singh, visited the UK recently, he put his seal on a new version of history, saying

> There is no doubt that our grievances against the British Empire had a sound basis for, as the painstaking statistical work of the Cambridge historian Angus Maddison has shown, India's share of world income collapsed from 22.6 per cent in 1700, almost equal to Europe's share of 23.3 per cent at that time, to as low as 3.8 per cent in 1952. Indeed, at the beginning of the twentieth century, 'the brightest jewel in the British Crown' was the poorest country in the world. (Singh 2005)

The battle against historical revisionism – the sanitizing of British colonial exploits in India, for example – is ongoing. See, for example, Gopal 2006 on Ferguson 2004. 4 EIU 2005. 5 On the travails of the call centre, see Anant 2005.

4   Agarwal, 2011; Hyderabad.co.in, 2008. In 2008 the population of Hyderabad surpassed 8 million people. Agarwal writes that the official number of people in slums has plummeted, yet also warns that there may be a severe undercount of slums, because official counts only include, on average, 49.7% of actual informal and illegal settlements.

5   See the Hyderabad Municipality's own data at: http://www.ourmch.com/cdp/.

6   Names have been changed.

7   'The Food and Agriculture Organisation of the UN FAO recommends that WHO Ia [in which phorate is classed] and Ib pesticides should not be used in developing countries, and if possible class II should also be avoided' (MARI, CSA and CWS 2005: 15).

8   PAN, 2010.

9   Commission on Farmers' Welfare 2005: 80.

10   Patnaik 2005. Patnaik also notes that the total number of suicides up to 2004 is over 5,000 (data from police records up to 27 January 2002, presented by Kisan Sabha at a symposium on farmer suicides held at Hyderabad Andhra Pradesh, 3 February 2002 and attended by the author). The table has been partially updated by incorporating information for the entire year 2002, so

far available only for the districts of Warangal, Karimnagar and Nizamabad as reported in The Hindu, Hyderabad edition, 6 January 2003. For the other districts the figures given in the last column continue to refer to a single month, January 2002. Additional suicides numbering 1700 have taken place since then, for which the district break-up is not yet available (Patnaik 2003: 31). For more recent information, see Center for Human Rights and Global Justice, 2011..

11   Mohanty 2005.
12   UNDP India 2004: 42.
13   Kaur, 2010..
14   Devinder Sharma, personal communication, 25 August 2005.
15   *India Today*, 29 November 2004, New Delhi, available at: http://www.undp.org.in/hdrc/pc/Dec03/GreenRevolution.pdf.
16   Sainath, 2010..
17   Center for Human Rights and Global Justice, 2011..
18   Bunsha 2006. See also www.dsharma.org for more.
19   Phillips, Li and Zhang 2002.
20   Phillips et al. 2002.
21   Zhang et al., 2009.
22   Qin and Mortensen 2001.
23   Middleton et al. 2003: 1183.
24   BBC News 2003.
25   Meltzer et al., 2008.
26   Schneider 1987.
27   Fraser et al. 2005 presents a solid literature review.
28   Schneider 1987; Week in Review Desk 1985. Also Thompson and McCubbin 1987; Goodman and Redclift 1989; Buttel 1989.
29   Gallagher and Delworth 2003.
30   Housing Assistance Council, 2006.
31   Center for Rural Affairs, newsletters, various issues, available at http://www.cfra.org/. Egan 2002.
32   US Census Bureau 2010
33   I'm grateful to Sajja Srinivas for accompanying me here. His work, together with Vinod Jairath, on the way in which the British Department for International Development is mangling the water supply in this area will be well worth reading.
34   Sainath 2005b.
35   Sainath 1996: x.
36   Patnaik 2005.
37   Patnaik, 2010.
38   The Bank did not return calls or emails concerning its methodology for this research project.

39   Patnaik, 2007a.

40   Steinbeck 2002: 31–2.

41   Ravi Shankar and Maraty, 2009..

42   Ravi Shankar and Maraty, 2009..

43   Commission on Farmers' Welfare 2005: 8.

44   Commission on Farmers' Welfare 2005: 5.

45   Dogra, 2008.

46   United Nations, Department of Economic and Social Affairs 2005 on the cur-
     rentstate of global inequality.

47   Patnaik 2005.

48   The full text of this is available at www.stuffedandstarved.org.

49   According to Kang Ki Kab, Member of the National Assembly, Republic of
     Korea, who was at Lee's side at the time he died.

50   AFP 2003.

51   Watts 2003.

52   Ibid.

53   For those who have read the excellent *Omnivore's Dilemma* (Pollan 2006a),
     this is the same George Naylor. On the NFFC and Via Campesina, see Desma-
     rais 2002, 2003; Borras 2004.

54   George Naylor, untitled speech presented at the Asociación Nacional de
     Empresas Comercializadoras de Productores del Campo Conference, Mex-
     ico City, Mexico, 5 December 2000. Online at http://www.nffc.net/comm3.
     htm.

55   Malcolm 1985.

56   Friedman 1999.

57   FIAN 2006.

58   Ibid., and for South Africa see, e.g., http://www.landaction.org/display.
     php?article=217.

59   Some have argued that the violence in rural areas is actually an integral part
     of state policy, indistinguishable from the economics of agricultural change.
     The violence encourages the militant and organized rural poor to negotiate
     directly with the government (Sauer 2006).

60   Steinbeck 2002: 38.

61   Young-rae 2003.

62   And feel free to criticize them. I find his worry about 'too many people', for
     instance, objectionable.

Chapter 3

1   This is an appropriate metaphor – the foundations of neoclassical economics

are, after all, to be found in the mathematics of nineteenth-century high-energy physics, as applied to the world of production.

2   For some, NAFTA, on balance, hasn't been a disaster. In its report on NAF-TA's success, the World Bank suggested that NAFTA increased Mexico's economic growth rate by 0.5–0.7 percentage points (Lederman, Maloney and Servén 2003). It was a conclusion they were forced to modify downward, and which shouldn't, really, be there at all (Weisbrot, Rosnick and Baker 2004). In fact, the trends in the Mexican economy seem, at a general level, to have been exaggerated. NAFTA didn't deliver on its promises and clearly had an effect on the lives of rural communities, but the question is whether NAFTA was solely and exclusively to blame. See also Pacheco-Lopez 2005.

3   See Nadal 2000.

4   Nadal 2000: 31.

5   Mohanty, 2008.

6   Mohanty, 2008.

7   See table 2.6 in Nadal 2000.

8   The difference was made up through government payments to US farmers, who, as we shall see in the next chapter, are also struggling to survive.

9   Boyce 1999: 7.

10 For which President Clinton in the end offered a $50 billion bail-out. See Congressional Budget Office 2003 for a discussion on whether the crisis was caused by NAFTA. It likely wasn't.

11 At the point where marginal cost equals marginal price.

12 Henriques and Patel 2003.

13 Fiess and Lederman 2004: 2.

14 Puentes-Rosas, López-Nieto and Martínez-Monroy 2004, though see Borges et al. 1996 for slightly different figures. The rate is low compared to, say, India. In India, in 1990, the rates for men were 10.5, and for women 7.3 per 100,000. By 1998, India s was over 10 per 100,000 and climbing (WHO 2004).

15 Duran-Nah and Colli-Quintal 2000.

16 Instituto Nacional de Estadìstica, 2005.

17 For an overview, see Hanson 2003.

18 Agriculture is, in the words of Peter Rosset, different (Rosset 2006a).

19 The phrase is Schumpeter's (Schumpeter 1950).

20 See, e.g., Förster and Pearson 2002; Mann and Riley 2007.

21 United Nations 2005. In the US, Kennedy-era 'Trade Adjustment Assistance', designed to soften the blow of free-trade-related job losses, has come under repeated attack for being ineffective and inefficient. Most recently, see Beattie 2006.

22 As Amartya Sen notes:

The central issue of contention is not globalization itself, nor is it the use of the market as an institution, but the inequity in the overall balance of institutional arrangements – which produces very unequal sharing of the benefits of globalization. The question is not just whether the poor, too, gain something from globalization, but whether they get a fair share and a fair opportunity. There is an urgent need for reforming institutional arrangements – in addition to national ones – in order to overcome both the errors of omission and those of commission that tend to give the poor across the world such limited opportunities. (Sen 2002)

23 Not lime as in gin and tonic, but lime as in limelight – slaked calcium oxide.

24 When they took corn back with them from the New World, Europeans didn't know how to cook it properly. The result was that populations dependent on corn as a staple were prone to Pellagra – a disease of niacin deficiency. The disease remains a problem when corn is dropped into populations where it is the only thing available to eat, and with already-low levels of nutrition: refugees (WHO 2000).

25 Nadal and Wise 2004: 38.

26 Frontera NorteSur, 2011.

27 Hoover's Inc., 2011c.

28 In 2004 according to the company's reports.

29 Nadal and Wise 2004: 38.

30 For more on the long history of international agribusiness in Mexico see Barkin 1987.

31 Labor Council for Latin American Advancement and Public Citizen's Global Trade Watch 2004.

32 For a better grasp of recent Mexican history as it relates to trade and food, see Babb 2001; Barkin 1987; Fox 1992; Wessman 1984.

33 *The Financial Times* also reported that 'The bank is now working with the government on how to support the agricultural sector if, as is likely, barriers to maize imports are eliminated as part of the North American Free Trade Agreement. The bank will target money – and advice – on improving the quality of land through irrigation, while simultaneously offering income supports to the hardest-hit farmers' (Fraser 1992). This income support never materialized.

34 Kelly 2001: 90.

35 Lustig 1996, cited in Kelly 2001.

36 Schaeffer 1995: 256.

37 Barkin 1987. See also the overview in Wessman 1984 for perspectives on this.

38 At the end of a short-lived but effective series of food policy interventions. As Fox (1992) chronicles, the areas recording the best outcomes were ones in which policy structures were open-ended, and where peasants were able successfully to challenge rural power blocs. Under that 'ethics of urgency' (Žižek 2006), the needs of the rural majority became an impediment to

a broader, *national*, effort. In other words, in order to save the nation, its poorest members were shouldered with the largest burden. This, incidentally, isn't a uniquely Mexican phenomenon. It is global. For more on Brazil, for example, see chapter 7. For more on South Africa, see Bond 2000, Marais 2000; on India, Müller and Patel 2004; on Colombia, Mondragón 2000.

39   Babb 2001: 175.

40   Lasala Blanco 2003.

41   See the fine Babb 2001 for much more.

42   The policies of development adapted through the 1970s to 1990s didn't have to suffer the indignity of debate. As Babb notes: 'this trend has occurred in societies where a significant proportion of the population is illiterate (13 per cent in Mexico) ... the power of Mexican technocracy most assuredly does not derive from popular belief in the expertise of foreign trained economists' (Babb 2001: 20).

43   NAFTA, Annex 302.2 in Schedule of Mexico, tariff item 0713.33.02., cited in Nadal 2000: 27.

44   'That's what's so hard to explain,' says Ana De Ita, an analyst with the Centre for the Study of Change in the Mexican Countryside (CECCAM). 'At least, you can't explain this exclusively on the basis of production. But you can explain it, after the end of the peso crisis, if you look at the corn traders who had moved in. ADM, Cargill, Continental, Corn Products International. They were the ones who governed the maize market. The government counted the interests of farmers at nothing. El Campo No Aguanta Más wanted to re-negotiate this part of the treaty, and especially for tariffs around maize. The government response was 'We're going to put a tariff on white maize.' But white maize is only 8 per cent of the imports – the problem was with yellow maize, and that they didn't touch. And their only reason was to defend the transnationals who were importing maize.'

45   Folgarait 1991.

46   Pérez and Enciso 2003.

47   Fox 1992.

48   Pérez and Enciso 2003.

49   Pérez and Enciso 2003.

50   Neuwirth 2005; Davis 2004; Pithouse 2005; Žižek 2005 provide a good introduction to this topic. On the politics of migration, especially international migration, Saskia Sassen observes: 'refugee policies acknowledge indirectly that U.S. military activities abroad make the U.S. accountable, at least to some degree, for the fate of an ally's displaced people. Refugee entitlements carry such an acknowledgement. One might ask whether people displaced because of commercial developments by US corporations abroad, i.e. large-scale export crops, are entitled to certain indemnities for being forced to become emigrants' (Sassen 1988: 5). Among the pitiful indemnities refugees

receive at the moment is a short course in how to survive American food (Brimacombe 2006).

51 Pérez and Enciso 2003.

52 World Bank, 2010.

53 Cameron and Tomlin, 2000.

54 As Friedman 2004 has observed, the sucking sound can now be heard in Mexico.

55 Davis 2004.

56 Mohapatra, Ratha, and Silwal, 2011.

57 Hall and Patrinos 2005.

58 Lewis 2005:45.

59 Aitoro, 2011.

60 PolitiFact.com, 2010.

61 The Inter-American Commission on Human Rights (2003) reported that over 268 women and girls had been brutally murdered between 1993 and 2003, with more than 250 further persons missing in a border town inflected with epidemic and horrific levels of violence against women, from a range of sources.

62 del Rio-Navarro et al. 2004.

63 del Rio-Navarro et al. 2004. See also Jiménez-Cruz, Bacardí-Gascó, and Spindler 2003.

64 Agriculture and Agri-Food Canada 2005a.

65 Chopra and Darnton-Hill 2004: note 14.

66 Vega, 2010.

67 Hawkes 2006.

68 And, indeed, the continent – see Reardon and Berdegué 2002.

69 Lyons, 2007.

70 Chopra and Darnton-Hill 2004; Reardon and Berdegué 2002. See also Agriculture and Agri-Food Canada 2005b, 2005c.

71 Hawkes 2006.

72 Garcia and Buffa 2006.

73 http://video.google.com/videoplay?docid=818540535102292014.

74 For a historical treatment of financial policy and the effect on farmers in the US, see *The Wizard of Oz*, and then read Rockoff 1990. See also, Susman 1989 more generally.

75 Wikipedia gives a fine thought experiment to understand how petrodollars gave the US a free ride in the 1970s: http://en.wikipedia.org/wiki/Petrodollar_recycling, version dated 29 May 2006.

76 Susman 1989: 297.

77 As much as 40 per cent of loans came from non-farm banks.

78 Schneider 1986.

79 Susman 1989: 300.

80   Malcolm 1985; Schneider 1987; Week in Review Desk 1985. A similar story
     can be told of Mexico. The climb in suicide rates can be traced to this point in
     time. From 1970 to 1994, the rate increased 156 per cent (Borges et al. 1996).
     Mexico's outbreak of obesity, likewise, has been dated to before 1992 (Ar-
     royo et al. 2004). Even the widespread change in eating habits, from beans
     to wheat, has a long pre-NAFTA history. Wheat was the third most widely
     grown crop in Mexico (after corn and cotton) in the 1930s, and Mexico has
     for decades been a recipient of US wheat, as food aid or as cheap bulk com-
     modity (Perkins 1997:112).

81   Buchanan 2003.

82   And man responsible for the phrase 'Soviet Canuckistan' to describe Canada.

83   Buchanan 2003.

84   Center for Immigration Studies 2006. The immigration debate has since
     moved on, and attitudes have changed regarding free trade and its effects.
     In a 2011 Gallup poll,Jones, 2011. only 43% of Americans wanted immigra-
     tion decreased. 35% wanted it kept at current levels, and 18% wanted it
     increased.

85   Mishel, Bernstein and Boushey 2003. There has also been growing income
     equality, and a downward pressure on workers' wages in the United States.

86   LAO 2004. Or possibly the ninth-largest, using the CIA's methodology.

87   Source: US Bureau of Economic Analysis.

88   LAO 2006. Agriculture, 2010a.

89   USDA, 2007a.

90   USDA, 2007b.

91   http://www.ers.usda.gov/statefacts/CA.HTM

92   Agriculture, 2010b..

93   The organic market is also skewed: 1443 farmers together produce the total
     value of organic produce in the state: $149,137,000; 94 per cent is produced
     by just 314 farms.

94   Walker 2004 points this out wonderfully, and his book is highly recom-
     mended.

95   Walker 2004: 66 and passim.

96   Based on US Census 2008 American Community Survey dataset at http://
     www.census.gov.

97   Ahn, Moore, and Parker 2004.

98   According to California's Employment Development Department at http://
     www.labormarketinfo.edd.ca.gov.

99   Rothenberg's 1998 book, always moving, committed and engaged, is a fine
     source through which to follow this up, as is Hurston's 1999, for a fictional-
     ized and profoundly true account of African-American farm worker experi-
     ence in Florida.

100 Bonacich, Appelbaum et al, 2000.

101 Chang 2000.

102 See the 2004 data in ETC Group 2005b. The meatpacking industry has its own fascinating history of migrant labour. See, e.g., Stanley 1994 and of course, Upton Sinclair's *The Jungle* (Sinclair and Eby 2002).

103 Also La Via Campesina member organizations have participated in these mobilizations, such as El Proyecto de los Trabajadores Agricolas Fronterizas (The Border Agricultural Workers Project) in El Paso, Texas. Protests in following years were, however, muted. Díaz and Rodríguez, 2007..

104 McGhee, 2007.

105 Lashus, Loughran, and Candler, 2008.

106 Ferriss, Sandoval and Hembree 1997: 24. See also McWilliams 1936.

107 This quote in Matthiessen 1969: 225–6. Although there's a fair amount of fuss about the New Journalism revolution, McWilliams and Steinbeck have a strong claim to inaugurating that tradition, in the fields of California.

108 In a solidly Californian state, where registered Republicans outnumbered registered Democrats 3-1, Sinclair's candidacy flipped the state on its ear. By the time of the election, there were more registered Democrats than Republicans. California's big businesses lined up against him, raising $10 million to promote his Republican opponent. Louis B. Mayer, of MGM fame, headed a charge which included Southern California Edison, Southern Pacific Railroad, Standard Oil and Pacific Mutual. Media were crucial to the election like never before, with no newspapers endorsing Sinclair at all. Despite intimidation of Democratic voters, an unprecedented publicity blitz and widespread 'red-scare'-mongering, the greatest blow came when President Roosevelt, himself a Democrat, withheld his support from Sinclair's campaign. Sinclair lost the election, gaining 40 per cent of the vote, and retired from politics. The Democrats, however, consolidated their power in the state, winning the next gubernatorial election. See Mitchell 1992.

109 Ferriss, Sandoval and Hembree 1997: 148.

110 Martin 2003.

111 Ahn, Moore, and Parker 2004.

112 Shrek 2005.

113 Find out more at http://www.southcentralfarmers.org.

114 Becerra, Garvey, and Hymon, 2006.

115 See the website of South Central's Farmers at http://www.southcentralfarmers.com/

Chapter 4

1   This doesn't contradict the rise in tortilla prices after NAFTA in chapter 3.

While it's true that trade liberalization is often accompanied by a cut in entitlements for poor citizens and a rise in profits for traders, the history of international food trade has, undeniably, brought many people a historically unparalleled choice of foods.

2   Readman 200: footnote 149.

3   Abu-Lughod 1989.

4   Wood 2000. More generally see Cain and Hopkins 1980.

5   See Sweeney 2004.

6   Zenith International, 2008.

7   Zenith International 2006.

8   Denyer 1893.

9   Mintz 1985: 5–6.

10   Yeomans et al. 2000.

11   For more detail on sugar in tea, see Smith 1992. For more on tea in general, see Ukers 1935.

12   Mintz 1985: 53.

13   Denyer 1893: 38.

14   Men ate the lion's share of proteins and fats, while women were consigned to consume mainly bread and tea. See Oddy 1970.

15   As the doyen of food politics, Sidney Mintz, has observed. And if you only ever read one more book on food, make it Mintz's 1985 *Sweetness and Power*.

16   Denyer 1893: 38.

17   Central to this was the possibility, as sugar prices dropped, for middle-class, and eventually working-class, people to emulate the consumption styles of the aristocracy.

18   Mintz 1985: 137.

19   McCrae 2004. One reviewer, writing from Oxford University, writes that the Temperance movement has yet to have an impact on her workplace, where gin remains a daily fixture.

20   Mintz 1985: 137, footnote 101.

21   McCrae 2004.

22   See e.g. Denyer 1893: 33–4.

23   Labour Research Service, Women on Farms Project and Programme for Land and Agrarian Studies (University of the Western Cape) n.d.

24   Africa wasn't the only source of slaves – similar practices could be found in South Africa, where slaves were brought from Java (now Indonesia) by the Dutch to work in the Cape farms.

25   Talbot 1995.

26   See also Arrighi 1983, Friedland 1994.

27   Friedmann and McMichael 1989.

28   Friedmann 2006.

29   Irwin 1996, McMichael 1992, 1994 more generally.

30   Davis 2001: 297, 9.
31   Beaud 2001: 160.
32   Lenin 1970: 75.
33   It's a fear that persists. It's hard otherwise to explain why, today in the US, at least one in seven union organizers are fired illegally. See Schmitt and Zipperer 2007.
34   It is this observation that gave economics the moniker 'the dismal science'. He was particularly exercised by the consequences of population growth among Britain's working classes, and it was to them that his policy prescriptions were directed. Malthus has been treated somewhat unfairly respect of the reporting of his ideas. Take this oft-quoted passage, from the second edition of his essay:

> Instead of recommending cleanliness to the poor, we should encourage contrary habits. In our towns we should make the streets narrower, crowd more people into the houses, and court the return of the plague. In the country we should build our villages near stagnant pools, and particularly encourage settlements in all marshy and unwholesome situations. But above all, we should reprobate specific remedies for ravaging diseases. (Bk IV, ch. V: Malthus 1993: xix)

While this passage has been used to demonize Malthus, the context in which he wrote it was the presentation of a *reductio ad absurdum* of existing policy towards the encouragement of marriage. Malthus' solution to population, always directed at the poor, wasn't anything as Swiftian as this. Rather, he urged to poor to adopt 'moral restraint' – delaying marriage until they had resources to feed their offspring. And while his desires for a population free of misery were benign, the focus of his moral prescriptions on the poor earned him scorn in literary circles. Percy Bysshe Shelley decried Malthus as the 'apostle of the rich', saying that Malthus' logic licensed the rich to 'add as many mouths to consume the products of the labour of the poor as they please' (Shelley and Rolleston 1920: VII 32–3 cited in Pullen 2001). Byron, in *Don Juan*, wonders:

> "Had Adeline read Malthus? I can't tell; I wish she had: his book's the eleventh commandment, Which says, 'Thou shalt not marry,' unless well: This he (as far as I can understand) meant. 'Tis not my purpose on his views to dwell Nor canvass what so 'eminent a hand' meant; But certes it conducts to lives ascetic, Or turning marriage into arithmetic." Byron 1857: 377

Malthus' greatest achievement, though, was overlooked by the contemporary scions of literature. Coleridge missed it the best, in describing Malthus' essay as '350 pages to prove an axiom! ... a self-evident truth!' (Malthus 1993: xx). While it was self-evident that the poor were hungry, the link between poverty and fertility wasn't obvious at all. Malthus created a science, soon after the French Revolution had shown what hungry and poor people were capable of doing to the rich, around the reproductive lives of the poor. He made it possible to bind together food, sex and death in ways that erase the roots of poverty in politics and history and root it firmly in the untamed and fecund flesh of the destitute.

35 Hobsbawm 1978.

36 Note too that the labour required by the Industrial Revolution had itself been created by changes in rural social relations. English landlords had created the working class, by turning the peasants into people whose only asset was their labour. They had created markets for that labour. They'd seen the productivity of their land soar as a result of shifting from feudal to capitalist relations. See Wood 2000 for more on this. The surplus food produced thus had fuelled the growth of cities, of industry and, ultimately, of changes in society that broke the power of the upper class, by the time of the Great Reform Act of 1832. The landed rich, the men who incubated capitalism, were finally devoured by its new middle classes (Gunn, 2004).

37 See Thompson 1968 for the seminal description of the rise of 'class consciousness' in the Industrial Revolution. See Polanyi 1944 on Speenhamland and the Poor Laws.

38 See Davis 2006 for more etymology.

39 Dickens and Southwick 1996: ch. 2.

40 Roberts 1963, though see Henriques 1968 for a corrective.

41 Feinstein 1998.

42 Nicholas and Oxley 1993: 747–8.

43 Hobsbawm 1978.

44 A book that, according to interviews with Wall Street executives, remains relevant.

45 Marx 1852.

46 Meacham 1972 has a useful discussion on 'the impending sense of doom' and its historiography, though lacking a culturally and psychologically sensitive reading of middle-class fear.

47 James' 1963 treatise on Haiti remains essential reading.

48 Farmer 2006.

49 Davis 2001.

50 Perkins 1997: 127.

51 Even with the political and ideological commitment hardening, and with an ideology in place that offered to do a great deal of the thinking for policy makers, much remained up for grabs. There were wide-ranging struggles

over the instruments and institutions that would deliver on a US-led war with, and on, hunger. Within the US itself, for instance, the 1949 Brannan plan for agriculture, named for the Secretary of State, Charles F. Brannan, generated schisms within the farm lobby that have persisted until today. By proposing that large-scale agriculture receive the same amount of support that an 'efficient family farm' might receive, a wedge was driven between large-scale industrial agriculture and smaller farming operations within the United States. The plan was fiercely opposed by Republicans, on ideological and party-political grounds – with one GOP representative observing ahead of the 1950 congressional elections that 'if the Democrats get it through, they're in for life' (Christenson 1959; Krebs 2000). In the end, it came to naught, in no small part because by targeting farmers, rather than their commodities, the farm support programme proved inadequate to the task of producing the surpluses the government (and agribusinesses) felt were necessary to win the war on Communism.

52   Inaugural Address of Harry S. Truman, 20 January 1949.

53   See the treatment in Esteva 1992, but also Rist 2002; Cowen and Shenton 1996.

54   Friedmann 1982.

55   Indeed, the US government itself admits as much, albeit forty years later. According to the Congressional Budget Office, 'US aid spending has tended to follow the nation's strategic priorities. In the 1940s, Europe received the most US assistance as war-torn European nations rebuilt their national economies and infrastructures. In the 1950s and 1960s, Asian countries— particularly South Korea, Taiwan and South Vietnam—received about half of US bilateral assistance' (Congressional Budget Office 1997).

56   Friedmann 1982: 265.

57   Butz, incidentally, would likely have continued with this brand of folksy wisdom had he not been forced to resign from his post in 1976 after making the following remark: 'I'll tell you what the coloreds want. It's three things: first, a tight pussy; second, loose shoes; and third, a warm place to shit.' The remark wasn't widely publicized, for the sake of propriety, but there's no indication that his racism didn't inflect his policy decisions.

58   This was, in turn, precipitated by the Arab-led OPEC's decision to suspend export of oil to countries that had supported Israel in the Yom Kippur war.

59   United Nations 1974.

60   Although the roles in this oil-for-food programme invert the ones with which we are today more familiar in Iraq, the goals were the same – to secure both a position for the US government in world affairs and inputs for the domestic US economy.

61   And not just in the Global South – the US and Sweden were sterilizing their own populations until the 1970s too, and California is currently mooting

plans to force-sterilize women prison inmates. We're not as far away from these concerns as we might like to think.

62 See Goldzimmer 2003 on Export Credit Agencies.

63 Chang 2002.

64 For more on structural adjustment, debt and neoliberal economic policy see George 1994 and Bello et al. 1999.

65 The US and UK are the most often cited examples, but as Kelsey 1995 notes, the neoliberal experiments were global, and often related to changes in the production of food.

66 Berthelot 2001.

67 It's a course of action that remains contentious, most recently because it has been used by China to win concessions and control resources through lending principally in Africa (Beattie and Yeh 2007).

68 UNCTAD 1996.

69 Countries that have deviated from the constitution have experienced, dramatically and quickly, far better changes in development indicators than those that have toed the line. In the words of then-World Bank President James Wolfensohn, 'Cuba has done a great job on education and health, and it does not embarrass me to admit it' (Lobe 2001). One imagines that it might have embarrassed him just a little, since countries that have ignored international development advice, and especially those that have engaged in redistribution for equality, have seen gains come speedily to the poorest.

Chapter 5

1   Carney 1995.

2   World Bank Independent Evaluation Group, 2007.

3   Arcal and Maetz 2000.

4   McMichael 2006.

5   Cullather and Gleijeses 1999.

6   Muse 2007.

7   While lacking the trappings of a formalized colonial system, the United States enjoyed a similar *de facto* empire. Zinn 2003.

8   See also Enloe 1989 and Friedland 1994: 175, 180. As Dick Walker notes, not all agribusinesses are behemoths (Walker 2004). A longer study would point this out more thoughtfully, but in the meantime, I can't recommend a better introduction than Walker's study of the California agribusiness system, particularly the attention he pays to capital.

9   Carnegie 1903.

10 Krebbs 1999.

11   Murphy 2006.

12   ETC Group 2005a.

13   ETC Group, 2008.

14   ETC Group, 2008.

15   ETC Group, 2008.

16   O'Brien 2006. Jones, 2010.

17   See Lopez et al 2002, and Mamen et al 2004.

18   Taylor 1999.

19   Wise, 2011.

20   See e.g. http://www.publicintegrity.org/lobby/default.aspx for details on
      the revolving door.

21   Fernandez-Cornejo and Schimmelpfennig 2004.

22   Monsanto Inc. 2005.

23   Not that investors can't, at times, be as credulous as the general public. But
      investors can sue.

24   Hoover's Inc., 2011a.

25   Bird 2000.

26   Bird 2000; see also http://www.kzwp.com/lyons/index.htm.

27   After all, food system giants need credit just like small farmers do. It's just
      that they're better able to acquire it than the poor.

28   OpenSecrets.org, 2011.

29   The United States isn't the only country in which this practice happens, of
      course. It happens worldwide, but in many other countries it's illegal, which
      results, incidentally in a curious double standard. When they are caught
      accepting donations from corporations, governments elsewhere are dubbed
      'untransparent' by NGOs in the business of pointing fingers in this way. The
      lesson for the unscrupulous is to legalize and regulate the practices of politi-
      cal graft, rather than outlaw them altogether.

30   Levenstein 1996.

31   Connor 2001, 1997; Lieber 2000. This said, the mind-boggling numbers
      ought not to beguile. While juries can impose fines as high as they can count,
      the actual sums paid in restitution for this kind of corporate crime are a frac-
      tion of the penalty. The US Government Accounting Office puts the fraction
      at around 7 per cent. Mendoza and Sullivan 2006.

32   See also Kneen 1995.

33   Heffernan 2000.

34   Heller 1961.

35   ashington's address available at http://avalon.law.yale.edu/18th_century/
      washing.asp.

36   Lieber 2000.

37   Isikoff 1985. I'm indebted to Bovard's (1995) fine exposé on this matter,
      which I commend to readers, and which has directed me to many of the

journalistic sources on HFCS.

38 Isikoff 1985.

39 Perkins 1997.

40 Pincus 1963.

41 USDA, 2010b.

42 USDA, 2010a.

43 Barnes 1987.

44 This figure has been falling since the early 2000's. Mostly, HFCS ends up in soft drinks, and there has been a marked growth in the market for diet, as opposed to high-sugar, beverages. The consumption of refined sugar has remained stable at around 64 pounds per capita annually since the mid-1980's.

45 USDA, 2011.

46 Hoover's Inc., 2011b; Gill, 2011.

47 Quoted in Bovard 1995.

48 Isikoff 1985.

49 Duara 1996

Chapter 6

1 Jacobs 1890.

2 Crookes 1899: 38 cited in Shapin 2006.

3 Mishra 2006.

4 Rao 2006.

5 Nehru 1984: vol. 4 p.65. See also Tharoor 2003.

6 According to the FAOSTAT database at the Food and Agricultural Organization of the United Nations.

7 Perkins 1997: 175 and Shiva 1989: 55.

8 Perkins 1997: 175.

9 Belair Jr 1965. For more on this thesis and its origins, see the excellent Perkins 1997.

10 Ahlberg 2003. For more on food riots see Walton and Seddon 1994.

11 Time Magazine 1964 cited in Ahlberg 2003: 211.

12 Speech, Orville Freeman, 'Growing Nations, New Markets,' 15 February 1967, Department of Agriculture Administrative History, vol, II, documentary supplement, chapter IV: 5, 19, in Ahlberg 2003: 149.

13 Shiva 1989: 30.

14 Belair Jr 1965.

15 Congressional Record, 89th Congress, 2nd session, 1966, 112, part 16: 21105, in Ahlberg 2003: 138.

16 Cleaver 1972, 1977.

17 Notably the Maoist Naxalites, whose abortive 1967 rural uprising has its legacy in contemporary India.

18 For more on the 'anti-politics of development', of how development transforms political problems into technological ones, see the classic Ferguson 1990.

19 Dharmadhikary, Sheshadri and Rehmat 2005.

20 Shiva 1989: 78.

21 Shiva 1989: 177.

22 Samu, 2009.

23 Samu, 2009.

24 UNDP India 2004: 42.

25 Department of Agriculture, 2011.

26 See http://censusindia.net/; Dharmadhikary, Sheshadri and Rehmat 2005: xvii. Many thanks to Biju Mathew for giving me his copy of this report.

27 Heller 2001.

28 Data following Bajpai 2003.

29 FAO, 2007.

30 http://data.worldbank.org/indicator/SH.STA.STNT.ZS

31 In 2002, 8 per cent of children in China were underweight, not stunted. 21.8 per cent of children under five were stunted – but there is great geographic variation. For example, in Beijing only 7% of children under five were stunted, while in the rural region of Guizhou, 56 per cent of children were stunted. FAO, 2002.

32 Müller and Patel 2004.

33 Nayak 2002.

34 Sharma 1999.

35 See Müller and Patel 2004: 40 for more.

36 Ministry of Finance and Company Affairs – Government of India 2003.

37 Müller and Patel 2004: iii.

38 Sen 1981.

39 Sharma 2005.

40 Reid 2005.

41 Howard 2003.

42 These are a set of rules so contrary to economic good sense that they've even been repudiated by an economic advisor to the US trade team who negotiated the original WTO, Jagdish Bhagwati. See Bhagwati 2004: 182–3.

43 A fuller discussion of intellectual property rights is available at http://stuffedandstarved.org/ip.

44 Slogan: 'Win in the Flat World'. Perhaps they have been reading Thomas Friedman.

45 Kadidal 1997; McGirk 1995.

46 BBC News 2005.

47 Mishra 2006.

48 Mishra 2006.

49 Mishra 2006.

50 Prahalad 2006.

51 In his book, C. K. Prahalad praises, for example, the cause of Hindustan Lever, who, together with the World Bank, are in the business of selling soap to the poor in order to keep them hygienic and healthy. This is a little wishful – the leading proximate cause of ill-health for poor Indians isn't dirty hands, it's the absence of clean water to wash them with. Trouble is, there's very little money to be made in giving water to the poor, as an increasing number of private companies are discovering. See e.g. Vidal 2006.

52 World Health Organization, 2011.

53 Indeed, the Green Revolution has a hand in creating this situation – with its obsession with providing macronutrients recall that its key crops were wheat, rice and maize; crops that had traditionally been sources of micronutrients in local diets were exterminated as 'weeds'.

54 Connor 2006.

55 Centre for Sustainable Agriculture et al. 2006. Note, too, that old Green Revolution crops were themselves the subject of declining yields in some cases. Cassman and Pingali 1995.

56 See Shiva 2006, who also provides a solid critique of surveys carried out in the area claiming the benefits of the crop.

57 Behere and Behere, 2008.

58 Black 2007.

59 Anand 2005.

60 See e.g. Stone 2007, who points out that in Gujarat, farmers are reclaiming the right to experiment with seed, and beginning to re-skill themselves. Crucially, this depends on their own appropriation and innovation of GM technology.

61 Birchall 2005.

62 'The reforms we announce today will speed up and simplify the process of bringing better agricultural products, developed through biotech, to consumers, food processors and farmers,' Mr Quayle told a crowd of executives and reporters in the Indian Treaty Room of the Old Executive Office Building. 'We will ensure that biotech products will receive the same oversight as other products, instead of being hampered by unnecessary regulation' (Vidal 2005).

63 Coons, 2010.

64 Heard et al. 2003; Hawes et al. 2003; Zeki 2003; Perry et al. 2003; Roy et al. 2003; Haughton et al. 2003; Brooks et al. 2003; Firbank 2003; Champion et al. 2003.

65 Soil Association 2003.

66   See Langer 2001.

67   Starkman, 2011.

68   Butler 1769: lines 1278–82.

69   Quist and Chapela 2001; Independent Science Panel et al. 2003; Walsh 2004.

70   Monbiot 2002a, 2002b.

71   Walsh 2004.

72   Walsh 2004.

73   Vidal 2005.

74   Novartis 2005.

75   Press and Washburn 2000. Press and Washburn note that when David Quist
      was invited to an 'open forum' to discuss the agreement between the univer-
      sity and Novartis, Quist took notes which, upon being observed by a mem-
      ber of the University's public relations department, were impounded by the
      dean for several months.

76   Thompson 2000.

77   See also Morales and Verhaag 2004.

78   Smith 2003.

79   Gillis 2003.

80   Sainath 2005a.

81   Or indeed any of the contributors to Hickey and Mittal 2003.

82   Arsenault 2006.

83   CORE 2003.

84   Available at http://www.core-online.org/features/voices_video.htm.

85   See the World Bank data: http://data.worldbank.org/indicator/SP.POP.
      GROW/countries/ZG-ZQ-CF-ZA?display=graph

86   FAO Stat data shows, for example, that consumption of cereals and produce
      per person per day is up by 10 per cent today from 1969–71. Not only are
      more calories available, but those calories come from more protein and fat
      than previously – a sign of an improved diet.

87   See the World Bank data: http://data.worldbank.org/indicator/AG.PRD.
      FOOD.XD/countries/1W-ZG-ZA-ZQ?display=graph

88   See Watts 1983; Scott 1976 for classic studies.

89   SADC-FANR Vulnerability Assessment Committee 2002b.

90   SADC-FANR Vulnerability Assessment Committee 2002a.

91   UNDP 2002.

92   SADC-FANR Vulnerability Assessment Committee 2002c.

93   WFP 2002.

94   Devereux 2002.

95   Jubilee Research 2002.

96   OAU 1981.

97   World Bank 1981.

98   Arrighi 2002.

99   Danaher and Riak 1995.

100 Weiss 2002.

101 Toufe 2002.

102 Nickson 2004.

103 Driessen 2004.

104 My research in Makhathini was conducted with Harald Witt and Matt Sch-
     urr, both of the University of KwaZulu-Natal in 2005. I am grateful to them
     and to the research team of Nonhlanhla Dlamini, Dumisani Nyathi, and
     Aoibheann O'Sullivan for making this collaboration possible.

105 Horsch 2003.

106 Bradbury 2000; Toufe 2002.

107 And this points to the poverty of racial politics in Europe and North America.

108 Thirtle et al. 2003.

109 Greenberg and African Centre for Biosafety 2004 has more on the global
     context of GM cotton.

110 See www.gatesfoundation.org for the foundation's own reporting of its own
     documents.

111 It's worth noting that Microsoft has benefited from the same kind of patent
     protection that keeps the biotech companies in business. Of course, there
     are other solutions for African hunger, just as there are other operating sys-
     tems than Windows. Indeed, one of the most popular alternatives to Win-
     dows even has an African name (though the work of a great deal of inter-
     national collaboration). The Ubuntu operating system is widely regarded
     as one of the most versatile, easy and friendly versions of Unix. It's also free
     and at least a little bit homegrown. But, like the solutions to African hunger,
     the Gates Foundation seems more ready to align with proprietary and more
     expensive solutions.

112 Heim 2006.

113 Vidal, 2010.

114 http://www.nyeleni.org/?lang=en is the website for the 2007 Food Sover-
     eignty conference in Mali at which some of these solutions were discussed.

115 Morgan 2004.

116 For instance: an egg and a steak are sitting in the park. All of a sudden, they
     see a vast crowd running towards them, saliva dripping from their lips. 'Run
     for your life', says the egg. 'Nah, you run,' says the steak. 'They won't even
     recognize me.'

117 Sinclair and Thompson 2001.

118 Rosset and Benjamin 1994.

119 Those who argue that GM is the only way to solve problems in agriculture,
     whether to do with pests, or with the vast amount of fuel needed to sustain
     industrialized agriculture ought to bear this in mind. See e.g. in this ex-
     change Avery et al. 2005; Fedoroff and Brown 2004; Pimentel 2004.

120 Peter Rosset, personal communication, 17 September 2005.
121 Nicholls et al. 2002.
122 Rosset and Benjamin 1994.
123 Though see Funes et al. 2002.
124 Few countries have experienced this to the extent that the US has. Williams 2006 documents and Wilson et al. 2002 offers important insight on racism in the location of these operations.
125 UNDP 2005.
126 Nilda Peres at the University of Havana heads this exciting initiative.
127 Patel 2012.
128 Fukuoka 1978.
129 See Holt-Gimenez 2006.

Chapter 7

1 Dahl 1973: 144.
2 To begin with, we have no idea whether the cocoa in chocolate is produced by child slaves. In Côte d'Ivoire, where just under half the world's cocoa is grown, UNICEF and the US State Department estimated that around 15,000 children were enslaved on farms. In Côte d'Ivoire, according to a report by Global Exchange,

> Ten major exporters, led by US companies Cargill and ADM, control the cocoa sector in the Ivory Coast. The biggest cocoa bean buyer during the 2001/2002 season was the Cargill group, which purchased 13 per cent of the total crop. American rival Archer Daniels Midland ADM was number two, with 10 per cent of the crop, followed by France's Bollore group with eight per cent.

With cocoa prices going through the floor, and yet with cocoa being the primary means of earning foreign exchange, and with the oligopoly on price run by cocoa traders, there's little room for manoeuvre. The squeeze is transmitted through an axle of evil, from the market, through the local employment market, onto the bodies of children in Côte d'Ivoire. The response of the cocoa and chocolate manufacturers association was to develop a 'code of conduct', which, to date, seems not to have been implemented. The issue has fallen out of the media spotlight. And we can return to chomping our chocolate without care (Global Exchange 2005).
3 Greenpeace International 2006.
4 Davidson 1999. Sorosiak 2000 suggests that the word *shoyu* might in turn be

related to the ancient Chinese *sho*.

5   This isn't unique – there are other plants similarly named for their processed yield, such as sugar beet and sugar cane. But it's striking that these plants also occupy a place of near ubiquity in our modern food system.

6   Hymowitz and Shurtleff 2005.

7   Sears 2000.

8   WorldWatch Institute 2006. See also the excellent Greenpeace report (Greenpeace International 2006), which was released as this book was being completed.

9   WWF 2004; Drewnowski 2000. See also www.SoyStats.com/2010

10   Finlay 2004.

11   Stock 1996; Primmer 1939; Gilbert and Howe 1991 on helpful ways of thinking about New Deal agricultural policies.

12   Windish 1981: 98. Windish has the date as 1938, Finlay as 1935.

13   Windish 1981: 31.

14   For its seventy-fifth anniversary celebrations, the Ford Motor Company released a publication entitled *Henry Ford and the Beanstalk*. See also Lewis 1995.

15   Windish 1981:32.

16   The industrial uses of soy were limited, though they owed much to the post-WWI settlement, in which the US appropriated German industrial patents as part of its reparations. Soy was important in Manchuria because of its industrial uses (Deasy 1939).

17   Finlay 2004.

18   Munn 1950: 223–4.

19   Josling and Tangerman 2003.

20   Tubiana 1989.

21   One of her followers was John Harvey Kellogg, whose brother, Will Keith, founded the cereal company as a way of encouraging Americans to follow the Seventh Day Adventist health fad.

22   They might take a dim view of soy's post-war culinary success being attributable to its use as a meat-extender in sausages.

23   This was, incidentally, the year after Brazil abolished slavery. See below.

24   Bock 1979; Cowen and Shenton 1996.

25   Frank 1969.

26   de Sousa and Busch 1998.

27   See also Welch 2006.

28   Forman 1971.

29   Forman 1971.

30   de Sousa and Busch 1998.

31   It's not coincidental that the soy boom began in Rio Grande do Sul. The climate there is similar to that of the soy-growing areas of the US, and the

varieties planted there were ones that had been developed for production in the US.

32   Hasse and Bueno 1996: 99.

33   Friedmann and McMichael 1989: 109.

34   And, incidentally, fewer seabirds, and less guano, which was also a major Peruvian export at the time.

35   Warnken 1999.

36   These are season-average data, though. The price in 1972 spiked to $12/bushel.

37   The wheat programme was, however, unsuccessful, and farmers soon turned to year-round soy growth.

38   Hillman and Faminow 1987.

39   de Sousa and Busch 1998.

40   Warnken 1999.

41   See Wittman 2005, especially chapter 1.

42   Helfand 1999.

43   Folha Online 2004.

44   Folha Online 2004.

45   Mccarthy 2005; Lloyd's List 2005.

46   Diaz 2004b; Mccarthy and Buncombe 2005.

47   Mccarthy 2005.

48   Lazzarini and Filho 1997: 22.

49   Diaz 2004a.

50   Thompson 2003.

51   Astor 2003.

52   The price of land has been increasing in Mato Grosso. This has complicated the picture, as Mozambique plans to open up 50-year concessions to Brazilian soy and cotton farmers.

53   Warnken 1999: 35 cited in Cassel and Patel 2003: 26.

54   Mccarthy and Buncombe 2005. It was for his rather cavalier attitude to the deforestation that Greenpeace awarded Maggi the Golden Chainsaw award. According to Greenpeace, he refused to accept it when ambushed at a school and ducked out the back, to chants of 'Maggi, Maggi, accept it, accept it'. Maggi has since arrested eighty-four people on charges of illegal logging, including his environment secretary. Despite this, there's a strong local, and international, feeling that Maggi is the architect behind illegal logging in the state and surrounds (Blount and Tornaghi 2005).

55   It's important, too, not to take these figures at face value. They themselves constitute an intervention in an ongoing debate between the US and Brazil, in which the goings-on in Mato Grosso have, to a greater or lesser extent in the US, come to epitomize the predations of the entire industry.

56   The system of agriculture which soy supports also affects water quality in

Europe. Because of the tilt towards importing cheap animal feed from Brazil, European livestock farming has become more intensive, resulting in a range of environmental problems linked to animal waste (Chapecó Declaration 2005).

57 Greenpeace International 2006.

58 Fearnside 2001.

59 We might also want to be a little sceptical about the statistics. The Brazilian government claims that 16 per cent of the Amazon is occupied. But a recent study suggests that the figure is closer to 50 per cent. Similar errors might apply elsewhere (Hay 2004, and more recently Barreto et al. 2005).

60 Kamalurre Mehinaku 2006.

61 In more recent years, Blairo Maggi has begun to work with various environmental groups. He sees emerging carbon markets as a profitable use of conserved Amazonian forests in Matto Grosso, saying that if Reduced Emissions from Deforestation and Forest Degradation (REDD) trading is allowed in Brazil, it will be "much much more profitable than soybeans." As of 2011, the program has yet to be fully established.

62 This is an awkward term, especially in the Brazilian context. The burdens facing indigenous people are different from those facing, for example, Afro-Brazilians, and, especially in a country so vast, there are considerable variations in the shape and structure of racism. On some of this complexity, see Harris 1956, kindly recommended to me by Angus Wright.

63 Cassel and Patel 2003, passim.

64 Reporter Brazil, 2009.

65 Cassel and Patel 2003, passim.

66 Hall 2004.

67 SAPA/AFP 2004.

68 ILO 2004: 16.

69 *The Economist* 2005b.

70 Lilley 2004.

71 SAPA/AFP 2004.

72 And, as Peine astutely notes, vice versa – the environmental movement plays an important role in the imagination of Brazilian soy producers.

73 http://www.organicconsumers.org/corp/veneman.cfm.

74 I search hard for a *reductio ad absurdum* here, but toe-curling conflicts of interest seem increasingly to be a prerequisite for senior positions in the White House.

75 A similar situation prevails in Brazil.

76 House Committee on Agriculture, 2011.

77 Memarsadeghi and Patel 2003.

78 *Farm Subsidies Database*, Environmental Working Group. Online at http://www.ewg.org/farm/, cited in Memarsadeghi and Patel 2003. The new farm

bill has yet to run its course, so full-term averages aren't yet computable.

79   Poulin 2003 and see, in a different industry but similar pattern, Bacheva, Kochladze, and Dennis 2006.

80   Greenpeace International 2006.

81   Emelie Peine, personal communication, 5 July 2005.

82   American Soybean Association 2004.

83   Delta Farm Press 2004. Across a range of industries in the farm sector, one can find vast industry-sponsored farming organizations ranged against smaller, but more independent, organizations. Compare, for example, the tensions between the National Cattlemen's Beef Association and Ranchers-Cattlemen Action Legal Fund (R-CALF); the American Farm Bureau Federation and the National Farmers' Union; and the National Corn Growers Association and the American Corn Growers Association. The former of these pairings are large, usually pro-free trade and have stronger connections to industry than their smaller, less well-funded and protectionist opponents. See Dreibus 2005 for more.

84   Buanain and Silveira 2002 see also discussion in Cassel and Patel 2003: 32.

85   Jaccoud, Lemos de Sá and Richardson 2003.

86   GRR 2004.

87   McMichael 2003. See also discussion Wittman 2005: 44.

88   Martins 2006.

89   Martins 2006; Wright and Wolford 2003; Harnecker 2003.

90   As Wittman 2005 notes, while these statistics are cited for the entire country, the movement has an uneven coverage across the country, and uneven successes as it experiments against the different geographies, histories and concerns of communities in different areas.

91   Sauer 2006.

92   http://www.mstbrazil.org/?q=node/86. Wittman goes on to note that:

Lula promised to re-settle 400,000 families during his first term and regularize the land tenure situation of another 130,000. The numbers of families actually settled so far are much less than expected. In 2003, not even 30,000 were settled of the proposed 115,000 families, and between January and December 2004 the government expropriated only enough land to settle 25,000 families, although they insist that they settled more than 68,000 out of the 115,000 planned for 2004. (Wittman 2005)

93   Wright and Wolford 2003; Harnecker 2003.

94   Wittman 2005. I'm tremendously grateful to Hannah Wittman, not only for pointing me in the right direction on many occasions, but for brokering the introduction to the settlement.

95   Brazilian land law is based on the Napoleonic code, not English law. Within

this lies a crucial difference. Under Napoleonic law, land is considered to have a social value, one that is lost to society if the landowner underutilizes, or does not use, the land. Although, under World Bank supervision (Sauer 2006; Borras 2003), the Brazilian government has tried to shift customs of land ownership towards the English model, important rights still remain, even if these rights are often obstructed or suppressed.

96   Wittman 2005: 106. 93 MST-MT Caderno do Núcleo No. 9, Julho de 2002, Cuiabá – MT and Caderno de Núcleo no. 11,Outubro 2002. cited in Wittman 2005: footnote 88.

97   MST-MT *Caderno do Núcleo* No. 9, Julho de 2002, Cuiabá – MT and *Caderno de Núcleo no. 11, Outubro* 2002. cited in Wittman 2005: footnote 88.

98   Heredia et al. 2006.

99   Heller 2001.

100   Wright and Wolford 2003: 48.

101   Friends of the MST 2006b.

102   Lloyd's List 2005.

103   Wright and Wolford 2003; Harnecker 2003.

104   Wright and Wolford 2003; Harnecker 2003; Sauer 2006; Martins 2006; Rosset 2006b.

105   For more on ecological citizenship in Brazil, see Wittman 2005.

106   Friends of the MST 2006a.

107   See Greenpeace International 2006.

108   Vomhof Jr 2005.

109   PR Newswire, 2010.

110   Gardner and Halweil 2000 cited in Chopra and Darnton-Hill 2004.

Chapter 8

1   Nemerov 1967. I am indebted to Mintz 1995 for finding this poem.

2   Mathews 1996.

3   Or possibly 9 September, depending on the source: see Mathews 1996, Urbanski 2002.

4   Saunders 1917.

5   Terdiman 1985, observes the origins of consumerism in the department stores of France, and Benjamin's *Arcades Project* is a singularly important work for those wanting to know more (Benjamin and Tiedemann 1999). Saunders' innovation in grocery retailing lies both in its targeting of working people and, unlike department stores, in the way in which the environment was configured so directly to make shoppers look at everything on display.

6   Humphery 1998: 60 – thanks to Rachel Schwartz for pointing this out.

7   Bakan 2004.
8   Strauss 1924.
9   Perhaps its closest modern-day descendent is online shopping.
10   *The Economist* 1978.
11   Ginsberg's *A Supermarket in California* is the poem that best captures this mood. Ginsberg 2001.
12   As readers of Foucault will appreciate, schools and prisons and barracks are spaces which are also monitored. But none are grounds of such rapid and concentrated surveillance while, at the same time, so successfully conferring the illusion of liberty.
13   Herrington 1996.
14   Lowrey, 2008.
15   Bellizzi and Hite 1992.
16   Ibid.; Crowley 1993.
17   Bellizzi, Crowley, and Hasty 1983; Crowley, 1993.
18   Bellizzi, Crowley, and Hasty, 1983. Turley and Milliman 2000: 196.
19   Lowrey, 2008.
20   Kreidler and Joseph-Mathews, 2009.
21   See also, *The Economist* 2005c. Michon, Chebat and Turley 2005; Koch and Koch 2003; Caldwell and Hibbert 2002; Mattila and Wirtz 2001; Chebat, Vaillant and Gelinas-Chebat 2000; Yalch and Spangenberg 2000; Turley and Milliman 2000.
22   Donate at www.eff.org – they're good people doing important work.
23   For more, see: http://www.computerbytesman.com/privacy/safewaycard.htm.
24   Evans 1999. Of course, all this information doesn't come without its ethical trouble. Consider the case of Mrs 'Brown', a woman who has young children because she buys nappies, who spends £90 on a single weekly Friday visit to the supermarket, when she also buys two bottles of gin. Mitchell 1996 in Evans 1999.
25   The real logical conclusion is to dispense with the store itself and have you shop online.
26   Seideman 1994.
27   Gillette is looking to protect its razor blades through this kind of technology.
28   Larson, Bradlow and Fader 2005. I am grateful to Alison Bing for bringing this to my attention.
29   Of course, the self-service revolution didn't extinguish these roles overnight, and the Great Depression saw a return for some of these roles, particularly the need for credit (Lentz 1989).
30   Walmart, 2011., Perry, 2011.
31   *The Economist* 2001.
32   Job creation at Walmart has generally been decreasing. http://walmartstores.

com/pressroom/news/9182.aspx

33   In 2007, $188 million was awarded to workers in Pennsylvania. In 2008, $54.25 million was awarded to 100,000 current and former employees in Minnesota who did not receive pay for missed breaks and off-the-clock work. The same year, Walmart settled a US$352 million lawsuit, consisting of 63 cases in 42 states, for forcing employees to work off the clock. In 2010, Walmart settled a suit by agreeing to pay US$86 million for failing to pay thousands of workers during paid vacation, overtime, and other wages in California.

34   Rudnitsky 1982.

35   Walmart, 2011.

36   Wal-Mart 2005.

37   'Associate' is the term Walmart prefers to 'employee', but there isn't a strong reason to dignify this obfuscatory and disingenuous term with repetition.

38   This anecdote is recounted in Sam Walton's autobiography. For critique, see also Frank 2006.

39   According to the industry intelligence company Planet Retail. http://www.planetretail.net/default.asp?PageID=EAlert&Article=45027&Date=2006-02-10.

40   According to Walmart's own 2010 corporate factsheet.

41   Greenhouse 2004 in Miller 2004.

42   *The Economist* 2001.

43   Even after Walmart (previously Wal-Mart) dropped the hyphen in 2008, they kept "gimmy a squiggly" in their morning cheer because saying 'squiggly' raised worker's spirits.

44   Miller 2004.

45   Greenhouse 2005.

46   Featherstone 2003.

47   Vicini, 2011; Totenberg, 2011.. It is, and I feel silly for having to point this out, possible both to be discriminated against and to make it to a management position. The law is, however, an ass Dickens, 1839.

48   Mitchell 2005.

49   Reich 2005.

50   Mitchell 2005.

51   Mattera et al. 2004, Mattera, 2011.

52   Stone 1997; also Goetz and Swaminathan 2004 and Fleming and Goetz, 2011.

53   *Information from 2007 South African Agricultural Census.*

54   Wijeratna 2005: 2.

55   Collins 1995: 224.

56   This workshop facilitated by Nonhlanhla Dlamini on 26 January 2005, and I'm indebted to her for her translation.

57   See Monsalve-Suárez 2006 for more on gender and agrarian politics.

58   Huws 2003.

59   Jiang, 2011.

60   Miller, 2008.

61   See Reardon and Berdegué 2002. Large foreign retailers, like Walmart and Carrefour, have been kept out of India. They have been lobbying for entry, and at time of publication, there is rumor that this ban may soon end. Indian merchants suggest that such stores would have to drastically change their layout and selling models to adapt to weak infrastructure. Nelson, 2011.

62   Johnson 2007.

63   Carrefour Group, 2010.

64   Kamath and Godin 2001.

65   Carrefour Group, 2010.

66   See the 2011 Indian census: http://indiafacts.in/india-census-2011

67   Reardon and Berdegué 2002.

68   Gorton, Sauer, and Supatpongkul, 2011; Uncles and Kwok, 2009; Market Research, 2011.

69   Sheehan and Newman 2002.

70   This also has strong impacts on the links between obesity and household location. One study in Michigan found that obesity was up to 9 per cent higher in rural than urban children. See Jensen et al. 2006. Note that the USDA sanctified food deserts as an operating term in 2009 USDA, 2009a. 'Food deserts' is an unlovely phrase, not least because it suggests that there's no food at all to be found in these areas, rather than recognizing that food is available and that people fight back as best they can against the widely available processed and unhealthy food that siphons cash out of communities, exploiting at the same time as it fills bellies.

71   Caplovitz 1964. See also Kolodinsky and Cranwell 2000.

72   The Economist 1992.

73   Kane 1984 in Eisenhauer 2001:130.

74   The Economist 1992.

75   Morland, Diez Roux and Wing 2006.

76   Cummins and Macintyre 2006. Corroborated in three studies cited by Sallis and Glanz 2006. Booth, Pinkston and Carlos Poston 2005 have a comprehensive review of the literature to date.

77   United States Department of Agriculture 2000.

78   The Economist 2005a.

79   This applies more generally to debates around 'standards'. For more, see Friedmann 2005b.

80   Stagl 2002.

81   See, more widely, Richard Manning's excellent 2004a book.

82   See Gibson-Graham 2003.

83   Sperry 1985. Central to the programme, as Sperry notes, is the education of

girls, a realization that has dawned much more slowly in the world of development professionals.

84 Certainly, there are some places where markets are inappropriate – every proponent of markets can admit that. And markets in land, particularly in the Global South, are contenders for strong circumscription of market forces. See Borras 2003 and Courville, Patel and Rosset 2006b more generally for a range of reasons why.

85 Walmart's own corporate fact sheet states that the average full-time horly wage for Walmart associates is $11.75. Since Walmart everyone is an "associate" at Walmart, including CEO Mike Duke who in 2010 received US$18.7 million (1,201 times the annual income of the average sales associate), the mean wage is higher than the median wage. See http://walmartwatch.org/get-the-facts/fact-sheet-wages/ for more information.

86 See: http://walmartwatch.org/get-the-facts/fact-sheet-health-care/ for more.

87 Data from the People's Grocery.

88 It's a contradiction. But remember that the aim here is not to get local fresh food instead of supermarketed food – the challenge is to get any kind of fresh food at all into West Oakland.

89 Leather 1996. For more on the Black Panthers in Oakland, see Patel 2011.

Chapter 9

1 I'm grateful to Mintz 1985 for reminding me.

2 Omahen 2003.

3 The war in Iraq has led to 600,000 excess deaths (Burnham et al. 2006), up from the 100,000 estimate in 2004 (Roberts et al. 2004). See also Smith Fawzi et al. 1997. Note, too, that fast food has, through its wrapping, provided soldiers in Iraq with that rarest of commodities – stationery upon which to write home (Valerie 2003). It's a choice that the manufacturers never intended.

4 Menzies 2002, Chenoweth 1996–9: 113 – I am grateful to David Szanton for bringing this to my attention.

5 Lind 1753: 192–3.

6 OED 1992.

7 Thompson and Cowan 1995: 41.

8 Nasrallah 2003.

9 Thompson and Cowan 1995: 42.

10 Brillat-Savarin, author of the definitive book on taste in 1825, would not

have approved. His third aphorism: 'The fate of nations depends on what they eat' (Brillat-Savarin 1970 [1825]: 13).

11   Thompson and Cowan 1995: 44.

12   Ibid.: 45.

13   Mintz 1995: 10.

14   Pendergrast 2000: 201. The original story is to be found in Fast 1990, 1960.

15   Labbi 2003. See also PA Newswire 2003; Burger King Corporate Information 2006.

16   Drummond, Wilbraham and Hollingsworth 199; Cannon 2005: 702.

17   Leitzmann and Cannon 2005: 790; McCance and Widdowson 1956.

18   Friedmann 1994: 259.

19   McMichael and Kim 1994: 33.

20   Perkins 1997.

21   Frozen food was far from an instant success. It was hampered by the limited number of freezers and also, for example in Australia, because the US-sized containers wouldn't fit in Australian-sized freezers. Since comparatively few families owned freezers, the majority of frozen meals were sold for consumption on the same day. Groves 2004.

22   Strömberg 2002.

23   Betty Godfrey, 'Kitchen TV a Joy to Housewives', *Australian Home Beautiful* November 1956: 25. Cited in Groves 2004.

24   See Spigel 1992 for more. Incidentally, TV dinners have grown by 150 calories since the 1950s (Anonymous 2003a).

25   Roberts et al. 1999. Some reports, citing A.C. Nielsen data which I have been unable to obtain, have put the figure at nearer two in three US families having dinner in front of the TV.

26   Monbiot 2005a.

27   This in turn was a symptom of British policies of divide and rule, pitting Indians against Africans and engendering persistent racial divisions (Jagarnath 2006), which in turn were resisted through Black Consciousness – see Biko and Stubbs 1978; Biko and Malan 1997.

28   There are a number of other creation myths around bunny chow, with some people dating its origins before apartheid, arguing that it was invented by indentured Indian labourers, who hadn't the time or resources to make their own bread, and so purchased white peoples', before marching off into the fields. Even if this is the case, the argument, that bunny chow was a food born of resistance, oppression and the white domination of space still holds.

29   Depending on what you're after, there are three temples of bunny in Durban – for the traditional vegetarian version in a working-class, multiracial atmosphere, Little Gujerat (sic) on Aliwal Street is the place. For the best chicken bunny, it's Govenders, and for mutton it's Goundens, within a 100 yards of one another in the Glenwood auto-repair district.

30 For more on this, see Counihan and Kaplan 1998; Counihan and Van Esterik 1997.

31 See the WHO country profiles available at http://www.who.int/countries/. While the US and South African levels are very similar, there is a difference in the gender distribution. In the US, 30.2% of males are overweight or obese, and females are only slightly higher at 33.2%. In South Africa, however, obesity and overweight are only present in 23.3% of males, while 42.8% of females are classified as such.

32 Lichtarowicz 2004.

33 Harris 2006.

34 Morland et al. 2002; Booth, Pinkston and Carlos Poston 2005.

35 King et al. 2005: footnote 12.

36 Many commentators have covered this in depth, and for more see Baranowski et al. 2003; Schor 2004; Henderson and Kelly 2005; Wartella 1995.

37 See, e.g., Wartella 1995.

38 And that's not the least of it. See, for an early example, Packard 1957, who describes a 1950s study in which children learn to sing music from beer commercials before they sing 'The Star Spangled Banner'. Children babysat by TV are more likely to come from families of colour, and the poor. But the result holds for all families, rich or poor. More than two hours with the TV on, even if it is not watched, collapses the possibilities for doing other things, increasing the likelihood of obesity. The TV merely needs to be turned on for it to have its effect. In this, the paediatric data is supported in turn by ethnographic study. For more on Sustain, visit http://www.sustainweb.org/. For more on marketing to children, see McGinnis et al. 2006.

39 Luo and Hu, 2002 cited in Cheng 2004.

40 Ji, 2008.

41 Parvanta et al., 2010; Cairns, Angus, and Hastings, 2009.

42 Hoffman et al. 2000.

43 Brownell and Horgen 2004.

44 Segrave 2002.

45 Ellaway, Macintyre and Bonnefoy 2005; King et al. 2005.

46 Powell, Slater and Chaloupka 2004.

47 Krenichyn 2006; Veitch et al. 2006.

48 Lipman 2006; Pendola and Gen 2007; Lopez-Zetina, Lee and Friis 2006; Ong and Blumenberg 1998.

49 Schlosser 2001 covers the impact of fast food wonderfully.

50 Fast food for poor people isn't new (Carlin 1995). See Jackson and Heeps 2006.

51 See Offer 1998, which, frankly, I was disappointed to read, given his superlative work on the Agrarian Interpretation of the First World War (Offer 1991).

52 Olshansky et al. 2005, who cite in support of their case, Oeppen et al. 2002

on life expectancy, Daviglus et al. 2004 on Medicare expenses, and on total costs, Wolf et al. 1998 and Allison et al. 1999.

53 Breslow 2006. To derive his conclusions, he used data from the Metropolitan Life Insurance Company, whose actuaries had a keen interest in the rate of expiry of their clientele. The link between obesity on the one hand and kidney, respiratory, neurological and cardiovascular disease on the other was one that, almost immediately, drew links between morbidity, body size, class and the quality of 'insured lives'.

54 Mokdad et al. 2003.

55 See, e.g. Cheng 2004: 395 for China.

56 This is defined as a body mass index (BMI) of greater than 30, where BMI = weight in kilograms ÷ height in metres 2. Oliver 2005 offers a fine account of the unsavoury and arbitrary history of the BMI.

57 Campos et al. 2006a: 55.

58 Defined as a BMI of 40 or more.

59 Campos et al. 2006a, 2006b; Oliver 2005.

60 If you can get it, do read Saguy and Riley 2005 – it's a fantastic and important dissection of the obesity literature. The authors would do the world a great service by making it freely available.

61 Saguy and Almeling 2005: 28.

62 Obesity in children is more often seen as the fault of a 'bad mother,' rather than a structural issue where the probability of eating well is much less than that of eating poorly. This trope is revealed both when mothers are directly blamed, or when they are quoted as the sole and heroic solution to the obesity 'epidemic.'Rothblum and Solovay, 2009.

63 Critser 2000: 43.

64 Rothblum and Solovay, 2009..

65 Rohter 2005; Anonymous 2005.

66 On the UK, see Connolly et al. 2000, and for the situation in the US see Brown et al.'s 2004 review.

67 Urbina 2006.

68 Darnton-Hill, Nishida and James 2004. Danaei et al., 2011.

69 The Leisure Database Company, 2011., Data from *The 2011 IHRSA Global Report on the State of the Health Club Industry.*

70 DSSV, 2009.

71 IHRSA, 2010.

72 Atkins and Linde 1977: 24–5. For a fine review, see Shapin 2004. Making a similar observation about blame is Lobstein 2006: 75.

73 Cannon 2004: 67.

74 Anonymous 2003b; CNN 2005.

75 Ballantyne, 2009.

76 Swithers, Ogden, and Davidson, 2011.

77   *The Economist* 2004. See also Lang 2005 for an anti-nutraceutical.

78   Hein 2007.

79   Stevenson 2002.

80   Online at http://www.naafa.org.

81   Bell and Valentine 1997. It was an event of a piece with feminism that saw the effects of patriarchy written on womens' bodies, and that those bodies were battlefields. Despite the fight, it remains the case that obese women are discriminated against. Averett and Korenman 1996.

82   An aesthetic satirized to great effect in the *Zoolander* motion picture, with its 'Derelicte' collection.

83   For more on this back and forth, see Gilman, 2008.

84   Alicia 2004; Klimis-Zacas and Wolinsky 2004.

85   Orbach 2006 argues that fat, after all, is a feminist issue.

86   And in Belize, young women now discriminate between the curvaceous 'Coca-Cola' and the less desirable 'Fanta' body type, reflecting the different shapes of the bottles in which these modern beverages arrive, as Anderson-Fye 2004 notes. For more on this see e.g. Becker 2004; Becker et al. 2002, 2005; and Littlewood 2004.

87   I thought I'd come up with this pun first, but Macduff 2006 clearly beat me to it.

88   http://www.slowfood.com/international/4/where-we-are#risultati

89   See the full manifesto at: http://www.slowfoodusa.org/about/manifesto. html.

90   Friedmann 2005a.

91   Mintz and Friedmann 2004.

92   Even though he might have misspelled it 'massala'. See Cook 2001.

93   Salone del Gusto.it, 2010.

94   Parasecoli 2003:33 notes a further play on words – that the Gambero Rosso was the place where Pinocchio was defrauded of his gold coins by the Cat and the Fox.

95   *Barossa Slow Program*, Slow Food, South Australia, 2004, cited in the excellent Peace 2006: 52.

96   Ong and Blumenberg 1998; Ehrenreich 2001.

97   Jeffress with Mayanobe 2001.

98   It's a striking demonstration of what has been termed 'globalization from below', of international links against corporate food. But internationalism isn't something that one is born with, and sometimes the lessons aren't easy. Bové's home in Larzac has learned internationalism. During the Algerian war for independence, the French took Algerian prisoners of war back to a military base in Larzac. Anti-war protesters from the cities tried to enlist the support of local farmers. The farmers initially responded with indifference. After all, it wasn't their fight. But as the farmers themselves began to feel

the predations of the broader war, and with the French military buying up farms surrounding its base, the farmers caught a whiff of what was going on elsewhere. They fought back locally, squatting camps near the military base (Bové 2001). And in the process, they came to understand their fight as linked to the one they'd disavowed. On one of the sheep trails in Larzac is a wooden plaque, on which is carved a public apology, by the farmers, for ignoring the prisoners of war in France's Guantanamo. They have since begun a programme to bring Algerian children to study in Larzac and have provided food to a number of industrial workers' strikes across France (Diamond 2001). See more generally Notes From Nowhere 2003.

99 Levenstein 1988.
100 Bové and Dufour 2005: 66.
101 Weinstein 2005.
102 Woodruff Atkinson, 2008.
103 MST-MT Caderno do Núcleo No. 9, Julho de 2002, Cuiabá MT and Caderno de Núcleo no. 11,Outubro 2002. cited in Wittman 2005: footnote 88.

Chapter 10

1 Andersen 2005.
2 Dharmadhikary, Sheshadri and Rehmat 2005; Nadal and Wise 2004; Valerie 2002; Barlow and Clarke 2002; Manning 2004a.
3 Halweil 2004.
4 Peck (2006) offers a comprehensive review of the structural vulnerabilities of the food system.
5 Smith et al. 2005: ii.
6 Pirog and Benjamin 2003.
7 Manning 2004b, and the fine Manning 2004a more widely.
8 Lawrence et al. 2005.
9 Klare 2006. See Klare 2001 for more.
10 http://www.greens.org.nz/food-revolution/.
11 The stifling and criminalization of dissent is increasing, for those opposed not only to corporate globalization, but war and injustice the world over.
12 Cox 2005.
13 This comes from the Centers for Disease Control. See, for example, its web page at: http://www.cdc.gov/ncidod/diseases/food/index.htm. Also see Cox 2005 for more.
14 EPA 2003.
15 The resource inefficiencies of the meat industry are also immense. To produce 1 ton of grain to feed to cattle, 1,000 tons of water are required. To

produce 1 ton of beef takes 7 tons of grain. Lawrence et al. 2005 is a very good introduction to the issue.

16 In the US over the course of a year, meat eaters produce 1.5 tons of CO_2 more than vegetarians (Steinfeld et al. 2006).

17 Hilton et al. 2004 and Hilton 2006.

18 Louthan 2003.

19 GRAIN 2006. See also Connor 2006; Lucas 2007.

20 Worm et al. 2006. And aquaculture is heir to the same problems as agriculture, with the industry heir to its own pollution, social dislocation, diminishing returns and even the development of genetically modified fish.

21 Chavez 1984.

22 See Windfuhr and Jonsén 2005 for a longer exegesis and McMichael's forthcoming piece for analysis.

23 Via Campesina 2003.

24 FAO 2006b.

25 That rights without obligations might be considered 'nonsense on stilts' is an idea belonging to Jeremy Bentham. I've written a little more about this in Patel 2007. The US successfully opposed the right to food at the World Food Summit in Rome in 2002, despite being alone among 182 nations. The UN itself resists the idea of peasant rights, and it is a deficit against which Via Campesina continues to campaign.

26 Oliver 2005.

27 Predictably, food companies have tried to make capital out of this already. The slogan on a recently spotted bottle of Tabasco®: 'How Food Gets Attention'.

28 There are powerful arguments against eating any. See, for example, Torres and Torres 2005.

29 Pollan 2006b.

30 Cited in Walker 2004: 186.

31 Fukuoka et al. 1978; Altieri 1987.

32 Simple organic farming can feed the world – see Halweil 2006. Fukuoka suggests even higher yields from more sophisticated forms of farming.

33 It's like parkour, the art of traversing urban space that transforms bleak modern architecture into a playground. But with potted plants. More at http://www.guerillagardening.org.

34 Taylor, Madrick and Collin 2005.

35 Rubin, Jatana and Potts 2006.

36 To find out more about Mrs Perumal's situation, visit: http://www.stuffedandstarved.org/.

37 Organic stores in South Korea and Japan have long understood the importance of locally grown food, and of the importance of having a connection with the producer. Some go so far as to display a photo of the producer,

together with their address and mobile phone number, an informative move, but one that also shrinks people to the size of labels.

38   Sabine and Sigrid 2001.

39   Learn more, and find out the multiplier effects in your own town – visit the New Economics Foundation's site at http://www.pluggingtheleaks.org/.

40   Kantor 2001.

41   DeLind and Ferguson 1999: 197.

42   Walsh 2006.

43   See the Education Rights Project (www.erp.org.za) for more. Of course, the aid and debt industry in Africa is dysfunctional. Aid to Africa has been beset by corruption and scandal and looks likely to remain so. But trade and investment don't seem to be helping either. The flimsy 'Equator Principles', which call for a minimum of ethical and environmental integrity when investing, are being flouted not only by the World Bank and IMF, but now by new Chinese lending to Africa as well, of course, as by African governments. And, over the entirety of the Global South in 2005, $527 billion more went to the Global North than they received. See United Nations 2006. On the Equator Principles see, e.g., *Financial Times* 2006.

44   Courville, Patel and Rosset 2006.

45   BBC News 2006. And this for a school that should have been equipped by government in the first place.

46   Powell 2007.

47   Which has been well covered by Michael Pollan, particularly in his correspondence with Whole Foods' CEO John Mackey at http://www.michaelpollan.com/article.php?id=80.

48   Renard 2005; Bacon 2005; Fridell 2006; Lewis 2005; Martínez-Torres 2006. For instance, a key study of coffee growers in Mexico refutes one of Fair Trade's claims 'that it helps to prevent migration. The logic here is that by increasing the price of coffee, farmers will be encouraged to stay in rural areas. But the coffee price has been so low for so long, the damage has already been done. Campesinos have already been scooped up in a rural exodus to the city in search of better work, to the extent that there are fewer wage labourers around. Wage rates have increased, meaning that rural workers get a little more to work on coffee plantations than the pittance they got before. But for farmers to have enough money to hire labour to actually produce coffee, and take advantage of the fair-trade price, some coffee-farming families have had to send someone to the US. From there, they send home remittances to keep the farm alive. And sometimes it just isn't worth it. In the words of a woman who stayed to run the business while her husband went to the US: 'When he went to the US, I realized how much we invested in coffee. The truth is that coffee production isn't working for us. We're making fools of ourselves' (Lewis 2005: 57). Hers is a common cry.

49 This would seriously affect the profits of coffee traders, processors and re-tailers. It's a threat that has been headed off by other high-street coffee vendors, who are currently setting up their own in-house certification processes. It's an invitation to trust a poacher who has hired himself as a gamekeeper.

50 This might seem to run contrary to Margaret Mead's oft quoted 'Never doubt that a small group of thoughtful, committed citizens can change the world. Indeed, it is the only thing that ever has.' To my ear, it smacks just a little of elitism, and insofar as it is true, reflects small groups of people who have usually done things for the worse. Every progressive victory that I can think of, from liberation struggles to civil rights, involved not a handful of people, but hundreds of thousands. (See Patel 2005 for more.)

51 The Mondragón collective and Participatory Economics offer two visions among many for this kind of democracy.

52 Even the World Bank, in its 2008 World Development Report, agrees.

53 See Hart 2002; Courville, Patel and Rosset 2006, the latter available free at www.foodfirst.org/promisedland, for more.

54 In the UK, Jamie Oliver has led the charge; in the US, Ann Cooper has been doing the same; and many a school yard has benefited from the experiments in Berkeley, California, involving Chez Panisse chef Alice Waters and the Edible Schoolyards project. Marco Flavio Marinucci's Cook Here and Now site offers an exemplary education for the rest of us, out of school.

55 Monbiot 2005b makes the strong case against biofuels. It's a position echoed by many of Via Campesina's constituent organizations, who battle the reign of large-scale plantations for other reasons. See www.stuffedandstarved.org/biofuel, for more.

56 See, e.g., Parry et al. 2004; Fischer et al. 2005. I am grateful to Jeff Purcell for these references.

57 Debt relief would benefit citizens in both rich and poor countries, but not the banks that profit from the cycle of debt (Anderson and The Global Economic Justice Task Force of the Institute for Policy Studies 2006).

58 Ahn and Ahmadi 2004, Reynolds, 2009..

59 Diamond 2003: 285.

60 Nancy 2000 – thanks to Sharad Chari for pointing me this way.

References

Aaron, Rita, Abraham Joseph, Sulochana Abraham, Jayaprakash Muliyil, Kuryan George, Jasmine Prasad, Shantidani Minz, Vinod Joseph Abraham, and Anuradha Bose. 2004. Suicides in Young People in Rural Southern India. *Lancet* 363 (9415): 1117

Abu-Lughod, Janet L. 1989. *Before European Hegemony: The World System A.D. 1250–1350.* New York: Oxford University Press. AFP. 2003. *Thousands Protest in Bangladesh over Farmer's Suicide at WTO Meet.* Dhaka: Agence France Presse, 12 September.

Agarwal, Bina. 1994. *A Field of One's Own: Gender and Land Rights in South Asia.* Cambridge South Asian Studies. Cambridge: Cambridge University Press.

Agarwal, Siddharth. 2011. The state of urban health in India; comparing the poorest quartile to the rest of the urban population in selected states and cities. *Environment and Urbanization* 23 (1):13-28.

Agriculture and Agri-Food Canada. 2005a. Instant Noodle's Consumption is Higher than that of Beans and Rice. *Agri-Food News from Mexico*, 1 November 2004–31 January 2005. http://atn-riae.agr.ca/latin/e3362.htm.

———. 2005b. Wal-Mart and Liverpool Reinforce their Position in the Mexican Retail Market. *Agri-Food News from Mexico*, 1 November 2004–31 January 2005. http://atnriae.agr.ca/latin/e3362.htm.

———. 2005c. Wal-Mart Mexico Reaches Historic Record Sales During 2004. *Agri-Food News from Mexico*, 1 November 2004–31 January 2005. http://atnriae.agr.ca/latin/e3362.htm.

Ahlberg, Kristin Leigh. 2003. 'Food Is a Powerful Tool in the Hands of This Government': The Johnson Administration and PL 480, 1963–1969 (Israel, Vietnam, India). Ph.D Dissertation, Department of History, University of Nebraska, Lincoln, Nebraska.

Ahn, Christine, and Brahm Ahmadi. 2004. Beyond the Food Bank. *Food First Backgrounder* 10 (4).

Ahn, Christine, with Melissa Moore and Nick Parker. 2004. Migrant Farmworkers: America's New Plantation Workers. *Food First Backgrounder* 10 (2). Oakland, CA: Institute for Food and Development Policy/Food First.

Aitoro, Jill R. 2011. Virtual border fence project canceled. *Washington Business Journal*, 14 January.

Alicia, Weissman. 2004. Weight Control. In Sana Loue and Martha Sajatovic (eds.), *Encyclopedia of Women's Health*. New York: Kluwer Academic/Plenum Publishers.

Allison, D. B., R. Zannolli and K. M. Narayan. 1999. The Direct Health Care Costs of Obesity in the United States. *American Journal of Public Health*. 89: 1194–9.

Altieri, Miguel A. 1987. *Agroecology: The Scientific Basis of Alternative Agriculture.* Boulder: Westview Press.

American Soybean Association. 2004. *Return of Organization Exempt from Income Tax (990 Filing for 503c3 Organization).* OMB No. 1545-0047. Internal Revenue Service.

Anand, Tuhina. 2005. *Greenpeace Files Complaint against Mahyco Monsanto's Misleading Ad.* New Delhi: agencyfaqs!

Anant, Birjinder. 2005. Sketches of Bombay: At the Call Centers. *Samar* 21. http://www.samarmagazine.org/archive/article.php?id=205.

Andersen, Hans Christian. 2005. *The Complete Stories.* London: British Library.

Anderson, Sarah, and The Global Economic Justice Task Force of the Institute for Policy

PB024MQ Stuffed & Starved NEW MARGINS 2/21/08 4:45 PM Page 349 Studies. 2006. *Debt Boomerang 2006: How Americans Would Benefit from Cancellation of Impoverished Country Debts*. Washington, DC: Institute for Policy Studies. http://www.ips-dc.org/boomerang/DB2006.pdf.

Anderson-Fye, Eileen P. 2004. A 'Coca-Cola' Shape: Cultural Change, Body Image, and Eating Disorders in San Andrés, Belize. *Culture, Medicine and Psychiatry* 28 (4): 561–95.

Angus, Ian, and Simon Butler. 2011. *Too Many People? Population, Immigration and the Environmental Crisis*. Chicago, IL: Haymarket Books.

Anonymous. 1945. On the Business Horizon. *Barron's National Business and Financial Weekly*, 14 May: 5.

———. 2003a. Appetite-Controlling Hormone Shows Promise. *Tufts University Health & Nutrition Letter* 21 (9): 3.

———. 2003b. *Diet Watchers*. Farmington: Global Information Inc.

———. 2004 *The Only True Mother Goose Melodies*. Project Gutenberg, 2004-01-01 (cited). Available from http://www.gutenberg.org/etext/4901.

———. 2005. *Editor's Note*. New York Times, 28 January.

Appleby, Louis. 2000. Suicide in Women. *Lancet* 355 (9211): 1203.

Arcal, Yon Fernández de Larrinoa, and Materne Maetz. 2000. *Multilateral Trade Negotiations on Agriculture: A Resource Manual*. Rome: Food and Agriculture Organization of the United Nations.

Arrighi, Giovanni. 1983. *The Geometry of Imperialism: The Limits of Hobson's Paradigm*. London: Verso.

———. 2002. The African Crisis: World Systemic and Regional Aspects. *New Left Review* 15: 5–36.

Arroyo, Pedro , Alvar Loria, and Oscar Méndez. 2004. Changes in the Household Calorie Supply during the 1994 Economic Crisis in Mexico and its Implications on the Obesity Epidemic. *Nutrition Reviews* 62 (7 (Part 2)): S163–S168.

Arsenault, Raymond. 2006. *Freedom Riders: 1961 and the Struggle for Racial Justice, Pivotal Moments in American History*. New York: Oxford University Press.

Astor, Michael. 2003. Groups Clash Over Soybean Boom in Brazil. *Associated Press Online*, Querencia, Brazil, 18 December.

Atkins, Robert C., and Shirley Linde. 1977. *Dr Atkins' Superenergy Diet*. New York: Bantam Books.

Averett, Susan, and Sanders Korenman. 1996. The Economic Reality of the Beauty Myth. *Journal of Human Resources* 31 (2): 304–30.

Avery, A. A., C. S. Prakash, A. McHughen, A. R. Trewavas, T. R. DeGregori and David Pimentel. 2005. What Kind of Farming Works Best? (and Response). *Science* 307 (5714): 1410–11.

Babb, Sarah. 2001. *Managing Mexico: Economists from Nationalism to Neoliberalism*. Princeton: Princeton University Press.

Bacheva, Fidanka , Manana Kochladze and Suzanna Dennis. 2006. *Boom Time Blues: Big Oil's Gender Impacts in Azerbaijan, Georgia and Sakhalin*. Washington, DC: Gender Action. http://www.genderaction.org/images/boomtimeblues.pdf.

Bacon, Christopher. 2005. Confronting the Coffee Crisis: Can Fair Trade, Organic, and Specialty Coffees Reduce Small-Scale Farmer Vulnerability in Northern Nicaragua? *World Development* 33 (3): 497–511.

Bajpai, Nirupam. 2003. India: Towards the Millennium Development Goals. In UNHD Programme (ed.), *Background Paper for Human Development Report 2003*.

Bakan, Joel. 2004. *The Corporation: The Pathological Pursuit of Profit and Power*. New York: The New Press.

Baldwin, James. 1963. *The Fire Next Time*. New York: Vintage.

Baranowski, Tom, Karen W. Cullen, Theresa Nicklas, Deborah Thompson and Janice

Baranowski. 2003. Are Current Health Behavioral Change Models Helpful in Guiding Prevention of Weight Gain Efforts? *Obesity Resesarch* 11 (Supplement): 23S–43S.

Barkin, David. 1987. The End to Food Self-Sufficiency in Mexico. *Latin American Perspectives* 14 (3, Agriculture and Labor): 271–97.

Barlow, Maude, and Tony Clarke. 2002. *Blue Gold: The Fight to Stop the Corporate Theft of the World's Water*. New York: New Press.

Barnes, John 1987. Anatomy of a Rip-Off. *New Republic*, 2 November 1987: 20–1.

Barreto, Paulo, Carlos Souza Jr, Anthony Anderson, Rodney Salomão, Wiles Janice and Ruth Noguerón. 2005. *Human Pressure in the Brazilian Amazon: Imazon – Amazon Institute of People and the Environment*. http://www.imazon.org.br/upload/ea_3e.pdf.

Baumel, Phil, Bob Wisner, Mike Duffy and Don Hofstrand. 2000. *Brazilian Soybeans – Can Iowa Farmers Compete?* Available from http://www.extension.iastate.edu/agdm/articles/baumel/BaumelDecoo.htm.

BBC News. 2003. Farmers 'More Likely to Be Suicidal'. BBCNews.com, 25 February.

———. 2005. India Wins Landmark Patent Battle. BBCNews.com, 9 March.

———. 2006. Tesco Upset by Voucher Auctions. BBC, 13 March. Available from http://news.bbc.co.uk/2/hi/uk_news/education/4802556.stm.

Beattie, Alan. 2006. Drive to Inoculate US Workers against Globalisation's Threats. *Financial Times*, 16 October.

Beattie, Alan, and Andrew Yeh. 2007. China Treads on Western Toes in Africa. *Financial Times*, 12 January.

Beaud, Michel. 2001. *A History of Capitalism, 1500–2000*. New York: Monthly Review Press.

Becerra, Hector, Megan Garvey, and Steve Hymon. 2006. L.A. Garden Shut Down; 40 Arrested. *Los Angeles Times*, 14 June.

Becker, Anne E. 2004. Television, Disordered Eating, and Young Women in Fiji: Negotiating Body Image and Identity during Rapid Social Change. *Culture, Medicine and Psychiatry* 28 (4): 533–59.

Becker, Anne E., Rebecca A. Burwell, David B. Herzog, Paul Hamburg and Stephen E. Gilman. 2002. Eating Behaviours and Attitudes Following Prolonged Exposure to Television among Ethnic Fijian Adolescent Girls. *British Journal of Psychiatry* 180 (6): 509–14.

Becker, Anne E., Stephen E. Gilman and Rebecca A. Burwell. 2005. Changes in Prevalence of Overweight and in Body Image among Fijian Women between 1989 and 1998. *Obesity Research*. 13 (1): 110–17.

Behere, P. B., and A. P. Behere. 2008. Farmers' suicide in Vidarbha region of Maharashtra state: A myth or reality? *Indian journal of psychiatry* 50 (2):124-7.

Belair Jr, Felix. 1965. U.S. Urged to Drop Surplus Exports. *New York Times*, 19 July: 11.

Bell, David, and Gill Valentine. 1997. *Consuming Geographies: We Are Where We Eat*. London, New York: Routledge.

Bellizzi, J. A., A. E. Crowley and R. W. Hasty. 1983. The Effects of Color in Store Design. *Journal of Retailing* 59 (1): 21–45.

Bellizzi, Joseph A., and Robert E. Hite. 1992. Environmental Color, Consumer Feelings, and Purchase Likelihood. *Psychology & Marketing* 9: 347–63.

Bello, Walden F., Shea Cunningham, and Bill Rau. 1999. *Dark Victory: The United States and Global Poverty*. Oakland, CA: Food First Books.

Benjamin, Walter, and Rolf Tiedemann. 1999. *The Arcades Project*. Cambridge, MA: Belknap Press.

Berthelot, Jacques 2001. *L'Agriculture, talon d'Achille de la mondialisation: clés pour un accord agricole solidaire à l'OMC*. Paris: L'Harmattan.

Bhagwati, Jagdish N. 2004. *In Defense of Globalization*. New York: Oxford University Press.

Biko, Steve, and Robin Malan. 1997. *The Essential Steve Biko*. Cape Town: D. Philip Publishers.

Biko, Steve, and Aelred Stubbs. 1978. *I Write What I Like*. London: Penguin, 1988.

Birchall, Jonathan. 2005. Monsanto to Settle Bribery Charges. *Financial Times*, 8 January.

Bird, Peter 2000. *The First Food Empire – A History of J. Lyons & Co.* Chichester: Phillimore & Co.

Black, Richard. 2007. *Growing Pains of India's GM Revolution*. BBCNews.com, 7 February.

Blount, Jeb, and Cecilia Tornaghi. 2005. Brazil's 'Chainsaw' Governor Vows Reform: Environment Secretary Arrested. Half of Amazon Forest Cleared in 2003–04 Was Harvested in Mato Grosso State. *Montreal Gazette*, 4 June: 20.

Bock, Kenneth. 1979. Theories of Progress, Development, Evolution. In T. Bottomore and R. Nisbet (eds.), *A History of Sociological Analysis*. London: Heinemann.

Bonacich, Edna, Richard P. Appelbaum with Ku-Sup Chin, Melanie Myers, Greg Scott, Goetz Wolff. 2000. *Behind the Label: Inequality in the Los Angeles Apparel Industry*. Berkeley: University of California Press.

Bond, Patrick. 2000. *Elite Transition: From Apartheid to Neoliberalism in South Africa*. London: Pluto Press.

Bonvecchio, Anabelle, Margarita Safdie, Eric A Monterrubio, Tiffany Gust, Salvador Villalpando, and Juan A Rivera. 2009. Overweight and obesity trends in Mexican children 2 to 18 years of age from 1988 to 2006. *Salud Publica de Mexico* 51:S586-S594.

Booth, Katie M., Megan M. Pinkston and Walker S. Carlos Poston. 2005. Obesity and the Built Environment. *Journal of the American Dietetic Association* 105: S110–S117.

Borges, Guilherme, Haydée Rosovsky, Cecilia Gómez and Reyna Gutiérrez. 1996. Epidemiología del Suicidio en México de 1970 a 1994. *Salud Pública de México*: 197–206.

Borras, Saturnino M. 2003. Questioning the Pro-Market Critique of State-Led Agrarian Reforms. *European Journal of Development Research* 15 (2i): 105–28.

———. 2004. *La Vía Campesina: An Evolving Transnational Social Movement*. Amsterdam: Transnational Institute. http://www.tni.org/reports/newpol/campesina.pdf.

Bourdieu, Pierre. 1986. *Distinction: A Social Critique of the Judgement of Taste*. London: Routledge & Kegan Paul.

Bovard, James. 1995. *Archer Daniels Midland: A Case Study in Corporate Welfare*. Washington, DC: Cato Institute.

Bové, José. 2001. A Farmers' International? *New Left Review* (12): 89–101.

Bové, José, and Francois Dufour. 2005. *Food for the Future*. Translated by J. Birrell. Cambridge: Polity Press.

Boyce, James K. 1999. *The Globalization of Market Failure? International Trade and Sustainable Agriculture*. Amherst: Political Economy Research Institute, University of Massachusetts.

Bradbury, Mark 2000. Normalising the Crisis in Africa. *Journal of Humanitarian Assistance*. http://www.jha.ac/articles/a043.htm.

Brass, Tom. 2000. *Peasants, Populism and Postmodernism: The Return of the Agrarian Myth*. London: Frank Cass.

Breslow, Lester. 2006. Public Health Aspects of Weight Control. *International Journal of Epidemiology* 35 (1): 10–12.

Brillat-Savarin, Jean-Anthelme. 1970 [1825]. *The Physiology of Taste*. Translated by A. Drayton. London: Penguin Books.

Brimacombe, Ian. 2006. Refugees Taught how to Eat American Food. BBCNews.com, 31 July.

Brinkman, Henk-Jan, Saskia de Pee, Issa Sanogo, Ludovic Subran, and Martin W. Bloem. 2010. High Food Prices and the Global Financial Crisis Have Reduced Access to Nutritious Food and Worsened Nutritional Status and Health. *The Journal of Nutrition* 140 (1):153S-161S.

Brooks, D. R., D. A. Bohan, G. T. Champion, A. J. Haughton, C. Hawes, M. S. Heard, S. J. Clark, A. M. Dewar, L. G. Firbank, J. N. Perry, P. Rothery, R. J. Scott, I. P. Woiwod, C. Birchall, M. P. Skellern, J. H. Walker, P. Baker, D. Bell, E. L. Browne, A. J. G. Dewar,

C. M. Fairfax, B. H. Garner, L. A. Haylock, S. L. Horne, S. E. Hulmes, N. S. Mason, L. R. Norton, P. Nuttall, Z. Randle, M. J. Rossall, R. J. N. Sands, E. J. Singer and M. J. Walker. 2003. Invertebrate Responses to the Management of Genetically Modified Herbicidetolerant and Conventional Spring Crops. I. Soil-surface-active Invertebrates. *Philosophical Transactions of the Royal Society – Series B – Biological Sciences* 00358 (01439): 1847–63.

Brown, Arleen F., Susan L. Ettner, John Piette, Morris Weinberger, Edward Gregg, Martin F. Shapiro, Andrew J. Karter, Monika Safford, Beth Waitzfelder, Patricia A. Prata and Gloria L. Beckles. 2004. Socioeconomic Position and Health among Persons with Diabetes Mellitus: A Conceptual Framework and Review of the Literature. *Epidemiologic Reviews* 26(1): 63–7.

Brownell, Kelly D., and Katherine Battle Horgen. 2004. *Food Fight: The Inside Story of the Food Industry, America's Obesity Crisis, and What We Can Do About It*. New York: McGraw-Hill.

Buanain, Antonio Marcio, and Jose Maria da Silveira. 2002. Structural Reforms and Food Security in Brazil. In *UNICAMP Discussion Paper Prepared for FAO World State of Food and Agriculture 2000*.

Buchanan, Patrick J. 2003. Who Killed California? *WorldNet Daily Commentary*, 30 July.

Bundy, Colin. 1979. *The Rise and Fall of the South African Peasantry*. Berkeley: University of California Press.

Bunsha, Dionne. 2006. Villages for Sale in Vidarbha. *The Hindu* 23 (5).

Burger King Corporate Information. *Global Facts* 2006. Available from http://www.bk.com/CompanyInfo/bk_corporation/fact_sheets/global_facts.aspx.

Burnham, Gilbert, Riyadh Lafta, Shannon Doocy and Les Roberts. 2006. Mortality after the 2003 Invasion of Iraq: A Cross-sectional Cluster Sample Survey. *The Lancet* 368 (9545): 1421–8.

Bush, George W. 2008. President Bush Discusses Economy, Trade Maryland Heights, Missouri May 2, 2008.

———. 2008. Press Conference by The President. Rose Garden, White House, Washington DC, April 29, 2008.

Butler, Samuel. 1769. *Hudibras: In Three Parts, Written in the Time of the Late Wars*, Glasgow: Robert and Andrew Foulis.

Buttel, Frederick H. 1989. The US Farm Crisis and the Restructuring of American Agriculture: Domestic and International Dimensions. In D. Goodman and M. Redclift (eds.), *The International Farm Crisis*. New York: St Martin's Press, pp. 46–83.

Byron, Lord. 1857. *Don Juan, In Sixteen Cantos, with Notes, Complete Edition*. Halifax: Milner and Sowerby.

Cain, P. J., and A. G. Hopkins. 1980. The Political Economy of British Expansion Overseas, 1750–1914. *The Economic History Review* 33 (4): 463–90.

Cairns, Georgina, Kathryn Angus, and Gerard Hastings. 2000. *The extent, nature and effects of food promotion to children: a review of the evidence to December 2008*. World Health Organization, WHO Press 2009. Available from http://hdl.handle.net/1893/2418.

Caldwell, C., and S. A. Hibbert. 2002. The Influence of Music Tempo and Musical Preference on Restaurant Patrons' Behavior. *Psychology & Marketing* 19 (11): 895–917.

California Department of Food and Agriculture. 2010a. California Agricultural Exports California Department of Food and Agriculture.

———. 2010b. California agricultural resource directory. *California agricultural resource directory*.

Cameron, Maxwell A., and Brian W. Tomlin. 2000. *The making of NAFTA : how the deal was done*. Ithaca, N.Y.: Cornell University Press.

Campos, Paul, Abigail Saguy, Paul Ernsberger, Eric Oliver and Glenn Gaesser. 2006a. The

Epidemiology of Overweight and Obesity: Public Health Crisis or Moral Panic? *International Journal of Epidemiology* 35 (1): 55–60.

———. 2006b. Response: Lifestyle Not Weight Should Be the Primary Target. *International Journal of Epidemiology* 35 (1): 81–2.

Cannon, G. 2004. Why the Bush Administration and the Global Sugar Industry Are Determined to Demolish the 2004 WHO Global Strategy on Diet, Physical Activity and Health. *Public Health Nutrition* 7: 369.

Cannon, Geoffrey. 2005. The Rise and Fall of Dietetics and of Nutrition Science, 4000 BCE–2000 CE. *Public Health Nutrition* 8: 701.

Caplovitz, David. 1964. *The Poor Pay More*. New York: Free Press of Glencoe.

Carlin, Martha. 1995. Provisions for the Poor: Fast Food in Medieval London. *Franco-British Studies: Journal of the British Institute in Paris* 20: 35–48.

Carnegie, Andrew. 1903. How to Succeed in Life. From the *Pittsburg Bulletin*, reprinted from the *New York Tribune*. http://www.clpgh.org/exhibit/neighborhoods/oakland/oak_n751.html

Carney, Dan. 1995. Dwayne's World. *Mother Jones*, July–August 1995: 47. http://www.motherjones.com/news/special_reports/1995/07/carney.html.

Carrefour Group. 2010. Financial Report. Nanterre: Carrefour.

Cassel, Amanda, and Raj Patel. 2003. Agricultural Trade Liberalization and Brazil's Rural Poor: Consolidating Inequality. Oakland, CA: Institute for Food and Development Policy/Food First.

Cassman, K. G., and P. L. Pingali. 1995. Intensification of Irrigated Rice Systems: Learning from the Past to Meet Future Challenges. *GeoJournal* 35 (3): 299–305.

Center for Human Rights and Global Justice. 2011. Every Thirty Minutes: Farmer Suicides, Human Rights, and the Agrarian Crisis in India. New York: NYU School of Law.

Center for Immigration Studies. 2006. *New Poll: Americans Prefer House Approach on Immigration*. Washington, DC: Center for Immigration Studies. http://www.cis.org/articles/2006/2006poll.html.

Center for Responsive Politics. 2011. 'Lobbying Database.' Retrieved July, 2011, from http://www.opensecrets.org/lobby/index.php

Centre for Sustainable Agriculture. 2006. '*Bt Cotton – No Respite for Andhra Pradesh Farmers More than 400 Crores of Losses': Report of Kharif 2005 Performance of the Crop, vis-à-vis NPM Approach to Cotton*. March. Secunderabad: Centre for Sustainable Agriculture. http://biosafetyinfo.net/file_dir/194479208544473669de2c6.pdf.

Champion, G. T., M. J. May, S. Bennett, D. R. Brooks, S. J. Clark, R. E. Daniels, L. G. Firbank, A. J. Haughton, C. Hawes, M. S. Heard, J. N. Perry, Z. Randle, M. J. Rossall, P. Rothery, M. P. Skellern, R. J. Scott, G. R. Squire and M. R. Thomas. 2003. Crop Management and Agronomic Context of the Farm Scale Evaluations of Genetically Modified Herbicidetolerant Crops. *Philosophical Transactions of the Royal Society – Series B – Biological Sciences* 00358 (01439): 1801–19.

Chang, Grace. 2000. *Disposable Domestics: Immigrant Women Workers in the Global Economy*. Cambridge, MA: South End Press.

Chang, Ha-Joon. 2002. *Kicking Away the Ladder: Development Strategy in Historical Perspective*. London: Anthem.

Chapecó Declaration. 2005. *ExchangeProject: 'WTO and Brazil-European Food Flows' Flemish and Brazilian Farmers Want to Participate in Decision-making*. Wervel, 15 March. Available from: http://www.wervel.be/EN/dossiers/fm_200505/fm_200505_0405.htm

Chari, Sharad. 2004. *Fraternal Capital: Peasant Workers, Self-Made Men and Globalization in Provincial India*. Delhi: Permanent Black.

Chavez, Cesar. 1984. *What the Future Holds for Farm Workers and Hispanics*. Speech given at the Commonwealth Club of California. 9 November. Available from http://

commonwealthclub.org/archive/20thcentury/84-11chavez-speech.html

Chebat, J. C., D. Vaillant and C. Gelinas-Chebat. 2000. Does Background Music in a Store Enhance Salespersons' Persuasiveness? *Perceptual and Motor Skills* 91 (2): 405–24.

Cheng, Tsung O. 2004. Childhood Obesity in China. *Health & Place* 10 (4): 395–6.

Chenoweth, Gene M. 1996–9. Melaka, 'Piracy' and the Modern World System. *Journal of Law and Religion* 13 (1): 107–25.

Chopra, Mickey, and Ian Darnton-Hill. 2004. Tobacco and Obesity Epidemics: Not So Different After All? *British Medical Journal* 328 (7455): 1558–60.

Christenson, Reo M. 1959. *The Brannan Plan: Farm Politics and Policy.* Ann Arbor: University of Michigan Press. *Cincinnati Enquirer.* 2005. Hearings for Farmers Help Right a Wrong. *Cincinatti Enquirer,* 6 March. http://bfaa-us.org/HearingsFor FarmersHelpRightAWrong_Enquirer_3-6-2005.pdf.

Cleaver, Harry. 1977. Food, Famine and International Crisis. *Zerowork* 2. Fall: 1-47. http://www.eco.utexas.edu/facstaff/Cleaver/357Lcleaverfood.pdf.

Cleaver, Harry M. 1972. The Contradictions of the Green Revolution. *The American Economic Review* 62 (1/2): 177–86.

CNN (Cable News Network). 2005. *CNN in the Money.* CNN.com, 26 November.

———. 2006. *Thousands March for Immigrant Rights.* CNN.com, 1 May.

Collins, Jane L. 1995. Gender and Cheap Labor in Agriculture. In P. McMichael (ed.), *Food and Agrarian Orders in the World-Economy.* Westport: Greenwood Press.

Commission on Farmers' Welfare. 2005. *Report of the Commission on Farmers' Welfare, Government of Andhra Pradesh.* Available from New Delhi: Macroscan. http://www.macroscan.org/pol/apr05/pol070405Andhra_Pradesh.htm

Congressional Budget Office. 1997. *The Role of Foreign Aid in Development.* Washington, DC: Congressional Budget Office.

———. 2003. *The Effects of NAFTA on US-Mexican Trade and GDP.* Washington, DC: Congressional Budget Office.

Connolly, V. N. Unwin, P. Sherriff, R. Bilous and W. Kelly. 2000. Diabetes Prevalence and Socioeconomic Status: A Population Based Study Showing Increased Prevalence of Type 2 Diabetes Mellitus in Deprived Areas. *Journal of Epidemiology and Community Health* 54 (3): 173–7.

Connor, John M. 1997. The Global Lysine Price-Fixing Conspiracy of 1992–1995. *Review of Agricultural Economics* 19 (2): 412–27.

———. 2001. *Global Price Fixing: Our Customers Are the Enemy.* Boston: Kluwer Academic Publishers.

Connor, Steve. 2006. Farmers Use as Much Pesticide with GM crops, US Study Finds. *Independent,* 27 July.

Cook, Robin. 2001. Robin Cook's Chicken Tikka Masala Speech: Extracts from a Speech by the Foreign Secretary to the Social Market Foundation in London. *Guardian,* 19 April.

Coons, Rebecca. *EPA Fines Monsanto* [8 July] 2010. Available from Accessed from LexisNexis on July 5th. .

CORE, New York Chapter of Core Inc. 2003. *Return of Organization Exempt from Income Tax (990 Filing for 503c3 Organization).* OMB No. 1545-0047.Internal Revenue Service.

Costa, P.T.M., and International Labor Organization (ILO). 2009. *Fighting forced labour: The example of Brazil.* Geneva.

Counihan, Carole Marie, and Steven L. Kaplan. 1998. *Food and Gender: Identity and Power, Food in History and Culture,* vol. 1. Amsterdam: Harwood Academic Publishers.

Counihan, Carole, and Penny Van Esterik. 1997. *Food and Culture: A Reader.* New York: Routledge.

Courville, Michael, Raj Patel and Peter Rosset. 2006. *Promised Land: Competing Visions of Agrarian Reform.* Oakland, CA: Food First Books.

Cowen, M. P., and R. W. Shenton. 1996. *Doctrines of Development*. London: Routledge. Cox, Stan. 2005. 'Agroterrorists' Needn't Bother. *CounterPunch*. http://www.counterpunch.org/cox12152005.html.

Critser, Greg. 2000. Let Them Eat Fat. *Harper's Magazine* 300 (1798): 41–7.

Crookes, Sir William. 1899. *The Wheat Problem. Based on remarks made in the presidential address to the British Association at Bristol in 1898. Revised with an answer to various critics … With two chapters on the future wheat supply of the United States, by Mr. C. Wood Davis … and the Hon. John Hyde.* John Murray: London.

Crowley, A. E. 1993. The Two-Dimensional Impact of Color on Shopping. *Marketing Letters* 4 (1): 59–69.

Cullather, Nick, and Piero Gleijeses. 1999. *Secret History: The CIA's Classified Account of Its Operations in Guatemala, 1952–1954*. Stanford: Stanford University Press.

Cummins, Steven, and Sally Macintyre. 2006. Food Environments and Obesity—Neighbourhood or Nation? *International Journal of Epidemiology* 35 (1): 100–4.

Dahl, Ronald. 1973. *Charlie and the Chocolate Factory*. Harmondsworth: Penguin.

Danaher, Kevin, and A Riak. 1995. Myths of African Hunger. *Backgrounder*, Spring. San Francisco, CA: Food First Books.

Danaei, G., M. M. Finucane, C. J. Paciorek, Y. Lu, G. M. Singh, J. K. Lin, F. Farzadfar, M. Rao, M. J. Cowan, L. M. Riley, G. A. Stevens, Y. H. Khang, M. K. Ali, C. A. Robinson, and M. Ezzati. 2011. National, regional, and global trends in fasting plasma glucose and diabetes prevalence since 1980: Systematic analysis of health examination surveys and epidemiological studies with 370 country-years and 27 million participants. *The Lancet* 378 (9785):31-40.

Darnton-Hill, I., C. Nishida and W. P. T. James. 2004. A Life Course Approach to Diet, Nutrition and the Prevention of Chronic Diseases. *Public Health Nutrition* 7: 101.

Davidson, Alan. 1999. *The Oxford Companion to Food*. Oxford: Oxford University Press.

Daviglus, M. L., K. Liu, L. L. Yan et al. 2004. Relation of Body Mass Index in Young Adulthood and Middle Age to Medicare Expenditures in Old Age. *Journal of the American Medical Association*. 292: 2743–9.

Davis, Mike. 2001. *Late Victorian Holocausts: El Niño Famines and the Making of the Third World*. London: Verso.

———. 2004. Planet of Slums: Urban Involution and the Informal Proletariat. *New Left Review* 26: 5–34.

———. 2006. *Planet of Slums*. London: Verso.

Deasy, G. F. 1939. The Soya Bean in Manchuria. *Economic Geography* 15 (3): 303–10. del Rio-Navarro, Blanca E., Oscar Velazquez-Monroy, Claudia P. Sanchez-Castillo, Agustin Lara-Esqueda, Arturo Berber, Guillermo Fanghanel, Rafael Violante, Roberto Tapia-Conyer and W. Philip T. James. 2004. The High Prevalence of Overweight and Obesity in Mexican Children. *Obesity Research* 12 (2): 215–23.

DeLind, Laura B., and Anne E. Ferguson. 1999. Is This a Women's Movement? The Relationship of Gender to Community-supported Agriculture in Michigan. *Human Organization* 58 (2): 190.

Delta Farm Press. 2004. Soybean Producers Slam Import Stance. *Delta Farm Press*, 18 March.

Denyer, C. H. 1893. The Consumption of Tea and Other Staple Drinks. *Economic Journal* 3 (9): 33–51.

Department of Agriculture, Government of Punjab. 2011. Production of FoodGrains in 2010-11: A Record Harvest in Pubjab.

Desmarais, Annette-Aurélie. 2002. The Via Campesina: Consolidating an International Peasant and Farm Movement. *Journal of Peasant Studies* 29 (2): 91–124.

———. 2003. The Vía Campesina: Peasants Resisting Globalization. Doctoral Dissertation, Department of Geography, University of Calgary, Calgary, Alberta.

de Sousa, I. S. F., and L. Busch. 1998. Networks and Agricultural Development: The Case of Soybean Production and Consumption in Brazil. *Rural Sociology* 63 (3): 349–71.

Devereux, Stephen. 2000. *Famine in the Twentieth Century*. Brighton: Institute for Development Studies.http://www.ids.ac.uk/ids/bookshop/wp/wp105.pdf.

———. 2002. *State of Disaster: Causes, Consequences and Policy Lessons from Malawi*. Johannesburg: ActionAid. http://actionaidusa.org/ pdf/THE%20MALAWI%20STATE%20 OF%20DISASTER%20Final.pdf

Dharmadhikary, Shripad, Swathi Sheshadri and Rehmat. 2005. *Unravelling Bhakra: Assessing the Temple of Resurgent India: Report of a study of the Bhakra Nangal Project*. Badwani (MP): Manthan Adhyayan Kendra.

Diamond, Norm. 2001. 'Seattle on the Tarn': French Solidarity Against Capitalist Globalization. *New Politics* 8 (2): 111.

———. 2003. The Roquefort Rebellion. In Notes From Nowhere (eds.),*We Are Everywhere: The Irresistible Rise of Global Anticapitalism*. London: Verso.

Díaz, Jesse , and Javier Rodríguez. 2007. Undocumented in America. *New Left Review* 47:93-106.

Diaz, Kevin. 2004a. Grown in Brazil: Tariffs, Subsidies are Epic Struggle; U.S. and Brazilian Farmers Say the Other Side Has All the Advantages. *Star Tribune*, 7 March: 13a.

———. 2004b. Grown in Brazil: Soybeans and Asphalt Could Transform a Farmer into a President; Already the 'Soybean King,' His Plan for Getting Crops Moving on New Roads Is Paving the Way. *Star Tribune*, 7 March: 12.

Dickens, Charles. 1996/1839. *Oliver Twist*. Edited by Robert Southwick. Harlow: Longman.

Dogra, Bharat. 2008. The loan waiver that failed. *Infochange Agriculture*.

Dreibus, Tony. 2005. *Feuding Farmers: A Series of Articles on Farm Organizations By DTN Originally Published on Sept. 26 to 30*. Washington, DC: American Corn Growers Association. Available from http://www.acga.org/News/2005/feudingfarmers.htm.

Drewnowski, Adam. 2000. Nutrition Transition and Global Dietary Trends. *Nutrition* 16 (7–8): 486–7.

Driessen, Paul. 2004. CORE Mocks Environmentalists in Cancun. In *Environment News*, 1 January. Chicago: The Heartland Institute.

Drummond, J. C. B., Anne Wilbraham and Dorothy Hollingsworth. 1991. *The Englishman's Food: A History of Five Centuries of English Diet*. London: Pimlico.

DSSV. 2011. *Fitnessmarkt in Japan*. Arbeitgebervergand deutscher Fitness- und Gesundheits-Anlagen 2009 [cited 19 August 2011]. Available from http://www.dssv.de/index. php?id=492.

Duara, Prasenjit 1996. *Rescuing History from the Nation: Questioning Narratives of Modern China*. Chicago: University of Chicago Press.

Duran-Nah, J. J., and Colli-Quintal J. 2000. Intoxicación Aguada por Plaguicidas. *Salud Pública de México* 42 (1): 53–5.

Economist, The. 1978. American Supermarkets; Not So Super. *The Economist*, 18 November.

———. 1992. Shops in Inner Cities – A Sip of Something Good. *The Economist*, 10 October.

———. 2001. Wal Around the World. *The Economist*, 8 December.

———. 2004. Fancy That, Healthy Ketchup. *The Economist* (US edn), 13 December.

———. 2005a. Making a Meal of It; Packaged Food. *The Economist*, 7 May.

———. 2005b. The Amazon's Texan Saviour. *The Economist*, 28 May.

———. 2005c. Warfare in the Aisles. *The Economist*, 2 April.

Egan, Timothy. 2002. Pastoral Poverty: Seeds of Decline. *New York Times*, 8 December.

Ehrenreich, Barbara. 2001. *Nickel and Dimed: On (Not) Getting by in America*. New York: Metropolitan Books.

Eisenhauer, Elizabeth. 2001. In Poor Health: Supermarket Redlining and Urban Nutrition. *GeoJournal* 53 (2): 125. EIU (Economist Intelligence Unit – Business India Intelligence).

2005. Information Technology. *Business India Intelligence*, 14 September.

Ellaway, Anne, Sally Macintyre, and Xavier Bonnefoy. 2005. Graffiti, Greenery, and Obesity in Adults: Secondary Analysis of European Cross Sectional Survey. *British Medical Journal* 331: 611–12.

Enloe, Cynthia H. 1989. *Bananas, Beaches and Bases: Making Feminist Sense of International Politics*. Berkeley: University of California Press.

EPA (United States Environmental Protection Agency). 2003. *Federal Register 12 February 2003*. Washington, DC: U.S. Government Printing Office.

Escobar-Chaves, S. Liliana, Susan R. Tortolero, Christine M. Markham, Barbara J. Low, Patricia Eitel and Patricia Thickstun. 2005. Impact of the Media on Adolescent Sexual Attitudes and Behaviors. *Pediatrics* 116 (1): 303–26.

Esteva, G. 1992. Development. In W. Sachs (ed.), *The Development Dictionary: A Guide to Knowledge as Power*. London: Zed Books.

ETC Group, Action Group on Erosion, Technology and Concentration. 2005a. Global Seed Industry Concentration – 2005. In *Communiqué*. Ottawa: ETC Group. http://www.etcgroup.org/documents/Comm90GlobalSeed.pdf.

———. 2005b. Oligopoly, Inc. 2005: Concentration in Corporate Power. In *Communiqué*. Ottawa: ETC Group, Action Group on Erosion, Technology and Concentration. http://www.etcgroup.org/upload/ publication/44/01/oligopoly2005_16dec.05.pdf.

———. 2008. *Who owns nature? : corporate power and the final frontier in the commodification of life*. Winnipeg, MB: ETC Group.

EU Directorate-General for Agriculture and Rural Development. 2010. *Agriculture in the European Union: Statistical and Economic Information 2009*. Print.

Eurostat. 2009. *European Business: facts and figures* (No. 18130-8147). Luxembourg: Statistical Office of the European Communities.

Evans, Martin. 1999. Food Retailing Loyalty Scheme – and the Orwellian Millennium. *British Food Journal* 101 (2): 132–47.

FAO, Food and Agricultural Organization of the United Nations. 2002. *Nutrition country profile: China*. Food and Agricultural Organization of the United Nations 2002 [cited 10 August 2011]. Available from http://www.fao.org/ag/agn/nutrition/chn_en.stm

———.2006a. *The State of Food Insecurity in the World 2006*. Rome: Food and Agricultural Organization of the United Nations.

———. 2006b. *Women and Sustainable Food Security*. Rome: Prepared by the Women in Development Service, FAO Women and Population Division.

———. 2007. *India Country Facts*. Food and Agricultural Organization of the United Nations 2007 [cited 9 August 2011]. Available from http://www.fao.org/countries/55528/en/ind/.

———.2010. The State of Food Insecurity in the World, 2010: Addressing Food Insecurity in Protracted Crisis. Rome: Food and Agricultural Organization of the United Nations.

———. 2011. *The State of Food Insecurity in the World: How does international price volatility affect domestic economies and food security?* Rome: Food and Agricultural Organization of the United Nations.

———. 2011. *Food and Agricultural commodities production*. Retrieved July 12, 2011, from FAOSTAT: http://faostat.fao.org/site/339/default.aspx

Farmer, Paul. 2006. *The Uses of Haiti*. Monroe: Common Courage.

Farrell, Diana , and Eric Beinhocker. 2007. Next Big Spenders: India's Middle Class. *BusinessWeek*, May 19, 2007.

Fast, Howard. 1960. *The Howard Fast Reader: A Collection of Stories and Novels*. New York; Crown Publishers.

———. 1990. *Being Red*. Boston: Houghton Mifflin.

Fearnside, P. M. 2001. Soybean Cultivation as a Threat to the Environment in Brazil.

Environmental Conservation 28 (1): 23–38.

Featherstone, Liza. 2003. Wal-Mart Execs' Testimony Could Help Sex Bias Suit. *Women's Enews*, 1 May.

Fedoroff, Nina V., and Nancy Marie Brown. 2004. *Mendel in the Kitchen: A Scientist's View of Genetically Modified Foods*. Washington, DC: Joseph Henry.

Feinstein, Charles H. 1998. Pessimism Perpetuated: Real Wages and the Standard of Living in Britain during and after the Industrial Revolution. *The Journal of Economic History* 58 (3): 625–58.

Ferguson, James. 1990. *The Anti-politics Machine: 'Development', Depoliticization, and Bureaucratic Power in Lesotho*. Cambridge: Cambridge University Press.

Ferguson, Niall. 2004. *Colossus: The Price of America's Empire*. New York: Penguin Press.

Fernandez-Cornejo, Jorge, and David Schimmelpfennig. 2004. Have Seed Industry Changes Affected Research Effort? *Amber Waves* 2(1): 14–19.

Ferriss, Susan, Ricardo Sandoval and Diana Hembree. 1997. *The Fight in the Fields: Cesar Chavez and the Farmworkers Movement*. New York: Harcourt-Brace.

FIAN (Foodfirst Information and Action Network). 2006. *Annual Report: Violations of Peasants' Human Rights: A Report on Cases and Patterns of Violations 2006*. Heidelberg: Foodfirst Information and Action Network.

Fiess, Norbert, and Daniel Lederman. 2004. Mexican Corn: The Effects of NAFTA. *Trade Note* (18). 24 September. Washington, DC: World Bank.

Financial Times. 2006. Editorial: Wolves in Africa. *Financial Times*, 25 October.

Finlay, Mark R. 2004. Old Efforts at New Uses: A Brief History of Chemurgy and the American Search for Biobased Materials. *Journal of Industrial Ecology* 7 (3–4): 33–46.

Firbank, L. G. 2003. Introduction. *Philosophical Transactions of the Royal Society – Series B – Biological Sciences* 00358 (01439): 1777–9.

Fischer, Günther, Mahendra Shah, Francesco N. Tubiello and Harrij van Velthuizen. 2005. Socio-economic and Climate Change Impacts on Agriculture: An Integrated Assessment, 1990–2080. *Philosophical Transactions of the Royal Society- Series B* 360 (1463): 2067–83.

Flanagan, Meredith, and Laura Inoyue. 2006. *US Small Farmers and Racism*. Boston: Oxfam America. http://www.oxfamamerica.org/ whatwedo/where_we_work/united_states/ news_publications/food_farm/art2569.html

Fleming, David A., and Stephan J. Goetz. 2011. Does Local Firm Ownership Matter? *Economic Development Quarterly* 25 (3):277-281.

Fletcher, Michael A. 1999. USDA, Black Farmers Settle Bias Lawsuit. *Washington Post*, Wednesday 6 January: A1.

Folgarait, Leonard. 1991. Revolution as Ritual: Diego Rivera's National Palace Mural. *Oxford Art Journal* 14 (1): 18–33.

Folha Online. 2004. *China Wants Direct Imports of Brazilian Soy – Mato Grosso Governor*. http://www.folha.uol.com.br, 1 June.

Forman, Shepard. 1971. Disunity and Discontent: A Study of Peasant Political Movements in Brazil. *Journal of Latin American Studies* 3 (1): 3–24.

Förster, Michael, and Mark Pearson. 2002. *Income Distribution and Poverty in the OECD Area: Trends and Driving Forces*. Paris: OECD.

Fox, Jonathan. 1992. *The Politics of Food in Mexico: State Power and Social Mobilization*. Ithaca: Cornell University Press.

Frank, Andre Gunder. 1969. *Capitalism and Underdevelopment in Latin America: Historical Studies of Chile and Brazil*. New York: Monthly Review Press.

Frank, T. A. 2006. How Much Should We Hate Wal-Mart? *Washington Monthly*, April.

Fraser, C. E., K. B. Smith, F. Judd, J. S. Humphreys, L. J. Fragar and A. Henderson. 2005. Farming and Mental Health Problems and Mental Illness. *International Journal of Social Psychiatry* 51 (4): 340–9.

Fraser, Damian. 1992. Mexico's Growing Intimacy with the World Bank. *Financial Times*, 3 March: 7.

Fridell, Gavin. 2006. Fair Trade and Neoliberalism: Assessing Emerging Perspectives. *Latin American Perspectives* 33 (6): 2–28.

Friedland, William H. 1994. The Global Fresh Fruit and Vegetable System: An Industrial Organization Analysis. In P. McMichael (ed.), *The Global Restructuring of Agro-Food Systems*. Ithaca: Cornell University Press.

Friedman, Thomas L. 1999. *The Lexus and the Olive Tree*. New York: Farrar, Straus and Giroux.
———. 2004. What's That Sound? *New York Times*, 1 April: 23.

Friedmann, Harriet. 1982. The Political Economy of Food: The Rise and Fall of the Postwar International Food Order. *American Journal of Sociology* 88 (Supplement: Marxist Inquiries: Studies of Labor, Class, and States): S248–S286.
———. 1994. Distance and Durability: Shaky Foundations of the World Food Economy. In P. McMichael (ed.), *The Global Restructuring of Agro-Food Systems*. Ithaca: Cornell University Press.
———. 2005a. Biodiversity and Cultural Diversity in North American Foods. *Food News*. www.foodnews.ca. Archived at: http://www.slowfoodforum.org/archive/index.php/t-1018.html.
———. 2005b. From Colonialism to Green Capitalism: Social Movements and Emergence of Food Regimes. In F. H. Buttel and P. McMichael (eds.), *New Directions in the Sociology of Development*. Oxford: Elsevier.
———. 2006. From Colonialism to Green Capitalism: Social Movements and Emergence of Food Regimes. In Frederick H. Buttel and Philip McMichael (eds.), *New Directions in the Sociology of Global Development* (Research in Rural Sociology and Development, volume 11). Oxford: Elsevier.

Friedmann, Harriet, and Philip McMichael. 1989. Agriculture and the State System: The Rise and Decline of National Agricultures, 1870 to the Present. *Sociologia Ruralis* 29 (2): 93–117.

Friends of the MST. 2006a. Against Barbarism, Study; Against Individualism, Solidarity. *MST Informa* 117. http://www.mstbrazil.org/?q=node/331.
———. 2006b. For the first time, MST Landless Worker defends doctoral thesis. *Press Release*. http://www.mstbrazil.org/?q=doctoralmst.

Frontera NorteSur. 2011. *Tortilla Kings Claim New Mexico Conquest*. New Mexico State University 2011 [cited 12 July 2011]. Available from http://frontera.nmsu.edu/2011/04/15/tortilla-kings-claim-new-mexico-conquest/.

Fukuoka, Masanobu, Larry Korn, Chris Pearce and Tsune Kurosawa. 1978. *The One-Straw Revolution: An Introduction to Natural Farming*. Emmaus: Rodale.

Funes, Fernando, Luis Garcia, Martin Bourque, Nilda Perez and Peter Rosset. 2002. *Sustainable Agriculture and Resistance: Transforming Food Production in Cuba*. Oakland, CA: Food First Books.

Gale, Jason. 2010. India's Diabetes Epidemic Cuts Down Millions Who Escape Poverty. *Bloomberg.com*, 7 November.

Gallagher, Elizabeth, and Ursula Delworth. 2003. The Third Shift. Juggling Employment, Family, and the Farm. *Journal of Rural Community Psychology* 12 (2): 21–36.

Garcia, Ruben, and Andrea Buffa. 2006. *Watch Out Wal-Mart! Mexican Progressives Target Wal-Mart After Its Involvement in the Presidential Election*, 16 October. Available from: http://www.commondreams.org/views06/1016-30.htm.

Gardner, Gary, and Brian Halweil. 2000. Overfed and Underfed: The Global Epidemic of Malnutrition. In J. A. Peterson (ed.),*WorldWatch Paper*. Washington, DC: WorldWatch Institute.

Gautami, S., R. V. Sudershan, Ramesh V. Bhat, G. Suhasini, M. Bharati and K. P. C. Gandhi.

2001. Chemical Poisoning in Three Telengana Districts of Andhra Pradesh. *Forensic Science International* 122 (2–3): 167.

George, Susan. 1994. *A Fate Worse than Debt*. New York: Penguin.

Ghosh, Jayati. 2011. *Commodity speculation and the food crisis*. Word Development Movement 2010 [cited 18 October 2011]. Available from http://www.wdm.org.uk/sites/default/files/Commodity%20speculation%20and%20food%20crisis.pdf.

Gibson-Graham, J. K. 2003. Enabling Ethical Economies: Cooperativism and Class. *Critical Sociology* 29 (2): 123.

Gilbert, Jess, and Carolyn Howe. 1991. Beyond 'State vs. Society': Theories of the State and New Deal Agricultural Policies. *American Sociological Review* 56 (2): 204–220.

Gill, Dee. 2011. ADM Hit by Vote on Ethanol Subsidies; Shares are Likely Oversold. In *Forbes.com*: Forbes.

Gill, Gerard J., John Farrington, Edward Anderson, Cecilia Luttrell, Tim Conway, N. C. Saxena and Rachel Slater. 2003. *Food Security and the Millennium Development Goal on Hunger in Asia*. London: Overseas Development Institute.

Gillis, Justin. 2003. Debate Grows Over Biotech Food: Efforts to Ease Famine in Africa Hurt by U.S., European Dispute. *Washington Post*, 30 November.

Gilman, Sander L. 2008. *Fat : a cultural history of obesity*. Malden, MA: Polity.

Ginsberg, Allen. 2001. A Supermarket in California. In L. Pockell (ed.), *The 100 Best Poems of All Time*. New York: Warner Books.

Global Exchange. 2005. *The News on Chocolate Is Bittersweet: No Progress on Child Labor, but Fair Trade Chocolate Is on the Rise*. San Francisco: Global Exchange. http://www.globalexchange.org/campaigns/fairtrade/cocoa/chocolatereport2005.pdf.

Goetz, Stephan J., and Hema Swaminathan. 2004. *Wal-Mart and County-Wide Poverty*. University Park: Department of Agricultural Economics and Rural Sociology, The Pennsylvania State University. http://cecd.aers.psu.edu/pubs/PovertyResearchWM.pdf.

Goldzimmer, Aaron. 2003. *Worse than the World Bank? Expert Credit Agencies – The Secret Engine of Globalization*. Oakland, CA: Institute for Food and Development Policy/Food First.

Goodman, David, and Michael Redclift (eds.), 1989. *The International Farm Crisis*. New York: St Martin's Press.

Gopal, Priyamvada. 2006. The Story Peddled by Imperial Apologists is a Poisonous Fairytale. *Guardian*, 28 June.

Gorton, M., J. Sauer, and P. Supatpongkul. 2011. Wet Markets, Supermarkets and the "Big Middle" for Food Retailing in Developing Countries: Evidence from Thailand. *World Development* 39 (9):1624-1637.

GRAIN. 2006. Fowl Play: The Poultry Industry's Central Role in the Bird Flu Crisis. In *Grain Briefing*. Barcelona: GRAIN. http://www.grain.org/go/birdflu.

Greenberg, Stephen, and African Centre for Biosafety. 2004. 'The Venoms of Scorpions And Spiders …' *Global Agriculture and Genetically Modified Cotton in Africa*. Johannesburg: African Centre for Biosafety. http://www.gmwatch.org/archive2.asp?arcid=4571.

Greenhouse, Steven. 2004. In-House Audit Says Wal-Mart Violated Labor Laws. *New York Times*, 13 January: A16.

———. 2005. Labor Dept. Is Rebuked over Pact With Wal-Mart. *New York Times*, 1 November: A14.

Greenpeace International. 2006. *Eating Up the Amazon*. Amsterdam: Greenpeace International. http://www.greenpeace.org/forests.

Gregoire, A. 2002. The Mental Health of Farmers. *Occupational Medicine* 52 (8): 471–6.

Gresser, Charis, and Sophia Tickell. 2002. *Mugged: Poverty in Your Coffee Cup*. Oxford: Oxfam International. http://www.maketradefair.com/ en/index.php?file=16092002163229.htm.

Grievink, Jan-Willem. 2003. The Changing Face of the Global Food Industry. Paper read at OECD Conference, The Hague, 6 February. http://www.agribusiness accountability. org/pdfs//275_Changing%20Face%20of%20the%20Global%20Food%20Supply%20 Chain.pdf.

Groves, Derham. 2004. Gob Smacked! TV Dining in Australia Between 1956 and 1966. *Journal of Popular Culture* 37 (3): 409.

GRR (Rural Reflection Group). 2004. *Greenwash from the Soya Industry*. http://iguazu.grr. org.ar/textencing3.html.

Gunn, Simon. 2004. Class, Identity and the Urban: The Middle Class in England, c. 1790–1950. *Urban History* 31 (1): 29–47.

Hall, Gillette, and Harry Anthony Patrinos. 2005. *Indigenous Peoples, Poverty and Human Development in Latin America: 1994–2004*. Houndmills: Palgrave/Macmillan.

Hall, Kevin G. 2004. Slavery Exists Out of Sight in Brazil. *Knight Ridder Tribune Business News*, 5 September. http://www.knightridder.com/ papers/greatstories/wash/brazilslavery1.html.

Hall, Lee. 2005. Aliens on Spaceship Earth: The Controversial Sierra Club Elections. *Bender's Immigration Bulletin* 10: 1091–116.

Halweil, Brian. 2004. *Eat Here: Reclaiming Homegrown Pleasures in a Global Supermarket*. New York: W. W. Norton.

———. 2006. Can Organic Farming Feed Us All? *WorldWatch Magazine* 19 (3): 18–24.

Hanson, Gordon H. 2003. *What Has Happened to Wages in Mexico Since NAFTA? Implications for Hemispheric Free Trade*. Cambridge, MA: National Bureau of Economic Research.

Harnecker, Marta. 2003. *Landless People: Building a Social Movement*. São Paulo: Editora Expressão Popular.

Harris, Marvin. 1956. *Town and Country in Brazil*. Columbia University Contributions to Anthropology. No. 37. New York: Columbia University Press.

Harris, Paul. 2006. 37 Million Poor Hidden in the Land of Plenty. *Observer*, 19 February.

Hart, Gillian. 2002. *Disabling Globalization: Places of Power in Post-Apartheid South Africa*. Berkeley: University of California Press.

Harvard School of Public Health. 2011. *How to Spot Added Sugar on Food Labels*. Harvard University 2011 [cited 17 June 2011]. Available from http://www.hsph.harvard.edu/ nutritionsource/healthy-drinks/added-sugar-on-food-labels/index.html.

Hasse, Geraldo (text and research), and Fernando Bueno (photography). 1996. *O Brasil da Soja – Abrindo Frontieras, Semeando Cidades*. Translated by B. Becker and L. Becker. Porto Alegre: L&PM.

Haughton, A. J., G. T. Champion, C. Hawes, M. S. Heard, D. R. Brooks, D. A. Bohan, S. J. Clark, A. M. Dewar, E. L. Browne, A. J. G. Dewar, B. H. Garner, L. A. Haylock, S. L. Horne, N. S. Mason, R. J. N. Sands, L. G. Firbank, J. L. Osborne, J. N. Perry, P. Rothery, D. B. Roy, R. J. Scott, I. P. Woiwod, C. Birchall, M. P. Skellern, J. H. Walker, P. Baker and M. J. Walker. 2003. Invertebrate Responses to the Management of Genetically Modified Herbicide-tolerant and Conventional Spring Crops. II. Within-field Epigeal and Aerial Arthropods. *Philosophical Transactions of the Royal Society – Series B – Biological Sciences* 00358 (01439): 1863–78.

Hawes, C., A. J. Haughton, J. L. Osborne, D. B. Roy, S. J. Clark, J. N. Perry, P. Rothery, D. A. Bohan, D. R. Brooks, G. T. Champion, A. M. Dewar, M. S. Heard, I. P. Woiwod, R. E. Daniels, M. W. Young, A. M. Parish, R. J. Scott, L. G. Firbank and G. R. Squire. 2003. Responses of Plants and Invertebrate Trophic Groups to Contrasting Herbicide Regimes in the Farm Scale Evaluations of Genetically Modified Herbicide-tolerant Crops. *Philosophical Transactions of the Royal Society – Series B – Biological Sciences* 00358 (01439): 1899–914.

Hawkes, Corinna. 2006. Uneven Dietary Development: Linking the Policies and Processes of

Globalization with the Nutrition Transition, Obesity and Diet-related Chronic Diseases. *Globalization and Health* 2 (4). Available at http://www.globalizationandhealth.com/content/2/1/4.

Hay, Andrew. 2004. *Half of Brazil's Amazon Jungle Occupied, According to Study*. Reuters, 24 November.

Heard, M. S., C. Hawes, G. T. Champion, S. J. Clark, L. G. Firbank, A. J. Haughton, A. M. Parish, J. N. Perry, P. Rothery, R. J. Scott, M. P. Skellern, G. R. Squire and M. O. Hill. 2003. Weeds in Fields with Contrasting Conventional and Genetically Modified Herbicide-tolerant Crops. I. Effects on Abundance and Diversity. *Philosophical Transactions of the Royal Society – Series B – Biological Sciences* 00358 (01439): 1819–33.

Heffernan, William D. 2000. Concentration of Food Ownership and Control in Agriculture. In F. Magdoff, J. B. Foster and F. H. Buttel (eds.), *Hungry for Profit: The Agribusiness Threat to Farmers, Food and the Environment*. New York: Monthly Review Press.

Heim, Kristi. 2006. Want to Work for the Gates Foundation? *Seattle Times*, 17 October.

Hein, Kenneth. 2007. Coke and L'Oreal Partner on New Health Beverage. *Brandweek*, 12 March.

Helfand, Steven M. 1999. The Political Economy of Agricultural Policy in Brazil: Decision Making and Influence from 1964 to 1992. *Latin American Research Review* 34 (2): 3–41.

Heller, Joseph. 1961. *Catch-22: A Novel*. New York: Simon & Schuster.

Heller, Patrick. 2001. Moving the State: The Politics of Democratic Decentralization in Kerala, South Africa, and Porto Alegre. *Politics & Society* 29 (1): 131–63.

Henderson, V. R., and B. Kelly. 2005. Food Advertising in the Age of Obesity: Content Analysis of Food Advertising on General Market and African American Television. *Journal of Nutrition Education and Behavior* 37 (4): 191–6.

Hendrickson, Mary, and William D. Heffernan. 2007. *Concentration of Agricultural Markets*: Department of Rural Sociology, University of Missouri.

Hendrickson, Mary, William D. Heffernan, Philip H. Howard and Judith B. Heffernan. 2001. Consolidation in Food Retailing and Dairy. *British Food Journal* 103 (10): 715–28.

Henriques, Gisele, and Raj Patel. 2003. *Agricultural Trade Liberalization and Mexico*. Oakland, CA: Institute for Food and Development Policy.

Henriques, Ursula. 1968. How Cruel Was the Victorian Poor Law? *The Historical Journal* 11 (2): 365–71.

Heredia, Beatriz, Leonilde Medeiros, Moacir Palmeira, Rosângela Cintrão and Sérgio Pereira Leite. 2006. Regional Impacts of Land Reform in Brazil. In M. Courville, R. Patel and P. Rosset (eds.), *Promised Land: Competing Visions of Agrarian Reform*. Oakland, CA: Food First Books.

Herrington, J. D. 1996. Effects of Music in Service Environments: A Field Study. *Journal of Services Marketing* 10: 26.

Hickey, Ellen, and Anuradha Mittal. 2003. *Voices from the South: The Third World Debunks Corporate Myths on Genetically Engineered Crops*. San Francisco and Oakland, CA: a joint project of Food First/Institute for Food and Development Policy and Pesticide Action Network North America.

Hillman, Jimmye S., and Merle D. Faminow. 1987. Brazilian Soybeans: Agribusiness 'Miracle'. *Agribusiness* 3 (1): 3.

Hilton, David A. 2006. Pathogenesis and Prevalence of Variant Creutzfeldt-Jakob Disease. *The Journal of Pathology* 208 (2): 134–41.

Hilton, David A, Azra C. Ghani, Lisa Conyers, Philip Edwards, Linda McCardle, Diane Ritchie, Mark Penney, Doha Hegazy and James W. Ironside. 2004. Prevalence of Lymphoreticular Prion Protein Accumulation in UK Tissue Samples. *The Journal of Pathology* 203 (3): 733–9.

Hobsbawm, E. J. 1978. *The Age of Revolution: Europe, 1789–1848*. London: Abacus.

Hoffman, Daniel J., Ana L. Sawaya, Ieda Verreschi, Katherine L. Tucker and Susan B. Roberts. 2000. Why Are Nutritionally Stunted Children at Increased Risk of Obesity? Studies of Metabolic Rate and Fat Oxidation in Shantytown Children from São Paulo, Brazil. *American Journal of Clinical Nutrition* 72 (3): 702–7.

Holt-Gimenez, Eric. 2006. *Campesino A Campesino: Voices from Latin America's Farmer to Farmer Movement for Sustainable Agriculture.* Oakland, CA: Food First Books.

Holt-Giménez, Eric, and Raj Patel. 2009. *Food Rebellions! Crisis and the hunger for justice.* Oxford: Fahamu.

Hoover's Inc. 2011a. Altria Group, Inc. In-depth records.

———. 2011b. Archer-Daniels-Midland Company, In-depth Record.

———. 2011c. Gruma, S.A.B. de C.V. In-depth Records.

Hoppe, Robert, and Keith Wiebe. 2003. Agricultural Resources and Environmental Indicators: Land Ownership and Farm Structure. In R. Heimlich (ed.), *Agricultural Resources and Environmental Indicators, 2003.* Washington, DC: US Department of Agriculture.

Horsch, Robert. 2003. *Testimony of Dr. Robert Horsch, Vice President of Product and Technology Cooperation, Monsanto Company, St. Louis, MO.* Before the House Science Committee, Subcommittee on Research, Plant Biotechnology Research and Development in Africa: Challenges and Opportunities. Washington, DC: House Committee on Science and Technology. 12 June.

House Committee on Agriculture. 2011. *2008 Farm Bill.* US Government 2011 [cited 15 August 2011]. Available from http://agriculture.house.gov/singlepages.aspx?NewsID=1387&LSBID=23&RBSUSDA=T.

Housing Assistance Council. 2006. Poverty in Rural America. Washington DC: Housing Assistance Council.

Howard, Patricia. 2003. *The Major Importance of 'Minor' Resources: Women and Plant Biodiversity.* London: International Institute for Environment and Development Natural Resources Group and Sustainable Agriculture and Rural Livelihoods Programme. http://www.farmingsolutions.org/pdfdb/GK112.pdf.

Humphery, Kim. 1998. *Shelf Life: Supermarkets and the Changing Cultures of Consumption.* Cambridge: Cambridge University Press.

Hurston, Zora Neale. 1999. *Their Eyes Were Watching God: A Novel.* New York: Perennial Classics.

Huws, Ursula. 2003. *The Making of a Cybertariat: Virtual Work in a Real World.* New York: Monthly Review Press.

Hyderabad.co.in. 2011. *Hyderabad Demographics* 2008 [cited 23 June 2011]. Available from http://www.hyd.co.in/demographics/

Hymowitz, T., and W. R. Shurtleff. 2005. Debunking Soybean Myths and Legends in the Historical and Popular Literature. *Crop Science* 45 (2): 473–6.

ILO, International Labour Organization. 2004. Waiting in Correntes: Forced Labour in Brazil. *World of Work – The Magazine of the International Labour Organization* 50: 14–16.

———. 2005. A Global Alliance Against Forced Labour: Global Report under the Follow-up to the ILO Declaration on Fundamental Principles and Rights at Work 2005. Geneva: International Labour Organization.

Independent Science Panel, Miguel Altieri, Michael Antoniou, Susan Bardocz, David Bellamy, Elizabeth Bravo, Joe Cummins, Stanley Ewen, Edward Goldsmith, Brian Goodwin, Mae-Wan Ho, Malcolm Hooper, Vyvyan Howard, Brian John, Marijan Jos˘t, Lim Li Ching, Eva Novotny, Bob Orskov, Michel Pimbert, Arpad Pusztai, David Quist, Peter Rosset, Peter Saunders, Veljko Veljkovic, Roberto Verzola and Oscar B. Zamora. 2003. *The Case for a GM-Free Sustainable World* London: Institute for Science and Society. http://www.i-sis.org.uk/ispr-summary.php.

IAASTD, International Assessment of Agricultural Knowledge, Science and Technology for

Development. 2008. Executive Summary of the Synthesis Report. Johannesburg: IAASTD.

IHRSA. 2011. *Brazil Fitness Centers Spread as Brazilians Get Health Concerned*. IHRSA Industry News 2010 [cited August 19 2011]. Available from http://ihrsa-industry-news.blogspot.com/2010/07/brazil-fitness-centres-spread-as.html.

Instituto Nacional de Estadìstica, Geografìa e Inform·tica. 2005. *Estadìsticas de intentos de suicidio y suicidios*. Aguascalientes, Ags.: Instituto Nacional de Estadìstica, Geografìa e Inform·tica.

Inter-American Commission on Human Rights. 2003. *The Situation of the Rights of Women in Ciudad Juárez, Mexico: The Right to be Free from Violence and Discrimination*. OEA/Ser.L/V/II.117. 7 March 2003. Washington, DC: Inter-American Commission on Human Rights.

Irwin, Douglas A. 1996. *Against the Tide: An Intellectual History of Free Trade*. Princeton: Princeton University Press.

Isikoff, Michael. 1985. Andreas: College Drop-Out to Global Trader. *The Washington Post*, 8 December 1985: H 11.

Jaccoud, D'Alembert , Rosa Lemos de Sá, and Sarah Richardson. 2003. *Sustainability Assessment of Export-led Growth in Soy Production in Brazil*. WWF – Worldwide Fund for Nature. Available at http://www.bothends.org/strategic/soy25.pdf.

Jackson, Kevin, and Richard Heeps. 2006. *Fast: Feasting on the Streets of London*. London: Portobello Books.

Jacobs, Joseph. 1890. *English Fairy Tales*. London. http://www.pitt.edu/~dash/type-0328jack.html.

Jagarnath, Vashna. 2006. *Sydenham: A Social Historical Study of the Impact Apartheid Race Legislation*. Durban: Department of History and Internet Studies, University of Kwa-Zulu-Natal.

James, C. L. R. 1963. *The Black Jacobins; Toussaint L'Ouverture and the San Domingo Revolution*. 2nd edn. New York: Vintage Books.

Jeffress, Lynn, with Jean-Paul Mayanobe. 2001. A World Struggle Is Underway: An Interview with José Bové. *Z Magazine*, June.

Jensen, E. B., K. A. Schafft and C. C. Hinrichs. 2006. *Examining Prevalence of Childhood Obesity and School Wellness Initiatives within Pennsylvania's Food Deserts*. Paper read at Annual Meeting of the Rural Sociological Society, August 9–12. Louisville, KY.

Ji, C. Y. 2008. The prevalence of childhood overweight/obesity and the epidemic changes in 1985-2000 for Chinese school-age children and adolescents. *Obesity Reviews* 9 (01):78-81.

Jiang, Steven. 2011. Tension, security high in China's 'jeans capital' after riots. *CNN World*, June 17.

Jiménez-Cruz, A., M. Bacardí-Gascón and A. A. Spindler. 2003. Obesity and Hunger among Mexican-Indian Migrant Children on the US–Mexico Border. *International Journal of Obesity* 27: 740–7.

Johnson, Jo. 2007. India Opens Western-style Supermarkets. *Financial Times*, 30 January.

Jones, David. 2010. Top four brewers make up half global beer market. *Reuters*, 8 February.

Jones, Jeffrey M. 2011. *Americans' Views on Immigration Holding Steady*. Gallup 2011 [cited 5 August 2011]. Available from http://www.gallup.com/poll/148154/Americans-Views-Immigration-Holding-Steady.aspx

Josling, T, and S. Tangerman. 2003. Production and Export Subsidies in Agriculture: Lessons from GATT and WTO Disputes Involving the US and EC. In E.-U. Peters-Mann and M. A. Pollack (eds.), *Transatlantic Trade Disputes: The EU, the US, and the WTO*. Oxford: Oxford University Press. Jubilee Research. 2002. *IMF Boss Blames World Bank and EU for Malawi Blunder*. 4 July. http://www.jubileeresearch.org/worldnews/africa/

malawi040702.htm.

Kadidal, Shayana. 1997. United States Patent Prior Art Rules and the Neem Controversy: a Case of Subject-matter Imperialism? *Biodiversity and Conservation* 7 (1): 27–39.

Kamalurre Mehinaku. 2006. 'We Respect Whites but They Don't Respect Us'. *Guardian*, 6 September.

Kamath, Purnima, and Catherine Godin. 2001. French Carrefour in South-east Asia. *British Food Journal* 103 (7): 479–94.

Kantor, Linda Scott. 2001. Community Food Security Programs Improve Food Access. *Food Review* 24 (1): 20–6.

Kar, Debyani. 2005. The Tsunami's Aftermath: Reconstruction or Economic Opportunism? *Foreign Policy in Focus commentary*, 23 June. http://www.fpif.org/commentary/2005/0506tsunami_body.html.

Kaur, Mallika. 2010. The Paradox of India's Bread Basket: Farmer Suicides in Punjab. *The Fletcher Journal of Human Security* XXV:39-60.

Kelly, Thomas J. 2001. Neoliberal Reforms and Rural Poverty. *Latin American Perspectives* 28 (3): 84–103.

Kelsey, Jane. 1995. *The New Zealand Experiment: A World Model for Structural Adjustment?* Auckland: Auckland University Press.

King, T., A. M. Kavanagh, D. Jolley, G. Turrell, and D. Crawford. 2005. Weight and Place: A Multilevel Cross-sectional Survey of Area-level Social Disadvantage and Overweight/Obesity in Australia. *International Journal of Obesity* 0307-0565/05: 1–7.

Klare, Michael T. 2001. *Resource Wars: The New Landscape of Global Conflict*. New York: Metropolitan Books.

———. 2006. *The Coming Resource Wars*, 7 March 2006. TomPaine.com. Available from http://www.tompaine.com/articles/2006/03/07/ the_coming_resource_wars.ph.

Klein, Naomi. 2000. *No Logo: No Space, No Choice, No Jobs, Taking Aim at the Brand Bullies*. London: Flamingo.

Klimis-Zacas, Dorothy, and Ira Wolinsky. 2004. *Nutritional Concerns of Women*. 2nd edn. Boca Raton: CRC Press.

Kneen, Brewster. 1995. *Invisible Giant: Cargill and Its Transnational Strategies*. Halifax, Nova Scotia: Fernwood Publishing.

Koch, C., and E. C. Koch. 2003. Preconceptions of Taste Based on Color. *Journal of Psychology* 137 (3): 233–42.

Kolodinsky, Jane, and Michele Cranwell. 2000. *The Poor Pay More? Now They Don't Even Have a Store to Choose From: Bringing a Supermarket Back to the City*. Paper read at American Council on Consumer Interests, 46th Annual Conference, 22–5 March. http://cnr.consumerinterests.org/files/public/poor.PDF.

Krebbs, A. V. 1999 Corporate Agribusiness: Economic Concentration is Thy Name. *The Agribusiness Examiner* 55, 17 November. http://www.electricarrow.com/CARP/agbiz/agex-55.html.

Krebs, A. V. 2000. *Agribusiness Examiner #76*. June 1. Everett, WA: Corporate Agribusiness Research Project. http://www.electricarrow.com/CARP/agbiz/agex-76.html.

Kreidler, N. B., and S. Joseph-Mathews. 2009. How green should you go? understanding the role of green atmospherics in service environment evaluations. *International Journal of Culture, Tourism, and Hospitality Research* 3 (3):228-245.

Krenichyn, Kira. 2006. 'The Only Place to Go and Be in the City': Women Talk about Exercise, Being Outdoors, and the Meanings of a Large Urban Park. *Health & Place* 12 (4): 631–43.

Labbi, Theola. 2003. U.S. Troops Order Comfort, With Fries on the Side: Soldiers Looking for a Taste of Home Make for a Booming Business at Iraq's First Burger King. *Washington Post*, 19 October: 25.

Labor Council for Latin American Advancement, and Public Citizen's Global Trade Watch.

2004. *Another Americas Is Possible: The Impact of NAFTA on the U.S. Latino Community and Lessons for Future Trade Agreements*. Washington, DC: Public Citizen's Global Trade Watch. http://www.citizen.org/documents/LatinosReportFINAL.pdf.

Labour Research Service, Women on Farms Project, and Programme for Land And Agrarian Studies (University of the Western Cape). n.d. *Behind the Label: A Workers' Audit of the Working and Living Conditions on Selected Wine Farms in the Western Cape*. Cape Town: LRS/WFP/PLAAS.

Lang, Tim. 2005. Food Control or Food Democracy? Re-engaging Nutrition with Society and the Environment. *Public Health Nutrition* 8: 730.

LAO, Legislative Analyst's Office. 2004. *Cal Facts: California's Economy and Budget in Perspective*. Sacramento, CA: Legislative Analyst's Office.

———. 2006. *Cal Facts: California's Economy and Budget in Perspective*. Sacramento, CA: Legislative Analyst's Office.

Lappé, Frances Moore and Joseph Collins. 1977. *Food First: Beyond the Myth of Scarcity*. Boston: Houghton-Mifflin.

Lapper, Richard. 2007. US Migrant Workers Send Home $62.3bn. *Financial Times*, 15 March.

Larson, Jeffrey S., Eric Bradlow and Peter Fader. 2005. An Exploratory Look at Supermarket Shopping Paths. *International Journal of Research in Marketing*. 22 (4): 395–414.

Lasala Blanco, Narayani Donativo. 2003. *Las negociaciones del maíz en el Tratado de Libre Comercio de América del Norte*. Mexico: Centro de Estudios Internacionales, El Colegio de México, México DF.

LaSalle, Tim J., and Paul Hepperly. 2008. Regenerative Organic Farming: A Solution to Global Warming. Kutztown, PA Rodale Institute.

Lashus, K. R., R. F. Loughran, and M. S. Candler. 2008. Fear the ICE Man: Lessons From the Swift Raids to Warm You Up-The New Government Perspective on Employer Sanctions. *Nova law review*. 32 (2):391-422.

Lawrence, Robert S., Polly Walker, Pamela Rhubart-Berg, Shawn McKenzie and Kristin Kelling. 2005. Public Health Implications of Meat Production and Consumption. *Public Health Nutrition* 8: 348–56.

Lazzarini, Sérgio Giovanetti, and Paulo Faveret Filho. 1997. *Grupo André Maggi: Financiando um novo corredor de exportação*. São Paulo: USP/FEAC.

Leather, Suzi. 1996. *The Making of Modern Malnutrition: An Overview of Food Poverty in the UK*. London: Caroline Walker Trust.

Lederman, Daniel, William F. Maloney and Luis Servén. 2003. *Lessons from NAFTA for Latin American and Caribbean (LAC) Countries: A Summary of Research Findings*. Washington, DC: World Bank.

Leitzmann, Claus, and Geoffrey Cannon. 2005. Dimensions, Domains and Principles of the New Nutrition Science. *Public Health Nutrition* 8: 787.

Lenin, Vladimir Ilyich. 1970. *Imperialism, the Highest Stage of Capitalism: A Popular Outline*. New edn, Little Lenin Library, vol. 15. New York: International Publishers.

Lentz, Charles M. 1989. Grocery Shopping in the 1930s. *Michigan History* 73 (2): 14–15.

Levenstein, Harvey. 1988. *Revolution at the Table: The Transformation of the American Diet*. Oxford: Oxford University Press.

———. 1996. The Politics of Nutrition in North America. *Neuroscience & Biobehavioral Reviews* 20 (1): 75.

Lewis, D. A. 1995. Henry Ford and His Magic Beanstalk. *Michigan History* 79 (3): 10–17.

Lewis, Jessa M. 2005. *Strategies for Survival: Migration and Fair Trade-Organic Coffee Production in Oaxaca, Mexico*. Working Paper 118. June. San Diego: The Center for Comparative Immigration Studies, University of California, San Diego. http://www.ccis-ucsd.org/ publications/wrkg118.pdf.

Lex. 2011. Russia Wheat Ban Worked. *Financial Times*, May 31 2011

Lichtarowicz, Ania. 2004. *S Africans 'as Fat as Americans'.* BBCNews.com, 29 October.

Lieber, James B. 2000. *Rats in the Grain: The Dirty Tricks and Trials of Archer Daniels Midland.* New York: Four Walls Eight Windows.

Lilley, Sasha. 2004. *Paving the Amazon with Soy – World Bank Bows to Audit of Maggi Loan.* Corpwatch.org, 16 December. Available from http://www.corpwatch.org/article.php?id=11756.

Lind, James, Physician to the Royal Hospital at Haslar. 1753. *A Treatise of the Scurvy. In three parts. Containing an inquiry into the nature, causes, and cure, of that disease.* Edinburgh.

Lipman, Barbara. 2006. *A Heavy Load: The Combined Housing and Transportation Burdens of Working Families.* Washington D.C.: Center for Housing Policy. http://www.nhc.org/pdf/pub_heavy_load_10_06.pdf.

Littlewood, Roland. 2004. Commentary: Globalization, Culture, Body Image, and Eating Disorders. *Culture, Medicine and Psychiatry* 28 (4): 597–602.

Lloyd's List. 2005. Trouble Looms for Brazil Soya. *Lloyd's List*, 8 August: 10.

Lobe, Jim. 2001. *Learn from Cuba, Says World Bank.* Interpress Service, 30 April.

Lobell, David B., Wolfram Schlenker, and Justin Costa-Roberts. 2011. Climate Trends and Global Crop Production Since 1980. *Science.*

Masters, Michael M. 2009. Testimony of Michael W. Masters before the Committee on Homeland Security and Governmental Affairs, United States Senate . Washington DC, 5 August 2009.

Lobstein, Tim. 2006. Commentary: Obesity – Public Health Crisis, Moral Panic or a Human Rights Issue? *International Journal of Epidemiology* 35 (1): 74–6.

Lopez, Rigoberto A., M. Azzam Azzeddine and Lirón-España Carmen. 2002. Market Power and/or Efficiency: A Structural Approach. *Review of Industrial Organization* 20 (2): 115–26.

Lopez-Zetina, Javier, Howard Lee and Robert Friis. 2006. The Link Between Obesity and the Built Environment. Evidence from an Ecological Analysis of Obesity and Vehicle Miles of Travel in California. *Health & Place.* 12(4): 656-664.

Louthan, David. 2003. They Are Lying About Your Food: A Worker from the Mad Cow Meat Plant Speaks Out. *CounterPunch.* http://www.counterpunch.org/louthan01202004.html.

Lowrey, Tina M. 2008. Brick & mortar shopping in the 21st century. Paper read at Conference on Advertising and Consumer Psychology, 2008, at New York.

Lucas, Caroline. 2007. Bird Flu's Link with the Crazy Trade in Poultry. *Financial Times*, 26 February: 15.

Lustig, Nora. 1996. Solidarity as a Strategy of Poverty Alleviation. In W. Cornelius, A. Craig and J. Fox (eds.), *Transforming State–Society Relations in Mexico.* La Jolla: Center for US–Mexican Studies, University of California, San Diego.

Lyons, John. 2007. Southern Hospitality: In Mexico, Wal-Mart is Defying Its Critics. *The Wall Street Journal*, 5 March 2007.

Macduff, Ian. 2006. Your Pace or Mine? Culture, Time, and Negotiation. *Negotiation Journal* 22 (1): 31–45.

Malcolm, Andrew D. 1985. Deaths on the Iowa Prairie: 4 New Victims of Economy. *New York Times*, 11 December.

Malthus, Thomas Robert. 1993. *An Essay on the Principle of Population*, ed. with an introduction by Geoffrey Gilbert. Oxford: Oxford University Press.

Mamen, Katy, Steven Gorelick, Helena Norberg-Hodge and Diana Deumling. 2004. *Ripe for Change: Rethinking California's Food Economy.* Berkeley, CA: International Society for Ecology and Culture.

Mann, Michael, and Dylan Riley. 2007. Explaining Macro-regional Trends in Global Income Inequalities, 1950–2000. *Socio-Economic Review* 5(1): 81–115.

Manning, Richard. 2004a. *Against the Grain: How Agriculture Has Hijacked Civilization*. New York: North Point Press.

——. 2004b. The Oil We Eat: Following the Food Chain Back to Iraq. *Harpers*. 308 (1845): 37–45.

Marais, Hein. 2000. *South Africa: Limits to Change*. London: Zed Books.

Marcu, M. 2009. 'The EU-27 population continues to grow.' *Population and Social Conditions*. Print.

MARI, Warangal, Secunderabad CSA and Secunderabad CWS. 2005. *Killing and Poisoning –Pests or Human Beings? Acute Poisoning of Pesticide Users through Pesticide Exposure/ Inhalation*. Secunderabad: CSA-India.

Market Research. 2011. Supermarkets & Hypermarket Retailing in China: A Market Analysis. MarketResearch.com.

Markets and Markets. 2011. *Global Weight Loss & Diet Management Products & Services Market (2010-2015)*. Markets and Markets 2011 [cited 16 June 2011]. Available from http://www.marketsandmarkets.com/PressReleases/global-weight-loss-diet-management-products-services-market.asp.

Martin, Philip L. 2003. *Promise Unfulfilled: Unions, Immigration, and the Farm Workers*. Ithaca: ILR Press.

Martínez-Torres, Maria Elena. 2006. *Organic Coffee: Sustainable Development by Mayan Farmers*. Athens: Ohio University Center for International Studies.

Martins, Monica Dias. 2006. Learning to Participate: The MST Experience in Brazil. In M. Courville, R. Patel and P. Rosset (eds.), *Promised Land: Competing Visions of Agrarian Reform*. Oakland, CA: Food First Books.

Marx, Karl. 1852. Free Trade and The Chartists. *New York Daily Tribune*, 25 August.

Mathews, Ryan. 1996. Introduction: Background of a Revolution and the Birth of an Institution. *Progressive Grocer* 75 (12): 29.

Mattera, Philip. 2011. Shifting the Burden for Vital Public Services: Walmart's Tax Avoidance Schemes. Washington, DC.

Mattera, Philip, and Anna Purinton, with Jeff McCourt, Doug Hoffer, Stephanie Greenwood and Alyssa Talanker. 2004. *Shopping for Subsidies: How Wal-Mart Uses Taxpayer Money to Finance Its Never-Ending Growth*. Washington, DC: Good Jobs First. http://www.goodjobsfirst.org/pdf/wmtstudy.pdf.

Matthiessen, Peter. 1969. *Sal si puedes; Cesar Chavez and the New American Revolution*. New York: Random House.

Mattila, A. S., and J. Wirtz. 2001. Congruency of Scent and Music as a Driver of In-store Evaluations and Behavior. *Journal of Retailing* 77 (2): 273–89.

McCance, R. A., and Elsie M. Widdowson. 1956. *Breads, White and Brown: Their Place in Thought and Social History*. London: Pitman Medical Pub. Co.

Mccarthy, Michael, and Andrew Buncombe. 2005. The Rape of the Rainforest ... And This Is the Man Behind It. *Independent*, 20 May: 36–7.

Mccarthy, Michael. 2005. How Demand for Soya Drives the Destruction. *Global News Wire – Europe Intelligence Wire – Financial Times*, 20 May.

McCrae, Niall. 2004. The Beer Ration in Victorian Asylums. *History of Psychiatry* 15 (2): 155–75.

McGhee, Tom. 2007. Meatpacker Swift to be sold for $225 million. *Denver Post*, 29 May.

McGinnis, J. Michael, Jennifer Appleton Gootman, and Vivicia I. Kraak, eds. 2006. *Food Marketing to Children and Youth: Threat or Opportunity?* Washington, DC: The National Academies Press. http://books.nap.edu/openbook.php?record_id=11514&page=R1.

McGirk, Tim. 1995. India Turns Its Back on Western Ways. *Independent*, 29 September: 16.

McMichael, Philip. 1992. Tensions between National and International Control of the World Food Order: Contours of a New Food Regime. *Sociological Perspectives* 35 (2, Studies in the New International Comparative Political Economy): 343–65.

———. 1994. *The Global Restructuring of Agro-food Systems: Food Systems and Agrarian Change*. Ithaca: Cornell University Press.

———. 2003. Food Security and Social Reproduction: Issues and Contradictions. In I. Bakker and S. Gill (eds.), *Power, Production, and Social Reproduction: Human Insecurity in the Global Political Economy*. New York: Palgrave Macmillan.

———. 2006. Globalization and the Agrarian World. In G. Ritzer (ed.), *The Blackwell Companion to Globalization*. Oxford: Blackwell.

———. forthcoming. Food Sovereignty, Social Reproduction, and the Agrarian Question. In A. H. Akram-Lodhi and C. Kay (eds.), *Peasant Livelihoods, Rural Transformation and the Agrarian Question*. London: Routledge.

McMichael, Philip, and Chul-Kyoo Kim. 1994. Japanese and South Korean Agricultural Restructuring in Comparative and Global Perspective. In P. McMichael (ed.), *The Global Restructuring of Agro-food Systems*. Ithaca: Cornell University Press.

McWilliams, Carey. 1936. Gunkist Oranges. *Pacific Weekly*, 20 July.

Meacham, Standish. 1972. 'The Sense of an Impending Clash': English Working-Class Unrest before the First World War. *The American Historical Review* 77 (5): 1343–64.

Meltzer, H., C. Griffiths, A. Brock, C. Rooney, and R. Jenkins. 2008. Patterns of suicide by occupation in England and Wales: 2001-2005. *British Journal of Psychiatry* 193 (1):73-76.

Memarsadeghi, Sanaz, and Raj Patel. 2003. Agricultural Restructuring and Concentration in the United States: Who Wins, Who Loses? Oakland, CA: Institute for Food and Development Policy/Food First.

Mendez, Michelle A., Carlos A. Monteiro and Barry M. Popkin. 2005. Overweight Exceeds Underweight among Women in Most Developing Countries. *American Journal of Clinical Nutrition* 81 (3): 714–21.

Mendoza, Martha, and Christopher Sullivan. 2006. Corporations Stiffing Government on Fines. *Associated Press*, 19 March. http://www.commondreams.org/headlines06/0319-08.htm.

Menzies, Gavin. 2002. *1421: The Year China Discovered the World*. London: Bantam.

Michon, R., J. C. Chebat, and L. W. Turley. 2005. Mall Atmospherics: The Interaction Effects of the Mall Environment on Shopping Behavior. *Journal of Business Research* 58 (5): 576–83.

Middleton, Nicos, David Gunnella, Stephen Frankel, Elise Whitley and Daniel Dorling. 2003. Urban–Rural Differences in Suicide Trends in Young Adults: England and Wales, 1981–1998. *Social Science and Medicine* (57): 1183–94.

Miller, Darlene. Forthcoming. Local Suppliers and South African Retail Expansion in Africa. *South African Labour Bulletin*.

Miller, Darlene. 2008. Food Frontiers in Zambia: Resistance and Partnership in Shoprite's Retail Empire. *AfricaFiles* 8 (3).

Miller, George. 2004. *Everyday Low Wages: The Hidden Price We All Pay For Wal-Mart – A Report by the Democratic Staff of the Committee on Education and the Workforce U.S. House of Representatives – Representative George Miller (D-CA), Senior Democrat*. Washington, DC: Democratic Staff Committee on Education and the Workforce, US House of Representatives.

Ministry of Finance and Company Affairs – Government of India. 2003. *Economic Survey 2002–2003*. New Delhi: Ministry of Finance and Company Affairs.

Mintz, Sidney W. 1985. *Sweetness and Power: The Place of Sugar in Modern History*. New York: Penguin.

———. 1995. Food and Its Relationship to Concepts of Power. In P. McMichael (ed.), *Food and Agrarian Orders in the World-Economy*. Westport: Greenwood Press.

Mintz, Sidney, and Harriet Friedmann. 2004. *1750: Colonialismo e Prima Mondializzazione'. Atlante dell'allimentazione e della gastronomia*. Torino: Unione Tipografico-Editrice Torinese.

Mishel, Lawrence, Jared Bernstein and Heather Boushey. 2003. *The State of Working America: 2002–03*. Ithaca: ILR Press.

Mishra, Sourav. 2006. Revised Menu: India Looks to Open Agriculture to US Corporates. *Down to Earth: Science and Development Online*, 10 March. http://www.downtoearth.org.in/full6.asp?foldername=20060315&filename=news&sec_id=4&sid=3.

Mitchell, Donald. 2008. A Note on Rising Food Prices. Washington DC: World Bank Development Prospects Group

Mitchell, Greg. 1992. *The Campaign of the Century: Upton Sinclair's Race for Governor of California and the birth of Media Politics*. New York: Random House.

Mitchell, Stacy. 2005. *Responding to Reich on Wal-Mart*. http://www.newrules.org/retail/news_slug.php?slugid=288.

Mohanty. B. B. 2005. 'We Are Like the Living Dead': Farmer Suicides in Maharashtra, Western India. *Journal of Peasant Studies* 32 (2): 243–76.

Mohanty, Mritiunjoy. 2008. Small Farmers and the Doha Round: Lessons from Mexico's NAFTA Experience. *La Chronique Des Amériques* 12.

Mohapatra, Sanket, Dilip Ratha, and Ani Silwal. 2011. Migration and Development Brief. Washington D.C.: World Bank.

Mokdad, Ali H., Earl S. Ford, Barbara A. Bowman, William H. Dietz, Frank Vinicor, Virginia S. Bales and James S. Marks. 2003. Prevalence of Obesity, Diabetes, and Obesity-Related Health Risk Factors, 2001. *Journal of the American Medical Association* 289 (1): 76–9.

Monbiot, George. 2002a. *The Covert Biotech War*. http://www.monbiot.com/archives/2002/11/19/the-covert-biotech-war/.

———. 2002b. *The Fake Persuaders*. http://www.monbiot.com/ archives/2002/05/14/the-fake-persuaders/.

———. 2005a. *How Much Energy Do We Have?* ZNet, 9 December. Available from http://www.zmag.org/sustainers/content/2005-12/09monbiot.cfm.

———. 2005b. The Most Destructive Crop on Earth Is No Solution to the Energy Crisis. *Guardian*, 6 December.

Mondragón, Hector. 2000. *U.S. Fuelling the Fires in Colombia*. Available from http://www.nadir.org/nadir/initiativ/agp/free/colombia/mondrag1.htm.

Monsalve-Suárez, Sofía. 2006. *Gender and Land*. In M. Courville, R. Patel and P. Rosset (eds.), *Promised Land: Competing Visions of Agrarian Reform*. Oakland, CA: Food First Books.

Monsanto Inc. 2005. *Seminis. Acquisition, Investor Conference Call 2005*. Available from www.monsanto.com/monsanto/content/investor/ financial/presentations/2005/01-24-05_low.pdf.

Morales, Michel, and Bertram Verhaag. 2004. *Life Running out of Control*. Munich: DENKmal-Films.

Morgan, Faith. 2004. *The Power of Community: How Cuba Survived Peak Oil*. Yellow Springs, OH: AlchemyHouse Productions Inc. in association with The Community Solution.

Morland, Kimberly, Ana V. Diez Roux and Steve Wing. 2006. Supermarkets, Other Food Stores, and Obesity: The Atherosclerosis Risk in Communities Study. *American Journal of Preventive Medicine* 30 (4): 333.

Morland, Kimberly, Steve Wing, Ana Diez Roux and Charles Poole. 2002. Neighborhood Characteristics Associated with the Location of Food Stores and Food Service Places. *American Journal of Preventive Medicine* 22 (1): 23.

Müller, Anders Riel and Raj Patel. 2004. *Shining India? Economic Liberalization and Rural Poverty in the 1990s*. Oakland, CA: Institute for Food and Development Policy/Food First.

Munn, Alvin A. 1950. Production and Utilization of the Soybean in the United States. *Economic Geography* 26 (3): 223–4.

Murphy, Sophia. 2006. *Concentrated Market Power and Agricultural Trade*. Ecofair Trade Discussion Paper 1. August. http://www.tradeobservatory.org/library.cfm?refid=89014.

Muse, Toby. 2007. Colombians Want Banana Execs Extradited. *Associated Press*, 17 March.

Nadal, Alejandro, and Timothy A. Wise. 2004. *The Environmental Costs of Agricultural Trade Liberalization: Mexico-U.S. Maize Trade Under NAFTA*. Medford, MA: Working Group on Development and Environment in the Americas, Global Development And Environment Institute, Tufts University.

Nadal, Alejandro. 2000. *The Environmental and Social Impacts of Economic Liberalization on Corn Production in Mexico: A Study Commissioned by Oxfam GB and WWF International September 2000*. Oxford: Oxfam GB. http://www.oxfam.org.uk/what_we_do/issues/livelihoods/downloads/corn_mexico.pdf.

Nancy, Jean-Luc. 2000. *Being Singular Plural*. Translated by R. D. Richardson and A. E. O'Byrne. Stanford: Stanford University Press.

Nasrallah, Nawal. 2003. *Delights from the Garden of Eden: A Cookbook and a History of the Iraqi Cuisine*. Bloomington: AuthorHouse.

Navdanya and Navdanya International, International Commission on the Future of Food and Agriculture, and The Center for Food Safety. 2011. A Global Citizens Report on the State of GMOs- False Promises, Failed Technologies. Navdanya International.

Nayak, Bhabani Shankar. 2002. *Public Distribution System and Food Security in Orissa: A Case Study of Kalahandi District*. Department of Political Science, University of Hyderabad, Hyderabad.

Nehru, Jawaharlal. 1984. *Selected Works of Jawaharlal Nehru*. New Delhi: Jawaharlal Nehru Memorial Fund.

Nelson, Dean. 2011. India opens doors to supermarket giants - with strings attached. *The Telegraph*, June 05.

Nemerov, Howard. 1967. Grace to be Said at the Supermarket. In H. Nemerov, *Blue Swallows*. Chicago: Chicago University Press.

Neruda, Pablo. 1952. La United Fruit Co. In P. Neruda. *Poesia Politica (Discursos Politicos)*. Santiago de Chile: Editora Austral.

Nestle, Marion. 2002. *Food Politics: How the Food Industry Influences Nutrition and Health*. Berkeley: University of California Press.

Neuwirth, Robert. 2005. *Shadow Cities: A Billion Squatters, a New Urban World*. New York: Routledge.

Neven, David, and Thomas Reardon. 2004. The Rise of Kenyan Supermarkets and the Evolution of Their Horticulture Product Procurement Systems. *Development Policy Review* 22 (6): 669–99.

NHS Information Centre. 2010. National Child Measurement Programme: England, 2009/10 school year Leeds: The NHS Information Centre, Lifestyles Statistics.

Nicholas, Stephen, and Deborah Oxley. 1993. The Living Standards of Women during the Industrial Revolution, 1795–1820. *The Economic History Review* 46 (4): 723–49.

Nicholls, Clara Ines, Nilda Pérez, Luis Vasquez and Miguel A. Altieri. 2002. The Development and Status of Biologically Based Integrated Pest Management in Cuba. *Integrated Pest Management Reviews* 7 (1): 1–16.

Nickson, Elizabeth 2004. Green Power, Black Death. *National Post*, 9 January: A12.

Nord, Mark, Margaret Andrews and Steven Carlson. 2006. *Household Food Security in the United States, 2005*. Washington, DC: United States Department of Agriculture.

Nord, Mark, Alisha Coleman-Jensen, Margaret Andrews, and Steven Carlson. 2010. Household Food Security in the United States, 2009. Washington, DC: U.S. Dept. of Agriculture, Economic Research Service.

Notes From Nowhere. 2003. *We Are Everywhere: The Irresistible Rise of Global Anti-capitalism*. London: Verso.

Novartis. 2005. *Annual Report*. Basel: Novartis A.G. O'Brien, Chris. 2006. The Perils of Globeerization. Washington, DC: Foreign Policy in Focus. http://www.fpif.org/fpiftxt/3637.

OAU (Organization of African Unity). 1981. *The Lagos Plan of Action for the Economic Development of Africa 1980–2000*. Geneva: OAU.

Oddy, D. J. 1970. Working-class Diets in Late Nineteenth-Century Britain. *The Economic History Review* 23 (2): 314–23.

OED. 1992. *The Oxford English Dictionary*. 2nd edn, on compact for the IBM PC. Oxford: Oxford University Press.

Oeppen J. and J. Vaupel. 2002. Broken Limits to Life Expectancy. *Science*. 296: 1029–31. Offer, Avner. 1991. *The First World War: An Agrarian Interpretation*. New York: Clarendon Press.

————. 1998. Epidemics of Abundance: Overeating and Slimming in the USA and Britain Since the 1950s. In *University of Oxford, Discussion Papers in Economic and Social History*. Oxford: Oxford University. O'Hara, Sabine, U. and Stagl Sigrid. 2001. Global Food Markets and Their Local Alternatives: A Socio-Ecological Economic Perspective. *Population & Environment* 22 (6): 533–54.

Oliver, J. Eric. 2005. *Fat Politics: The Real Story behind America's Obesity Epidemic*. New York: Oxford University Press.

Olshansky, S. Jay, Douglas J. Passaro, Ronald C. Hershow, Jennifer Layden, Bruce A. Carnes, Jacob Brody, Leonard Hayflick, Robert N. Butler, David B. Allison and David S. Ludwig. 2005. A Potential Decline in Life Expectancy in the United States in the 21st Century. *New England Journal of Medicine* 352 (11): 1138–45.

Omahen, Sharon. 2003. New food products lifeblood of industry. *Georgia Faces*. June 26. http://georgiafaces.caes.uga.edu/getstory.cfm?storyid=1885.

Ong, Paul, and Evelyn Blumenberg. 1998. Job Access, Commute and Travel Burden among Welfare Recipients. *Urban Studies* 35 (1): 77–93.

OpenSecrets.org. 2011. *Lobbying: Altria Group*. Center For Responsive Politics 2011 [cited 20 July 2011]. Available from http://www.opensecrets.org/lobby/client_reports.php?id=D000000067&year=2005.

Orbach, Susie. 2006. Commentary: There is a Public Health Crisis – It's Not Fat on the Body but Fat in the Mind and the Fat of Profits. *International Journal of Epidemiology* 35: 67–9.

PA Newswire. 2003. Fast Food Comes to Iraq. *Sydney Morning Herald*, 21 April.

Pacheco-Lopez, Penelope. 2005. The Effect of Trade Liberalization on Exports, Imports, the Balance of Trade, and Growth: The Case of Mexico. *Journal of Post Keynesian Economics* 27 (4): 595–619.

Packard, Vance. 1957. *The Hidden Persuaders*. London: Longmans, Green and Co. Ltd.

Page, Jeremy. 2007. Indian Children Suffer More Malnutrition than in Ethiopia. *The Times*, 22 February.

PAN. 2011. *Phorate - Registration, import consent and bans*. PAN Pesticides Database 2010 [cited June 26 2011]. Available from http://www.pesticideinfo.org/Detail_ChemReg.jsp?Rec_Id=PC33402.

Parasecoli, Fabio. 2003. Postrevolutionary Chowhounds: Food, Globalization, and the Italian Left. *Gastronomica* 3 (3): 29–39.

Parry, M. L., C. Rosenzweig, A. Iglesias, M. Livermore and G. Fischer. 2004. Effects of Climate Change on Global Food Production under SRES Emissions and Socio-economic Scenarios. *Global Environmental Change* 14: 53–67.

Parvanta, S. A., J. D. Brown, X. Zhao, S. Du, C. R. Zimmer, and F. Zhai. 2010. Television Use and Snacking Behaviors Among Children and Adolescents in China. *Journal of Adolescent Health* 46 (4):339-345.

Passel, J. S. 2009. *A Portrait of Unauthorized Immigrants in the United States*: Pew Research Center. Retrieved March 20, 2012 from http://pewresearch.org/pubs/1190/portrait-unauthorized-immigrants-states

Patel, Rajeev. 2005. Book Review: Faulty Shades of Green. *Review of Radical Political Economics* 37 (3): 379–86.

———. Transgressing rights: La Vía Campesina's call for Food Sovereignty. *Feminist Economics* 13 (1): 87–93.

Patel, Raj. 2010. Mozambique's Food Riots - The True Face of Global Warming. *The Observer*, 5 September 2010.

———. 2011. "Survival Pending Revolution: What the Black Panthers Can Teach the US Food Movement." In *Food movements unite! : strategies to transform our food systems*, edited by Eric Holt-Gimenez. pp 115-137. Oakland: Food First Books

———. 2012. *What Cuba Can Teach Us About Food and Climate Change*. Slate, 5 April 2012. http://www.slate.com/articles/health_and_science/future_tense/2012/04/agro_ecology_lessons_from_cuba_on_agriculture_food_and_climate_change_.html

Patnaik, Utsa. 2001. Falling Per Capita Availability of Foodgrains for Human Consumption in the Reform Period in India. *Akhbar* 2, October.

———. 2004. *The Republic of Hunger*. New Delhi: SAHMAT (Safdar Hashmi Memorial Trust). http://www.macroscan.com/fet/apr04/ pdf/Rep_Hun.pdf.

———. 2003. *Global Capitalism, Deflation and Agrarian Crisis in Developing Countries*. Geneva: United Nations Research Institute for Social Development.

———. 2005. *Theorizing Food Security and Poverty in the Era of Economic Reforms*. Public Lecture in the series 'Freedom from Hunger', India International Centre, New Delhi. 12 April, 2005. Revised November 2005. http://www.mfcindia.org/utsa.pdf.

———.2007a. Aspects of Poverty and Employment - Neoliberalism and Rural Poverty in India. *Economic and political weekly*. 42 (30):3132.

———. 2007b. Aspects of Poverty and Employment: Neoliberalism and Rural Poverty in India *Economic and Political Weekly* 42 (30).

———. 2010. Trends in Urban Poverty under Economic Reforms: 1993-94 to 2004-05. *Economic and political weekly*. 45 (4):42.

Peace, Adrian. 2006. Barossa Slow: The Representation and Rhetoric of Slow Food's Regional Cooking. *Gastronomica* 6 (1): 51–9.

Peck, Helen. 2006. *Resilience in the Food Chain: A Study of Business Continuity Management* in the Food and Drink Industry: Final Report to the Department for Environment, Food and *Rural Affairs*. July 2006. Shrivenham: The Resilience Centre, Department of Defence Management & Security Analysis, Cranfield University.

Pendergrast, Mark. 2000. *For God, Country and Coca-Cola: The Definitive History of the Great American Soft Drink and the Company that Makes It*. 2nd edn. New York: Basic Books.

Pendola, Rocco, and Sheldon Gen. 2007. BMI, Auto Use, and the Urban Environment in San Francisco. *Health & Place* 13 (2): 551–556.

Pérez, Matilde, and Angélica Enciso. 2003. El campo ante el TCLAN. *La Jornada*, 1 February.

Perkins, John H. 1997. *Geopolitics and the Green Revolution: Wheat, Genes and the Cold War*. Oxford: Oxford University Press.

Perry, J. N., D. B. Roy, I. P. Woiwod, L. G. Firbank, G. R. Squire, D. R. Brooks, D. A. Bohan, G. T. Champion, R. E. Daniels, A. J. Haughton, C. Hawes, M. S. Heard, M. O. Hill, M. J. May and J. L. Osborne. 2003. On the Rationale and Interpretation of the Farm Scale Evaluations of Genetically Modified Herbicide-tolerant crops. *Philosophical Transactions of the Royal Society – Series B – Biological Sciences* 00358 (01439): 1779–800.

Perry, Mark. 2011. Walmart: The Most Successful Retailer in History. *Daily Markets*.

Phillips, M. R., X. Li and Y. Zhang. 2002. Suicide Rates in China, 1995–99. *Lancet* 359 (9309): 835–40.

Phillips, M. R., Yang G., Zhang Y., Wang L., Ji H., and Zhou M. 2002. Risk Factors for Suicide in China: A National Case-control Psychological Autopsy Study. *Lancet* 360 (9347): 1728–36.

Pimentel, D. 2004. Changing Genes to Feed the World. *Science* 306 (5697): 815.

Pincus, John. 1963. The Cost of Foreign Aid. *The Review of Economics and Statistics* 45 (4): 360–7.

Pirog, Rich, and Andrew Benjamin. 2003. *Checking the Food Odometer: Comparing Food Miles for Local Versus Conventional Produce Sales to Iowa Institutions*. Ames: Leopold Center for Sustainable Agriculture. http://www.leopold.iastate.edu/pubs/staff/files/food_travel072103.pdf.

Pithouse, Richard. 2005. *The Left in the Slum: The Rise of a Shack Dwellers' Movement in Durban, South Africa*. Durban: University of KwaZulu-Natal History and African Studies Seminar Series. http://www.history.ukzn.ac.za.

Pochna, Peter. 2003. Paramus, N.J., Hooters Waitresses File Harassment Suit. *Knight Ridder Tribune Business News*, 9 April.

Polanyi, Karl. 1944. *The Great Transformation*. Boston: Beacon Press. Pollan, Michael. 2006a. Mass Natural. *New York Times*, 4 June.

———. 2006b. *The Omnivore's Dilemma: A Natural History of Four Meals*. New York: Penguin Press.

PolitiFact.com. 2011. *Republic Mike Pence says Obama cut budget for illegal immigration effort. False.* . St.Petersburg Times 2010 [cited 5 August 2011]. Available from http://www.politifact.com/truth-o-meter/statements/2010/may/05/mike-pence/republican-says-obama-cut-budget-illegal-immigrati/.

Population Reference Bureau. 2007. *2007 World Population Data Sheet*. Washington, DC. Retrieved June, 2011 from http://www.prb.org/Publications/Datasheets/2007/2007WorldPopulationDataSheet.aspx

Poulin, Richard. 2003. Globalization and the Sex Trade: Trafficking and the Commodification of Women and Children. *Canadian Women Studies/Les Cahiers de la femme* 22 (3–4): 38–43.

Powell, Bonnie Azab. 2007. Whole Foods' Second Banana on Being Green. *Corporate Board Member Magazine,* January/February.

Powell, Lisa M., Sandy Slater, and Frank J. Chaloupka. 2004. The Relationship between Community Physical Activity Setting and Race, Ethnicity and Socioeconomic Status. *Evidence-Based Preventive Medicine* 1 (2): 135–44.

PR Newswire. 2010. Cargill Recognized by McDonald's USA for Its Animal Welfare and Environmental Efforts. *PR Newswire, United Business Media,* October 21.

Prabhu, Pingali. 2007. Westernization of Asian diets and the transformation of food systems: Implications for research and policy. *Food Policy* 32 (3):281-298.

Prahalad, C. K. 2006. *The Fortune at the Bottom of the Pyramid: Eradicating Poverty Through Profits*. Upper Saddle River: Pearson Education.

Press, Eyal, and Jennifer Washburn. 2000. The Kept University. *Atlantic Monthly*, 285 (3): 39–54.

Pretty, J. N., J. I. L. Morison, and R. E. Hine. 2003. Reducing food poverty by increasing agricultural sustainability in developing countries. *Agriculture, Ecosystems & Environment* 95 (1):217-234.

Primmer, George H. 1939. United States Soybean Industry. *Economic Geography* 15 (2): 205–11.

Puentes-Rosas, Esteban, Leopoldo López-Nieto and Tania Martínez-Monroy. 2004. La mortalidad por suicidios: México 1990–2001. *Revista Panamericana de Salud Pública/Pan American Journal of Public Health* 16 (2): 102–9.

Pullen, John 2001. A History of Malthus Scholarship. *Working Paper Series in Economics* (2001–3). http://www.une.edu.au/economics/ publications/ECONwp01-3.PDF.

Qin, P., and Preben Bo Mortensen. 2001. Specific Characteristics of Suicide in China. *Acta Psychiatrica Scandinavica* 103 (2).

Quist, D, and I. Chapela. 2001. Transgenic DNA Introgressed into Traditional Maize Landraces in Oaxaca, Mexico. *Nature* 414: 541–3.

Rai, Kartik. 2003. Agrarian Crisis and Distress in Rural India. *People's Democracy* 27 (20).

Rao, M. Rama 2006. Bush on Indo–US Friendship. *Asian Tribune*, 4 March.

Ravi Shankar, K., and P. Maraty. 2009. Concerns of India's farmers. *Outlook on Agriculture* 38 (1):96-100.

Readman, Paul. 2001. The Liberal Party and Patriotism in Early Twentieth Century Britain. *Twentieth Century British History* 12 (3): 269–302.

Reardon, T., and J. A. Berdegué. 2002. The Rapid Rise of Supermarkets in Latin America: Challenges and Opportunities for Development. *Development Policy Review* 20: 371–88.

Reed, Matthew. 2001. Fight the Future! How the Contemporary Campaigns of the UK Organic Movement Have Arisen from Their Composting of the Past. *Sociologia Ruralis* 41 (1): 131–45.

Reich, Robert. 2005. Don't Blame Wal-Mart. *New York Times*, 28 February.

Reid, Tim. 2005. The Nixon Tapes II: Gandhi 'the Witch'. *The Times*, 30 June.

Renard, Marie-Christine. 2005. Quality Certification, Regulation and Power in Fair Trade. *Journal of Rural Studies* 21 (4): 419–31.

Reporter Brazil. 2009. Brazil of Biofuels: Impacts of Crops on Land, Environment and Society. *Centro de Monitoramento de Agrocombustiveis* 1 - Soy and Castor Bean:5.

Reynolds, Richard. 2009. *On guerrilla gardening : a handbook for gardening without boundaries.* London: Bloomsbury.

Rist, Gilbert. 2002. *The History of Development: From Western Origins to Global Faith.* London: Zed Books.

Roberts, David. 1963. How Cruel Was the Victorian Poor Law? *The Historical Journal* 6 (1): 97–107.

Roberts, Donald F., Ulla G. Foehr, Victoria J. Rideout and Mollyann Brodie. 1999. *Kids and Media @ the New Millennium: A Comprehensive Analysis of Children's Media Use.* Menlo Park, CA: Henry J. Kaiser Family Foundation.

Roberts, Les, Riyadh Lafta, Richard Garfield, Jamal Khudhairi, and Gilbert Burnham. 2004. Mortality Before and After the 2003 Invasion of Iraq: Cluster Sample Survey. *The Lancet* 364 (9448): 1857–64.

Rockoff, Hugh. 1990. 'The Wizard of Oz' as a Monetary Allegory. *The Journal of Political Economy* 98 (4): 739–60.

Rohter, Larry. 2005. Beaches for the Svelte, Where the Calories Are Showing. *New York Times.* 13 January.

Rosset, Peter M. 2006a. *Food is Different: Why We Must Get the WTO Out of Agriculture.* London: Zed Books.

———. 2006b. Moving Forward: Agrarian Reform as Part of Food Sovereignty. In M. Courville, R. Patel and P. Rosset (eds.), *Promised Land: Competing Visions of Agrarian Reform.* Oakland, CA: Food First Books.

Rosset, Peter, and Medea Benjamin. 1994. *The Greening of the Revolution: Cuba's Experiment with Organic Agriculture.* Melbourne: Ocean Press.

Rosset, Peter, and Maria Elena Martinez. 2005. The Democratisation of Aid. *Red Pepper*, 31 July. http://viacampesina.org/main_en/ index.php?option=com_content&task=view&id=14&Itemid=31.

Rothblum, Esther D., and Sondra Solovay. 2009. *The fat studies reader.* New York: New York University Press.

Rothenberg, Daniel. 1998. *With These Hands: The Hidden World Of Migrant Farmworkers.* Berkeley and Los Angeles: University of California Press.

Roy, D. B., D. A. Bohan, A. J. Haughton, M. O. Hill, J. L. Osborne, S. J. Clark, J. N. Perry, P. Rothery, R. J. Scott, D. R. Brooks, G. T. Champion, C. Hawes, M. S. Heard, and L. G. Firbank. 2003. Invertebrates and Vegetation of Field Margins Adjacent to Crops Subject to Contrasting Herbicide Regimes in the Farm Scale Evaluations of Genetically Modified

Herbicide-tolerant Crops. *Philosophical Transactions of the Royal Society –Series B – Biological Sciences* 00358 (01439): 1879–99.

Rubin, Guy, Nina Jatana and Ruth Potts. 2006. *The World on a Plate: Queens Market. The Economic and Social Value of London's Most Ethnically Diverse Street Market*. London: New Economics Foundation. http://www.neweconomics.org/gen/z_sys_publicationdetail.aspx?pid=222.

Rudnitsky, Howard. 1982. How Sam Walton Does It. *Forbes*, 16 August: 42–4. SADC-FANR Vulnerability Assessment Committee. 2002a. *Lesotho Emergency Food Security Assessment Report*. http://www.sadc.int/ english/fanr/food_security/Documents/Lesotho/July%20-%20August%202002%20Lesotho%20%20Emergency%20Assessment%20Report.pdf.

———. 2002b. *Malawi Emergency Food Security Assessment Report*. http://www.fews.net/resources/gcontent/pdf/1000156.pdf.

———. 2002c. *Zambia Emergency Food Security Assessment Report*. http://www.fews.net/resources/gcontent/pdf/1000158.pdf.

Saguy, Abigail, and Rene Almeling. 2005. *Fat Devils and Moral Panics: News Reporting on Obesity Science*. http://www.soc.ucla.edu/faculty/ saguy/saguyandalmeling.pdf.

Saguy, Abigail C., and Kevin W. Riley. 2005. Weighing Both Sides: Morality, Mortality, and Framing Contests over Obesity. *Journal of Health Politics Policy and Law* 30 (5): 869–923.

Sainath, P. 1996. *Everybody Loves a Good Drought: Stories from India's Poorest Districts*. New Delhi: Penguin Books.

———. 2005a. The Unbearable Lightness of Seeing. *The Hindu*, 5 February.

———. 2005b. Whose Suicide Is It, Anyway? *India Together*. 25 June. http://www.indiatogether.org/2005/jun/psa-whosesui.htm.

———. 2010. Of luxury cars and lowly tractors. *The Hindu*, December 27.

Sallis, James E., and Karen Glanz. 2006. The Role of Built Environments in Physical Activity, Eating, and Obesity in Childhood. *Future Child* 16 (1): 89–108.

Salone del Gusto.it. 2010. Record Attendance for the Eighth Salone del Gusto. *Salone del Gusto 2010*.

Salzman, Avi. 2009. U.S. Food Aid: We Pay for Shipping. *Bloomberg Businessweek*.

Samu, K. 2009. Agriculture: Farmers' Suicide - 2009. In *Human Rights Documentation*. New Delhi, India: Indian Social Institute.

SAPA/AFP, South African Press Association/Agence France-Presse. 2004. *Murder Puts Spotlight on Brazil's Slave Trade*, 30 July.

Sassen, Saskia. 1988. *The Mobility of Labor and Capital: A Study in International Investment and Labor Flow*. Cambridge: Cambridge University Press.

Sauer, Sérgio 2006. The World Bank's Market-Based Land Reform in Brazil. In M. Courville, R. Patel and P. Rosset (eds.), *Promised Land: Competing Visions of Agrarian Reform*. Oakland, CA: Food First Books.

Saunders, Clarence. 1917. *Self Serving Store*, Patent number 1,242,872. 9 October. Arlington, VA: United States Patent Office.

Sawaya, A. L., G. Dallal, G. Solymos, M. H. de Sousa, M. L. Ventura, S. B. Roberts and D. M. Sigulem. 1995. Obesity and Malnutrition in a Shantytown Population in the City of São Paulo, Brazil. *Obesity Research* 3 (2): 107S–115S.

Schaeffer, Robert. 1995. Free Trade Agreements: Their Impact on Agriculture and the Environment. In P. McMichael (ed.), *Food and Agrarian Orders in the World-Economy*. Westport: Greenwood Press.

Schlosser, Eric. 2001. *Fast Food Nation: What the All-American Meal Is Doing to the World*. London: Allen Lane.

Schmitt, John, and Ben Zipperer. 2007. *Dropping the Ax: Illegal Firings during Union Election Campaigns*. Washington, DC: Center for Economic and Policy Research. http://www.cepr.net/documents/publications/unions_2007_01.pdf.

Schneider, Keith. 1986. Upheaval in U.S. Food Industry Forces a Hard Look at Its Future. *New York Times*, 9 October: A1.

———. 1987. Rash of Suicides in Oklahoma Shows that the Crisis on the Farm Goes On. *New York Times*, 17 August: 13.

Schor, Juliet. 2004. *Born to Buy: The Commercialized Child and the New Consumer Culture*. New York: Scribner.

Schumpeter, Joseph Alois. 1950. *Capitalism, Socialism, and Democracy*. 3rd edn. London: George Allen & Unwin.

Scott, James C. 1976. *The Moral Economy of the Peasant: Rebellion and Subsistence in Southeast Asia*. New Haven: Yale University Press.

Seager, Ashley. 2006. Starbucks, the Coffee Beans and the Copyright Row that Cost Ethiopia £47m. *Guardian*, 26 October.

Sears, Barry 2000. *The Soy Zone*. New York: HarperCollins.

Segrave, Kerry 2002. *Vending Machines: An American Social History*. Jefferson: McFarland & Company, Inc.

Seideman, Tony. 1993. Bar Codes Sweep the World. *American Heritage of Invention and Technology* 8 (4).

Sen, Amartya Kumar. 1981. *Poverty and Famines: An Essay on Entitlement and Deprivation*. New York: Oxford University Press.

———. 2002. How to Judge Globalism. *The American Prospect* 13 (1), January 1–14.

Shapin, Steven. 2004. The Great Neurotic Art. *London Review of Books* 26 (15).

———. 2006. Tod aus Luft. *London Review of Books* 28 (2).

Sharma, Devinder. 1999. *Selling Out: The Cost of Free Trade for India's Food Security*. London: UK Food Group. Available from http://www.ukfg.org.uk/docs/Selling%20Out%20Indias%20Food%20Security.doc.

———. 2005. A Lost Opportunity. *Deccan Herald*, 11 July.

Sheehan, Molly O'Meara and Peter Newman. 2002. What Will It Take to Halt Sprawl? *World Watch* 15 (1): 12.

Shelley, Percy Bysshe, and T. W. Rolleston. 1920. *A Philosophical View of Reform*. New York: Oxford University Press.

Shields, D. A. 2010. *Consolidation and Concentration in the U.S. Dairy Industry*. Washington, DC: Congressional Research Service.

Shiva, Vandana. 1989. *The Violence of the Green Revolution: Ecological Degradation and Political Conflict in Punjab*. Dehra Dun: Research Foundation for Science and Ecology.

———. 2006. *The Pseudo-science of Biotech Lobbyists: The Baseless Barfoot–Brookes Claim that Farmers and the Environment Have Benefited from GMO's*. Available from: http://www.ourworldisnotforsale.org/showarticle.asp?search=1316

Shrek, Aimee. 2005. Farmworkers in Organic Agriculture: Toward a Broader Notion of Sustainability. *Sustainable Agriculture Newsletter* 2005 17(1). http://www.sarep.ucdavis.edu/newsltr/v17n1/sa-1.htm.

Sinclair, Minor, and Martha Thompson. 2001. *Cuba: Going Against the Grain: Agricultural Crisis and Transformation*. Washington, DC: Oxfam America.

Sinclair, Upton, and Clare Virginia Eby. 2002. *The Jungle: An Authoritative Text, Contexts and Backgrounds, Criticism*. New York: Norton.

Singh, Manmohan. 2005. *Address by Prime Minister Dr Manmohan Singh at Oxford University, in acceptance of an Honorary Degree from Oxford University*, 8 July. Available at: http://www.hindu.com/nic/0046/pmspeech.htm.

Smith, Alison, Paul Watkiss, Geoff Tweddle, Alan McKinnon, Mike Browne, Alistair Hunt, Colin Treleven, Chris Nash and Sam Cross. 2005. *The Validity of Food Miles as an Indicator of Sustainable Development: Final Report Produced for DEFRA*. London: DEFRA. http://statistics.defra.gov.uk/esg/reports/foodmiles/final.pdf.

Smith, Jeffrey M. 2003. *Seeds of Deception: Exposing Industry and Government Lies about the Safety of the Genetically Engineered Foods You're Eating.* Fairfield: Yes Books.

Smith, Woodruff D. 1992. Complications of the Commonplace: Tea, Sugar, and Imperialism. *Journal of Interdisciplinary History* 23 (2): 259–78.

Smith Fawzi, Mary C., Walid Aldoori, Wafaie W. Fawzi and Nagib Armijo-Hussein. 1997. The Gulf War, Child Nutrition and Feeding Practices in Iraq. *Nutrition Research* 17 (5): 775.

Soil Association. 2003. *Soil Association Comments on Farm-scale GM Trials.* Bristol: Soil Association. Available from http://www.soilassociation.org/web/sa/saweb.nsf/librarytitles/190E2.HTML.

Sorosiak, Thomas. 2000. Soybean. In K. F. Kiple and C. O. Kriemhild (eds.), *The Cambridge World History of Food.* Cambridge: Cambridge University Press.

Sperry, Charles W. 1985. What Makes Mondragón Work? *Review of Social Economy.* 43 (3): 345–56.

Spigel, Lynn. 1992. *Make Room for TV: Television and the Family Ideal in Postwar America.* Chicago: University of Chicago Press.

Stagl, Sigrid. 2002. Local Organic Food Markets: Potentials and Limitations for Contributing to Sustainable Development. *Empirica* 29 (2): 145.

Stanley, Kathleen. 1994. Industrial and Labor Market Transformation in the U.S. Meatpacking Industry. In P. McMichael (ed.), *The Global Restructuring of Agro-Food Systems.* Ithaca: Cornell University Press.

Starkman, Naomi. 2011. *Consumer Rights Victory as US Ends Opposition to GM Labeling Guidelines.* ConsumersUnion.org 2011 [cited July 6 2011]. Available from http://www.consumersunion.org/pub/core_food_safety/017858.html.

Steinbeck, John. 2002. *The Grapes of Wrath.* New York: Penguin Books.

Steinfeld, Henning, Pierre Gerber, Tom Wassenaar, Vincent Castel, Mauricio Rosales and Cees de Haan. 2006. *Livestock's Long Shadow: Environmental Issues and Options.* Rome: Food and Agriculture Organization of the United Nations.

Stevenson, Seth. 2002. I'd Like To Buy the World a Shelf-Stable Children's Lactic Drink. *New York Times,* 10 March.

Stock, Catherine McNicol. 1996. *Rural Radicals: Righteous Rage in the American Grain.* Ithaca: Cornell University Press.

Stone, Glenn Davis. 2007. Agricultural Deskilling and the Spread of Genetically Modified Cotton in Warangal. *Current Anthropology* 48 (1): 67–103.

Stone, Kenneth E. 1997. *Impact of the Wal-Mart Phenomenon on Rural Communities.* Chicago: Farm Foundation. Available from http://www.seta.iastate.edu/ retail/publications/10_yr_study.pdf.

Strauss, Samuel. 1924. Things are in the Saddle. *Atlantic Monthly,* November: 577–88.

Strömberg, David 2002. *Distributing News and Political Influence.* Institute for International Economic Studies, University of Stockholm. Available from http://rincewind.iies.su.se/~stromber/wbbook.pdf.

Strydom, John, Anthony Osler, Angela Shaw, Claire Clark and Chrisi van Loon. 2005. *Quiet Food: From Fast Food to Slow Food to Quiet Food.* Cape Town: Double Storey.

Susman, Paul. 1989. Exporting the Crisis: U.S. Agriculture and the Third World. *Economic Geography* 65 (4, Trade Theories, Scale, and Structure): 293–313.

Sweeney, Nick. 2004. Do You Atkins? (Letter to Editor). *London Review of Books* 26 (18).

Swithers, S. E., S. B. Ogden, and T. L. Davidson. 2011. Fat substitutes promote weight gain in rats consuming high-fat diets. *Behavioral Neuroscience* 125 (4):512-518.

Talbot, John M. 1995. The Regulation of the World Coffee Market: Tropical Commodities and the Limits of Globalization. In P. McMichael (ed.), *Food and Agrarian Orders in the World-Economy.* Westport: Greenwood Press.

Tandon, Aditi. 2006. Kin of Indebted Farmers Finally Get to Speak – Tribunal Records Suicide

Accounts in Punjab. *Chandigarh Tribune*, 2 April.

Tang, Ke, and Wei Xiong. 2011. Index Investment and Financialization of Commodities. Princeton University.

Taylor, C. Robert 1999. *Economic Concentration in Agribusiness*. Testimony to the United States Senate Committee on Agriculture, Nutrition and Forestry. Washington, DC, 26 January.

Taylor, John, Matina Madrick, and Sam Collin. 2005. *Trading Places: The Local Economic Impact of Street Produce and Farmer's Markets*. London: London Development Agency, London Food and the Mayor of London, New Economics Foundation. http://www.neweconomics.org/gen/uploads/w2rrxbb4htuk3t55fbvmhh551412200511434I.pdf.

Terdiman, Richard. 1985. *Discourse/Counter-Discourse: The Theory and Practice of Symbolic Resistance in Nineteenth-century France*. Ithaca: Cornell University Press.

Tharoor, Shashi. 2003. *Nehru: The Invention of India*. New York: Arcade Publishing. Thirtle, Colin, Lindie Beyers, Yousouf Ismael and Jenifer Piesse. 2003. Can GMTechnologies Help the Poor? The Impact of Bt Cotton in Makhathini Flats, KwaZulu-Natal. *World Development* 31 (4): 717–32.

The Leisure Database Company. 2011. Fitness Industry Stands Strong Despite Downward Economic Trend.

Thompson, Don. 2000. Universities Criticized for Research Contracts with Private Firms. *Associated Press Wire*, 16 May. http://www.biotech-info.net/universities_criticized.html.

Thompson, Edward Palmer. 1968. *The Making of the English Working Class*. Harmondsworth: Penguin Books.

Thompson, Elizabeth A., and Hamilton I. McCubbin. 1987. Farm Families in Crisis: An Overview of Resources. *Family Relations* 36 (4, Rural Families: Stability and Change): 461–7.

Thompson, James. 2003. Soybean King Turns Soybean Governor. *Soybean Digest*, 1 March: 4.

Thompson, Susan J., and J. Tadlock Cowan. 1995. Durable Food Production and Consumption in the World-Economy. In P. McMichael (ed.), *Food and Agrarian Orders in the World-Economy*. Westport: Greenwood Press.

Time Magazine. 1964. Too Many People, Too Little Food. *Time Magazine*, 31 July: 29.

Torres, Bob, and Jenna Torres. 2005. *Vegan Freak: Being Vegan in a Non-Vegan World*. Colton: Tofu Hound Press.

Totenberg, Nina. 2011. Supreme Court Limits Wal-Mart Discrimination Case. *NPR.org*, June 20.

Toufe, Zaynep. 2002. Let Them Eat Cake: TV Blames Africans for Famine. *Fairness and Accuracy in Reporting*. http://www.fair.org/extra/0211/famine.html.

Tubiana, Laurence. 1989. World Trade in Agricultural Products: From Global Regulation to Market Fragmentation. In D. Goodman and M. Redclift (eds.), *The International Farm Crisis*. New York: St Martin's Press.

Turley, L. W., and R. E. Milliman. 2000. Atmospheric Effects on Shopping Behavior: A Review of the Experimental Evidence. *Journal Of Business Research* 49 (2): 193–211.

Ukers, William H. 1935. *All About Tea*. New York: Tea and Coffee Trade Journal Co.

Uncles, M. D., and S. Kwok. 2009. Patterns of store patronage in urban China. *J. Bus. Res. Journal of Business Research* 62 (1):68-81.

UNCTAD. 1996. *UNCTAD and WTO: A Common Goal in a Global Economy*. <TAD/INF/PR/9628 08/10/96>. Geneva: United Nations Conference on Trade and Development.

———.2011. Price Formation in Financialized Commodity Markets. Geneva: United Nations Conference on Trade and Development.

UNDP (United Nations Development Programme). 2002. *Human Development Report 2002: Deepening Democracy in a Fragmented World*. New York: Oxford University Press.

———.2005. *Human Development Report 2005: International Cooperation at a Crossroads: Aid, Trade and Security in an Unequal World*. New York: Oxford University Press.

UNDP India (United Nations Development Programme). 2004. *Human Development Report – Punjab*. New Delhi: Government of Punjab.

United Nations. 1974. *Declaration on the Establishment of a New International Economic Order*, New York: United Nations General Assembly.

———. 2006. *International Financial System and Development: Report of the Secretary-General*. New York: United Nations General Assembly.

United Nations, Department of Economic and Social Affairs. 2005. *The Inequality Predicament: Report on the World Social Situation 2005* [A/60/117/Rev.1 ST/ESA/299]. New York: United Nations.

US Census Bureau. 2007. Industry Statistics Sampler. Retrieved June, 2011, from http://www.census.gov/econ/industry/

USDA, United States Department of Agriculture. 2000. *Glickman Announces National Standards for Organic Food*. Washington, DC: Department of Agriculture. http://www.usda.gov/news/releases/2000/12/0425.htm.

———. 2007a. Census of Agriculture. Washington DC: United States Department of Agriculture.

———. 2007b. Census of Agriculture Table 11: Selected Characteristics of Irrigated and Nonirrigated Farms: 2007 and 2002. Washington DC: United States Department of Agriculture.

———. 2007c. Table 7. Hired Farm Labor - Workers and Payroll. Washington D.C: USDA. Retrieved June, 2011, from http://www.agcensus.usda.gov/Publications/2007/Full_Report/Volume_1,_Chapter_2_US_State_Level/index.asp

———. 2009a. Access to Affordable and Nutritious Food: Measuring and Understanding Food Deserts and Their Consequences. Washington DC: USDA.

———. 2009b. *Global Food Markets: Global Food Industry Structure*. USDA Economic Research Service [cited 29 July 2011]. Available from http://www.ers.usda.gov/Briefing/GlobalFoodMarkets/Industry.htm.

———. 2010a. Sugar and Sweeteners Yearbook Table 3b: World raw sugar price, ICE Contract 11 nearby futures price, monthly, quarterly, and by calendar and fiscal year. Washington D.C.: United States Department of Agriculture.

———. 2010b. Sugar and Sweeteners Yearbook Table 4: U.S. raw sugar price, duty-fee paid, New York, monthly, quarterly, and by calendar and fiscal year. Washington DC: United States Department of Agriculture.

———. 2011. Sugar and Sweeteners Yearbook Table 27: U.S. use of field corn, by crop year. Washington D.C.: United States Department of Agriculture/Economic Research Service. Retrieved July 19, 2011, from www.ers.usda.gov/briefing/sugar/data/table27.xls

US GAO. 2009. *Agricultural Concentration and Agricultural Commodity and Retail Food Prices*. Retrieved from http://www.gao.gov/products/GAO-09-746R.

Urbanski, Al. 2002. Piggly Wiggly. *Progressive Grocer* 81 (1): 55.

Urbina, Ian. 2006. Rising Diabetes Threat Meets a Falling Budget. *New York Times*, 16 May.

Valerie, Alvord. 2003. MREs Providing More Than Food; With No Room for Stationery, Troops in Combat Use Meal Packaging to Write Home. *USA Today*: A.13.

Valerie, Grim. 2002. The High Cost of Water: African American Farmers and the Politics of Irrigation in the Rural South, 1980–2000. *Agricultural History* 76 (2): 338.

Van Der Hoek, W., F. Konradsen, K. Athukorala and T. Wanigadewa. 1998. Pesticide Poisoning: A Major Health Problem in Sri Lanka. *Social Science and Medicine* 46 (4–5): 495.

Vega, Margarita. 2010. Piden freno a obesidad y diabetes. *Reforma*, 13 October 2010.

Veitch, Jenny, Sarah Bagley, Kylie Ball, and Jo Salmon. 2006. Where Do Children Usually Play? A Qualitative Study of Parents' Perceptions of Influences on Children's Active Free-play. *Health & Place* 12(4): 383–393.

Via Campesina. 2003. *What is Peoples' Food Sovereignty?* Available from: http://www.via-campesina.org/art_english.php3?id_article=216.

———. 2005. *Press Release of Regional Conference on Tsunami*. 19 February. http://viacampe-sina.org/main_en/index.php?option=com_content&task=view&id=28&Itemid=31.

Vicini, James. 2011. Factbox: Wal-Mart Discrimination Case. *Reuters*.

Vidal, John. 2005. Ignacio Chapela: Enemy of the State. *The Guardian*, 19 January.

———. 2006. Big Water Companies Quit Poor Countries. *The Guardian*, 22 March.

———. 2010. Why is the Gates foundaiton investing in GM giant Monsanto? *The Guardian*, September 29.

———. 2011. *Why is the Gates foundation investing in GM giant Monsanto?* The Guardian 2011 [cited October 19 2011]. Available from http://www.guardian.co.uk/global-develop-ment/poverty-matters/2010/sep/29/gates-foundation-gm-monsanto.

Virilio, Paul. 1986. *Speed and Politics: An Essay on Dromology, Semiotext(e) Foreign Agents Series*. New York: Columbia University Press.

Vomhof Jr, John. 2005. McDonald's Names Cargill 'Supplier of the Year'. *Minneapolis/St. Paul Business Journal*, 12 December.

Vorley, Bill. 2003. *Food, Inc.: Corporate Concentration from Farm to Consumer*. London: IIED. http://www.ukfg.org.uk/docs/UKFG-Foodinc-Nov03.pdf.

Walker, Richard A. 2004. *The Conquest of Bread: 150 years of Agribusiness in California*. New York: New Press.

Wal-Mart. 2005. *Annual Report*. Bentonville, AK: Wal-Mart.

Walmart. 2011. Building the Next Generation Walmart...Responsibly. In *Global Responsibility Report*. Bentonville, AK: Walmart.

Walsh, Fiona. 2006. Supermarket Chain's Scheme to Help African Growers Bears Fruit. *Guardian*, 29 May.

Walsh, Sharon. 2004. Berkeley Denies Tenure to Ecologist Who Criticized University's Ties to the Biotechnology Industry. *The Chronicle of Higher Education*, 7 January: A10.

Walton, John, and David Seddon. 1994. *Free Markets and Food Riots: The Politics of Global Adjustment*. Oxford: Blackwell.

Wang, Y., M. A. Beydoun, B. Caballero, L. Liang, and S. K. Kumanyika. 2008. Will all Ameri-cans become overweight or obese? Estimating the progression and cost of the US obe-sity epidemic. *Obesity Obesity* 16 (10):2323-2330.

Warnken, Philip F. 1999. *The Development and Growth of the Soybean Industry in Brazil*. Ames: Iowa State University Press.

Wartella, Ellen. 1995. The Commercialization of Youth: Channel One in Context. *Phi Delta Kappan* 76 (6): 448.

Watts, Jonathan. 2003. Field of Tears. *Guardian*, 16 September.

Watts, Michael. 1983. *Silent Violence: Food, Famine, and Peasantry in Northern Nigeria*. Berke-ley: University of California Press.

Week in Review Desk. 1985. The Hands of Anger, Frustration, Humiliation. *New York Times*, 15 December: 5.

Weinstein, Miriam. 2005. *The Surprising Power of Family Meals: How Eating Together Makes Us Smarter, Stronger, Healthier, and Happier*. Hanover: Steerforth Press.

Weisbrot, Mark, David Rosnick and Dean Baker. 2004. *Getting Mexico to Grow With NAFTA: The World Bank's Analysis*. http://www.cepr.net/publications/nafta_2004_10.htm.

Weiss, Rick. 2002. Starved for Food, Zimbabwe Rejects U.S. Biotech Corn. *Washington Post*, 31 July.

Welch, Cliff. 2006. Keeping Communism Down on the Farm: The Brazilian Rural Labor Movement during the Cold War. *Latin American Perspectives* 33 (3): 28–50.

Wessman, James W. 1984. The Agrarian Question in Mexico. *Latin American Research Review* 19 (2): 243–59.

WFP, World Food Programme. 2002. *Food Shortages in Lesotho: The Facts*. www.wfp.org/newsroom/in_depth/Africa/sa_lesotho020705.htm.

Which? 2004. *Cereal Offenders*. London: Which? http://www.which.net/campaigns/food/nutrition/0403cerealoffenders_rep.pdf.

Which? 2006. Some Cereal More than Half Sugar. In *Which?* London.

WHO (World Health Organization). 2000. *Pellagra and Its Prevention and Control in Major Emergencies*. Geneva: World Health Organization. Available from http://whqlibdoc.who.int/hq/2000/WHO_NHD_ 00.10.pdf.

———. 2004. *Suicide Rates (per 100,000) by Gender, India, 1980–1998*.

———. 2011. "*Obesity and Overweight*" World Health Organization 2011 [cited June 15th 2011]. Available from http://www.who.int/mediacentre/factsheets/fs311/en/index.html.

———.2011. *Micronutrient Deficiency: Vitamin A*. WHO 2011 [cited 10 August 2011]. Available from http://www.who.int/nutrition/topics/vad/en/

Wijeratna, Alex. 2005. *Rotten Fruit: Tesco Profits as Women Workers Pay a High Price*. Johannesburg: ActionAid.

Williams, Heather. 2006. Fighting Corporate Swine. *Politics & Society* 34 (3): 369–98.

Williams, Raymond. 1973. *The Country and the City*. New York: Oxford University Press.

Wilson, Sacoby M., Frank Howell, Steve Wing and Mark Sobsey. 2002. Environmental Injustice and the Mississippi Hog Industry. *Environmental Health Perspectives* 110 (Supplement 2): 195–201.

Windfuhr, Michael, and Jennie Jonsén. 2005. *Food Sovereignty: Towards Democracy in Localized Food Systems*. Rugby: ITDG Publishing.

Windish, Leo G. 1981. *The Soybean Pioneers, Trailblazers ... Crusaders ... Missionaries ...* Galva: no publisher named.

Wise, Timothy A. 2011. Still Waiting for the Farm Boom: Family Farmers Worse Off Despite High Crop Prices. In *GDAE Policy Brief 11-01*. Medord, MA: Tufts University, Global Development and Environment Institute.

Wittman, Hannah. 2005. The Social Ecology of Agrarian Reform: The Landless Rural Worker's Movement and Agrarian Citizenship in Mato Grosso, Brazil. Ph.D Dissertation. Ithaca: Department of Development Sociology, Cornell University.

Woodruff Atkinson, Sarah J. 2008. Family meal influence dietary quality of students in grade six, seven, and eight from Ontario and Nova Scotia, Library and Archives Canada, Ottawa.

Wolf, A. M. and G. A. Colditz. 1998. Current Estimates of the Economic Costs of Obesity in the United States. *Obesity Research*. 6: 97–106.

Wood, Ellen Meiksins. 2000. The Agrarian Origins of Capitalism. In F. Magdoff, J. B. Foster and F. H. Buttel (eds.), *Hungry for Profit: The Agribusiness Threat to Farmers, Food and the Environment*. New York: Monthly Review Press.

World Bank. 1981. *Accelerated Development in Sub-Saharan Africa: An Agenda for Action*. Washington, DC: World Bank.

———. 2005. *Global Economic Prospects 2006: Economic Implications of Remittances and Migration*. Washington, DC: World Bank.

———. 2010a. Rising Global Interest in Farmland: Can it Yield Sustainable and Equitable Benefits? Washington D.C.: World Bank.

———. 2010b. Migration and Remittances Factbook 2011. http://siteresources.worldbank.org/INTPROSPECTS/Resources/334934-1199807908806/Mexico.pdf.

———. 2011a. *GDP (current US$) Data Table*. [cited 17 June 2011]. Available from http://data.worldbank.org/indicator/NY.GDP.MKTP.CD.

———. 2011b. *The World Bank: Mexico Data*. [cited 1 August 2011]. Available from http://data.worldbank.org/country/mexico.

World Bank Independent Evaluation Group. *World Bank assistance to agriculture in Sub-Saharan Africa : an IEG review*. World Bank 2007.

World Summit on Food Security. 2009. Declaration of the World Summit on Food Security. Rome: Food and Agriculture Organization of the United Nations.

WorldWatch Institute. 2006. *State of the World Report*. Washington, DC: WorldWatch Institute.

Worm, Boris, Edward B. Barbier, Nicola Beaumont, J. Emmett Duffy, Carl Folke, Benjamin S. Halpern, Jeremy B. C. Jackson, Heike K. Lotze, Fiorenza Micheli, Stephen R. Palumbi, Enric Sala, Kimberley A. Selkoe, John J. Stachowicz and Reg Watson. 2006. Impacts of Biodiversity Loss on Ocean Ecosystem Services. *Science* 314 (5800): 787–90.

Wright, Angus Lindsay, and Wendy Wolford. 2003. *To Inherit the Earth: The Landless Movement and the Struggle for a New Brazil*. Oakland, CA: Food First Books.

WWF (WorldWide Fund for Nature). 2004. *Fakten zum Soja-Anbau in Südamerika: WorldWide Fund for Nature*. www.panda.org/downloads/forests/factsheetsoyfootprint-aug04.doc.

Yalch, R. F., and E. R. Spangenberg. 2000. The Effects of Music in a Retail Setting on Real and Perceived Shopping Times. *Journal of Business Research* 49 (2): 139–47.

Yeomans, M. R., A. Jackson, M. D. Lee, B. Steer, E. Tinley, P. Durlach and P. J. Rogers. 2000. Acquisition and Extinction of Flavour Preferences Conditioned by Caffeine in Humans. *Appetite* 35 (2): 131–41.

Young-rae, Cho. 2003. *A Single Spark: The Biography of Chun Tae-il*. Seoul: Dolbegae Publishers Co.

Zeki, Semir. 2003. Preface. *Philosophical Transactions of the Royal Society – Series B – Biological Sciences* 00358 (01439): 1775–7.

Zenith International. 2006. *Soft Drinks to Overtake Hot Drinks Globally*. Zenith International Ltd, 31 March. Available from: http://www.zenithinternational.com/news/press_release_detail.asp?id=152.

———.2011. *Global Soft Drinks Report*. Zenith International, November 2008 2008 [cited 7 August 2011]. Available from http://www.zenithinternational.com/reports_data/117/Global+Soft+Drinks+Report.

Zinn, Howard. 2003. *A People's History of the United States: 1942–Present*. New edn. New York: HarperCollins.

Žižek, Slavoj. 2005. Knee Deep. *London Review of Books* 26 (17).

———. 2006. Jack Bauer and the Ethics of Urgency. *In These Times*, 27 January.

Acknowledgements

A book about the global food system needed a world to write it. At times, that world felt like Cornell University's Department of Development Sociology. Bob Torres, Saadia Toor, Kelly Dietz, Dia Mohan, Malinda Seneviratne, Ayca Cubukcu, Anna Zalik, Rachel Bezner-Kerr, Kai and Annyce Schafft, Tracy Aagaard, Vern Long, Mikush Schwam-Baird, the DSA, *Catholic Worker*, the editorial staff at *The Cobbler* and the Ithaca Sharks Affinity group all helped me to think much more clearly and live more bravely. Rachel Schwartz shared her insight on supermarkets. Shelley Feldman, Ravi Kanbur, Steve Kyle and Peter Katzenstein put analytical tools in my hands which, I hope, I haven't misused.

In India, the good folk at Focus on the Global South's India office, particularly Meena Menon and Benny Kuruvilla, set me on the right path. Chukki Nanjundaswamy and Sheshar Reddy at the Karnataka State Farmers Association took time from their meetings to discuss La Via Campesina and their vision of food sovereignty, and a range of people from the KRRS, BKU and Centre for Sustainable Agriculture took time to talk. Devinder Sharma and his colleagues, P. Sainath, Ramanjaneyulu and all at the Centre for Sustainable Agriculture, the staff at CRRID, Jayathi Ghosh and Utsa Patnaik at JNU's Economics department pointed me to invaluable writing. On the way, Banubhai Patel, Swarn, Livleen, Gurtaj, Mila Kahlon, Jasveen and Vinod Jairath all provided refuge, food, conversation, generosity and pointers about where to go next, and how to understand it. Sajja Srinivas, Biju Mathew and Sangeeta Kamat fed, educated and challenged me, as did Shalmali Guttal, who has long been a beacon in honest, clear, sharp and straightforward thinking about globalization.

I'd not have been able to raid Italy's bounties without the Commission on the Future of Food, so thanks to Vandana Shiva,

Miguel Altieri, Debi Barker, Wendell Berry, Marcello Buiatti, Peter Einarsson, Elena Gagliasso, Bernward Geier, Edward Goldsmith, Benny Haerlin, Colin Hines, Vicki Hird, Andrew Kimbrell, Tim Lang, Frances Moore Lappé, Caroline Lucas, Jerry Mander, Helena Norberg-Hodge, Kristen Corselius, Sandra Sumane, and Percy Schmeiser, Caroline Lockhart and Chiara Boni. Carlo Petrini at Slow Food and Gianluca Brunori at the University of Pisa took time to answer uncomfortable questions about cultures of pleasure. Marco Flavio Marinucci and Alison Bing have always provided that culture, and Alana Ferry provided a home for it in Rome.

Another group thinking about food met most recently in Brazil, and my thanks to Renato S. Maluf, Jorge O. Romano, Adriano Campolina, Claudia Schmitt, Jacques Berthelot, Roberto I. Escalante Semerena, Maria Clara Couto Soares and Bruno Losch who provided sounding boards to some of the arguments here. Particular thanks to Corinna Hawkes, ActionAid, Brazil, and John Wilkinson for guidance on this history of soy, and to Christine Dann for her excavation of Lee Kyung Hae's thought, and profound engagement with issues of justice, race and environment. Laura Carlsen offered sage advice and a much-appreciated last-minute quote. Laura Davis provided further insights into a Britain that seems increasingly remote, as did Robert Vint, and Katharine Ainger's work at the *New Internationalist* and as part of the Notes from Everywhere Collective is required reading.

In Brazil, Maria Rita Reis, Jason Peilemeyer and all at the Terra de Direitos office took time to show us the contradictions of GM soy. Geraldo and Dulcinéia from MST SRI, the staff at the MST offices in Cuiabá and Rondonopolis, and the residents of the 14 de Agosto settlement took time to house, feed, talk and inebriate us. Maria Luisa and Zé took us in at short notice, and with warm generosity. Thanks too to the staff of Cargill and Bunge in Paranaguá for soy-related goodies, and ADM in Cuiabá for a tour of their processing plant.

Razack Karriem and most especially Emelie Peine made time

to fill my deep ignorance, travel, sherpa, fix and think through some of the deepest issues in this book. Without Emelie's transnational insight and scholarship, many of the links between Brazil and the US would have eluded me – indeed, most of Brazil would have. Hannah Wittman came to my rescue through her subtle knowledge and appreciation for the MST, and entertaining the manuscript with far more kindness than it deserved.

Ana De Ita and the staff at Ceccam, Peter Rosset and Sofia Monsalve (and family) have always guided, and did so with aplomb and friendship in Mexico, and with the manuscript after it was done. In Thailand, Greenpeace, the Assembly of the Poor and the staff of Focus on the Global South, especially Nicola Bullard, provided grist for the mill, and power to the elbow even if, alas I wasn't able to squeeze much of it in. David Dunkley at the WTO proved himself the Peoples' Librarian.

In New York, Radhika Balakrishnan made it possible to present early ideas both at Marymount Manhattan College and, with the kind support of Anwar Shaikh, at the New School. Mark Ash at the USDA's ERS helpfully provided data on soy production. The Polson Institute for International Development and the Cornell Branch of the Telluride Association housed and nurtured early versions of this book, Kolya Abramsky provided helpful insight from Binghamton, and Jeff Purcell references from Ithaca. Michael Watts, Iain Boal and especially Ignacio Chapela among other Retort group members bounced ideas. Sharmila Rudrappa at the University of Texas at Austin was kind enough to invite me to an event at the South Asia Institute, at which I was able to learn from Jagdish Bhagwati that there's no such thing as a Gujarati Marxist. Lee Hall and Michael Dorsey helped with key issues of race and environmentalism. Steven Schapin, whose thoughts on food are always to be savoured, Daryll Ray, Tom Hayden, Jan-Willem Grievink, Richard Watts and Elizabeth Saguy provided helpful references, quotes, ideas and permissions. Harriet Friedmann provided warm, delicious and always challenging food for thought.

The staff and interns at the Institute for Food and Development Policy/ Food First pushed these ideas along and provided invaluable research support, and especial thanks to Alexa Delwiche, Amanda Cassel, Sanaz Memarsadeghi, Max Eisenburger, Anders Riel Müller, Paulina Novo and Marilyn Borchardt for permission to use the work I was involved in while there.

Sandy Nichols provided advice on migrant labour in California, Joe Costello, Brad Templeton, Ryan Ismert, Carol Park, Will Kopp, Kara Holstrom, Joe Quirk, Michael Courville, Anirvan Chatterjee, Barnali Ghosh, the denizens of the Sanchez Annex Writers Grotto in San Francisco, Tezozomoc, the Vaquero family and all at South Central Farm, Brahm Ahmadi and Malaika Edwards at the People's Grocery, Terry Baird, Myriam Rahman and the good folk at Arizmendi, and Chris Loss at The Culinary Institute of America all provided deeply appreciated help on the West Coast.

Jun Borras and Eric Ross at the Institute for Social Studies shared insight on land and foundations. Paul Nicholson and Nico Verhagen at Via Campesina, in various conversations, provided clear thinking around politics, and Naomi Klein and Avi Lewis likewise on the world of media and activism.

In Korea, thanks to Bokrae Seo Lee and family, Sohi Jeon, Kang Ki Kap, the KPA, KoPA and residents of Chodae district, in Dangjin, Chungnam province. Chul-Kyoo Kim's thoughts were especially lucid, but I'd not have left square one without Chad Futrell and Hyunok Lee, who, again, taught me much, and supported me often and generously, before, during and after my visit, and who continue to inspire, and whose comments on the manuscript improved it considerably.

Although the bulk of this book was written in Durban, South Africa, it wouldn't have moved very far without the help of the 'Searching for South Africa' group in Cape Town, especially Dan Moshenberg and Shereen Essof. Mickey Chopra at the Medical Research Council pointed to important work. Louis and Chrisi Van Loon generously hosted me at the Ixopo Buddhist retreat, so that I could learn about Quiet Food. Mangaliso Kubheka and Thobekile

Radebe, among others in the Landless Peoples' Movement, the Church Land Programme, the Advisory team to the National Land Committee (especially Stephen Greenberg, who pointed me to valuable resources on supermarkets), and the activists of GE Free Africa abetted and encouraged me.

Few could want for a better place to work and write than the University of KwaZulu-Natal, and thanks to all there, particularly Vishnu Padayachee, Julian May, and Harald Witt who together with Matt Schnurr at UKZN, with the support of Dumisani Nyathi, Nonhlanhla Dlamini and Aoibheann O'Sullivan, I worked in Makhathini. A range of visiting and permanent scholars from the Centre for Civil Society helped, as did a range of staff in the History, Economic History and Development Studies departments. Claire Ichou, David Ntseng and Sally Smyth, whom it was a pleasure to supervise, taught me much. Helen Poonen was a sine qua non of Durban life. Anthony Collins, Amanda Alexander, Tapera Kapuya, Bana Bose, Sharad Chari, Ismail Khan, Fazel Khan, Richard Ballard, Mark Hunter, Gill Hart, David Szanton, S'bu Zikode, System Cele and the University of Abahlali baseMjondolo all provided witting or unwitting support. Special thanks to Julian Brown for suffering through the manuscript. Living in Durban wouldn't have been possible, though, without Richard Pithouse and Vashna Jagarnath, whose skills in sharing music, poetry, food and life have left me a better person.

Chris Brooke, constant friend and careful reader, recognized in an early draft some paragraphs from a talk he made it possible for me to give at Oxford University's Corporate Power group. Without his and Josephine Crawley Quinn's editorial and muse-like skills, and a high combined (if unevenly distributed) capacity for alcohol, the book would be a far bigger mess than it is.

Many of the best and most irrelevant anecdotes were excised by blue pencil, or the threat of it, and few pencils are sharper than those wielded by Philip Gwyn Jones, ably supported by Laura Barber and the team at Portobello Books. Thanks, too, to Jackie Newman for invaluable permissions sleuthing, and to Jim Gifford at HarperCollins Canada, Sophy Williams at Black Inc books, Jos Baijens at Uitgeverij De Wereld, and Valerie Merians at Melville House Books for taking a chance on me. Their support not only made the first edition a success, but a second edition possible. Though little would have been achieved in the writing of the second edition without the research skills of Meredith Palmer.

Still, the story of a militant vegetarian priest, naked, jangling in self-righteousness at the paltry number of cows saved by his businessmen friends is one that I'll take to my grave. I still have the priest's business card given to me by his agent ('he's great at weddings'). Karolina Sutton at ICM was, I think, more successful, and I couldn't have wished for a better sherpa and comrade in the world of writing. Deep thanks to Palash Davé for the introduction.

Deepest thanks to Phil McMichael, for mentorship, support and giggles, who always suspected I had a book in me and was made to regret it by reading through interminable drafts. I wouldn't have been able to write this book without my family, Mum, Dad, Sanjeev, Ramona, Eshaan, Armaan; and most of all, I thank Mini Kahlon for inspiring, critiquing, editing, planning, feeding, strategizing, Jahaning and, well, everything.

Permissions

Index

Keep in touch with
Granta Books:

Visit granta.com to discover more.

GRANTA

THE VALUE OF NOTHING

How to Reshape Market Society and Redefine Democracy

THE *NEW YORK TIMES* BESTSELLER

'[A] penetrating and admirably concise guide to the follies of market fundamentalism.' John Gray, *Observer*

If the full environmental, social, health and economic costs of a burger were taken into account, the average BigMac would retail at £150. There's something broken at the heart of the price system. How do we fix it?

'Patel combines sociology and neuroeconomics to ask the most fundamental question of the season: why do things cost what they do?' *Prospect*

'This is Raj Patel's great gift: he makes even the most radical ideas seem not only reasonable, but inevitable. A brilliant book.' *Naomi Klein*

'Patel offers us a whole new way to think about price and value. Bracingly written and full of surprises, *The Value of Nothing* is itself invaluable.' *Michael Pollan*

'Raj Patel takes an axe to the ideology of market fundamentalism in this broad ranging polemic . . . a bang up-to-date, tightly argued and timely study that deserves to be read by anyone concerned with the state of the world today.' *Tribune*